Children's
Literature
Review

Guide to Gale Literary Criticism Series

For criticism on	Consult these Gale series
Authors now living or who died after December 31, 1999	*CONTEMPORARY LITERARY CRITICISM (CLC)*
Authors who died between 1900 and 1999	*TWENTIETH-CENTURY LITERARY CRITICISM (TCLC)*
Authors who died between 1800 and 1899	*NINETEENTH-CENTURY LITERATURE CRITICISM (NCLC)*
Authors who died between 1400 and 1799	*LITERATURE CRITICISM FROM 1400 TO 1800 (LC)* *SHAKESPEAREAN CRITICISM (SC)*
Authors who died before 1400	*CLASSICAL AND MEDIEVAL LITERATURE CRITICISM (CMLC)*
Authors of books for children and young adults	*CHILDREN'S LITERATURE REVIEW (CLR)*
Dramatists	*DRAMA CRITICISM (DC)*
Poets	*POETRY CRITICISM (PC)*
Short story writers	*SHORT STORY CRITICISM (SSC)*
Literary topics and movements	*HARLEM RENAISSANCE: A GALE CRITICAL COMPANION (HR)* *THE BEAT GENERATION: A GALE CRITICAL COMPANION (BG)* *FEMINISM IN LITERATURE: A GALE CRITICAL COMPANION (FL)* *GOTHIC LITERATURE: A GALE CRITICAL COMPANION (GL)*
Asian American writers of the last two hundred years	*ASIAN AMERICAN LITERATURE (AAL)*
Black writers of the past two hundred years	*BLACK LITERATURE CRITICISM (BLC)* *BLACK LITERATURE CRITICISM SUPPLEMENT (BLCS)*
Hispanic writers of the late nineteenth and twentieth centuries	*HISPANIC LITERATURE CRITICISM (HLC)* *HISPANIC LITERATURE CRITICISM SUPPLEMENT (HLCS)*
Native North American writers and orators of the eighteenth, nineteenth, and twentieth centuries	*NATIVE NORTH AMERICAN LITERATURE (NNAL)*
Major authors from the Renaissance to the present	*WORLD LITERATURE CRITICISM, 1500 TO THE PRESENT (WLC)* *WORLD LITERATURE CRITICISM SUPPLEMENT (WLCS)*

ISSN 0362-4145

volume 134

Children's Literature Review

Excerpts from Reviews,
Criticism, and Commentary
on Books for Children
and Young People

Tom Burns
Project Editor

GALE
CENGAGE Learning

Detroit • New York • San Francisco • New Haven, Conn • Waterville, Maine • London

GALE
CENGAGE Learning™

Children's Literature Review, Vol. 134

Project Editor: Tom Burns

Editorial: Dana Barnes, Elizabeth Cranston, Kristen Dorsch, Jeffrey W. Hunter, Jelena O. Krstović, Michelle Lee, Thomas J. Schoenberg, Noah Schusterbauer, Lawrence J. Trudeau

Data Capture: Frances Monroe, Gwen Tucker

Indexing Services: Laurie Andriot

Rights and Acquisitions: Margaret Chamberlain-Gaston, Sue Rudolph, Misty Warren

Composition and Electronic Capture: Amy Darga

Manufacturing: Cynde Bishop

Product Manager: Marc Cormier

For product information and technology assistance, contact us at **Gale Customer Support, 1-800-877-4253.** For permission to use material from this text or product, submit all requests online at **www.cengage.com/permissions.** Further permissions questions can be emailed to **permissionrequest@cengage.com**

Gale
27500 Drake Rd.
Farmington Hills, MI, 48331-3535

LIBRARY OF CONGRESS CATALOG CARD NUMBER 76-643301

ISBN-13: 978-0-7876-9609-2
ISBN-10: 0-7876-9609-9

ISSN 0362-4145

This title is also available as an e-book.
ISBN-13: 978-1-4144-3755-2
ISBN-10: 1-4144-3755-2
Contact your Gale sales representative for ordering information.

Printed in the United States of America
1 2 3 4 5 6 7 12 11 10 09 08

Contents

Preface vii

Acknowledgments xi

Literary Criticism Series Advisory Board xv

Preface

Literature for children and young adults has evolved into both a respected branch of creative writing and a successful industry. Currently, books for young readers are considered among the most popular segments of publishing. Criticism of juvenile literature is instrumental in recording the literary or artistic development of the creators of children's books as well as the trends and controversies that result from changing values or attitudes about young people and their literature. Designed to provide a permanent, accessible record of this ongoing scholarship, *Children's Literature Review* (*CLR*) presents parents, teachers, and librarians—those responsible for bringing children and books together—with the opportunity to make informed choices when selecting reading materials for the young. In addition, *CLR* provides researchers of children's literature with easy access to a wide variety of critical information from English-language sources in the field. Users will find balanced overviews of the careers of the authors and illustrators of the books that children and young adults are reading; these entries, which contain excerpts from published criticism in books and periodicals, assist users by sparking ideas for papers and assignments and suggesting supplementary and classroom reading. Ann L. Kalkhoff, president and editor of *Children's Book Review Service Inc.,* writes that "*CLR* has filled a gap in the field of children's books, and it is one series that will never lose its validity or importance."

Scope of the Series

Each volume of *CLR* profiles the careers of a selection of authors and illustrators of books for children and young adults from preschool through high school. Author lists in each volume reflect:

- an international scope

- representation of authors of all eras

- the variety of genres covered by children's and/or YA literature: picture books, fiction, nonfiction, poetry, folklore, and drama

Although the focus of the series is on authors new to *CLR,* entries will be updated as the need arises.

Organization of the Book

A *CLR* entry consists of the following elements:

- The **Author Heading** consists of the author's name followed by birth and death dates. The portion of the name outside the parentheses denotes the form under which the author is most frequently published. If the author wrote consistently under a pseudonym, the pseudonym will be listed in the author heading and the author's actual name given in parentheses on the first line of the biographical and critical information. Also located here are any name variations under which an author wrote, including transliterated forms for authors whose native languages use non-roman alphabets. Uncertain birth or death dates are indicated by question marks.

- A **Portrait of the Author** is included when available.

- The **Author Introduction** contains information designed to introduce an author to *CLR* users by presenting an overview of the author's themes and styles, biographical facts that relate to the author's literary career or critical responses to the author's works, and information about major awards and prizes the author has received. The introduction begins by identifying the nationality of the author and by listing genres in which s/he has written for children and young adults. Introductions also list a group of representative titles for which the author or illustrator being profiled is best known; this section, which begins with the words "major works include," follows the genre line of the introduction. For seminal figures, a listing of major works about the author follows when appropriate, highlighting important biographies about the author or illustrator that are not excerpted in the entry. The centered heading "Introduction" announces the body of the text.

- **Criticism** is located in three sections: **Author Commentary** (when available) **General Commentary** (when available), and **Title Commentary** (commentary on specific titles).

The **Author Commentary** presents background material written by the author or by an interviewer. This commentary may cover a specific work or several works. Author commentary on more than one work appears after the author introduction, while commentary on an individual book follows the title entry heading.

The **General Commentary** consists of critical excerpts that consider more than one work by the author or illustrator being profiled. General commentary is preceded by the critic's name in boldface type or, in the case of unsigned criticism, by the title of the journal. *CLR* also features entries that emphasize general criticism on the oeuvre of an author or illustrator. When appropriate, a selection of reviews is included to supplement the general commentary.

The **Title Commentary** begins with the title entry headings, which precede the criticism on a title and cite publication information on the work being reviewed. Title headings list the title of the work as it appeared in its first English-language edition. The first English-language publication date of each work (unless otherwise noted) is listed in parentheses following the title. Differing U.S. and British titles follow the publication date within parentheses. When a work is written by an individual other than the one being profiled, as is the case when illustrators are featured, the parenthetical material following the title cites the author of the work before listing its publication date.

Entries in each title commentary section consist of critical excerpts on the author's individual works, arranged chronologically by publication date. The entries generally contain two to seven reviews per title, depending on the stature of the book and the amount of criticism it has generated. The editors select titles that reflect the entire scope of the author's literary contribution, covering each genre and subject. An effort is made to reprint criticism that represents the full range of each title's reception, from the year of its initial publication to current assessments. Thus, the reader is provided with a record of the author's critical history. Publication information (such as publisher names and book prices) and parenthetical numerical references (such as footnotes or page and line references to specific editions of works) have been deleted at the discretion of the editors to provide smoother reading of the text.

- A complete **Bibliographical Citation** of the original essay or book precedes each piece of criticism.

- Selected excerpts are preceded by brief **Annotations,** which provide information on the critic or work of criticism to enhance the reader's understanding of the excerpt.

Special Features: Entries on Illustrators

Entries on authors who are also illustrators will occasionally feature commentary on selected works illustrated but not written by the author being profiled. These works are strongly associated with the illustrator and have received critical acclaim for their art. By including critical comment on works of this type, the editors wish to provide a more complete representation of the artist's career. Criticism on these works has been chosen to stress artistic, rather than literary, contributions. Title entry headings for works illustrated by the author being profiled are arranged chronologically within the entry by date of publication and include notes identifying the author of the illustrated work. In order to provide easier access for users, all titles illustrated by the subject of the entry are boldfaced.

CLR also includes entries on prominent illustrators who have contributed to the field of children's literature. These entries are designed to represent the development of the illustrator as an artist rather than as a literary stylist. The illustrator's section is organized like that of an author, with two exceptions: the introduction presents an overview of the illustrator's styles and techniques rather than outlining his or her literary background, and the commentary written by the illustrator on his or her works is called "Illustrator's Commentary" rather than "Author's Commentary." All titles of books containing illustrations by the artist being profiled are highlighted in boldface type.

Indexes

A **Cumulative Author Index** lists all of the authors who have appeared in *CLR* with cross-references to the biographical, autobiographical, and literary criticism series published by Gale. A complete list of these sources is found facing the first page of the Author Index. The index also includes birth and death dates and cross-references between pseudonyms and actual names.

A **Cumulative Topic Index** lists the literary themes and topics treated in the series as well as in *Literature Criticism from 1400 to 1800, Nineteenth-Century Literature Criticism, Twentieth-Century Literary Criticism, Contemporary Literary Criticism,* and the *Contemporary Literary Criticism* Yearbook, which was discontinued in 1998.

A **Cumulative Nationality Index** lists all authors featured in *CLR* by nationality, followed by the number of the *CLR* volume in which their entry appears.

A **Cumulative Title Index** lists all author titles covered in *CLR*. Each title is followed by the author's name and corresponding volume and page numbers where commentary on the work is located.

Citing *Children's Literature Review*

When citing criticism reprinted in the Literary Criticism Series, students should provide complete bibliographic information so that the cited essay can be located in the original print or electronic source. Students who quote directly from reprinted criticism may use any accepted bibliographic format, such as University of Chicago Press style or Modern Language Association style.

The examples below follow recommendations for preparing a bibliography set forth in *The Chicago Manual of Style,* 14th ed. (Chicago: The University of Chicago Press, 1993); the first example pertains to material drawn from periodicals, the second to material reprinted from books.

Frederick, Heather Vogel. "Cynthia Rylant: A Quiet and Reflective Craft." *Publishers Weekly* 244, no. 29 (21 July 1997): 178-79. Reprinted in *Children's Literature Review.* Vol. 86, edited by Scot Peacock, 125-26. Detroit: Gale, 2003.

Strong, Pauline T. "Playing Indian in the Nineties: *Pocahontas* and *The Indian in the Cupboard.*" In *Hollywood's Indian: The Portrayal of the Native American in Film,* edited by Peter C. Rollins and John E. O'Connor, 73-81. Lexington: The University Press of Kentucky, 1998. Reprinted in *Children's Literature Review.* Vol. 86, edited by Scot Peacock, 125-26. Detroit: Gale, 2003.

The examples below follow recommendations for preparing a works cited list set forth in the *MLA Handbook for Writers of Research Papers,* 5th ed. (New York: The Modern Language Association of America, 1999); the first example pertains to material drawn from periodicals, the second to material reprinted from books.

Frederick, Heather Vogel. "Cynthia Rylant: A Quiet and Reflective Craft." *Publishers Weekly* 244. 29 (21 July 1997): 178-79. Reprinted in *Children's Literature Review.* Ed. Scot Peacock. Vol. 86. Detroit: Gale, 2003. 125-26.

Strong, Pauline T. "Playing Indian in the Nineties: *Pocahontas* and *The Indian in the Cupboard.*" *Hollywood's Indian: The Portrayal of the Native American in Film.* Eds. Peter C. Rollins and John E. O'Connor. Lexington: The University Press of Kentucky, 1998. 73-81. Reprinted in *Children's Literature Review.* Ed. Scot Peacock. Vol. 86. Detroit: Gale, 2003. 125-26.

Suggestions are Welcome

In response to various suggestions, several features have been added to *CLR* since the beginning of the series, including author entries on retellers of traditional literature as well as those who have been the first to record oral tales and other folklore; entries on prominent illustrators featuring commentary on their styles and techniques; entries on authors whose works are considered controversial; occasional entries devoted to criticism on a single work or a series of works; sections in author introductions that list major works by and about the author or illustrator being profiled; explanatory notes that provide information on the critic or work of criticism to enhance the usefulness of the excerpt; more extensive illustrative material, such as holographs of manuscript pages and photographs of people and places pertinent to the careers of the authors and artists; a cumulative nationality index for easy access to authors by nationality; and occasional guest essays written specifically for *CLR* by prominent critics on subjects of their choice.

Readers who wish to suggest new features, topics, or authors to appear in future volumes, or who have other suggestions or comments are cordially invited to call, write, or fax the Associate Product Manager:

Associate Product Manager, Literary Criticism Series
Gale
27500 Drake Road
Farmington Hills, MI 48331-3535
1-800-347-4253 (GALE)
Fax: 248-699-8054

Acknowledgments

The editors wish to thank the copyright holders of the excerpted criticism included in this volume and the permissions managers of many book and magazine publishing companies for assisting us in securing reproduction rights. We are also grateful to the staffs of the Detroit Public Library, the Library of Congress, the University of Detroit Mercy Library, Wayne State University Purdy/Kresge Library Complex, and the University of Michigan Libraries for making their resources available to us. Following is a list of the copyright holders who have granted us permission to reproduce material in this volume of *CLR*. Every effort has been made to trace copyright, but if omissions have been made, please let us know.

COPYRIGHTED EXCERPTS IN *CLR*, VOLUME 134, WERE REPRODUCED FROM THE FOLLOWING PERIODICALS:

American Scholar, v. 72, no. 2, spring, 2003. Copyright © 2003 by the author. Reprinted by permission.—*Associated Press,* November 24, 2003. Copyright © 2003. All rights reserved. Reprinted with permission of the *Associated Press.*—*Booklist,* v. 88, March 1, 1992; v. 90, May 15, 1994; v. 91, October 1, 1994; v. 94, November 15, 1997; v. 95, September 1, 1998; v. 95, April 1, 1999; v. 96, September 15, 1999; v. 96, February 15, 2000; v. 98, January 1-15, 2002. Copyright © 1992, 1994, 1997, 1998, 1999, 2000, 2002 by the American Library Association. All reproduced by permission.—*Bulletin of the Center for Children's Books,* v. 32, May, 1979; v. 55, January, 2002; v. 56, December, 2002; v. 57, March, 2004; v. 58, November, 2004; v. 59, December, 2005; v. 59, February, 2006. Copyright © 1979, 2002, 2004, 2005, 2006 by The University of Chicago. All reproduced by permission.—*Children's Literature,* v. 30, 2002. Copyright © 2002 The Johns Hopkins University Press. Reproduced by permission.—*Children's Literature Association Quarterly,* v. 25, fall, 2000. Copyright © 2000 Children's Literature Association. Reproduced by permission.—*Chronicle,* v. 26, March, 2004 for a review of "*The Amulet of Samarkand,* by Jonathan Stroud" by Michael M. Jones; v. 27, February, 2005 for a review of "*The Golem's Eye: The Bartimaeus Trilogy, Book Two,* by Jonathan Stroud" by Don D'Ammassa; v. 27, March, 2005. Copyright © 2004, 2005 *Chronicle.* All reproduced by permission of the respective authors.—*College Literature,* v. 23, June, 1996. Copyright © 1996 by West Chester University. Reproduced by permission.—*Explicator,* v. 64, winter, 2006. Copyright © 2006 by Helen Dwight Reid Educational Foundation. Reproduced with permission of the Helen Dwight Reid Educational Foundation, published by Heldref Publications, 1319 18th Street, NW, Washington, DC 20036-1802.—*French Review,* v. 50, December, 1976. Copyright © 1976 by the American Association of Teachers of French. Reproduced by permission.—*Guardian Unlimited,* December 13, 2003, for "The Djinni's Tale" by Diana Wynne Jones; January 12, 2004. Copyright © 2003, 2004 Guardian Newspapers Limited. Reproduced by permission of the author and *Guardian News Service, LTD.*—*History Today,* v. 55, November 1, 2005. Copyright © 2005 *History Today Ltd.* Reproduced by permission.—*Horn Book Magazine,* v. 79, November-December, 2003; v. 81, January-February, 2005; v. 82, March-April, 2006. Copyright © 2003, 2005, 2006 by *The Horn Book, Inc.,* Boston, MA, www.hbook.com. All rights reserved. All reproduced by permission.—*Independent on Sunday (London, England),* December 7, 2003. Copyright © 2003 *Independent Newspapers (UK) Ltd.* Reproduced by permission.—*Instructor,* v. 113, January-February, 2004. Copyright © 2004 by Scholastic Inc. Reprinted by permission.—*Kirkus Reviews,* v. 71, October 1, 2003; v. 72, August 1, 2004; v. 73, December 15, 2005. Copyright © 2003, 2004, 2005 by The Kirkus Service, Inc. All rights reserved. All reproduced by permission of the publisher, *Kirkus Reviews and Kirkus Associates, L.P.*—*KLIATT,* v. 39, May, 2005. Copyright © 2005 by *KLIATT.* Reproduced by permission.—*Lion and the Unicorn,* v. 27, 2003. Copyright © 2003 The Johns Hopkins University Press. Reproduced by permission.—*Magpies,* v. 12, March, 1997. Copyright © 1997 *Magpies Magazine.* Reproduced by permission.—*MLN,* v. 91, December, 1976. Copyright © 1976 The Johns Hopkins University Press. Reproduced by permission.—*Modern Language Review,* v. 87, July 1, 1992 for a review of "*The Count of Monte Cristo,* by Alexandre Dumas, edited by David Coward" by Timothy Unwin. Copyright © 1992 Timothy Unwin. Reproduced by permission of the author.—*New York Times Book Review,* November 14, 2004; August 20, 2006. Copyright © 2004, 2006 by The New York Times Company. Both reprinted with permission.—*Papers on French Seventeenth-Century Literature,* v. 26, 1999. Copyright © 1999 Gunter Narr Verlag Tubingen. Reproduced by permission.—*Poetics Today,* v. 13, spring, 1992. Copyright © 1992 by The Porter Institute for Poetics and Semiotics, Tel Aviv University. All rights reserved. Used by permission of the publisher, Duke University Press.—*Publishers Weekly,* v. 239, February 24, 1992; v. 241, May 16, 1994; v. 242, March 20, 1995; v. 243, September 30, 1996; v. 245, August 3, 1998; v. 245, August 31, 1998; v. 246, March 1, 1999; v. 248, July 16, 2001; v. 249, October 21, 2002; v. 250, July 14, 2003; v. 251, January 19, 2004; v. 251, August 16, 2004; v. 253, January 23, 2006. Copyright © 1992, 1994, 1995, 1996, 1998, 1999, 2001, 2002, 2003, 2004, 2006 by Reed Publishing USA. All reproduced from *Publishers Weekly,* published by the Bowker Magazine Group of Cahners Publishing Co., a division of Reed Publishing USA, by permission.—*Reading Today,* v. 18, April-May, 2001. Copyright © 2001 International Reading Association. Reproduced

COPYRIGHTED EXCERPTS IN *CLR*, VOLUME 134, WERE REPRODUCED FROM THE FOLLOWING BOOKS:

Gale Literature Product Advisory Board

The members of the Gale Literature Product Advisory Board—reference librarians from public and academic library systems—represent a cross-section of our customer base and offer a variety of informed perspectives on both the presentation and content of our literature products. Advisory board members assess and define such quality issues as the relevance, currency, and usefulness of the author coverage, critical content, and literary topics included in our series; evaluate the layout, presentation, and general quality of our printed volumes; provide feedback on the criteria used for selecting authors and topics covered in our series; provide suggestions for potential enhancements to our series; identify any gaps in our coverage of authors or literary topics, recommending authors or topics for inclusion; analyze the appropriateness of our content and presentation for various user audiences, such as high school students, undergraduates, graduate students, librarians, and educators; and offer feedback on any proposed changes/enhancements to our series. We wish to thank the following advisors for their advice throughout the year.

Alexandre Dumas (père)
1802-1870

French novelist, playwright, essayist, short-story writer, nonfiction writer, autobiographer, and author of juvenile fiction.

The following entry presents an overview of Dumas's career through 2006.

INTRODUCTION

Dumas *père* ("the elder") has remained one of the most enduringly popular novelists of the past two centuries. Among his many novels of adventure and romance, often set in a context of French history and featuring historically real figures, the best known to modern readers are *Les trois mousquetaires* (1844; *The Three Musketeers*) and *Le comte de Monte-Cristo* (1844-1845; *The Count of Monte-Cristo*), both of which have been adapted to film in numerous productions. Dumas is credited with popularizing the French historical romance in the mid-nineteenth century and has been called the French Walter Scott (whose Waverly novels set in old England served as an important influence). Dumas is often disparagingly compared to his contemporaries Victor Hugo and Honoré de Balzac, who have maintained the highest literary accolades while Dumas has been relegated to the status of popular—but not literary—novelist and dramatist. His prolific output over the course of a long career includes more than three hundred published titles, the majority of which have sunk into obscurity. However, several excerpts, abridgements, and adaptations of Dumas' works are more familiar to modern readers. A long excerpted section of his novel *Le vicomte de Bragelonne* (1848-1850) has been published separately as *The Man in the Iron Mask*. His 1844 short story for children "L'Histoire d'un Casse-Noisette," adapted from a story by E. T. A. Hoffman, was the basis for *The Nutcracker,* the perennial Christmas ballet by Russian composer Pytor Ilyich Tchaikovsky. In the late twentieth century, a number of adaptations from Dumas' works were published as children's texts, among them *Captain Pamphile's Adventures* (1971), *When Pierrot Was Young* (1975), and *The Nutcracker* (1977). Dumas is referred to as Alexandre Dumas *père* in order to distinguish him from his son Alexandre Dumas *fils* ("the younger"), who was also a novelist and playwright.

BIOGRAPHICAL INFORMATION

Dumas was born July 24, 1802, in Villers-Cotterets, a small town in France. His mother, Marie-Louise-Elisabeth Labouret, was the daughter of an innkeeper. His father, Thomas-Alexandre Dumas Davy de la Pailleterie, born in Santo Domingo (now Haiti), was the son of a French marquis and a slave woman of African descent. Thomas-Alexandre had chosen to adopt his mother's surname, Dumas, rather than the more prestigious name of his father, before joining the French Revolution, whence he achieved the rank of general in Napoleon's army. In 1801 he quit the army in protest against Napoleon's absolutist regime and rejoined his wife in Villers-Cotterets. Soon after, Dumas was born. Dumas' father died when he was only three, leaving the family in a state of financial hardship. At an early age, Dumas began to work as an errand boy and clerk to help support his mother and sister. Hoping to make a name for himself as a playwright, he left his home town for Paris at the age of twenty-one. His admirable penmanship secured him a job as a copier of official letters for the Duke d'Orléans (who later became King Louis-Philippe of France). At the age of twenty-seven, Dumas' career as a playwright took off with the enormously successful production of *Henri III et sa cour* (1829) at the Comedie-Française theatre in Paris. Thenceforth, Dumas enjoyed immense success as a popular playwright of his day, though critics generally disparaged his work as lacking in literary merit. In 1842 he began collaborating on novels and plays with Auguste Maquet, a younger man and professor of history. Dumas generally relied on Maquet to generate first drafts, providing a rough sketch of story and characters, which Dumas then extensively elaborated and embellished upon to flesh out the story. Dumas also relied on the scholarly Maquet to conduct the historical research necessary for his novels, many of which are set among significant events of French history and feature historically real characters. Though Maquet was co-author of many of Dumas' most successful works, his name was never credited on any of their publications. With the publication of *The Three Musketeers,* co-authored with Maquet, in 1844, Dumas made the transition from popular playwright to popular novelist. Dumas' novels were first published serially in periodicals—a form known as the *roman-feuilleton*—over the course of a year or two, then released in book form. Over the years, Dumas came to collaborate with a number of other writers, most of whom worked under him and were not named as co-authors of his works. However, his working relationship with Maquet was the most extensive and long-lasting. Their friendship and collaborative work eventually broke down when, in 1857, Maquet took Dumas to court over questions of authorship and royalty payment for their many novels and plays. A scathing pamphlet entitled "The Novel Factory: Alexandre Dumas & Company," penned by Eugene de Mirecourt, circulated widely in 1845, accusing Dumas of falsely claiming authorship for works that were essentially produced factory-like by his stable of employed writers. Critics today have continued to debate questions of the nature and extent of Dumas' collaborative process. Over the course of his life, Dumas' personal life became notorious for his numerous affairs with a variety of women and his extensive financial debts, resulting in bankruptcy, which he incurred his despite outstanding success as an author. He fathered three children out of wedlock by three different women, though he eventually acknowledged his paternity of each child. His son Alexandre Dumas *fils,* born in 1824, went on to become an author in his own right, penning the novel and play adaptation *La Dame aux camélias* (1848, *Camille*). Dumas *père* died at the home of his son in Dieppe, on December 5, 1870, at the age of sixty-eight.

MAJOR WORKS

Possibly Dumas' best-known and most read work—particularly among young adult audiences—*The Three Musketeers* is set in seventeenth-century France, where the historically real figures of King Louis XIII and Queen Anne, as well as the powerful Cardinal Richelieu, are the sources of intrigue in which the novel's heroes become enmeshed. The story begins in the year 1625, when D'Artagnan, the novel's young hero, goes to Paris in hopes of joining the King's Musketeers, an elite Royal Guard renowned for their honor and skill. D'Artagnan soon proves his bravery and prowess as a swordsman to the three musketeers of the novel's title. The foursome subsequently form a deep bond of friendship, which they vow to uphold with their motto "All for one and one for all!" Each musketeer has specific character traits that remain consistent throughout the story. Porthos is a brutish man whose strengths are physical rather than mental, yet he maintains an endearing childlike innocence that counterbalances his

tendency to vanity. Athos, a man of few words and a great love of wine, maintains a quiet nobility and moral courage. Aramis embodies the contradictory impulses of the priest and the soldier, and remains a mystery even to his closest friends. D'Artagnan, the youngest of the four, providing the force of thought and reason, is a clever strategist in determining how best to meet the challenges they face during the course of their adventures. The central storyline of *The Three Musketeers,* which runs over five-hundred pages, concerns a conspiracy instigated by Richelieu to compromise the Queen by exposing her infidelity to the King. The Queen has secretly given to her lover, the Duke of Buckingham, a diamond necklace given her by the King. The nefarious Milady de Winter arranges to have two studs stolen from the necklace, while Richelieu convinces the King to insist his wife wear the necklace to a public event. Because D'Artagnan's lover, Constance Bonacieux, is the Queen's lady-in-waiting, he and his fellow musketeers are given the task of traveling to England to reclaim the gems for the Queen, and thus save her reputation. Their episodically-narrated adventures in carrying out this task prove to be steps in the education and maturing of D'Artagnan, who, by the end of the story, is wiser for having had these experiences. *Vingt ans après* (1845; *Twenty Years After, or, The Further Feats and Fortunes of a Gascon Adventurer*), finds the four musketeers middle-aged and dispersed throughout France. D'Artagnan, now serving Cardinal Mazarin, is asked to reunite his friends as personal bodyguards to the unpopular Cardinal. His efforts to do so are frustrated by the fact that Athos and Aramis now belong to an organization devoted to the overthrow of the Cardinal. The four friends nonetheless vow never to fight against one another, despite their differing political allegiances, "to be united in spite of all and forever." *Le vicomte de Bragelonne,* the third book of the musketeers cycle, is now known primarily for the excerpted ending section that has been published seperately under the title *The Man in the Iron Mask.* In *The Man in the Iron Mask,* the musketeers scheme to replace the corrupt King Louis IV with his twin brother Philippe, whose existence has remained a closely guarded secret, and who has been imprisoned since the age of nineteen, his face locked in an iron mask in order to conceal his identity. Though the switching of Philippe for Louis is briefly successful, in the end, the scheme fails and Philippe is returned to prison to spend the rest of his days sealed within the iron mask.

Aside from the original *Three Musketeers,* Dumas' next most popular work is *The Count of Monte-Cristo,* which is widely regarded as the author's masterpiece. A novel of over one thousand pages, it is a story of brutal injustice and ruthless vengeance. Set in nineteenth-century France and loosely based on a true story drawn from Parisian police records, *The Count of Monte-Cristo* concerns the sufferings and triumphs of Edmond Dantès, a nineteen-year-old sailor engaged to the beautiful Mercédès and soon to be made a ship's captain. On the night of his engagement party in February 1815, Dantès is inexplicably arrested, accused of political conspiracy, and sentenced to imprisonment in the island prison of the Chateau d'If. Spending fourteen years in prison without a trial or contact with the outside world, Dantès befriends the Abbé Faria, a fellow prisoner and learned old priest who provides him with a scholarly education and helps him to figure out who is responsible for his undeserved punishment. When the old man dies, Dantès effects a clever escape from the island and finds his way to the islet of Monte Cristo, where he recovers a buried treasure bequeathed to him by Faria. Returning to French society as the mysterious and outstandingly wealthy Count of Monte-Cristo, Dantès devotes his life to enacting revenge against the men who betrayed him. In the process, he takes on a variety of disguises to carry out his intentions. While Dantès had believed himself to be carrying out the will of God in seeking revenge, he realizes in the end that he has unfairly punished the innocent children of his enemies. While Dumas was an extremely prolific author during his lifetime—a fact bolstered by his frequent reliance on collaborators and researchers—the Musketeer trilogy and *The Count of Monte-Cristo* represent the majority of his canon that still widely read today. These works have been co-opted by many young readers drawn to the text's emphasis on adventure and heroism, and have become so well-known that elements for the Musketeer and *Monte-Cristo* stories make regular appearances in contemporary pop culture. The popularity of the books with juvenile audiences has also been fostered by several "Classics Illustrated" adaptations of the texts, which present condensed versions of the narrative, recounted in comic book format with full illustrations. A few of Dumas' other young adult and juvenile works have also witnessed modern revisitings, including *Captain Pamphile's Adventures* and *The Nutcracker,* an adaptation by Dumas of the original fairy tale by E. T. A. Hoffmann.

CRITICAL RECEPTION

Critics have generally agreed that Dumas' enduring literary popularity is, in large part, due to his skill at creating action-packed stories of drama and suspense, while evoking an irresistible sense of adventure and romance. Though his characters typically lack the psychological depth that distinguishes much literary fiction, they have been recognized as well-drawn and appealing, embodying easily recognizable personality types and such archetypal traits as courage, valor, and nobility. His prose style, however, has been regularly criticized as plodding, overly melodramatic, and inelegant. Dumas' representation of French history in his novels has also been widely debated. While many scholars have faulted his texts for historical inaccuracy and for reducing social and political forces to personal intrigues between powerful individuals, Dumas' supporters have lauded the author for skillfully integrating fictional narratives with historically real events and characters. Other reviewers have acknowledged that, while his representations of French history are not factually reliable, Dumas succeeded in celebrating the French national character through the glorification and romanticization of seventeenth-century France. Arthur F. Davidson has observed that *The Three Musketeers* owed its popularity to "the loyal comradeship of these seventeenth-century gallants, their reckless fighting, their impetuous lovemaking, which typified to the French public certain characteristics identified with France in her greatest days. . . . Dumas' intent is ever to glorify France and to bring out all that is most attractive in the French character." According to Davidson, Dumas succeeded in "catching to spirit of a particular epoch." Allen G. Wood, discussing *The Three Musketeers,* has remarked, "Dumas was less concerned with a given year than with an entire era, and brought it alive with adventurous deeds rather than documented accuracy." Wood has further applauded Dumas for utilizing historical settings as a means of tapping into a collective unconscious, asserting that *The Three Musketeers* "rewrites the past so that it can enter into the realm of the symbolic, the imaginary for the general masses." Critics have also attributed Dumas' lasting appeal to his exploration of enduring themes and universal archetypes. F. W. J. Hemmings has asserted that *The Count of Monte-Cristo* "is no doubt the greatest 'revenger's tragedy' in the whole history of the novel."

PRINCIPAL WORKS

Selected Works for Children and Young Adults

*Les trois mousquetaires. 8 vols. [with Auguste Maquet] (novel) 1844; translated into English anonymously as *The Three Musketeers,* 1846

†*Le comte de Monte-Cristo.* 18 vols. [with Auguste Maquet] (novel) 1844-1845; translated into English anonymously as *The Count of Monte-Cristo,* 1846

L'Histoire d'un Casse-Noisette [adaptor; from a story by E. T. A. Hoffman] (juvenile fiction) 1845

Vingt ans après. 10 vols. [with Auguste Maquet; translated by William Barron as *Twenty Years After, or, The Further Feats and Fortunes of a Gascon Adventurer* 1846] (novel) 1845

‡*Le vicomte de Bragelonne, ou Dix ans plus tard.* 26 vols. [with Auguste Maquet] (novel) 1848-1850; translated into English anonymously as *The Vicomte of Bragelonne; or, Ten Years Later,* 1857

Captain Pamphile's Adventures [based on the 1839 short story "Le Capitaine Pamphile"; translated and adapted by Douglas Munro] (juvenile fiction) 1971

When Pierrot Was Young [based on the 1854 short story "La Jeunesse de Pierrot; Le roi de Bohême"; translated and adapted by Douglas Munro; illustrations by Peter Farmer] (juvenile fiction) 1975

The Nutcracker [based on the 1844 short story "Histoire d'un casse-noisette"; translated and adapted by Douglas Munro; illustrations by Phillida Gili] (juvenile fiction) 1977

Selected Other Works

Henri III et sa cour [translated by Lord Francis Leveson Gower as *Catherine of Cleves,* 1831] (play) 1829

La tour de Nesle [with Grédéric Gaillardet; translated by George Almar as *The Tower of Nesle; or, The Chamber of Death,* 1932] (play) 1832

Le chevalier d'Harmental. 4 vols. [with Auguste Maquet] (novel) 1842; translated by P. F. Christin and Eugene Lies as *The Chevalier d'Harmental; or, Love and Conspiracy,* 1846

Les demoiselles de Saint-Cyr (play) 1843; translated as *The Ladies of Saint-Cyr; or, The Runaway Husbands,* 1870

Georges. 3 vols. (novel) 1843; translated by G. J. Knox as *George; or The Planter of the Isle of France,* 1846

Le chevalier de Maison-Rouge. 6 vols. [with Auguste Maquet] (novel) 1845; translated as *Marie Antoinette; or, The Chevalier of the Red House,* 1846

Les Frères corses. 2 vols. [*The Corsican Brothers*] (novella) 1845

Le reine Margot. 6 vols. [with Auguste Maquet; translated as *Marguerite de Valois*] (novel) 1845

La dame de Monsoreau. 8 vols. (novel) 1846; translated as *Diana of Meridor; or, The Lady of Monsoreau,* 1846; also translated as *Chicot, the Jester,* 1857

Les quarante-cinq. 10 vols. [with Auguste Maquet; translated as *The Forty-Five Guardsmen*] (novel) 1847-1848

Le collier de la reine. 11 vols. [with Auguste Maquet; translated as *The Queen's Necklace, or, The Secret History of the Court of Louis XVI*] (novel) 1849-1850

Ouvres complètes d'Alexandre Dumas. 17 vols. (novels, plays, fiction, and nonfiction) 1850-1857

Ange Pitou. 8 vols. [with Auguste Maquet] (novel) 1851; translated by Thomas Williams as *Six Years Later; or, The Taking of the Bastille,* 1851

Mes mémoires [translated and abridged by A. Craig Bell as *My Memoirs,* 1961] (autobiography) 1852-1855

Les Mohicans de Paris. 19 vols. (novel) 1854-1855; translated anonymously as *The Mohicans of Paris,* 1859

Ouvres complètes d'Alexandre Dumas. 225 vols. (novels, plays, fiction, and nonfiction) 1860-1865

Ouvres complètes. 38 vols. [edited by Gilbert Sigaux] (novels, plays, fiction, and nonfiction) 1962-1967

*Other notable editions of *The Three Musketeers* include the version translated by William Barrow in 1846; translated by Park Benjamin; translated by Jacques Le Clercq in 1951 (reissued, 2001); translated by Isabel Ely Lord in 1952; translated by Lord Sudley in 1952; illustrated by Edy Legrand in 1953; illustrated by C. Walter Hodges in 1957; abridged and adapted by Jane Carruth; illustrated by John Worsley in 1982; translated by Lowell Blair in 1984; abridged and adapted by Vincent Buranelli; illustrated by Hieronimus Fromm in 1985; and translated by Marcus Clapham and Clive Reynard in 1992, among many others.

†Other notable editions of *The Count of Monte-Cristo* include the version translated and adapted by Lowell Blair in 1981; illustrated by Mead Schaeffer in 1985; edited by David Coward in 1990; and abridged and adapted by Mitsu Yamamoto; illustrated by Marcos Studio in 1990, among many others. It was also adapted as a drama in 1848.

‡Other notable excerpted editions of this text have been published under the title *The Man in the Iron Mask,* including the version illustrated by Edy Legrand in 1964; edited by David Coward in 1991; and abridged and adapted by Paul Mantell in 1998, among many others.

GENERAL COMMENTARY

Arthur F. Davidson (essay date 1902)

SOURCE: Davidson, Arthur F. "The Great Novels (1843-1853)." In *Alexandre Dumas (père): His Life and Works,* pp. 216-56. Philadelphia, Penn.: J. B. Lippincott, 1902.

[In the following essay, Davidson provides a critical overview of some of Dumas's best known historical romance novels—including Les Trois Mousquetaires—*and discusses Dumas's methods of collaborative writing.]*

Dumas in the inventiveness of his plays, Dumas in his eager appetite for history, Dumas in his pleasant stories of travel—these we have seen. Combine the three, not forgetting the wondrous imagination which underlies them all—the dramatist, the historian, the *conteur*—and we have the qualities of Dumas as the writer of historical romance. For some while past he has cherished the idea of popularizing French history: he has dipped into it on different occasions, and each dip has convinced him that the subject was worth pursuing further. Did any one say that French history was dull? Perish the thought! The historians may have been dull, but that was their own stupid fault. Scotch history would doubtless have been liable to the same reproach had there been no Sir Walter Scott, and who would say that the annals of France were less eventful than those of Scotland? Nay, the opposite was being proved at this very time by Michelet, by Hugo, by De Vigny, by Mérimée. Pass over the first as an "historian" proper—romantic and picturesque, but still a professional historian: did not *Notre Dame, Cinq Mars,* and *Charles IX* attest the influence and value of the Waverley novels? Yet none of these three had really touched the popular level. Hugo had divagated into poetry and archaeology, the spirit of De Vigny's work was essentially aristocratic, Mérimée had produced a gem of exquisite art—a joy for ever to *connoisseurs,* too delicate for the general. For true popularity something on a larger scale was wanted, laid on with a thicker brush and in colours more vivid. For that business Dumas was the man, and the only man. His was the genius which could produce "the dramatic romance"—that form of novel which Victor Hugo dreamed of as forming "one long drama, divided into scenes, in which the descriptive parts serve as do the costumes and scenery of a theatrical piece." And just as in the theatre there is a *décorateur* whose function it is to see to the costumes and scenery, so in the dramatic romance—and more so as the affair is of greater length—it will be desirable to have a man for this purpose. By good fortune Dumas had lighted on the man—a student of history, an unwearied rummager of documents, whose name was Auguste Maquet. Originally a lecturer at the Collège Charlemagne, and for the last five or six years a writer—under the pseudonym of "Macqueat"—of stories and verses, Maquet's first association with his great partner arose from some help which Dumas had given to his drama *Bathilde* (1839), and it was this acquaintance which brought about the first of the great novels. For Maquet had written a short one-volume story called *Jean Buvat* dealing with the Cellamare conspiracy against the Regent Duc d'Orléans. Having tried in vain to place this story he brought it to Dumas, who took the little thing, expanded it into a long romance, named it *Le Chevalier d'Harmental,* and readily secured for it the *feuilleton* space of *Le Siècle*—at the same time paying Maquet twelve hundred francs for his share instead of the modest one hundred he had originally tried in vain to get. So began this most notable of literary partnerships. To catalogue the works which it produced in their order of publication would be merely to show that the popularization of French history did not proceed on a regular and progressive plan, but was effected bit by bit, the first often coming last and the last first, until at the end a sequence—not indeed of years but of epochs—found itself established, stretching from the reign of Charles IX to the French Revolution. Thus, after *Le Chevalier d'Harmental* (1843) Dumas went back to Louis XIII and wrote *Les Trois Mousquetaires* (1844) and its first sequel, *Vingt ans après* (1845). Then returning to the Regency period we have *Une Fille de Régent* (1845) to supplement *Le Chevalier d'Harmental,* after which we hark back to the reign of Charles IX in *La Reine Margot* and its continuation, *La Dame de Monsoreau.* Between this and its sequel, *Les Quarante-Cinq* (1848) come in two of the Revolution novels, *Le Chevalier de Maison Rouge* and *Joseph Balsamo* (1846), and so on. To us, however, it matters little in what order the slides of the magic lantern were originally made: we prefer to see them as a whole and as a series. To do this we may begin even a little earlier than the Saint Bartholomew.[1] For that exciting and terrible time *Les Deux Diane* and *Le Page du Duc de Savoie*[2] serve as a gentle preparation. The date is 1550, and the reign is that of Henri II, over whom the fair Diana of Poitiers still holds sway. Through all the fighting of that time—the loss of St. Quentin and the gain of Calais—we follow in one story the love of the young Comte de Montgomery (afterwards the famous defender of Domfront) for Diane de Castro, daughter of the King and Diane de Poitiers; in the other the devotion of Emanuel Philibert to his mistress Léona, who passes to all the world as his page Léone. Thus we come to the Treaty of Cateau Cambrésis, the death of King Henry mortally wounded in tournament by Montgomery, and the accession of François II. For the first time now Queen Catherine comes to the front. Hitherto, as the sovereign's wife she has for long years effaced herself before imperious Diana and gruff Montmorency the Constable; now as the sovereign's mother she begins a long delayed vengeance for neglect. This first son, indeed, she loved but little: he is too much the slave of his girl wife, beautiful Marie Stuart, and Marie is wholly influenced by the Guises, with whom Catherine has not yet made common cause. And so when the sickly François lies dying, it is Catherine who—coveting the crown for a second son more pliable, and perhaps for a third more loved than either—will forbid the skill of Ambrose Paré to intervene lest haply the King's life might be prolonged: rather let nature take its course, and let his reign be short. To him succeeds Charles, ninth of that name; the Queen-mother's grasp grows stronger and the scope of her dark deeds wider. As a Catholic she hates the heretics, as a mother she fears most of all men their leader Henri de Navarre, whom she foresees as a rival to her beloved Henri d'Anjou. To compass the death of this Béarnais is her whole desire. The story of **La Reine Margot** is the story of the duel between these two. On the one side all the devices of murder—the secret assassin, the drugs of Réné the Florentine, the lip-slave for Madame de Sauve, whose lips Henri often touches, the poisoned page of the book which, missing its intended victim, kills the King's favourite hound and more slowly the King himself. On the other side Henri of Navarre avoids the various snares, partly by his own shrewd opportunism—for when it is a question of "Mort, Messe, ou Bastille" he does not hesitate to profess himself a Catholic, just as on a famous future occasion he will declare that "Paris vaut bien une messe"; partly by the help of his wife, Queen "Margot," who is a good friend to her husband—though they each have their own love affairs and have passed their honeymoon as far away from each other as possible; and partly also by the good offices of his brother-in-law, King Charles, who—though for the most part a puppet in the hands of Catherine—asserts sometimes his right to be generous, and, while shooting through his window at the wretched Huguenots, keeps his kinsman beside him out of harm's way. Others were not so fortunate. The romantic La Mole—lover of Queen Margaret—and the jovial Coconnas had fraternized at their first meeting when they entered Paris on the eve of St. Bartholomew; then they fought each other desperately, as in duty bound, since the one was a Huguenot and the other a Catholic; finally they became bosom friends again, and both perished together—victims of that same dire Catherine.

"Le roi est mort! Vive le roi!" The throne of Charles IX is now occupied by his brother Henri III, summoned from Poland by courier after courier. The Queen-mother has failed to kill Henri of Navarre, but she has managed to postpone his reign and make him fly for his life. The new King, who oscillates between debauchery and superstition with occasional fits of Satanic kingliness, has enemies enough—his treacherous brother d'Anjou, the ambitious Henri de Guise, and the crafty Cardinal. His "minions" can amuse him and are good enough to fight with d'Anjou's "Gentlemen"; but how would he fare without Chicot

the Jester, wisest of fools, who baffles the conspirators at every turn—personating the King, hiding in the confessional-box, making brother Gorenflot drunk, preaching sermons, signing abdications, and what not? Wamba was nothing to him. As for the Dame de Monsoreau it is enough for us that she was loved by that brave Bussy d'Amboise, whose regrettable murder—brought about by the jealousy of his master d'Anjou—alone prevented him from adding d'Épernon to the many victims of his valour. D'Épernon, however, lives to form the Gascon bodyguard of Henri III, known as "Les Quarante-Cinq": and former personages reappear in new shapes. Now it is the Duchesse de Montpensier, sister of Guise, masquerading as a page-boy to help her brother: now it is Chicot, who for having trounced Mayenne has had to go into hiding for some years till we refind him in Robert Briquet—faithful as ever to his King, and a good friend also to Henri of Navarre, whom he accompanies to the siege of Cahors. A wonderful picture this siege gives of the future Henri IV, physically a coward and trembling with fear, yet by sheer force of will leading the attack as bravest of the brave. There are other battles and sieges too, notably that of Antwerp, which Anjou conducted while the fleet under Joyeuse gave help. Little glory did French arms gain there, nor was Anjou more successful in love than in war. For returning to France he fell in with Diane de Monsoreau, who had loved Bussy and had never forgiven the Duke for his death. Seeking now to entrap her he prepared retribution for himself. It was the old story—the laboratory, a little "aqua tofana," a mysterious illness, and farewell Duke of Anjou! With this **Les Quarante-Cinq** ends, and the Valois period of French history is done with. Before the curtain rises again forty years elapsed,[3] which cover the reign of Henri IV and the early part of Louis XIII. Obviously such an interval invites reflection and discussion on what has passed. The majority of readers are quite content: some few will be troubled by the pangs of the historical conscience; one will even go so far as to write a book to prove the "Historical Inaccuracies in **La Dame de Monsoreau.**" This poor man is much to be pitied, for he has begun a work which will never end. Let us rather grant at once to the author of dramatic historical romance the privilege of regulating facts and marshalling them for effect. Otherwise how can he realize that famous ideal which Dumas set before himself of "elevating history to the dignity of romance"? "Inaccuracies," then, or "elevations"—many such may be discovered: as a type one will suffice. History informs us that, between the death of Charles IX and the arrival of his brother Henri from Poland, some three or four months passed. But *La Reine Margot* teaches us better by showing how Catherine just secures the succession for her favourite son by bringing him back at the dramatic moment before Charles has yet quite ceased to breathe—an arrangement which every one will admit to be more effective. *Ex uno disce omnes*: yet these, and some "extra-historical" incidents, are but the acknowledged licences of fiction, with which none but a pedant will quarrel. The more important question is, What impression of the main characters and events of French history will these romances leave on a reader who knows French history only through them? Will such an one on the whole see right? Doubtless, yes. About the course of religious strife, of domestic intrigue, of foreign policy, he will gather little which serious history would have him unlearn. And as to the persons of the drama, admit that their characters are modelled on the traditional and popular view; it is always possible that this view, formed at or near the time itself, may be the truest. Dumas, of course, adopted it naturally and unconsciously as being the most suitable for his purpose: even had he been aware of another it is inconceivable that he would have hesitated between—let us say—a white-washed Catherine de Medicis, a passive instrument of Spanish policy, and the masterful woman of scheme and intrigue, spell and poison: the one was so colourless, the other so lurid. To name the Queen-mother is to name the strongest instance of a possible perversion of truth. Others are less questionable. Charles IX, Henri III, Henri IV—what historian can amend the characters of these kings as they are presented by the novelist, or what historian can draw their characters with more distinctness? And if any one wants to see how Dumas had advanced in historical knowledge since the days when he wrote *Henri III et sa Cour,* let him compare the Duc de Guise of that drama with the Duc de Guise of the Valois novels. Human nature, as Plato long ago observed, has been coined in very small pieces; and the sorting of these, to form a just estimate of character, involves so much balancing and counterbalancing that it ends in being perplexing without being any the more infallible. For Dumas it has to be said that whenever he touches history—in novels, plays, or studies—he has the true historical instinct; without either faculty or inclination for the drudgery of analysis he somehow arrives at a synthesis quite as convincing as any that can be reached by the most minute methods.

When the curtain rises again it is on a scene very different from that of the decadent Valois house. The gloom of secret stratagems and snares has been dispersed: a brighter and more buoyant air is felt at once, when on a morning of 1625—Louis XIII being King and Cardinal Richelieu his minister—a certain young Gascon appears in the township of Meung on a wonderful orange-coloured pony, which excited the jeers of Rochefort and gave the newcomer a first opportunity of showing his metal. To his sword also D'Artagnan owed his introduction to Athos, Porthos and Aramis, the three musketeers, who henceforth are four. "Queen's musketeers" really rather than "King's," since it is on them that Anne of Austria depends to protect her love for Buckingham from the hostile schemes of Richelieu, especially in that affair of the diamond studs, which—as Madame Bonacieux revealed—the Queen of France had given to her English lover. Hence the desperate journey to England undertaken by the four heroes with their four lackeys, when by one misadventure or another the rest drop out, and on D'Artagnan and his man Planchet rests the whole burden of saving the Queen's honour. How that was accomplished is a matter of history—or at any rate of romance. We know that D'Artagnan won his race against time and that the Queen was able to wear her diamonds when the King led her forth to open the ball at the Hôtel de Ville. We know also how Richelieu had vainly employed on this business the beautiful criminal "Milady," as he employed her again more successfully to bring about that "miracle for the salvation of France" which was wrought at Portsmouth by the dagger of Felton. For these reasons and for others of a more private nature the brotherhood had vowed a righteous vengeance against Milady, performed with due ceremony by the executioner of Bethune.

Not however to this sombre ending nor to the general unpleasantness of "Miladyism" does the story of the Musketeers owe its popularity. Rather it was the loyal comradeship of these seventeenth-century gallants, their reckless fighting, their impetuous love-making, which typified to the French public certain characteristics identified with France in her greatest days. Athos for dignity, Porthos for strength, Aramis for subtlety, D'Artagnan for wit and resourcefulness, all for a courage to which other virtue is quite secondary—such qualities fascinate readers of all nationalities, whether in the way of similarity or of contrast. It is not a question here of historical persons—they are less problematical, and the chief of them, Richelieu, is excellently drawn in his day of power—but rather of catching the spirit of a particular epoch; and this by common consent Dumas has done most admirably. Nor does any book illustrate better his power of assimilating material and improving upon it than the story of the Musketeers. The substance of the whole is to be found in the *Mémoires d'Artagnan* by Courtils de Sandras. There we have D'Artagnan and his three friends, as also Milady (lady-in-waiting to Queen Henrietta), de Vardes, Rochefort (called Rosnay), Madame Bonacieux and her spouse, the rivalry of the King's Musketeers with those of the Cardinal, and much else. The life of D'Artagnan himself represents three phases of character. At first he is the quarrel-seeking adventurer, swaggering in wine-shops, gambling in the ante-chambers of the King, leading wives astray and beating husbands. Then under Mazarin during the Fronde period he becomes more attached to intrigue both in love and in politics, and he is entrusted with confidential missions to England, where he spends much time. Later on, when Louis XIV has assumed power and the splendours of the Court have begun, D'Artagnan, now Capitaine-lieutenant of the Musketeers, appears as a punctilious and particular *gentilhomme,* most anxious to forget the wildness of his early fights and amours, He died in 1673, killed during the siege of Maestricht. Thus one may read in Courtils de Sandras,[4] from whose voluminous memoirs—without excluding other authorities of the same sort[5]—ransacked by himself or Maquet, Dumas borrowed freely, and at the same time discreetly. Over all he sprinkled the salt of his own wit: much he imagined and invented—such as the entertaining characters of Grimaud, Mousqueton, Bazin, and Planchet, or the details of the journey to Calais: some things he altered—ante-dating, e.g., by several years the birth of D'Artagnan, which seems really to belong to 1623, so that the young man could hardly have come from Béarn in 1625 except in the arms of his nurse: other things he suppressed if they were either discreditable to his heroes, gross in themselves, or likely to offend modern readers.[6] Dumas' intent is ever to glorify France and to bring out all that is most attractive in the French character. And here it may be noted, in passing, that of the two really detestable women in all his novels neither is French—Catherine de Medicis an Italian, Milady an English woman.

The historical landmark which ends *Les Trois Mousquetaires* is the murder of Buckingham (1629). When the story is resumed, after an interval of eighteen years, Louis XIII and his great Minister are dead; and France, groaning under the taxation of crafty and avaricious Mazarin, is divided into two parties, the Cardinalists and the Frondists. Among others whom Mazarin imprisoned was the Duc de Beaufort, grandson of Henri IV and Gabrielle d'Estrées: the escape of this nobleman—by the help of a certain colossal

pie, which concealed beneath its crust daggers and rope ladder—is the subject of several diverting pages. This, however, is incidental: the proper continuance of the first story belongs not to anti-Mazarin movements—D'Artagnan indeed is nominally in the Cardinal's service—but to the fortunes of the Musketeers in England, where by chance they found themselves, at first on different sides—since Athos and Aramis fought for King Charles, while the other two were agents from Mazarin to Cromwell; but soon all made common cause as loyal gentlemen to save the King. A noble though vain struggle, involving many desperate dealings with Milady's son, Mordaunt, who sought to avenge his mother's death, and after coming often near success perished at last in the waters, hurled down by the hand of Athos. Thus history, public and private, pursues its course, though—as is sometimes the way of sequels—*Vingt ans après* has not the charm of twenty years before.

It was often wondered what that last word of King Charles on the scaffold meant, "Remember," until Dumas found its meaning in an injunction to Athos that he should discover and use, when the proper time came, a treasure hidden in the vaults of Newcastle keep. Athos—or the Comte de La Fère, to be correct—did not forget; and having gone in 1660 to Newcastle he was negotiating with General Monk when D'Artagnan and his followers, disguised as fishermen, kidnapped the General, and having conveyed him in their smack over to Holland presented him to the exiled Charles II, by whose graciousness he was deeply impressed. All which things explain, in a way ignored by the generality of historians, the reason why Monk took so important a share in the Restoration.

So in 1660 begins the story of *Le Vicomte de Bragelonne,* Raoul, the son of Athos, a youth full of valour and promise, but short-lived and ill-fated. For, loving Louise de la Vallière, he came into rivalry with his royal master, whom Louise loved more; and so, broken-hearted, he left the King's service and went into a far country, where, fighting bravely, he perished; which calamity being announced, Athos, long distressed by his son's sorrow and by their separation, himself faded out of life. Thus the eldest of the Musketeers departed. And what of the others? Aramis, now General of the Jesuits, had renounced the sword for the cassock, after which, we remember, he had always hankered. In this capacity he must needs concern himself with a plot in favour of that luckless twin brother of Louis XIV who was languishing in the Bastille: the plot failed—though for one short day the King and the prisoner of the Bastille changed places—and the dangerous twin was secretly conveyed away to the Île Sainte Marguerite, to be known henceforth only as "the man in the iron mask." For these reasons, Aramis, as sharing in the treason of Fouquet, was to be seized: and with Aramis was involved Porthos, the innocent tool of his clever friend—Porthos, who helped to fortify Belleisle, picking up big boulders and flinging them about like pebbles—Porthos, who with less of boisterous swagger now than in early days, remained still the *bon enfant,* the good-natured giant, slow of wit, large of heart, cheerfully working for others without troubling to understand what it was all about. Never did more repugnant duty fall to D'Artagnan than when, as Captain of the King's Musketeers, he was sent to arrest his friends at Belleisle. By every means he sought to warn and save them, but a higher power and the secret orders of Colbert baffled his loyalty. Fate, it seems, had decreed that Porthos should die. See, then, this Titan driven to bay in his cavern, while he beats off his foes time after time and hurls at them that huge barrel of gunpowder, which exploding devastates all around. Amid the wreckage Porthos stands, holding off by strength of arm the granite masses which press upon him, until failing at last beneath the incumbent weight—"too heavy—too heavy!"—he falls buried in the ruin his own hands have wrought. How D'Artagnan afterwards died gloriously in battle has been already said: for Aramis—or Monsieur d'Herblay, about whom we care little—he recovered favour and found in diplomacy a suitable sphere for his special gifts. But the book is the book of Porthos—Porthos into whom Dumas put most of himself and of his father, and whose death he declared had stricken him with a heavy sorrow. The modern reader may draw back aghast at the six volumes of *Le Vicomte de Bragelonne,* but he will have missed the best part of the Musketeer cycle should he fail to read those pages which describe the end of Porthos— true epic pages such as Homer's self had not disowned.

The later part of the reign of Louis XIV is not dealt with by any novel of Dumas.[7] Again there is an interval of forty years before we come to the date of the two Regency romances, *Le Chevalier d'Harmental* and *Une Fille du Régent.* These are very similar in setting and in incident. Both revolve round plots formed against the Regent Duc d'Orléans; in both we see much of the "ape-like face" of Dubois, who scratches his nose while pondering, prowls about Paris in all disguises, and tracks down every sort of conspirator: in both the Regent figures, as a man of

pleasure indeed, whose *petits soupers* and other nocturnal amusements receive full attention, but as essentially merciful and generous, pardoning where Dubois was anxious to punish. The historical pivot of *Le Chevalier d'Harmental* is the Cellamare conspiracy of 1718 got up by the Spanish Ambassador and the Duchesse de Maine for the purpose of kidnapping the Regent in the interests of Philip of Spain; and the Chevalier, who has a private grudge against Orléans, is used by these people as their instrument. Similarly in the second story—which was suggested by an incident in the first—Hélène de Chaverny, a daughter of the Regent, is loved by a young Breton nobleman who has pledged himself to take her father's life—the relationship of course being unknown. The Regent, disguised as a Spanish duke, talks with the young man, for whom he has taken a great liking, and tries to dissuade him from so dangerous a design: meanwhile Dubois, with a bag of gold pieces on the table, interrogates the valet, and by the process of adding or taking away ten louis for each answer—according as it is valuable or not—soon succeeds in extracting all the information he requires. In both stories the reader is introduced to the interior of the Bastille, where M. de Launay presides and where various distinguished inmates are living as the guests of the State, for the most part pleasurably enough and with every kind of ingenious contrivance for communicating with one another. On the whole we are moving now in a more subtle and deceptive world: things are less often what they seem: love, less eager to satisfy itself at the moment, has become more elegant and artificial; hatred, more long-headed, marks down an enemy for distant vengeance rather than for immediate chastisement. It is a changed atmosphere since the days of the Musketeers, and no one runs any risk of confusing the seventeenth century with the eighteenth.

With the Regent's death in 1723 the reign of Louis XV, properly speaking, began: its history may be filled in from all the recognized authorities.[8] For the purpose of romance the chief interest belongs to its closing years, which form a sort of explanatory prologue to the Great Revolution. In 1770, then, the *Mémoires d'un Médecin* series opens with the five volumes called *Joseph Balsamo,* chiefly concerned with the doings of that remarkable impostor—the "archquack" of Carlyle's pages. The phenomena of occultism had always fascinated Dumas: he dabbled, at different times, in palmistry, phrenology, clairvoyance, spiritualism; especially he was attracted by that form of mesmeric development which is nowadays called hypnotism. To test the reality of this power he made several experiments[9] at the time when he was writing *Joseph Balsamo,* and with considerable success, though he admits that the subjects he operated on were always persons peculiarly liable to such influence—young girls or impressionable women. The conclusion he arrived at was this: "I believe that by the help of magnetism a bad man might do much harm, I doubt that a good man could do much good. . . . I consider that magnetism is an amusement but not yet a science." In the story of *Joseph Balsamo* the possibilities of magnetism are stretched to the uttermost demands of fiction. The "arch-quack" is seen with all his quackeries; only, he is a quack who believes in himself and in his mission to regenerate humanity by breaking up the existing order of things. As the head of a widespread society of Nihilists, whose motto is L.P.D. (lilia pedibus destrue), he directs the undermining of society's foundations: he pulls the strings with which the puppets are made to dance. As a showman he introduces to us, in one way or another, some famous people—Jean Jacques for example, and the querulous Thérèse (Rousseau by the way will have nothing to do with Balsamo, preferring to trust to the gentler process of time); a certain young surgeon called Marat, who is all for prompt and violent methods; the young Austrian princess just come to France to be the bride of the shy studious dauphin, who is more interested in the mechanism of clocks than in any affairs of Court; Madame Dubarry, with her pet negro Zamore and all her intrigues to keep her position; that eminent churchman, Cardinal de Rohan, whose eyes are dazzled by the sight of Balsamo making gold. Here too a beginning is made with the romantic story of Andrée de Taverney and her brother Philippe, when the one becomes a lady-in-waiting to the new Dauphiness and the other at first sight of Marie Antoinette conceives for her that devoted love which will last until she falls beneath the axe of the guillotine. But Dumas knows that there are flaws in magnetism; and so Balsamo, whose power depends mainly on the information supplied by the clairvoyance of his wife Lorenza Feliciani, comes near to an early and ignominious ending. For that lady when she has escaped from his influence goes off and betrays the secrets of the association to the Government, with the result that several of the conspirators are arrested and Balsamo himself only escapes by the help of Dubarry. Gloom, mystery, and a sense of impending cataclysm are the intended impressions of the book, which ends with the death of Louis XV in 1774.

Ten years later Balsamo, reappearing as the Comte de Cagliostro, resumed more openly his campaign against Royalty. He it was who engineered all that affair of the diamond necklace, using as his principal instruments Jeanne de la Motte, Cardinal de Rohan, and a certain Nicole Légay, whose marvellous resemblance to Marie Antoinette gave opportunity for employing her in affairs which would damage the reputation of the Queen. Many men there were who loved Marie Antoinette; none more than Philippe de Taverney, for whom she did not care at all, and the Comte de Charny, whom in her cold, proud way she loved. It was about her that these two friends quarrelled and fought, and it was to save her from the King's displeasure that Charny was made to marry Andrée de Taverney. But the scandal of the necklace—which after all the poor Queen had enjoyed for so short a while—was sedulously spread abroad by the Comte de Provence and other enemies, nor was it abated by the arrest of Rohan and Cagliostro, and the public whipping of La Motte.

Then we plunge straight into the Revolution. The *Ange Pitou*—who gives his name to the story and whose early life is partly a reproduction of Dumas' own boyish days—is not in himself a person of any consequence; but having come from Villers-Cotterets to Paris he found himself, July 14, 1789, engaged in the storming of the Bastille. Thence, among other rescued prisoners, came the *médecin* whose memoirs we are supposed to be reading, and whose ward Ange Pitou was. This Dr. Gilbert, a disciple of Balsamo and imprisoned for publishing revolutionary ideas, having now got himself appointed one of the Court physicians, did his best—as a moderate reformer—to advise the King and Queen for their welfare. But events moved too fast for advice—those well known events which no fiction can enhance—the rending in pieces of Foulon and Berthier, suspected of "cornering" bread; the arrival of the Flanders regiment at Versailles and the fatal banquet at which the tricolour was trodden under foot; the march of the hungry women from Paris, and the hurried journey of La Fayette to protect the palace from plunder and the sovereign from outrage.

More minutely *La Comtesse de Charny* describes all the efforts made to save Royalty by the sound sense of Gilbert, the self-sacrifice of Favras, the genius of Mirabeau. Everything is frustrated by the vacillation of the King and the obstinacy of the Queen, who is always *l'Autrichienne,* always distrusts the French, and looks to the foreigner for help. If omens could save the hapless woman she had been saved—the candles which go out one by one as she sits at the red-baize-covered table, the shuddering memory of a distant but unforgotten vision which passes over her as she sees the King absorbed in drawing improved designs for Dr. Guillotin's newly invented machine.

And meanwhile her enemies gain strength. Barnave impeaches Mirabeau; Robespierre's sad sallow face begins to dominate the Jacobin Club; D'Aiguillon and Marat hover about—Marat with his "yellow lips, flat nose, viper-like eyes, veins of mingled blood and poison." Whatever plans the Royal party form or unform, Balsamo-Cagliostro-Zanoni knows them all, his spies being present everywhere; and when the story ends, the King and Queen, arrested at Varennes and brought back on that "journey of sorrow" to Paris, have lost their last hope of freedom.

To end the Revolution series comes *Le Chevalier de Maison Rouge,* which opens finely thus: "C'était pendant la soirée du 10 Mars, 1793. Dix heures venaient de tinter à Notre Dame, et chaque heure, se detachant l'une après l'autre, comme un oiseau nocturne élancé d'un nid de bronze, s'était envolée triste, monotone et vibrante." The time is just before the fall of the Gironde. The King has perished; the Queen a prisoner, first in the Temple and then in the Conciergerie, awaits the same doom. To save her while there is yet time many schemes are on foot, at bottom of them all being the Chevalier de Maison Rouge, whom, as Philippe de Taverney, brother of Andrée de Charny, we have met before. To communicate with Marie Antoinette by means of a note wrapped in a carnation and to effect her escape by the opening of an underground passage, was the plan on which the Chevalier and his partner, citizen Dixmer, staked their last hope; that failing, Maison Rouge flung himself beneath the scaffold and by a self-inflicted death avoided surviving the Queen to whom he had given his life. But the name of the book does not imply its whole, or even its chief, interest. Besides the Chevalier and Dixmer, there is Dixmer's wife, Géneviève; and Maurice her republican lover; and above all Lorin, the friend of Maurice—and the best type of a Revolution patriot—gay, witty, generous, and faithful, who voluntarily joins his friends in the Salle des Morts that he may share their fate, and dies making an epigram and paying a compliment to Sanson.[10] The Chevalier himself—with his disguises, his escapes, and his plots—might well seem the creation of lawless fancy did not we know that his original was a real person. He was not of course the Count Fersen we hear of in history, nor was he such an ideal of chivalry as Dumas makes him to be; but he was a certain audacious and rather disreputable adventurer called Rougeville who—as his recently published history shows[11]—lived between 1761 and 1814, when he was shot by order of Napoleon as a spy and a traitor. On whatever documents the novel was based, the treatment of this character is not only an illustration of the old proverb about truth being stranger than fiction—for the adventures of the real Chevalier were quite as improbable as those of the imaginary—but also an example, not less remarkable than that afforded by the *Mémoires de D'Artagnan,* of the wonderful way in which Dumas could improve upon any material that fell into his hands.

About the writing of this book an anecdote is recorded by Blaze de Bury. Dumas often declared that, when once he had mapped out in his mind the scheme of a novel or a play the work was practically accomplished, since the mere writing of it presented no difficulty, and could be performed as fast as the pen could travel. Some one begged leave to dispute this assertion, and the result was a wager. Dumas had at that time in his head the plan of the *Chevalier de Maison Rouge,* of which he had not yet written a word, and he now made a bet of one hundred *louis* with his sceptical friend that he would write the first volume of the novel in seventy-two hours (including the time for meals and sleep). The volume was to be formed by seventy-five large foolscap pages, each page containing forty-five lines and each line fifty letters. In sixty-six hours Dumas had done the work—3,375 lines—in his fair flowing hand, disfigured by no erasures—and the bet was won with six hours to spare.

Yet no one surely would say that the *Chevalier de Maison Rouge* bears any marks of haste or inconsiderateness. On the contrary, it is, beyond doubt, the best of the Revolution novels, and not far from the best of all the novels. On closing it some retrospect and comparison is inevitable.[12] As a series these later romances fit not so well together as the earlier, nor individually do they hold so high a place in popular esteem. There are weak points. The juggleries of Joseph Balsamo, however thrilling in themselves, are a feeble peg on which to hang the French Revolution, seeming indeed but a trivial burlesque of dire realities; and this fact becomes clearer as the series advances. The peg gives way, and fiction has to glide—as in *Ange Pitou* and *La Comtesse de Charny*—more and more into a chronicle of facts. But the theory that Dumas had some special sense of the sixteenth and seventeenth centuries which he lacked when dealing with comparatively recent history is purely fanciful, and is falsified directly we get to the *Chevalier de Maison Rouge,* from which the Balsamo incubus has disappeared. Here the romance of history and its dignity are equally consulted. The Marie Antoinette of the preceding books—faithfully described by a pen which erred neither in being too sentimental nor too ungenerous—was not a lovable person: the Marie Antoinette of this last story, now in the extremity of fate, is treated with all the sympathy and respect which her womanhood, her rank, and her misfortune demand. The Republican Dumas will have nothing to do with "Madame Veto" or "Veuve Capet" or any other scurrility of the *sansculottes*: the woman we see in the prison and on the scaffold is still Marie Antoinette, Queen of France and daughter of kings.

To extol the **Chevalier de Maison Rouge** is not to belittle the romances of the Valois or Bourbon period—least of all that brilliant *épopée* of D'Artagnan and his friends. But the Musketeer books—while admirably adapted for continuity and for that "linked sweetness long drawn out" which the *feuilleton* requires—have also, it must be admitted, the defects of continuity. For one thing, inequalities are more marked: over so long a course good Homer has more chances of nodding—and nodding is infectious. For another, there is an absence of that finality which the mind of man craves for, even in fiction: there is indeed, except for the fate of all mortal things, no natural or necessary reason why these stories should ever end. To postulate a continuation is, artistically, a sign of weakness. *Les Trois Mousquetaires* does not perhaps demand a sequel, but it certainly invites one. It had better therefore be disengaged at once and set on its own pedestal, there to remain as a masterpiece, plausible in history, in imagination immense. For the rest, if it is permitted to assume that excellence, whether in a novel or a play (and remember that in Dumas the two are very close together) consists in a reasonable size, in compactness, in self-sufficiency, together with concentred interest, crisp and unflagging action, unity of movement towards an end—if this be admitted, then, flanking that first pedestal, two others must be set up—certainly no smaller in stature; and on the one must be placed **La Reine Margot,** on the other **Le Chevalier de Maison Rouge.** Whosoever bows before these will have done homage to the three greatest among the historical novels of Dumas.

Having now covered in some fashion or other so wide a stretch of ground—having traversed without halt fifteen thousand pages of fiction and a period of time close on two hundred and fifty years—one would gladly rest and be thankful. Dumas does not allow it. "When I write 'finis' to one book," says he cheerfully, "it just means that I am beginning another." There are novels and novels. In giving precedence to those which we call "great" the epithet has been presumed as proper to the ones mentioned, whether considered in their conception or their extent or their fame: it is not meant to signify an arbitrary barrier or to exclude the preferences of individual taste. Other romances, to say nothing of dramas and historical works, were appearing during the same years and in the same way—first as newspaper serials, then in book form. Without degenerating at this place into a catalogue we may give a passing word to one or two of these. In 1844 came *Ascanio* (a story chiefly concerned with Benvenuto Cellini), *Fernande,* and *Amaury* (modern and non-historical). The publication of the latter in *La Presse* was interrupted for a reason of interest as illustrating an unusual and pathetic connexion between fiction and real life. The heroine of the story was a girl dying of consumption, and Mademoiselle de Noailles, who happened also to be suffering from this fatal malady, was so vitally interested in following the fate of the imaginary patient as to aggravate her own dangerous condition. Therefore *Amaury,* on the request of M. de Noailles, was broken off, and was not resumed until after his daughter's death. It may be added—as showing how realistically Dumas utilized all his experience—that the physical symptoms traced minutely in the story were the result of observations made by him many years before during an illness of Felix Déviolaine, his cousin.

Les Frères Corses (1845) is a story well known, at any rate from its dramatized form, in this country. So also perhaps is **Le Bâtard de Mauléon** (1846),[13] the scene of which is chiefly Spain and the time the fourteenth century. Mauléon is supposed to meet old Froissart and to tell him his tale, "which," adds the author, "I have drawn from a *manuscrit inédit*"— one, no doubt, of those many unpublished MSS. which Dumas kept in his head and paraded for his own amusement and the tantalization of the ultra-inquisitive. It is a regular Froissart chronicle of the days of chivalry, having for its principal characters the Black Prince, Bertrand du Guesclin, Pedro of Navarre, and other warriors. There is also—but this has nothing to do with Froissart—a certain dog called "Allan," belonging to Don Frederick, the brother of Pedro the Cruel, "a slim wiry dog of the sierra, with a head pointed like that of a bear, piercing lynx-like eyes, legs fine and nervous as those of a deer." Now this beast was a portrait of Dumas' own dog "Mouton"—outwardly be it understood; for in moral qualities "Allan" was superior to his prototype, as was proved before long. About the antecedents of Mouton there had always been some mystery, and the friend from whom the dog came, parrying all questions, had contented himself with this advice: "Try first to attach him to you, and you will then see what he can do." The story of that attachment belongs to the book of *Mes Bêtes,* wherein we read that Mouton was a surly, unsociable brute, unresponsive to any attentions of his master, and such a terror to the neighbourhood that a request was made by the Mayor of Saint-Germain that he should not be taken abroad except on a chain. One day Dumas was writing that chapter of *Le Bâtard de Mauléon* which describes how the dog Allan, to protect Don Frederick, flew at the throat of a hostile Moor: in the distance Mouton was uprooting dahlias and paid no attention when commanded to desist. "Very well, you rascal," said Dumas, "just wait till I have finished this sentence!" The sentence having been written, Mouton received a vigorous kick, whereupon his true character appeared, and his "attachment" became a painful reality; for he turned and sprang on his master, who had just time to hold up both arms in self-defence, with the result that the dog's teeth closed on the right hand and munched it, until with the left he was gradually choked off. Then the misnamed Mouton was conducted back to his original owner, and Dumas, after a week's doctoring of his hand, resumed with difficulty *Le Bâtard de Mauléon.*

It would be inexcusable in the eyes of many to pass over without honourable mention that pretty romance which tells how the godson of Cornelius de Witt reared, amid much tribulation, the precious bulb which gained the prize at Haarlem. *La Tulipe Noire* (1850), if not a great novel, is a charming story; and memory retains easily its few, though vivid figures— William the Silent, Boxtel, Gryphus, his daughter, and the gentle Van Baerle, whose love is divided between Rosa and his tulips, until the two are reconciled in the "Tulipa Nigra Rosa Barlaeensis."

And there is yet one book—little known, little read— which enlightens, more than any other, that strange craving for the immeasurable and the impossible by which Dumas was always haunted. "What next?" was his eternal thought, as though he had hitherto touched only the fringe.

"Do the history of the world," said his son, not without irony.

"I have thought of that," was the reply quite serious; "but the objection is that you must either adhere to Biblical tradition, which only goes back some six or seven thousand years—and that would be too short; or else you must follow science—and that would be too long."

Eventually, however, he discovered a frame capable of holding some such gigantic picture as he desired to make. That frame was the old theme of the Wandering Jew, whose name—as it is given in French tradition—served as the title of the story. *Isaac Laquedem* (1853) is nothing but a fragment—a mere paltry two volumes out of a projected dozen, for it was stopped by the Censorship, and Dumas never resumed it again. But even as a fragment it is astounding. We see, first, the wanderer arriving in Rome in 1419 and joining himself to those pilgrims whose feet the Pope, by old custom, was wont to wash on Holy Thursday in each year. When it comes to his turn—he is the thirteenth—the Unknown falls at the Pontiff's knees, shows the brand upon his forehead, reveals himself as the accursed one who—for having refused the Christ bending under the Cross a moment's rest—had been condemned henceforth to wander through all countries and all ages, and finally begs the Holy Father to intercede for his pardon. This starting point having been established, the story plunges back into the remote past, traversing ancient Egypt, India, Persia, Greece, and Rome, comprising also Moses and the Prophets and the Old Testament history of the Jews, until it arrives at the New Testament and paraphrases the Gospel narrative with the miracles and sufferings of Christ—all in the most approved *feuilleton* style. It was as well, perhaps, that the Government should intervene to prevent the sacred drama of the Passion from being presented to the Parisian public in the same style as the story of the Musketeers, since the thing was bound to move scoffing in some and pain in others. But there is no doubting the good faith of Dumas himself: irreverence and inexpediency were as far from his view as the opposite qualities they connote. In all sincerity he had set himself to explain and adorn the mysteries of religion for the benefit of the man in the street; and this ingenuousness of treatment is only less astonishing than the magnitude of conception. What the future course of *Isaac Laquedem* would have been is but guess work. It is said—and is likely enough— that the author meant to have represented the Pope as securing for the criminal a conditional pardon—the condition being that he should still wander, but henceforth as the apostle of good, not of evil. In that case we can see how, after the interview with Paul II, the story would have started off again with the wide vista of the modern world before it, affording opportunities without end for the activity of the regenerate Jew. As it stands *Isaac Laquedem* is an inchoate epic of the human race, which can only be criticized by large marks of exclamation.

Marks of exclamation indeed punctuated Dumas all through his life. Sometimes they assumed a practical and hostile form. It was while these novels, greater and smaller, were appearing that an agitation was set on foot for the total abolition of Dumas. Ten years before he had been taken to task for appropriating in his plays the ideas and situations of other authors—mostly departed—whose reproachful spirits had been championed by Cassagnac. On this occasion the "ghosts" were not of the dead but of the living. Whence, it was asked, came this marvellous fertility of production—this output (some one had counted) of sixty volumes in one year? One gentleman in particular considered the thing a scandal, and being a dealer in scandals naturally took it up. This was "Eugène de Mirecourt," whose native name was Jacquot, less euphonius but quite adequate to its owner. With noble indignation he stigmatized as *mercantilisme littéraire* this wholesale production of books under the name of an eminent man who employed paid assistants to do the greater part of the work for him. Jacquot, it may be said, was not the first to start this quarry, for it had been done two years before (1842), rather cleverly, by one Louis de Loménie:[14] but Jacquot raised it to the dignity of a high literary question by bringing it before the Société des Gens de Lettres, and denouncing it as an imposture on the public, an injury to the assistants, who were merely paid like shop-hands but remained without name or fame, and finally as an outrage on the honour of literature. This was all very fine. But, as to the first point, the public did not care; as to the second, the assistants—or "secretaries," as they preferred to call themselves—worked under no compulsion and were at liberty to go away and make an independent name for themselves whenever and wherever they liked; while as to the dignity of literature, collaboration without naming was—whether good or bad—too common a practice in France for the Société to do anything but pass a vague resolution in favour of regulating it more definitely. Then Jacquot, discarding the cloak of literary and ethical purism, resorted to the more congenial sphere of personalities; and having invented an excellent catchpenny title he launched (1845) the pamphlet *Fabrique de Romans: Maison Alexandre Dumas et Cie.,* spicy enough to meet with a ready sale and libellous enough to incur a fortnight's imprisonment for its author. To refer to this *brochure* is the mere duty of the chronicler: it has in itself no importance, and neither then nor since has influenced any reputable critic.[15] For the measure of Jacquot's revelations was soon taken when he proceeded to biographize the celebrities of the day (*Les Contemporains*) at sixpence per head including the portrait, and fell foul of so many that he was constantly being fined or imprisoned, until from an amusement he came to be regarded as a nuisance and at last sought refuge from his various troubles within the walls of a monastery, where he died.[16] Peace however to his ashes! So far as Dumas is concerned, he occasionally happened to say what was true in regard to collaborations: his personal anecdotes—inspired it was believed, by resentment at failure to become one of the great man's "secretaries"—may be allowed to have a certain negative value, since, in the absence of other evidence, they afford a fair presumption to the contrary. All this is not to say that Dumas' collaborative methods require no comment, but only to bar at the outset that form of comment which assumes him to have been an impostor, incapable of writing anything good himself, and indebted for all his successes to the brains of others. Apart from this absurd contention, which none of the men who worked with him ever put forward even in times of discontent and open quarrel, there are certain points proper for consideration. To avoid confusion, it is necessary in the first place to exclude altogether those jobbing "operations" to which Dumas—especially in his later years—lent himself, and which belong to the category of "trafficking" not of collaboration. It was his nature to magnify and expand whatever he touched, and he probably persuaded himself that there might be an "extra-collaborative" just as there was an "extra-historic." Convinced that he was a focus from which all the rays of literature emanated, and that his sign-manual did in some magic way conduct his brain, he set his name to some books in which his own share was little or nothing, just as he wrote miscellaneous prefaces or lifted whole passages from other authors with a few introductory words of his own. He forgot—as he was reminded on a celebrated occasion[17]—that "there are degrees": the appreciation of degrees was his weakest point. These things—done sometimes to oblige a friend sometimes from the pressing need of money—must be regarded as disfiguring excrescences on the normal and legitimate form of collaboration. Ultimately, if the whole truth were known, they would resolve themselves into a sort of debtor and creditor account where the balance would be in Dumas' favour; he gave as freely and inconsiderately as he took, and while some of the publications bearing his name had little to do with him, it is equally certain that a great number appearing under other names were essentially his work.[18]

So much for the "extra-collaborative" department. Return now to legitimate collaboration: with it alone we are concerned in all the principal works of Dumas—those on which his reputation depends, and which come within the view of the ordinary reader. Such an one, if asked, "What do you think of the collaborators of Dumas?" would probably reply "I don't think about them at all:" And the answer would be conclusive. Still, there is no need to shirk the question. Maison Dumas et Cie.—why not? The fact, if not this way of putting it, was common enough in Paris at that time. It was brought about by the insistence of editors, publishers, and theatrical managers upon having some well known name with which to attract the public: and—all sophistry apart—the only difference between a commercial and a literary undertaking was that in the former the firm might bear the name of one who took no active part in it, whereas in the latter honesty demanded that the name on the cover of the book should indicate a real and a chief share in the work. To this condition the collaboration of Dumas conforms—that wonderful infusion of himself into others which, so far from belittling the man, has only in the course of time intensified the greatness of his individuality and power. Single-handed he might be as in *Henri III* or *Antony,* or many-handed as in the host of other works: it is only the conditions of authorship that are changed, not the person of the author. Faith divines this conclusion: curiosity would like to know how the thing was done. The various forms of collaboration may be reduced to two main classes, according to the nature of the principal partner's share. The first class includes those cases in which the subject of a play or a novel was brought to Dumas in an impossible or an imperfect state. Typical examples of this sort have been referred to in *La Tour de Nesle. Mademoiselle de Belleisle*[19] and *Le Chevalier d'Harmental,* in all which Dumas completed what was inchoate, strengthened what was puny, vitalized what was moribund. Sometimes he did more: he even resuscitated what was dead, as by recasting a play which had been hissed off the stage into that remarkable drama of his *Le Comte Hermann.* In all such cases where the book or the play would not otherwise have flourished, or perhaps even lived, who doubts that the giver of life is the real author? Sometimes, again, the suggestion from outside came in the course of conversation. In this way the novelist once had as a collaborator the learned Schlegel, who, meeting Dumas in 1838, told him from personal knowledge of certain events in the War of Liberation, which Dumas asked leave to make into a book and made into *Le Capitaine Richard.*

To the second category of collaboration belong those works in which Dumas was responsible for the subject, and in this class come all the books written in partnership with Maquet, except *Le Chevalier d'Harmental* and *Sylvandire,* the subjects of which Maquet suggested. In such cases, after discussing the plan with his partner, Dumas' habit was to draw up in outline a scheme of the whole, with the divisions and titles of chapters: then, when the assistant had filled in the outline, the MS. was handed to Dumas, who re-wrote it with such additions and alterations as he thought fit. The same course was followed in other books besides those written with Maquet. Edmond About has described[20] how he saw in 1858 at Marseilles the rough draft of *Les Compagnons de Jéhu* in which the master's original model had been developed by an assistant and which Dumas now took and wrote his romance from, elaborating it and *sémant l'esprit à pleines mains."*

This re-writing process resulted in such a prodigious amount of "Dumas" copy as to give rise to the legend that his "secretaries" had learned to imitate his handwriting so closely as to baffle detection—a superfluous theory and in some instances demonstrably false.[21] The re-writing signified in reality Dumas' appetite for appropriation, and it was a special feature of those works in which his share was greatest. This method, of course, was subject to exceptions, for occasionally time failed. and then the MS. would be delivered to the printer just as it was written by the collaborator. The last chapters, for example, of *Le Vicomte de Bragelonne* were printed from Maquet's copy because the newspaper in which the story was being published could not wait for the revised version. And similar things became more frequent in later years.

To the many writers who in their different degrees shared or lightened the labours of Dumas we would gladly devote some pages did space permit, but it must suffice to have mentioned their names—in the Bibliography—in connexion with the books or plays to which they belong. Probably, next to Maquet, the most substantial helpers were Paul Bocage and Paul Lacroix.[22] The latter—otherwise known as the "Bibliophile Jacob"—was a cordial friend and admirer, who speaking of his former relations with Dumas said: "I used to dress his characters for him and locate them in the necessary surroundings, whether in Old Paris or in different parts of France at different periods. When he was, as often, in difficulties on some matter of archaeology, he used to send round one of his secretaries to me to demand, say, an accurate account of the appearance of the Louvre in the year 1600. . . . I used to revise his proofs, make corrections in historical points and sometimes write whole chapters." These words show pretty well the nature of the services rendered by Dumas' assistants—services which neither did they exaggerate nor did he either deny or depreciate. But Maquet stands on a different footing from the rest: they were casual and intermittent, he alone for ten years worked closely and continuously with Dumas, and he alone was in the full sense a *collaborateur*. When Dumas was in Paris, there also was Maquet: when Dumas travelled Maquet accompanied him; when Dumas established himself at Saint-Germain, Maquet took up his quarters close by at Bougival, and between the two a ceaseless stream of messengers came and went bearing copy. In the course of time this *fidus Achates* developed powers of invention and description which made him far more than the mere searcher-out of facts he was at the outset—made him, in fact, an independent author who could, if need were, carry on the business of historical romance for himself. Yet never till the breach between them came did he claim a position of equality, and the claim which he then put forward was based primarily on financial rather than on literary grounds. Bankruptcy is a terrible solvent of friendship; and when Maquet, to whom considerable arrears of salary were due, found himself in the position of an ordinary creditor and entitled only to twenty-five per cent. which the other creditors of Dumas had agreed to accept, it occurred to him that he might assert his right to be "joint-author" instead of mere collaborator, a right which would involve the appearance of his name together with that of Dumas on the novels they had written together, and an equal share in any profits arising from these books. Twice the case came before the Courts, twice the opposing advocates thrashed it all out.[23] In both cases Maquet's claim was disallowed, though his share in the production of eighteen works was recognized, and with this barren honour he had to be content. The legal proceedings add nothing to what has already been said on the nature of the collaboration, but they leave us convinced of two things—first, that—as a matter of equity, Maquet ought to have been described as *co-auteur,* and secondly that—as a matter of literature—he was not the essential partner. Dumas without Maquet would have been Dumas: what would Maquet have been without Dumas? To illustrate this point more vividly, here is a little anecdote which, though it did not come out at the trial, is based on good authority. It concerns the story of *Ange-Pitou*—the last of their joint books. On this subject Maquet had been making researches at the library, and he came to Dumas with a mass of information about the hero, who was to be traced back to Louis Pithou, one of the authors of *La Satire Menippée.* "All right," said Dumas, "find out about him and let me have have the facts." Thereupon he made an agreement with *Le Constitutionnel* for the story, receiving—as was his wont—an instalment of the money in advance. As ill-luck would have it, a disagreement with Maquet—the beginning of their quarrel—supervened. Dumas, bound by contract to supply *Le Constitutionnel,* had no time to look up the antecedents of Ange Pitou, and for that matter he did not know where to look. And so like a brave man he cut the difficulty by constructing a Pitou whose early years were passed in Villers-Cotterets and whose early experiences were those of Alexandre Dumas! So little in reality did he, except as a luxury, depend on the help of others. Not that Maquet must be for a moment disparaged: his own historical novels, written after the separation—*La Belle Gabrielle, La Maison du Baigneur, Le Comte de Lavernie*—are quite good, especially the first. If their authorship were unknown they might well pass for joint work; only in that case they would have to be classed as what Dumas used pleasantly to call "one of my inferior books." It would have been strange indeed if Maquet, after ten years' association with his master, had not learned all there was to learn about the writing of novels.

But, leaving aside these vain questions and all the "indiscretions of the tribunals," we do better to remember the generally excellent relations—cordiality on the one side, admiration on the other—which prevailed between Dumas and his assistants, as well as the perfect good humour with which he met the rather savage attempts made to deprive him of even any share in the authorship of his books. Every one has heard how, after he had delighted a gathering of friends for some while with his talk and wit, he ended by saying, "I must be off now, for if I stay here talking any longer it will be reported to-morrow that I had collaborators to help me."

At a club one day an admirer, after complimenting him warmly on his books, ventured to say that he had found a geographical error in one of them.

"Indeed! which was that?"

Le Chevalier d'Harmental.

"The devil!" said Dumas, "I have not read it. Let me see, who was it wrote that for me? why, that rascal Auguste. I'll comb his hair for him! (*je lui laverai la tête*).

Assuming the story as reported to be authentic, it only shows the unreasoning prejudice to which Dumas was exposed that this little joke at his partner's expense should have been construed into a scandalous admission.

When the meticulous Quérard asserted that one part of **Monte Cristo** was written by Fiorentino and the other by Maquet, Dumas, after establishing the facts of the case, added with gentle irony: "After all, it was so simple to believe that I had written it."

While hunting up, at Bourg-en-Bresse, some particulars about the fate of the highway robbers described in **Les Compagnons de Jéhu,** he called on a magistrate of the place—a local antiquarian of some repute and self-esteem. This gentleman, who had heard all about the Maison Dumas, saw the opportunity for a score. "And so, M. Dumas," said he, "you are going to write a novel this time *yourself.*"

"Oh, yes," was the ready reply, "I got my valet do the last one, but as it was very successful the scoundrel demanded such an exorbitant rise of wages that to my great regret I have had to part with him."[24]

On all this subject the last word and the true word has perhaps been spoken by Blaze de Bury, who knew more about it than most people: "Dumas in a way collaborated with every one. . . . From an anecdote he made a story, from a story he made a romance, from a romance he made a drama; and he never let an idea go until he had extracted from everything that it could yield him. Admit—as the critics will have it—his collaboration, plagiarism, imitation: he possessed himself what no one could give him; and this we know because we have seen what his assistants did when they were working on their own account and separately from him."

Ultimately there is one question to put—Did Dumas need collaborators? The answer is No and Yes. As a matter of talent he did not, as a matter of temperament he did. Just as his imagination was quickened by the sight of places, so the exercise of his mind was made more agreeable by the friction of other minds. His expansive, sympathetic nature sought always communication with his fellows; alone on a desert island he would, we fancy, have pined away, bored even by himself. Indeed he rather resented any reserve in those with whom he came in contact. "Why don't you become my collaborator instead of Maquet?" he said to his son: "it would bring you in a couple of thousand or so per year, and all you would have to do is to raise objections, criticize my proposals, and give me embryo subjects which I would work out without your help."[25] No wonder, then, that Dumas not only wrote immensely himself but was the cause of writing in those around him. Thanks partly to the investigations of others, and chiefly to his own

confessions, we are able to give chapter and verse in many facts which concern the production of his books. We know how he got this idea or that, we know how he was helped by one or by another, we know a number of like details. But why or how from such materials and with such help so grand an edifice was raised—that remains a mystery. "The wind bloweth where it listeth." It is the same with whatever is great and effective in Nature or in Art: explanations of the process never explain the result.

Notes

1. The beginning must be fixed more or less arbitrarily in order to gain the best point for sequence of view. Otherwise it would be possible to start further back. *Le Bûtard de Manléon* concerns the reigns of John II and Charles V; the reign of Charles VI is treated in *Isabelle de Bavière*; that of Francis I in the semi-historic *Ascanio*.

2. In regard to these two companion books it should be stated that Maquet had no part in either; the first of them was, according to Parran, mainly the work of Paul Meurice.

3. So far as Dumas is concerned, Maquet's two novels, *La Belle Gabrielle* and *La Maison du Baigneur* to some extent fill this gap. Dumas himself treated the period later on in his studies of Henri IV and Louis XIII.

4. Or in the more handy and corrected abridgment, *D'Artagnan,* by Eugéne d'Auriac. Paris, 1846.

5. Such as the *Memoirs of La Porte, of Tallemant des Réaux, and of Madame de la Fayette.* A useful collection of all such documents, by Petitot, had recently been published (1829).

6. One of D'Artagnan's dealings with Milady might better perhaps have been omitted for this reason. Was it, one wonders, from squeamishness or from a patriotic dislike to see his hero worsted by the Englishwoman, that Dumas did not quote a certain letter attributed to Milady by Madame de la Fayette which was reported to run as follows: "(Elle lui répondit) que son nez l'incommoderait trop dans son lit, pour qu'il lui fût possible d'y demeurer ensemble"?

7. Maquet however wrote *Le Comte de Lavernie* as a connecting link between *Le Vicomte de Bragelonne* and *Le Chevalier d'Harmental.*

8. Dumas himself has treated it in other works not professedly "romances," e.g. *Louis XV et sa Cour,* and the *Mémoires d'une Aveugle* (Ma-

dame du Deffand), with its sequel, *Les Confessions de la Marquise*; also in his novel *Olympe de Clèves,* which might be called (like *Ascanio*) semi-historical, since—though the story of the actress-heroine is fictitious—a great many historical figures come in—Louis XV, Cardinal Fleury, Marshal Richelieu, etc.

9. Here is a characteristic one: "I was travelling in Burgundy in 1848 with my daughter. In the same carriage with us there happened to be a very charming lady of thirty or so. It was eleven o'clock at night, and in the course of conversation this lady mentioned that she had never in her life been able to sleep while travelling in a coach. I made no remark, but exercised my will upon her, and ten minutes later not only was she asleep but her head was resting on my shoulder. I then woke her up: she was equally astonished at having fallen asleep and at the position she had chosen in doing so."

There is no end to the *bonnes fortunes*—real or imaginary—of Dumas. *À propos* of his hypnotic powers he once told a story (according to an article of reminiscences in *La Nouvelle Revue* of August, 1899) about a certain Lady H., over whom his magnetic influence was so extraordinary that, on merely thinking how much he would like to see her, he presently observed her entering his room attracted by the suggestion. The rest of the story reads better in French. "Elle semblait endormie. En galant homme je la reconduisis chez elle, trois nuits de suite, en lui faisant remarquer que tout a une fin. Et, ma foi! quand elle vint pour la quatrième, je ne la reconduisis plus!"

10. In the novel Lorin dies with Maurice and Géneviève; in the play, by way of a happier ending, he secures their escape and remains to forfeit his own life.

11. *Le vrai Chevalier de Maison Rouge,* A. D. J. Gonzze de Rougeville, *d'après des documents inédits,* par G. Lenôtre (Paris, 1894).

12. We do not take account here of three later-written novels dealing with French history subsequent to the Revolution: *Les Compagnons de Jéhu,* and its sister book, *Les Blancs et les Bleus* (covering 1793-1800), and *Les Louves de Machecoul* (temp. 1832). Though these books are of considerable size, they can hardly otherwise be classed as "great novels."

13. *Le Bâtard de Mauléon* was refused by the manager of *La Presse* and appeared in *Le Commerce.*

14. *Galerie des Contemporains Illustrés* (vol. v.).

15. With the exception of Quérard, who was sometimes misled, and whose rash conjectures—for they are nothing more—on Dumas are the chief blot on his otherwise excellent bibliographical labours.

16. Whoever wants to see the quality of "Eugéne de Mirecourt" as a biographer should consult the *brochure* called *Confession d'un Biographe,* by Mazerolle, who describes the way in which these so-called biographies were compiled. The man who objected to Dumas' "manufactory" kept up an extensive one himself, and employed a number of assistants who were sent about Paris to pick up gossip and scandal concerning the subject of the biography whether in private houses or on the boulevard and in the café. *Rien n'était sacré pour un—Jacquot.*

17. In the Beauvallon trial at Rouen in 1846, when Dumas appeared as a witness, and being asked by the President what his profession was, said, "Dramatic author I should describe myself were I not in the country of Corneille." To which the judge's well known reply was, "Il y a des degrés."

18. A good example of this is given by Alfred Asseline (in the *Indépendance Belge* of November 20, 1870), where he tells how when writing his novel *L'Enlèvement d'Hélène* he found himself in a difficulty and went to Dumas for help. The "master" sat down and wrote the whole chapter for him—it was a description of a duel—to such good effect that when the story appeared every one praised the excellence of this chapter. "Needless to say," adds Asseline, "that Dumas never gave a hint to any one of what he had done, and generously left me to enjoy all the credit."

19. When Dumas had received from Brunswick the nucleus of *Mademoiselle de Belleisle* he let it lie for two or three years. Brunswick, despairing that anything would ever come of it, said to a friend: 'I wonder if I shall ever see that 300 francs Dumas promised me for my MS. I wish you would go and ask for the money." The friend went, taking with him an order from Brunswick entitling him to receive 300 francs. Thus reminded, Dumas unearthed the MS., and

taking the order, he added a cipher to the sum named, signed it and sent it back to Brunswick, authorizing him to receive from the Théâtre Français the first 3,000 francs of author's fees as soon as *Mademoiselle de Belleisle* should be produced.

20. Speech at the inauguration of the Dumas Monument (November 4, 1883).

21. The only instance of a genuinely puzzling resemblance is the case of Viellot, a secretary who joined Dumas about 1850 and gradually fell into an almost exact imitation of the master's handwriting.

22. The following are the works in which, according to M. Octave Uzanne, Paul Lacroix had most share: *Les Mariages du Père Olifus, La Femme au Collier de Velours, Olympe de Clèves, La Tulipe Noire, Isaac Laquedem.*

23. The *Gazette des Tribunaux* of January 20, 1858, and following days contains a long account of the proceedings. It appears that Maquet had, in 1848, made an agreement with Dumas by which he renounced all rights in their joint works in consideration of a payment of 145,000 francs. As only a small portion of this had hitherto been paid, the contention of Maquet's counsel was that the agreement was thereby invalidated; but the Court held otherwise.

24. This sort of anecdote is common enough. Oxford men may recall a story current some twenty-five years ago concerning the famous joint work of Liddell and Scott. The latter, it is known, died long before his partner; henceforth, whenever a mistake—more or less serious— was pointed out in the *Dictionary*, Liddell (it was said) would exclaim apologetically, "Ah! poor Scott!"

25. Dumas, however, in his *Souvenirs Dramatiques* (vol. ii.) allows some of the drawbacks of this system: "Of two collaborators one is generally a dupe, and that one is the man of talent. For your collaborator is like a passenger who has embarked on the same ship with you and who gradually reveals to you that he does not know how to swim; you have to keep him afloat when shipwreck comes—thereby running the risk of drowning yourself—and when you reach land he goes about everywhere declaring that without him you would have perished! . . . Often in a moment of weakness—either from good nature or because your self-love has been flat-

tered—you consent to look at the MS. which some young author presses upon you; when once you have said 'yes' to him, you will have no more peace."

Gamaliel Bradford (essay date 1926)

SOURCE: Bradford, Gamaliel. "Alexandre Dumas." In *A Naturalist of Souls: Studies in Psychography,* pp. 179-205. New York, N.Y.: Houghton Mifflin, 1926.

[*In the following essay, Bradford offers an appreciation of Dumas's personal character as well as the character of his writings.*]

Mr. Davidson, whose excellent volume on Dumas must be the foundation of any careful study of the subject, dismisses his author with the remark: 'Except for increasing the already ample means of relaxation, he did nothing to benefit humanity at large.' Is not this a rather grudging epitaph for the creator of ***Monte Cristo***? Are the means of relaxation so ample that we can afford to treat ***La Tour de Nesle*** and ***La Reine Margot*** as alms for oblivion? Would Stevenson have read ***Le Vicomte de Bragelonne*** six times, would you or I have read ***Les Trois Mousquetaires*** more times than we can count, if other relaxation of an equally delightful order were indeed so easily obtainable? In spite of the flood of historical novels and all other kinds of novels that overwhelmed the nineteenth century, story-tellers like Dumas are not born every day, nor yet every other day.

For he was a story-teller by nature, one who could make a story of anything, one who did make a story of everything, for the joy of his own childlike imagination. 'I am not like other people. Everything interests me.' The round oath of a man, the smile of a woman, a dog asleep in the sun, a bird singing in a bush, even a feather floating in the breeze, was enough. Fancy seized it and wove an airy, sunbright web about it, glittering with wit, touched with just a hint of pathos; and as we read, we forget the slightness of the substance in the grace and delicacy of the texture.

It is an odd thing, this national French gift of story-telling, of seeking by instinct the group-effect, as it were, of a set of characters, their composite relations to one another and the development of these relations in dramatic climax. English writers, from Chaucer down, dwell by preference on the individual character, force it only with labor and difficulty into the general framework, from which it constantly escapes in delightful but wholly undramatic human eccentricity. To the French habit of mind, such individuality is excrescent and distasteful. Let the characters develop as fully and freely as the action requires, no more. They are there for the action, not the action for them. Hence, as the English defect is dull diffusion and a chaos of disorder, so the French is loss of human truth in a mad eagerness for forcible situations, that is to say, melodrama.

Even in Hugo, in Balzac, in Flaubert, in Zola, one has an uneasy feeling that melodrama is not too far away. In Dumas it is frankly present always. The situation—something that shall tear the nerves, make the heart leap and the breath stop—for Dumas there lies the true art of dramatist and novelist. And what situations! No one ever had more than he the two great dramatic gifts, which perhaps are only one, the gift of preparation and the gift of climax. 'Of all *dénouements,* past, present, and I will say even to come,' writes Sarcey, 'that of *Antony* is the most brilliant, the most startling, the most logical, the most rapid; a stroke of genius.' *Henri III, Richard Darlington, La Tour de Nesle* are full of effects scarcely inferior. If one thinks first of the plays, it is only because in them the action is more concentrated than in the novels. But in novel after novel also, there is the same sure instinct of arrangement, the same masterly hand, masterly for obtaining the sort of effect which the author has chiefly in view.

And perhaps the melodrama is not quite all. The creatures are not always mere puppets, wire-pulled, stirring the pulse when they clash together, then forgotten. We hate them sometimes, sometimes love them, sometimes even remember them. Marguerite and Buridan are not wholly unreal in their wild passion. The scene of reconciliation between the Musketeers in the Place Royale has something deeper than mere effect. And these are only two among many. Under all his gift of technique, his love of startling and amazing, the man was not without an eye, a grip on life, above all, a heart that beat widely, with many sorrows and many joys.

Then the style is the style of melodrama, but it is also far more. No one knew better how and when to let loose sharp, stinging, burning shafts of phrase like the final speech of Antony, *'Elle m'a résisté; je l'ai assassinée,'*—shafts which flew over the footlights straight to the heart of every auditor. But these effects would be nothing without the varied movement of narration, the ease, the lightness, the grace—above all, the perpetual wit, the play of delicate irony,

which saves sentiment from being sentimental and erudition from being dull.

Dumas's style has been much abused, and in some ways deserves it. Mr. Saintsbury considers that the plays have 'but little value as literature properly so-called,' and that 'the style of the novels is not more remarkable as such than that of the dramas.' But how far more discerning and sympathetic is Stevenson's characterization of it: 'Light as a whipped trifle, strong as silk; wordy like a village tale; pat like a general's despatch; with every fault, yet never tedious; with no merit, yet inimitably right.' As for dialogue—that subtlest test of the novelist's genius—which neither Balzac, nor Flaubert, nor Zola could manage with flexibility or ease, Dumas may have used it to excess, but who has ever carried it to greater perfection? In M. Lemaître's excellent, if somewhat cynical, phrase, Dumas's dialogue has 'the wonderful quality of stringing out the narrative to the crack of doom and at the same time making it appear to move with headlong rapidity.' But let it string out, so it moves. And surely Dumas's conversations do move, as no others ever have.

In the hurry of modern reading, few people have time to get at Dumas in any but his best-known works. Yet to form a complete idea of his powers, one must take a much wider survey. All periods, all nations, all regions of the earth, came at one time or another under his pen. Of course this means an inevitable superficiality and inaccuracy. But one overlooks these defects, is hardly aware of them, in the ease, the spirit, the unfailing humanness of the narrative. Take a minor story like *L'Isle de Feu,* dealing with the Dutch in Java and with the habits and superstitions of the natives, snake-charming, spirit-haunting, etc. Everywhere there is movement, life, character, the wit of the *Impressions de Voyage,* the passion of *La Reine Margot.* And if Dumas does not quite anticipate the seductive melancholy of Loti's tropics, he gives hints of it which are really wonderful for a man who had never been south of latitude thirty.

Perhaps, outside of the historical novels, we may select four very different books as most typical of Dumas's great variety of production. First, in *Conscience l'Innocent,* we have a simple idyllic subject, recalling George Sand's country stories: peasant life, rural scenes, sweet pictures of Dumas's own village home at Villers-Cotterets, which he introduced into so many of his writings. Second, in the immense canvas of *Salvator,* too little appreciated, we have a picture of contemporary conditions, the Paris of Sue and

Hugo, treated with a vividness far beyond Sue and a dramatic power which Hugo never could command. Third, comes the incomplete *Isaac Laquedem,* the vast Odyssey of the Wandering Jew, in which the author planned to develop epically the whole history of the world, though the censorship allowed him to get no further than the small Biblical portion of it. Few of Dumas's books illustrate better the really soaring sweep of his imagination, and not many have a larger share of his *esprit.* Lastly, there is **Monte Cristo,** which, on the whole, remains, doubtless, the best example of what Dumas could do without history to support him. 'Pure melodrama,' some will say; in a sense, truly. Yet, as compared with the melodrama of, for instance, *Armadale* and *The Woman in White,* there is a certain largeness, a somber grandeur, about the vengeance of Dantès which goes almost far enough to lift the book out of the realm of melodrama, and into that of tragedy. And then there is the wit!

But it is on historical romance, whether in drama or fiction, that Dumas's popularity must chiefly rest. He himself felt it would be so, hoped it would be so; and his numerous references to the matter, if amusing, are also extremely interesting. He speaks of his series of historical novels as 'immense pictures we have undertaken to unroll before the eyes of our readers, in which, if our genius equalled our good will, we would introduce all classes of men from the beggar to the king, from Caliban to Ariel.' And again: 'Balzac has written a great work entitled "The Human Comedy." Our work, begun at the same time, may be entitled "The Drama of France."' He hopes that his labors will be profitable as well as amusing: 'We intentionally say "instruct" first, for amusement with us is only a mask for instruction. . . . Concerning the last five centuries and a half we have taught France more history than any historian.' And when some one gently insinuates that from a purely historical point of view his work cannot stand with the highest, he replies with his usual charming humor, 'It is the unreadable histories that make a stir; they are like dinners you can't digest; digestible dinners give you no cause to think about them on the next day.'

After all, humor apart, we must recognize the justice of Dumas's claim; and the enduring life and perpetual revival of the historical novel go far to support it. Mankind in general do love to hear about Henry IV, Richelieu, and the Stuarts, about Washington and Lincoln and Napoleon, and in hearing they do learn, even against their will. Pedants shake their heads. This birth-date is incorrect. That victory was not a victory

at all. When Dr. Dryasdust has given the slow labor of a lifetime to disentangling fact from fiction, how wicked to mislead the ignorant by wantonly developing fiction out of fact! As if Dr. Dryasdust really knew fact from fiction! As if the higher spiritual facts were not altogether beyond his ken and his researches! As if any two pedants agreed! Take the central fact of history, the point from which everything of importance and interest emanates—human character, the human soul. What pedant can reach it, can analyse it with his finest microscope? Napoleon was born on such a day, died on such a day, this he did, that he did. But was he in any sense patriotic, an idealist, a lover of France? Was he a suspicious, jealous, lascivious tyrant? Was he sometimes one, sometimes the other? State documents and gossiping memoirs give no final answer to these questions, only hints and cloudy indications bearing upon them, from which the genius of the historian must sketch a figure for itself. Therefore, as many historians, so many Napoleons, and in the end my Napoleon, your Napoleon. If so, why not Alexandre Dumas's Napoleon, said Dumas, having perhaps as much faculty of imaginative divination as you or I, or even as several historians whom we will not mention.

In fact, Dumas has undoubtedly taught the history of France to thousands who would otherwise have had little concern with it. And his characters live. Catherine de' Medici and her sons, Louis XIV, Mazarin, the Duc de Richelieu, Marie Antoinette—we know them as we know people whom we meet every day: in one sense, perhaps not at all; but in another sense, intimately. Great actions call for a large background, which should be handled with the wide sweep of the scene-painter, not with the curious minuteness of the artist in miniatures. The very abundance of these characters, the vastness of the canvas, help the reality, and in this matter of amplitude Dumas and Scott show their genius, and triumph over the petty concentration of later imitators. Nor are the characters wholly or mainly of Dumas's own invention less vivid than those historical; for Dumas learned from Scott the cardinal secret of historical romance, which Shakespeare did not grasp, that the action of the story should turn, not on real personages, but on fictitious heroes and heroines, whose fortunes can be moulded freely for a dramatic purpose. Dumas himself says somewhere that people complain of the length of his novels, yet that the longest have been the most popular and the most successful. It is so. We can wander for days in the vast galleries of the **Reine Margot** series, charmed with the gallantry of La Mole, the vivacity of Coconnas, the bravado of Bussy, above all, the inimitable wit and shrewdness of Chicot, who surely comes next to d'Artagnan among all Dumas's literary children. And d'Artagnan—what a broad country he inhabits! How lovely to lose one's self there in long winter evenings, meeting at every turn a saucy face or a gay gesture or a keen flash of sword that makes one forget the passage of time. 'I never had a care that a half-hour's reading would not dissipate,' said Montesquieu. Fortunate man! How few of us resemble him! But if a half-hour's reading of anything would work such a miracle, surely a novel of Dumas would do it.

As for the man himself, he happily created such characters as d'Artagnan and Chicot because he resembled them, and was in his own person as picturesque a figure as any that talks passion in his plays, or wit in the endless pages of his novels. I do not know that he had ever read Milton's oracular saying that he who would be a great poet should make his life a true poem; but, in any case, he pointed it aptly by showing that the best way to write romantic novels is to make a romantic novel of your own career. Born in 1802, in the most stirring period of French history, one quarter African by blood, he worked his way upward from bitter poverty and insignificance to sudden glory and considerable wealth. Ambitious for political as well as literary success he took a more or less active part in the various commotions of the second quarter of the century, so that he was able to say of himself with some truth and immense satisfaction, 'I have touched the left hand of princes, the right hand of artists and literary celebrities, and have come in contact with all phases of life.'

A great traveler, a great hunter, he had innumerable adventures by flood and field. Quick in emotion and quicker in speech, he made friends everywhere and some enemies. Peculiarly sensitive to the charms and caresses of women, he had no end of love-affairs, all more or less discreditable. Thoughtless, careless, full of wit, full of laughter, he traveled the primrose way, plucking kisses like spring blossoms, wrapping his cloak more tightly round him when he ran into winter storms of envy, jealousy, and mocking. What wealth he had he squandered, what glory, he frittered away. And as he was born in a whirlwind of French triumph, so he died, in 1870, in a wilder whirlwind of French ruin and despair.

The man's life was, indeed, a novel; and in writing his **Memoirs** he dressed it out as such, heightening, coloring, enriching the golden web of memory, as only he knew how to do; so that I am almost ready

to call these same memoirs the best of his works, even with *Les Trois Mousquetaires* and *La Tour de Nesle* in fresh remembrance. Such variety and vivacity of anecdote, such vivid, shifting portraiture of characters, such quick reality of incident, such wit always. But the best of it, unquestionably, is not Talma, nor Dorval, nor Hugo, nor the Duke of Orleans, but just Alexandre Dumas. It is said that once, when a friend asked him how he had enjoyed a party, Dumas replied, 'I should have been horribly bored, if it hadn't been for myself.' Readers of the **Memoirs** will easily understand how other society might have seemed dull in comparison.

From all the tangled mass of anecdote and laughter let us try to gather one or two definite lines of portraiture for the better understanding of this singular personage, 'one of the forces of nature,' as Michelet called him in a phrase which Dumas loved to repeat.

And to begin with the beginning. Did the creator of Buridan and Chicot have a religion, did he trouble himself with abstract ideas? You smile; and certainly he did not trouble his readers very much with these things. Yet in his own opinion he was a thinker, and a rather deep one. Read, in the preface to *Caligula,* how the public received with awe 'this rushing torrent of thought, which appeared to it perhaps new and daring, but solemn and chaste; and then withdrew, with bowed head, like a man who has at last found the solution of a problem which has vexed him during many sleepless nights.'

In his turbulent youth the author of **Antony** was a disbeliever, as became a brother of Byron and Musset; 'there are moments when I would give thee up my soul, if I believed I had one.' But in later years he settled down to the soberer view which appears in the dedication of 'La Conscience' to Hugo: 'in testimony of a friendship which has survived exile and will, I hope, survive death. I believe in the immortality of the soul.' And again and again he testified to the power of his early religious training, which 'left upon all my beliefs, upon all my opinions, so profound an impression that even today I cannot enter a church without taking the holy water, cannot pass a crucifix without making the sign of the cross.' Nor do these emotions spring from mere religiosity, but from an astonishingly, not to say crudely, definite form of belief: 'I know not what my merit has been, whether in this world or in the other worlds I may have inhabited before; but God has shown me especial favors and in all the critical situations in which I have found myself, he has come visibly to my assistance. Therefore, O God, I confess thy name openly and humbly before all skeptics and before all believers.' What revivalist of to-day could speak with more fervor? If only one did not suspect a bit of the irony that shows more clearly in the conversation with his old teacher, whose prayers Dumas had requested. 'My prayers?' said the abbé. 'You don't believe in them.'—'No, I don't always believe in them. That is very true; but don't worry: when I need them I will believe in them.' On the strength of that remark we might almost call Dumas the inventor of Pragmatism before Professor James.

And the irony is rooted in a truth of character. Dumas was a man of this world. He might dream of the other at odd moments, in vague curiosity; but by temperament he was a frank pagan, an eater, a laugher, a lover, a fighter, gorgeously in words, not wholly ineffectively in deeds, even after we have made the necessary discount from his own version of his exploits. He had inherited something of his father's magnificent physique and something of his father's courage. When he tells us that 'since I arrived at manhood, whenever danger has presented itself, by night or by day, I have always walked straight up to danger,' we believe him—with the discount aforesaid; and we believe him all the more, because like every brave man, he does not hesitate to confess fear. 'It was the first time I had heard the noise of grapeshot, and I say frankly that I will not believe any one who tells me that he heard that noise for the first time without perturbation.'

In truth, the religion, the courage, the fear—all, and everything else in the man, were a matter of impulse, of immediate emotion. He was quite aware of this himself. When he proposed his Vendée mission to Lafayette, the latter said to him, 'Have you reflected on what this means?'—'As much as I am capable of reflecting about anything: I am a man of instinct, not of reflection.' The extraordinary vanity of which he was justly accused, of which he accuses himself—'everybody knows the vain side of my character'—was only one phase of this natural impulsiveness. He spoke out what others think—and keep to themselves. Mr. Davidson has admirably noted that in Dumas's case vanity was perfectly compatible with humility. He had no absurdly exaggerated idea of his own powers. But he liked to talk about himself, to be conspicuous, to be the central figure on every stage. The African blood, of which he was not ashamed—'I am a mulatto,' he says repeatedly—told in him; the negro childlikeness. He was a child always, above all childlike in this matter of vanity. Readers of *Tom*

Sawyer will remember that that delightful youth, on hearing the beatific vision of Isaiah, which pictures such a varied menagerie dwelling in harmony, with a little child to lead them, had one absorbing wish: that he might be that child. Dumas was precisely like Tom Sawyer; witness this delightful prayer of his youth: 'Make me great and glorious, O Lord, that I may come nearer unto thee. And the more glorious thou makest me, the more humbly will I confess thy name, thy majesty, thy splendor.'

The same childlike temper, the fresh, animal instincts of a great boy, explain, if they do not excuse, the disorders of Dumas's life.

In this connection it is hardly necessary to do more than to point out his hopeless aberration from all Anglo-Saxon standards of propriety and decency. It would be easy to lash such aberration, but it is perhaps better to consider it in connection with the man's character as a whole, and to remember that his life was as far as possible from being a generally idle or dissipated one. He never smoked, cherishing, in fact, a grudge against tobacco, which he regarded as an enemy to true sociability. He was moderate in eating and drinking. Above all, he was an enormous worker. No man essentially vicious, no man who had not a large fund of temperance and self-control, could have produced a tithe of Dumas's legacy to posterity. But what is most interesting of all in this matter of morals is Dumas's entire satisfaction with himself. I doubt if any other human being would deliberately have ventured on a statement so remarkable as the following: 'When the hand of the Lord closes the two horizons of my life, letting fall the veil of his love between the nothingness that precedes and the nothingness that follows the life of man, he may examine the intermediate space with his most rigorous scrutiny, he will not find there one single evil thought or one action for which I feel that I should reproach myself.' Comment on this would only dim its splendor. Yet people say that the *Memoirs* of Dumas lack interest as human documents! He was an atrocious hypocrite, then, you think? Not the least in the world. Simply a child, always a child.

A child in money matters also. No one could accuse him of deliberate financial dishonesty; but to beg and borrow and never to pay was the normal condition of things. To promise right and left when cash was needed, then to find one's self entirely unable to fulfil one's promises—still childlike. Only, persons of that childlike temper, who have not genius, are apt to end badly. And then, after all, to write in cold blood that one has never had a single action to reproach one's self with! I trust the reader appreciates that passage as I do.

And if the child lacked a sense of money property, how should he be likely to have a sense of property in literature? Shakespeare, Schiller, dozens of others, had had ideas which were useful. Why not use them? A few persons had previously written on the history of France. Distinguished historical characters had left memoirs describing their own achievements. It would have been almost disrespectful to neglect the valuable material thus afforded. Let us quote the histories and borrow from the memoirs. As for mentioning any little indebtedness, life is not long enough for that. We make bold to think that what we invent is quite as good as what we take from others. So it is—far better. A careful comparison of *Les Trois Mousquetaires* with the original d'Artagnan *Memoirs* increases rather than diminishes one's admiration for the author of the novel.

But it will be said, even after borrowing his material, Dumas could not write this same novel without the assistance of a certain Maquet. Again the same child-like looseness in the sense of property. Could a genius be expected to write three hundred[1] volumes without helpers for the rough work? He must have hodmen to fetch bricks and mortar. And perhaps the builder, hurried and overdriven, may set the hodmen to lay a bit of wall here and there, may come to leave altogether too much to hodmen so that the work suffers for it. What matter? Had ever any Maquet or Gaillardet or Meurice, writing by himself, the Dumas touch? As Mr. Lang justly points out, no collaborator has been suggested for the *Memoirs* and I have already said that the *Memoirs* belong, in many respects, to Dumas's best, most characteristic work.

Then, a child is as ready to give as to take. So was Dumas. In money matters it goes without saying. He was always ready to give, to give to everybody everything he had, and even everything he had not and some one else had. 'Nature had already put in my heart,' he says of his childhood, 'that fountain of general kindliness through which flows away and will flow away, everything I had, everything I have, and everything I ever shall have.' But it was not only money, it was time and thought, labor and many steps. This same fountain of general kindliness was always at the service even of strangers. For instance, Dumas himself tells us that, happening once to be in a seaport town, he found a young couple just sailing for the islands and very desolate. He set himself to

cheer them up, and his efforts were so well received that he could not find it in his heart to leave them, though pressing business called him away. He went on board ship with them, and only returned on the pilot boat, in the midst of a gale and at the peril of his life, so says the story. Even in the matter of literary collaboration, Mr. Davidson justly points out that Dumas gave as well as took, and that the list of his debtors is longer than that of his creditors.

And in the highest generosity, that of sympathy and appreciation for fellow workers, the absence of envy and meanness in rivalry, Dumas is nobly abundant. He tells us so himself, not having the habit of concealing his virtues: 'Having arrived at the summit which every man finds in the middle of life's journey, I ask nothing, I desire nothing, I envy nothing, I have many friendships and not one single hatred.' More reliable evidence lies in the general tone of enthusiasm and admiration with which he speaks of all his contemporaries. Musset avoided him, Balzac insulted him; yet he refers to both with hearty praise very different from the damning commendations of the envious Sainte-Beuve. Lamartine and Hugo he eulogizes with lavish freedom, not only in the often-quoted remark, 'Hugo is a thinker, Lamartine a dreamer, and I am a popularizer'—a remark more generous than discriminating—but in innumerable passages which leave no possible doubt of his humility and sincerity. 'Style was what I lacked above everything else. If you had asked me for ten years of my life, promising in exchange that one day I should attain the expression of Hugo's 'Marion Delorme,' I should not have hesitated, I should have given them instantly.'

These things make Dumas attractive, lovable even, as few French writers are lovable. With all his faults he has something of the personal charm of Scott. Only something, however; for Scott, no whit less generous, less kindly, had the sanity, the stability, the moral character, why avoid the word? which Dumas had not. And in comparing their works—a comparison which suggests itself almost inevitably; 'Scott, the grandfather of us all,' said Dumas himself—this difference of morals strikes us even more than the important differences of style and handling of character. It is the immortal merit of Scott that he wrote novels of love and adventure as manly, as virile, as heart can wish, yet absolutely pure.

Now, Dumas has the grave disadvantage of not knowing what morals—sexual morals—are. Listen to him: 'Of the six hundred volumes (1848) that I have written, there are not four which the hand of the most scrupulous mother need conceal from her daughter.' The reader who knows Dumas only in *Les Trois Mousquetaires* will wonder by what fortunate chance he has happened on two volumes out of those 'not four.' But he may reassure himself. There are others of the six hundred which, to use the modern French perversion, more effective untranslated, the daughter will not recommend to her mother. The truth is, Dumas's innocence is worse than, say, Maupassant's sophistication. To the author of *La Reine Margot* love, so called, is all, the excuse, the justification, for everything. Marriage—*ça n'existe pas*; Dumas knew all about it. He was married himself for a few months—at the king's urgent suggestion. Then he recommended the lady to the ambassador at Florence with a most polite note, and she disappeared from his too flowery career. Therefore, Dumas begins his love-stories where Scott's end, and the delicate refinement, the pure womanly freedom of Jeannie Deans and Diana Vernon, is missing in the Frenchman's young ladies, who all either wish to be in a nunnery or ought to be.

The comparison with Scott suggests another with a greater than Scott; and like Scott, Dumas did not object to being compared with Shakespeare, who, by the way, has never been more nobly praised in a brief sentence than in Dumas's saying that 'he was the greatest of all creators after God.' There are striking resemblances between the two writers. Shakespeare began in poverty, lived among theatrical people, made a fortune by the theater. Only, being a thrifty English *bourgeois*, he put the fortune into his own pocket instead of into others'. Shakespeare made a continuous show of English history and bade the world attend it. Shakespeare begged, borrowed, and stole from dead and living, so that his contemporaries spoke of his

'Tiger's heart wrapped in a player's hide.'

Doubtless Maquet and Gaillardet would have been willing to apply the phrase to their celebrated collaborator. Thus far the comparison works well enough. But Shakespeare had a style which was beyond even that of '*Marion Delorme*.' And then, Shakespeare felt and thought as a man, not as a child; his brain and his heart carried the weight of the world.

What will be the future of Dumas? Will his work pass, as other novels of romantic adventure have passed? Three hundred years ago idle women—and men—read 'Amadis de Gaul' and the like, with passion. Says the waiting-woman in Massinger's *Guardian*:

'In all the books of *Amadis de Gaul*

The *Palmerins* and that true Spanish story,

The Mirror of Knighthood, which I have read often,

Read feelingly, nay, more, I do believe in't,

My lady has no parallel.'

Where are Amadis and the Palmerins now? Two hundred years ago the same persons read with the same passion the novels of Scudéry and La Calprenède. 'At noon home,' says Mr. Pepys, 'where I find my wife troubled still at my checking her last night in the coach in her long stories out of *Grand Cyrus,* which she would tell, though nothing to the purpose, nor in any good manner.' And hear Madame de Sévigné on *Cléopatre:* 'The style of La Calprenède is abominable in a thousand places: long sentences in the full-blown, romantic fashion, ill-chosen words—I am perfectly aware of it. Yet it holds me like glue. The beauty of the sentiments, the violent passions, the great scale on which everything takes place and the miraculous success of the hero's redoubtable sword—it carries me away, as if I were a young girl.' *Le succès miraculeux de leur redoutable épée;* if one tried a thousand times, could one express more precisely and concisely one's feelings about *Les Trois Mousquetaires*? Yet *Grand Cyrus* is dead, and *Cléopatre* utterly forgotten. No bright-eyed girl asks for them in any circulating library any more.

Shall d'Artagnan, 'dear d'Artagnan,' as Stevenson justly calls him—'I do not say that there is no character so well drawn in Shakespeare; I do say that there is none I love so wholly'—d'Artagnan, whose *redoutable épée* makes such delightful havoc among the nameless *canaille,* whose more redoubtable wit sets kings and queens and dukes and cardinals at odds and brings them to peace again—shall d'Artagnan, too, die and be forgotten? The thought is enough to make one close *Le Vicomte de Bragelonne* in the middle and fall a-dreaming on the flight of time and the changes of the world. And one says to one's self that one would like to live two or three centuries for many reasons, but not least, to read stories so absorbing that they will make one indifferent to the adventures of d'Artagnan.

1908

Note

1. Perhaps it would be well to explain the different numerical estimates of Dumas's works. As now published in the Lévy collection they fill about three hundred volumes, but in their original form they ran to twelve hundred, more or less.

Richard S. Stowe (essay date 1976)

SOURCE: Stowe, Richard S. "Other Fiction." In *Alexandre Dumas (père)*, pp. 127-34. Boston, Mass.: Twayne, 1976.

[*In the following essay, Stowe presents an overview of some of Dumas's lesser-known works of fiction, including* Georges, Les Frères corses, *and the Villers-Cotterêts novels.*]

The first impression received from a survey of Dumas's other nonhistorical fiction is of its variety. The high-spirited *Le Capitaine Pamphile* (1839) combines pirates, Huron Indians, and exotic animals with happy results. A year before that book Dumas had published his first contemporary novel, *La Salle d'armes*—actually a pair of short novels of which the more memorable is the first, *Pauline*. A moving tale filled with Romantic antitheses, it is the story of a young woman in love with a man who turns out to be a thief and murderer. *Amaury* (1844) is another love story, while *L'Histoire d'un Casse-Noisette* (1845) is an adaptation from E. T. A. Hoffmann, the source of Tschaikovsky's ballet *The Nutcracker.* Hoffman is the hero of *La Femme au Collier de velours* (*The Woman with the Velvet Necklace*), perhaps Dumas's most successful venture into the literature of the occult. This is an eerie mingling of dream and reality, a story of Hoffmann's love for a dancer that is completely in the vein of such tales by the German master as *Don Juan* or the three used by Offenbach in his opera. Dumas says that the story was first told to him by Nodier; the papers of Paul Lacroix left to the Arsenal Library show that he too at least had a hand in drawing up Dumas's scenario for it;[1] but the writing is emphatically Dumas near his best. Originally published alone (1851), it is now usually included with the macabre tales of vampires and severed heads that Dumas issued in 1849-50 under the collective title *Les Mille et un Fantômes* (*The Thousand and One Phantoms*), stories in which the occult merges with the terror and horror of the Gothic novel. A different kind of tale of Germanic origin is *Othon l'Archer,* a version of the legend opera-lovers will recognize as the source of Wagner's *Lohengrin. Isaac Laquedem* (1853) is the first and only volume of a projected "epic" novel in twenty-five volumes based on the legend of the Wandering Jew. This book recounts the story of Jesus; censorship forced abandonment of the rest of the series. *Le Père la Ruine* (1860), a somber story of Marne fishermen told with moving simplicity and sobriety, may well be Dumas's most sustained tragic work.

The list could go on but the point, we trust, is made. Among the many and varied works that compose Du-mas's nonhistorical fiction five merit a slightly longer look. All of them may be loosely categorized as *romans de moeurs,* but each is something more as well.[2] The subject of *Georges* is racial conflict; *Les Frères corses* is an absorbing psychological study with supernatural overtones; *Conscience l'Innocent, Catherine Blum,* and *Le Meneur de loups*—along with parts of *Ange Pitou*—constitute Dumas's fictional tribute to the town and region of his birth.

I. GEORGES

Georges appeared in 1843, just the year before *Les Trois Mousquetaires,* and perhaps partly for that reason has tended to remain less known and less read than it deserves to be. Not ranking among Dumas's masterpieces, it is nonetheless a solid, well-written book. Of particular interest today because of its subject matter, it offers typical Dumasian appeal also in its exotic setting and adventurous story.

Georges Munier, the hero, is one of two sons of Pierre Munier, a wealthy mulatto planter of the Isle of France—an island east of Madagascar known to-day as Mauritius. Despite his wealth and personal qualities, Pierre Munier had decided he could best live vis-à-vis the white ruling class of the island by complete subservience: "his entire life was spent apologizing for his birth." His sons were sent to Europe to school in 1810, not to return for fourteen years. Though only twelve when he left, the sensitive Georges had already borne all the affronts he could from the whites—in particular young Henri de Malmédie—and determined that, unlike his father, he would devote his life to a "war to the death against prejudice." To that end he spent his years in Paris and London developing his mental, moral, and physical capacities to the maximum, especially his force of will and self-control. Following his formal education, Georges travelled extensively in Greece and the Near East and won the crosses of the Légion d'Honneur and of Charles III of Spain for his bravery in the battle of Trocadero. His brother had a different kind of life, going to sea and eventually becoming a slave trader: "Indeed, by a strange coincidence, chance brought together in one family the man who had spent his life bowed down under the prejudice of color, the man who made his fortune by exploiting it, and the man who was ready to risk his life to fight it."

After his return Georges falls in love with Sara de Malmédie, cousin and fiancée of his enemy Henri, and she is drawn to him. When Georges, who has thus far remained incognito, reveals his identity at the English governor's ball, Sara alone among the creoles there remains sympathetic. Georges determines to win her; he goes through the formality of asking for her hand, but is neither surprised nor dissuaded by her uncle's refusal. Georges is asked by Laïza, a slave he has freed, to serve as leader of an uprising of the slaves. When he learns that Henri de Malmédie, whom he has deliberately insulted, refuses to fight a duel with him, a mulatto, Georges agrees to Laïza's request but is tricked and imprisoned by the governor.

The uprising fails for lack of a leader and because the English forestall it by lighting the city and leaving barrels of liquor about to tempt the invading blacks. Georges escapes from prison and joins the few hundred blacks who are fighting the English, but the cause is lost. Recaptured and condemned to death by the English, in another *coup de théâtre* Georges escapes again, with Sara, to his brother's boat. A sea chase ensues and battle is engaged, but the English are defeated and the governor goes down with his ship.

It is difficult to read this novel without feeling that in it Dumas, like his hero, is fighting a prejudice. Because the prejudice is one that Dumas himself occasionally encountered, more than one commentator has identified Dumas with Georges. J.-H. Bornecque, for example,[3] sees Georges as an anticipation of Edmond Dantès both as superman and as the author's vicarious instrument of vengeance against a mediocre or rejecting society. One would be reluctant to go farther than this, if even this far, since Dumas's life is manifestly so different from that of his character. Unquestionably he experienced slights and insults—some of the worst being found in Mirecourt's pamphlet—but there is little evidence to suggest that he was deeply wounded by them, even less to suggest that he brooded over them. Certainly he never experienced the kind of ostracism and rejection of which Georges was a victim. In a cogent essay, "Dumas et les Noirs," ("Dumas and the Blacks"), Léon-François Hoffmann[4] reminds readers that, unlike Georges, Dumas was readily accepted in all circles in which he moved—indeed adulated in many—and that in the memoirs and in his letters he gives no hint of defensiveness or sensitivity about his lineage. Correspondingly, Hoffmann adds, he does not seem to find it a matter for special pride either; he does not even state in his memoirs that the grandmother whose name he bore was black. Though Dumas in all probability ex-

pressed his honest convictions about racial prejudice in *Georges,* it seems at the very least unlikely that the book was a deeply felt crusade or personal vindication.

Hoffmann points out another aspect of the book that emerges with careful reading: it is not a "black" novel in the usual sense of the word. The hero is a mulatto, and the prejudice he fights is quite clearly that directed against his mixed blood. Georges and his father both own black slaves[5] and Jacques, the slave trader, is depicted as breaking the law but by no means as a reprehensible person. Indeed, slavery as an institution does not seem to be seriously questioned, and Dumas seems more attracted by the paradoxical contrast of views within the Munier family than moved to support or denounce any of them. Further, except for Laïza and his brother the blacks in the book are shown as inferior beings. It is not by accident that Pierre Munier's intelligence and other fine qualities shine forth when he is in the company of blacks—as opposed to the whites who force him automatically into his self-deprecatory role—or that the slaves planning a revolt should look to Georges for the leadership they apparently could not find in their own numbers. If Dumas's life offers little support for theories that his novel is a calculated attack on anti-black prejudice in the nineteenth century, the novel suggests that he tended to share rather than to challenge his century's views.

In the light of the foregoing one may argue that for Dumas slavery or the status of the black man (or even the mulatto) as such was not at issue in this book. George's mixed blood, rather, appears exactly comparable to Antony's illegitimacy or Kean's profession: it is the pretext for a prejudice that keeps a superior man from participating in society. Georges joins the company of outcast Romantic heroes, exceptional individuals barred from their due by the laws, conventions, or prejudices of men less gifted than they. Dumas does not deny the reality of the injustice; he deplores it. But as was true in *Antony,* his approach is from the standpoint of the specific individual in the concrete situation rather than on the level of principle.

II. *LES FRÈRES CORSES*

The Corsican Brothers is a brief work, scarcely more than a long short story. It is cast in the form of the anecdotes in the **Impressions de voyage** and is narrated throughout in the first person by Dumas, who consequently plays a small role. The other characters were also real people, whom Dumas met on a visit to Corsica[6] and in Paris on his return.

The story is a simple one that falls naturally into two parts. In Corsica Dumas is lodged in the home of the de Franchi family, in the room of Louis de Franchi, one of his hostess's twin sons. The other son, Lucien, shows him around the house and village (Sullacaro), and tells how his parents had ended a vendetta of many years by simultaneously killing—in different places—the last two members of the enemy family. In the course of conversation Lucien describes the almost telepathic communication that exists between him and Louis, though Louis has chosen to settle in Paris and "be French" while Lucien has vowed to remain always Corsican. Reference is also made to Louis's lack of skill with a pistol in contrast to Lucien's expertise. During his visit Dumas witnesses the peaceful settlement of a vendetta between two families in which Lucien, almost annoyed with himself for doing it, serves as arbiter. When Dumas returns to Paris he takes with him a letter of introduction to Louis de Franchi.

Back in Paris Dumas establishes contact with Louis, for whom he soon finds himself serving as second in a duel with a young man named Château-Renaud.[7] Before the duel Louis writes a letter to his mother telling her he is dying of a brain fever, and informs Dumas that the ghost of his father had visited him during the night and told him he would die at 9:10 A.M. Mortally wounded in the duel, it is precisely at that time that Louis dies.

About five days later Lucien arrives in Paris, having seen his brother in a vision or dream the night before his death. He also says he knows the rest of what happened and has come, with his mother's blessing, to avenge Louis's death. Château-Renaud accepts Lucien's terms for a duel at the same place and with the same weapons. Lucien remains utterly calm, kills Château-Renaud as he predicted he would, then throws himself into Dumas's arms, weeping for the first time in his life.

The first thing that strikes the reader of this tale is the simplicity and economy of its telling, qualities not often held to be Dumas's forte. It lacks the controlled spareness of Mérimée's Corsican stories, but Dumas has found and maintained exactly the right tone for himself. Descriptions are vivid, characters and atmosphere are sketched with precision and force; there is scarcely a superfluous detail or word, and the action moves smoothly and relentlessly to its climax. Nothing is overstated, nothing distracts from unity or mood.

It is this straightforwardness and restraint that help Dumas to make the supernatural elements so convincing. They are, quite simply, there; and the reader accepts them with no need for explanation or justification. Unlike the spectacular display of Joseph Balsamo's powers, these visions—or ghostly visits, who is to say?—somehow do not strain the credulity or clash with the sober realism of their context. Similarly, the very simplicity of the characters lends them a moving nobility that enlarges their humanity as it deepens the meaning of the tale.

III. THE VILLERS-COTTERÊTS NOVELS

"And, in point of fact, was it not in Villers-Cotterêts that I really and truly lived, since it was there that I waited for life?" So wrote Dumas in Chapter I of **Catherine Blum.** The affection he always felt for his native town, so apparent in even the most incidental allusions, overflowed in the 1850's in the series of novels Dumas based on recollections of his childhood and youth. The writing and publication of his memoirs occupied the first half of that decade and doubtless stimulated his memory, for the links between these novels and **Mes Mémoires** are many and close. By coincidence it was during the same period that Dumas wrote **Ange Pitou** and in that fact surely lies the explanation of its barely disguised transposition from his own life.

The earliest of the group, **Conscience l'Innocent,** is also the longest. Jean Manscourt received his nickname—the title of the book—because of his simplicity and absolute candor. After a quiet childhood in the village of Haramont, remote from the great events of the Napoleonic era, in 1813 Conscience—just eighteen—is called up for military service. His grandfather, who is dependent on him, tries unsuccessfully to buy a replacement. Knowing that a friend was discharged because of the loss of two fingers, Conscience chops off his right index finger. Accused of trying to avoid service, Conscience unhesitatingly admits his intent but persuades the authorities that he did not do it for himself. He escapes punishment and is taken on as a *soldat de train.* Eventually drawn into combat anyhow, he is blinded. His childhood sweetheart Mariette secures his release from the hospital in Laon and brings him home. Slowly his sight is regained. In 1815 when Napoleon passes through Villers-Cotterêts en route to Waterloo, Mariette and Conscience are in the throng waiting to greet him. The emperor speaks to them, gives Conscience a *croix de guerre* and Mariette an apronful of gold.

For about the first three-quarters of its length **Conscience l'Innocent** maintains a disarming simplicity and charm. Though idealized and sentimental, its depiction of peasant characters and life is sufficiently realistic and unaffected not to cloy. Conscience especially is well drawn, believable, and appealing despite his alarming perfection of character and fondness for talking to animals and flowers. Unfortunately, midway through the second volume the slight tale becomes unduly drawn out and repetitious and the ending is too contrived to satisfy.

Catherine Blum more successfully balances substance and length, at least partly, perhaps, because Dumas has concentrated all the action in a single day. A final chapter serves as epilogue to inform the reader of the longer-range consequences of the day's events.

Catherine returns to the home of her uncle Guillaume Watrin in Villers-Cotterêts after eighteen months in Paris learning millinery. During her absence she and her cousin Bernard Watrin realize that they love each other, but obstacles arise in their path. Bernard's mother opposes their marriage because Catherine is Protestant (her father was German); Louis Chollet, a Parisian, also seeks Catherine's hand; and a malevolent villager, Mathieu Gogolue, is trying to avenge an insult from Bernard. His plan for vengeance takes the form of a trick to deceive Bernard into thinking that Catherine is having clandestine meetings with Chollet. Mathieu's deception is eventually exposed, Mme Watrin is reconciled to the marriage, and all ends happily.

Like *Conscience l'Innocent, Catherine Blum* is a story whose chief merit is charm. It is again sentimental but its humor and brevity keep it from being maudlin or overly sweet. Perhaps its most surprising element is the cruelty shown by most of the characters toward the crippled Mathieu. Dumas apparently thought that Mathieu's viciousness was sufficient justification for the others' treatment of him and makes no attempt to excuse or conceal it. A modern reader might well find a major cause of Mathieu's meanness and vindictiveness in the attitudes of the others, and in Dumas's seeming lack of sympathy another example of the kind of acceptance of prevailing views that we observed in *Georges*.

Le Meneur de loups (*The Wolf-Leader*) joins Dumas's affection for his *petite patrie* to his predilection for tales of the supernatural. The story of a werewolf, it is a legend of the forest of Villers-Cotterêts told to him by old Mocquet, his father's *garde*. It has all the flavor of ghost stories told around a campfire, complete with the eerie reality of strange events in a

familiar setting. Dumas precedes it with a lively account of a real wolf-hunt that prepares the way beautifully by familiarizing the reader with the setting and subtly suggesting the mysteries to be revealed. The story itself is a mingling of local legend and the universal tale of a pact with the devil: the covetous and ambitious young sabotmaker Thibault trades his soul for the fulfillment of his wishes, but reaps only unhappiness as each desire leads to another until the tragic dénouement.

These three novels cannot be ranked among Dumas's important works, but they deserve to be less neglected than they have been—especially *Catherine Blum* and *Le Meneur de loups*. Besides their intrinsic attractiveness they reveal a side of Dumas which he himself always took seriously, and they demonstrate his ability to work on an intimate scale at subdued volume. All three are filled with beautiful evocations of nature—especially the forest—and suffused with love for his native corner of France. To read them is to discover a different Dumas and to understand the familiar one in different ways, as he turns from the dazzling colors of history and adventure to the tranquil contemplation of a quieter world that is no less rich for him.

> Why should I not love to speak of that immense bower of verdure, where every single object is fraught with memories of the past? I knew everyone and everything there; not only the people of the town, not only the stones of the houses, but even more the trees of the forest. . . . I will teach you the language of all those old friends of my youth, whether they be living or dead, and you will then understand with what gentle voices they breathe into my ear.[8]

Notes

1. Clouard, p. 244.

2. A further point in common is that all are among the works Dumas wrote without collaborators. The only one whose authorship is disputed at all is *Georges*. Mirecourt asserted that it had been written by Félicien Mallefille, but Dumas insisted that it was his own and there is little reason to doubt his word.

3. Bornecque, preface to *Monte-Cristo* (Garnier), pp. lxii ff.

4. Léon-François Hoffmann, introduction to his edition of *Georges* (Paris: Gallimard, Collection Folio, 1974).

5. Dumas's father too had a black servant, though obviously not a slave; cf. *Mes Mémoires*, Chap-

ter XVI, and Chapter 2 of *Le Meneur de loups.* A black servant accompanied Dumas on his trip to Spain (Cf. *De Paris à Cadix,* Chapter 2 and *passim*).

6. Clouard (p. 242) places Dumas's trip to Corsica in 1842, during his travels with Prince Napoleon. In the story Dumas specifies the date as early March, 1841.

7. Dumas gives the same name to one of the young dandies in the circle of Albert de Morcerf in *Le Comte de Monte-Cristo.*

8. "Prologue" (Chapter I) to *Catherine Blum.*

Selected Bibliography

PRIMARY SOURCES

The standard edition of Dumas is the *Oeuvres complètes* in 301 volumes published by Michel Lévy, later Calmann-Lévy, beginning in 1851. Unfortunately this edition is considerably less than definitive or really complete; it is unannotated and many volumes are exceedingly difficult to find. Most of Dumas has been reprinted, however, and at least the best-known works are readily obtainable in French or English. We have made no attempt to cull the mass of popular editions and translations, but list below the most authoritative and useful edited versions that have appeared in recent years.

Oeuvres d'Alexandre Dumas père. Ed. Gilbert Sigaux. 38 vols. Lausanne: Editions Rencontre, 1962-67. This series contains the following fifteen novels, all accompanied by excellent introductions:

Les Trois Mousquetaires.

Vingt Ans après.

Le Vicomte de Bragelonne.

Le Comte de Monte-Cristo.

Joseph Balsamo.

Le Collier de la Reine.

Ange Pitou.

La Comtesse de Charny.

Les Deux Diane.

La Reine Margot.

La Dame de Monsoreau.

Les Quarante-Cinq.

Le Chevalier de Maison-Rouge.

Les Blancs et les Bleus.

Les Compagnons de Jéhu.

Mes Mémoires. Ed. Pierre Josserand. 5 vols. Paris: Gallimard, collection "Mémoires du passé pour servir au temps présent," 1954-68.

Théâtre complet. Ed. Fernande Bassan. Many volumes projected. Paris: Lettres Modernes-Minard, Collection "Bibliothèque introuvable," 1974-.

Antony. Ed. Joseph Varro. Paris: Larousse, "Nouveaux Classiques Larousse," 1970.

Le Comte de Monte-Cristo. Ed. J.-H. Bornecque. 2 vols. Paris: Garnier, 1962.

Georges. Ed. Léon-François Hoffmann. Paris: Gallimard, Collection "Folio," 1974.

Kean. Adaptation by Jean-Paul Sartre (Dumas's text appended). Paris: Gallimard, 1954.

Les Trois Mousquetaires. Ed. Charles Samaran. Paris: Garnier, 1956. Rpt. 1966.

Vingt Ans après. Ed. Charles Samaran. Paris: Garnier, 1962.

Les Trois Mousquetaires. Vingt Ans après. Ed. Gilbert Sigaux. Paris: Gallimard, Bibliothèque de la Pléiade, 1962. Rpt. 1966.

Voyage en Russie. Ed. Jacques Suffel, preface by André Maurois. Paris: Hermann, 1960.

A NOTE ABOUT TRANSLATIONS

Substantially all of Dumas's fiction has been translated into English, some of it many times over during the past hundred years, and all but the most obscure novels can be located with relative ease. Translations of the plays, on the other hand, where they exist at all, are extremely difficult to find. An excellent abridged translation of Dumas's memoirs has been published under the title *The Road to Monte-Cristo* by Jules Eckert Goodman (New York: Scribner, 1956). A. C. Bell has also translated portions of the memoirs as well as a variety of other nonfictional works by Dumas. Abridged translations from the travel writings done by Alma Elizabeth Murch can likewise be recommended. *On Board the Emma* (London: Ernest Benn, 1929), R. S. Garnett's translation of *Les Garibaldiens,* is more complete than standard French versions as it incorporates material Dumas intended to include in reprintings but did not. Garnett has also translated Garibaldi's memoirs as edited and revised by Dumas (New York: D. Appleton, 1931).

SECONDARY SOURCES

Books and articles about Dumas are even more numerous than his own writings. Again we list only the most important or interesting among fairly recent works, plus a few still valuable earlier studies. Other books and articles consulted in the preparation of this volume are indicated in the footnotes.

Bassan, Fernande, and Sylvie Chevalley. *Alexandre Dumas père et la Comédie-Française.* Bibliothèque de Littérature et d'Histoire, no. 15. Paris: Lettres Modernes-Minard, 1972. Detailed and informative study of all matters relative to the production of Dumas's plays by this company.

Bell, A. Craig. *Alexandre Dumas: A Biography and Study.* London: Cassell, 1950. Not completely satisfactory as either biography or study, it nevertheless contains valuable bibliographies and much useful information, especially about Dumas's journalistic activities.

Blaze de Bury, [Ange] Henri. *Mes Études et mes souvenirs: Alexandre Dumas, sa vie, son temps, son oeuvre.* Paris: Calmann-Lévy, 1885. Sympathetic recollections of Dumas and interesting comments on his writings, especially the plays. One of the best nineteenth-century studies.

Bouvier-Ajam, Maurice. *Alexandre Dumas ou Cent Ans après.* Paris: Les Éditeurs Français Réunis, 1972. Lively, provocative study, especially interesting on Dumas's political ideas and methods of work, though some conclusions are debatable.

Clouard, Henri. *Alexandre Dumas.* Paris: Albin Michel, 1954. Unquestionably the best general study of the life and works of Dumas *père,* unfortunately without bibliography or index and never translated into English.

Europe, no. 48. Février-Mars 1970. A special issue of the magazine devoted to articles about Dumas on the occasion of the centenary of his death. All are interesting though of variable merit.

Gorman, Herbert. *The Incredible Marquis: Alexandre Dumas.* New York: Farrar and Rinehart, 1929. A quite reliable and very entertaining popular biography.

Maurois, André. *Alexandre Dumas: A Great Life in Brief.* Trans. Jack Palmer White. New York: Alfred A. Knopf, 1966. Good, readable introduction to Dumas's life, quite obviously adapted from parts of the next entry.

———. *Les Trois Dumas.* Paris: Hachette, 1957. Rpt. Le Livre de Poche, 1957. *The Titans, a Three-Generation Biography of the Dumas.* Trans. Gerard Hopkins. New York: Harper and Row, 1957. The authoritative biography of Dumas *père,* his father, and his son. Excellent bibliography and index in Hachette and Harper editions, omitted in Livre de Poche.

Mirecourt, Eugène de. *Fabrique de Romans, Maison Alexandre Dumas et compagnie.* Paris: Tous les Marchands de Nouveautés, 1845. The famous attack on Dumas.

Parigot, Hippolyte. *Alexandre Dumas père.* Paris: Hachette, "Les Grands Écrivains français," 1902. Still one of the very best studies of Dumas's work: balanced, perceptive, and fair.

———. *Le Drame d'Alexandre Dumas: Étude dramatique, sociale et littéraire.* Paris: Calmann-Lévy, 1899. Parigot's *thèse,* the classic and irreplaceable study of Dumas's plays.

Reed, Frank Wilde. *A Bibliography of Alexandre Dumas père.* London: J. A. Neuhuys, 1933. An indispensable key for entry into the bibliographical maze of Dumas's published works and a few unpublished ones. Ten typewritten supplements are owned by the British Museum.

Simon, Gustave. *Histoire d'une collaboration: Alexandre Dumas et Auguste Maquet.* Paris: Crès, 1919. One of the first attempts to study the question of Dumas's collaborations from documents, Simon's pro-Maquet conclusions have been effectively qualified by later scholars.

Allen G. Wood (essay date 1997)

SOURCE: Wood, Allen G. "Of Kings, Queens, and Musketeers." *Papers on French Seventeenth-Century Literature* 24, no. 46 (1997): 163-71.

[*In the following essay, Wood examines the enduring popularity of the* Three Musketeers *trilogy, commenting that,* "[t]he exploits of d'Artagnan and his three musketeer friends are perhaps better known and more read than works actually written during the reign of Louis XIII."]

The first half of the French seventeenth century remains vividly animated in the collective, popular imagination as the period of the Three Musketeers, even more than one hundred and fifty years after the publication of Alexandre Dumas' historical novel. The exploits of d'Artagnan and his three musketeer friends are perhaps better known and more read than works actually written during the reign of Louis XIII, for readers in France and indeed throughout the world. And the commercial success which Dumas enjoyed, as installment followed installment during the spring and summer of 1844 in *Le Siècle,* called for the sequels of *Vingt Ans Après* and the *Vicomte de Bragelonne,* which advanced the musketeers to the time of the Fronde, then to Louis XIV. Even today, the popularity of the musketeers is still apparent in the various film versions of this modern classic story. It is important to examine the dynamics of history and fiction contained within the novel in order to ascertain the mechanisms of historical transmission in novel form, and determine which elements of the seventeenth century are conveyed by the popular icon.

The intertextual links between Dumas' novel and the *Mémoires de M. d'Artagnan* by Gatien de Courtilz are described in many critical and editorial commentaries, in addition to speculations about the involvement of Auguste Maquet, one of Dumas' many hired writers, in the final draft of the *Trois Mousquetaires.* But rather than focus on questions of hypotextual, source material on one hand, or authorial collaboration on the other, which would only repeat well known information, this study will consider Dumas' text by itself and examine the ways in which it represents the historical period, the era which sets the scene for the narrative action. Dumas did not think of himself as a historian, but he did regard history as "un clou auquel j'accroche mes romans" (Maurois, 170). But where exactly is this historical nail in the *Trois Mousquetaires,* and how does the fiction hang from it?

The historical novel as genre was initiated by Scott, and popularized in 19th-century France by Balzac, Hugo, Vigny and Dumas, who appropriated French history for their fictional rewriting of history from the Middle Ages (*Notre Dame de Paris*) to the French Revolution (*Les Chouans*). Georg Lukacs reminds us that:

> What matters in the historical novel is not the re-telling of great historical events, but the poetic awakening of the people who figure in those events. What matters is that we should reexperience the social and human motives which led men to think, feel, and act just as they did in historical reality.
>
> (p. 43)

It is not a matter of canonizing history, but of popularizing it. While on the one hand the nineteenth century was institutionalizing the past, as presented in Ralph Albanese's study of Molière in the Republican school system, on the other hand fictive creations such as those of Dumas had great mass appeal because they did not claim to be scholarly or pedantic. It is important to be aware of all the various symbolic presentations of past mentalities, in addition to the more traditional documentary aspects of history.

The ahistoricity of this genre, and Dumas' work in particular, has long been noted, and it is clear that ". . . personne ne lit la trilogie de Dumas pour apprendre quelque chose sur le XVIIᵉ siècle." (Bem, p. 13) Jeanne Bem's article continues with a lengthy key which reveals that the major historical events related in the three novels had analogues in the nineteenth century, the true historical referent for the works. It must be noted, however, that such a reading of Dumas' text puts too great a privileged position on the major events of history. Moreover, and to the point at hand, only two of the twelve items in the key refer to the *Trois Mousquetaires.*

The novel's beginning is highly significant in indicating a precise historical period. Dumas, not particularly fond of subtlety, begins his novel with a matter of fact statement concerning date and place: "Le premier lundi du mois d'avril 1625, le bourg de Meung, où naquit l'auteur du *Roman de la Rose.* . . ." There are no transitions, but an abrupt and swift movement backward in time to a specific moment in the past, although, in fact, the exact date of the first Monday in April in 1625 is not provided. Dumas did not use this technique in *Vingt Ans Après* but returned to it in the *Vicomte de Bragelonne*: "Vers le milieu du mois de mai de l'année 1660, à neuf heures du matin, lorsque le soleil. . . ." After this initial date, however, the year is not mentioned again throughout the novel, until the final page, the "Epilogue," which closes the events of the work in a historical chronology containing three references to dates or years. In other words, within this framework which directly states a date in time, the historical period is evoked in a non-calendar fashion.

After stating that initial events in the novel occur in 1625, Dumas then has the task of recreating a world different from that of 1844, where the differences convey a plausible historicity indicating early seventeenth-century France. His second paragraph begins:

> En ce temps-là les paniques étaient fréquentes, et peu de jours se passaient sans qu'une ville ou l'autre enregistrât sur ses archives quelque événement de ce genre. Il y avait les seigneurs qui guerroyaient entre eux; il y avait le roi qui faisait la guerre au cardinal; il y avait l'Espagnol qui faisait la guerre au roi. Puis, outre ces guerres sourdes ou publiques, secrètes ou patentes, il y avait encore les voleurs, les mendiants, les huguenots, les loups et les laquais, qui faisaient la guerre à tout le monde. Les bourgeois s'armaient toujours contre les voleurs, contre les loups, contre les laquais . . . mais jamais contre le cardinal et l'Espagnol.

These multiple "paniques" make this a formidable, hostile environment, one which threatens the average citizen from multiple sources, in an inextricable web of opposing forces which ensnares all too easily. The wolves and Huguenots allude to a pre-1700 society, and references to king and cardinal specify even more accurately the period of Louis XIII. As for the dangers of thieves, lackeys, and warring lords, they provide a universal enough threat to indicate almost any time of the Ancien Regime. All the details in this list of "panics" give general support to the historical dating of the events as occurring in 1625, without being particularly precise.

Reference to a Spanish war with the king of France raises the first instance in the novel of historical anachronism. War with Spain did not break out until ten years later, in 1635. Although the historical novel as a genre presents a mixture of fact and fiction, of history and narrative, the phenomenon of anachronism presents an inappropriate fiction in an item which requires greater historical accuracy. Various critics have pointed out numerous anachronisms in the *Trois Mousquetaires,* which are important only to the extent that they reveal certain blindspots or inattentions. It is true that Dumas was no historian, nor was he writing for historians. Yet his novels are historical in that they capture the general essence of a period, and are highly plausible with regard to historical data, dealing with the realm of the *vraisemblable,* if not with the *vrai.* The question of perspective arises: "L'écriture historique sur le XVIIème siecle doit-elle passer par une vision moderne, Historique, scientifique et 'exacte' de ce qu'était la réalité du XVIIème, ou par la vision que les gens du XVIIème avaient de leur temps. . . ?" (Ronzeaud, p. 122) Anachronisms do occur as traces of a difference, as signs of fictionality. Yet they must be apparent to figure in the reading, whereas, indeed, those in the *Trois Mousquetaires,* like hairline cracks between the imaginary and the real, are likely not even to be perceived.

The fact that Mme de Combalet and the Duchesse d'Aiguillon are presented as two minor characters, when in fact they are two names for the same person in history, apparently escaped the author's attention. In addition, the Porte de la Conférence in Paris is mentioned at a time before the conference which gave it its name, and the rue Servandoni discussed at a time before the architect was even born. Marion de Lorme is alluded to as a mistress of Cardinal Richelieu when she was only fifteen—but, given her reputation, this detail may imply an improbability, rather

than an anachronism. The musketeers bathed in the sea when such an act was rare except in cases of illness, lord Winter threatens to have Milady transported to Botany Bay, discovered by Captain Cook one hundred fifty years later, and houses in Dumas' seventeenth-century Paris bore street numbers earlier than conventional history allows. Finally, many critics chide the reference to Papal infallibility in M. de Tréville's sarcastic comments to the king concerning Richelieu:

> —Son Eminence n'est pas Sa Sainteté, Sire.
>
> —Qu'entendez-vous par là, Monsieur?
>
> —Qu'il n'y a que le pape qui soit infaillible, et que cette infaillibilité ne s'étend pas aux cardinaux.
>
> (p. 94)

The reality of Papal infallibility was quite obviously an anachronism in the time of Louis XIII, but also in that of the *Trois Mousquetaires* in 1844. It was not until Pope Pious IX's proclamation in 1870 that this concept became church doctrine. Until that time it was simply an idea, like so many others, that could have been uttered at any time, without taint of anachronism.

Such lapses are minor, however, especially when the multiple authorship of Dumas' works (Maquet-Dumas) is considered, as well as the rapidity of its creation in installments for *Le Siècle,* and the great quantity of detail provided in the 700-800 page novel. Even when perceived by critical attention, the anachronisms carry little consequence, since Dumas only missed by a decade or two (some two hundred years later) his chronological target. Dumas corrected several mistakes present in the first drafts, corrections based on his own readings of the seventeenth century (Tallemant des Réaux, Mme de Lafayette, etc.). But he was no pedant, preferring a few errors which reveal his own historical fallibility, while not diminishing from his talents as a writer of narrative. Although Charles Samaran calls into question Dumas' historical accuracy, he also evokes a different kind of history at which Dumas excelled:

> Qui a, mieux que Dumas, fait sentir une époque, respirer l'air du temps, et pour cela, entrer dans le secret personnel, psychologique, moral, pittoresque, des gens et des choses, [ou] . . . mieux rendu le passé présent?
>
> (Introduction, *Trois Mousquetaires,* xxxiii)

Dumas was less concerned with a given year than an entire era, and brought it alive with adventurous deeds rather than documented accuracy.

With regard to the paragraph on the various *paniques* of the seventeenth century, although war and strife predominate at this initial stage of the novel, as the moral climate is established, it does not persist throughout the work. This is an early justification of force and a call for virile action in a world of sword-play and intrigue. The seventeenth century as presented in the *Trois Mousquetaires* is generally depicted with a certain nostalgia, as a pleasant enough world, especially for the brave of heart. In short, it is an idealized age of Louis XIII:

> Dumas' picture of the seventeenth century omits everything that would have made it a most uncomfortable age for any of his nineteenth-century readers were they to have been magically transported back into it. The epidemics, the famines, the injustices, the barbarous superstitions of the period have no place in his account. Even war is reduced to a gay picnic beneath the fortifications of La Rochelle.
>
> (Hemmings, p. 123)

The historical period is maintained much less by facts of History, that is, major personalities and events, than it is by the everyday details of custom and fashion. References every few pages to an item of clothing, a unit of currency, or a mode of transportation suffice, with the numerous allusions to king and cardinal, to keep the action well anchored in its historical moment, indicated as "ce temps là." But the *pourpoints* and *pistoles* would be mere stage props if there was not also the recreation of a past mentality, of the image of a real lived experience conveyed by the descriptions and the characters. The one historical item which predominates the others, and reveals a lifestyle different from that of the nineteenth century, is the sword.

The musketeers are swordsmen, sworn to defend the king, his honor, and their own *corps* by the use of arms. The seventeenth century appears at first in the novel as a time of great panic, were it not for men like d'Artagnan and the musketeers who are skilled at swordfighting. As heroes of the tale, they emerge from their violent encounters sometimes wounded, but ultimately victorious. In the *Trois Mousquetaires,* the seventeenth century is presented as a period of libidinal freedom, with different forces of law and order (especially of king and cardinal) fighting each other for control. The musketeers establish relationships with other men, friendship or enmity, by the sword, and their relations with women are carnal and tinged with scandal. D'Artagnan loves Mme Bonacieux, a married woman. The musketeers often

succeed one another in the beds of their mistresses, who act as intermediaries:

> Ces femmes dont les mousquetaires partagent le service ou la couche forment un pont entre eux: leur amitié, ou leur amour si l'on veut, s'exprime en entreprises communes et en corps partagés. La maîtresse commune sert de relais à de troublants messages, de dépositaire de charmants présents, de support à de singulières opérations.
>
> (Tranouez, p. 322)

The musketeers are free to fight and love, serving one father figure as they resist the unjust constraints, the Law of the Father abrogated by Cardinal Richelieu.

Such a portrayal of the seventeenth century is both historically plausible at the same time that it makes of the former French period an exotic, idealized time. It is depicted as a chaotic yet freer era, a time which calls for dramatic, violent action from those "ordinary" citizens who serve their king. Those in the middle of society (lesser nobles, bourgeois), like the four heroes, could make a difference, and participate in shaping the course of history, both the major events (La Rochelle), as well as some of the smaller details (*l'affaire des ferrets*).

The chaos of life in the 1620's is also contained in a series of unstable structures in the narrative, which call for vigilance on the part of characters or readers. In particular, a series of triads either expand or collapse, creating confusion in the structure, and occasionally danger on the level of plot action. The very title of the novel indicates three musketeers, yet the novel describes the adventures of four friends. The fact that d'Artagnan is not officially a musketeer seems a mere technicality. But the common theme of "one for all and all for one" makes it unclear whether there are four heroes, or one.

Even minor details present an unstable triad. In the first chapter, when d'Artagnan leaves home, he is shown as having three presents from his parents: a letter to M. de Tréville, some money, and a horse. Yet, in addition, he has also learned the secret for making a restorative balm to heal wounds, which he uses both in this first chapter and later in the novel (it is the one "present" which lasts longest). But the most unstable and therefore dangerous triad in the entire novel involves the king, queen, and cardinal. The ambiguity in the relationship between king and cardinal makes the "panic" of warring seigneurs preferable in its simplicity, for the ambiguity can ensnare those caught in the middle, like the musketeers. The cardinal dissembles in his statements of service to the king, while the monarch, who realizes the duplicity of Richelieu, relies upon him nonetheless. The queen, caught up in all their conspiracies and intrigues, is victimized by both. While most critics view the basic dichotomy of power between king and cardinal, some, like Patrick Brady, see in the novel a general fight between good and evil as incarnated in the figures of an innocent Anne of Austria and the ruthless Richelieu.

The historical aspects of the historical novel are primarily the marginalized events of the institutionalized historical discourse, in an inversion of events and character. The perspective in the historical novel is that of a relatively minor, even imaginary, historical figure whose experience involves the average, everyday reality which surrounds a great historical moment or event. In the *Trois Mousquetaires,* for example, d'Artagnan does come into contact with all three principal historical figures, Louis XIII, Anne of Austria, and Cardinal Richelieu, who play influential characters limited to minor roles in the novel. The three interviews are spaced throughout the novel, providing, if not much narrative suspense, a sense of historical awe, as the "average" d'Artagnan, is sought out (and with him, the readers) by each of the three great personnages.

Because of his skilled swordsmanship, d'Artagnan comes to the attention of the king extraordinarily soon after the young man arrives in Paris. It is plausible that d'Artagnan should meet the king, since he is attached to his service through M. de Tréville, but the encounter emphasizes the fictive aspect of history. In the sixth chapter the king is both pleased that his men beat those of the cardinal, while saddened at the schism in the country, occasioned by "deux partis en France, deux têtes à la royauté." (p. 81) D'Artagnan and the king meet face to face in the Louvre, although M. de Tréville and his men were requested to use a secret stairway to avoid the cardinal's surveillance. Once inside, d'Artagnan's actions arouse the admiration of the king, who asks d'Artagnan to relate his exploits.

D'Artagnan's role in recovering the queen's ten diamond tags or *ferrets* from England and in counterfeiting the other two which the cardinal had taken places him in a privileged historical position. As the cardinal, who played upon the suspicions of the king, set his trap for Anne at the ballet de la Merlaison, it was d'Artagnan alone among the attendees who real-ized the significance of the queen's appearance with the twelve diamonds. The author shifts the description from the heads of state to the unacknowledged hero who saved the queen:

> L'attention que nous avons été obligés de donner pendant le commencement de ce chapitre aux personnages illustres que nous y avons introduits nous a écartés un instant de celui à qui Anne d'Autriche devait le triomphe inouï qu'elle venait de remporter sur le cardinal, et qui, confondu, ignore, perdu dans la foule entassée à l'une des portes, regardait de là cette scène compréhensible seulement pour quatre personnes: le roi, la reine, Son Eminence et lui.

> (chpt. 22, p. 282)

D'Artagnan is rewarded, not with an interview with the queen, which would be far too dangerous, but with her arm. He is led into a darkened room adjoining one with the queen, when: "tout à coup une main et un bras adorables de forme et de blancheur passerent à travers la tapisserie" (p. 283) The hero is allowed one brief kiss of this great historical hand, at which time he is given a ring as a token of gratitude, before it is hastily withdrawn. As Michel Picard indicates, "C'est la Reine, évidemment, qui figure la part la plus sacrée et la plus interdite. . . ." (p. 61)

Finally, d'Artagnan's exploits bring him to the attention of Cardinal Richelieu, with whom the young swordsman has a most chilling interview (chapter 40). The reader suffers along with d'Artagnan under the gaze of His Eminence: "Nul n'avait l'œil plus profondément scrutateur que le cardinal de Richelieu, et d'Artagnan sentit ce regard courir par ses veines comme une fièvre." (p. 494). Richelieu is impressed with the young man's loyalty to the king, yet reminds him that he could easily destroy the young Gascon. The novel concludes with the Cardinal's great exploit, the destruction of La Rochelle, which continues the process of a fictive perspective bringing alive in narrative form the daily events and reality of a great historical moment.

The historical setting of the seventeenth century serves many functions in Dumas' nineteenth-century fiction. It recreates a time which is both familiar in its use of historical names and geographical places, yet marked by the great difference of the Revolution which makes of it an *Ancien Régime*. As such, the novel rewrites the past so that it can enter into the realm of the symbolic, the imaginary for the general masses. It evokes a time which calls for daring, even scandalous actions, of justified murderous and amorous affairs, in a release of libidinal energy. The characters and events in the *Trois Mousquetaires* are those of common life, of ordinary citizens, more closely related to the reading public. Social hierarchies are lessened, in a general move toward democratization. Material marginalized in academic, historical discourse is given primary consideration, and history is shaped by characters who are known for their actions, not for their birth. Whereas the institutionalized History developed in the nineteenth century was an instrument of closure and death, the historical novel opened up past periods and infused them with life.

One of the most significant uses of French seventeenth-century history in the *Trois Mousquetaires* involves the rewriting of history to foster nationalistic pride in the past, especially as portrayed in small details of history which reveal national character and the participatory role of the middle class. Along with other historical novels, Dumas' tale of the musketeers seeks to create a national myth of heroic valor and to put it into circulation as an object of exchange. The reader pays for a little bit of history, a piece of the national dream, as the body of seventeenth-century history became textualized, traded, possessed and finally consumed.

Works Cited

Albanese, Ralph. *Molière à l'Ecole républicaine.* Saratoga, CA: Anma Libri, 1992.

Bem, Jeanne. "D'Artagnan, et après", *Littérature,* 22 (mai 76): 13-29.

Brady, Patrick. "L'épée, la lettre, et la robe: Symbolisme dramatique et thématique des *Trois Mousquetaires*", *Acta Litteraria Academiae Scientiarum Hungaricae,* 23, 3-4 (1981): 215-225.

Dumas, Alexandre. *Les Trois Mousquetaires,* ed. Charles Samaran. Paris: Garnier, 1968.

Hemmings, F W J. *Alexandre Dumas: The King of Romance.* New York: Scribner's, 1979.

Lukacs, Georg. *The Historical Novel,* trans. Hannah and Stanley Mitchell. Boston: Beacon Press, 1962.

Maurois, André. *Les Trois Dumas.* Paris: Hachette, 1957.

Picard, Michel. "Pouvoirs du feuilleton ou d'Artagnan anonyme", *Littérature,* 50 (mai 1983): 55-78.

Ronzeaud, Pierre, éd. *Le Roman historique, Actes de Marseille.* Paris: Biblio 17, 1983.

Tranouez, Pierre. "Cave filium! Etude du cycle des *Mousquetaires" Poétique,* 71 (Sept. 1987): 321-331

Roger Macdonald (essay date November 2005)

SOURCE: Macdonald, Roger. "Behind the Iron Mask." *History Today* 55, no. 11 (November 2005): 30-6.

[*In the following essay, Macdonald investigates the origins of the protagonists of the Three Musketeers trilogy and* The Man in the Iron Mask.]

Long before the days of mass-produced paperbacks, Alexandre Dumas achieved sales of over one million for his Musketeers trilogy: *The Three Musketeers* (1844), *Twenty Years After* (1845) and *The Man in the Iron Mask* (1850). In an obituary notice published in 1870 after his death, aged sixty-eight, an American newspaper placed Dumas second only to Napoleon Bonaparte as the most famous man of the century. Yet the great French playwright and author, having set the Musketeers firmly on the road to immortality, had been compelled through circumstance to obfuscate their origins, until they came to be regarded as entirely fictional characters, when they were really based on flesh and blood. In doing so he also unwittingly distanced himself from clues to the true identity of the secret prisoner in the mask, a tale more extraordinary and terrible than even Dumas could devise.

In the late 1840s, when Dumas was at the height of his fame, accusations that he was a shameless plagiarist were gathering pace. The drama critic, Granier de Cassagnac compellingly demonstrated that the substance of two of Dumas' plays, *Henri III and His Court* (1829) and *Christine* (1830), came straight from the pages of Schiller. Jean-Baptiste Jacquot, an ambitious writer whose services had been spurned by Dumas, produced a pamphlet alleging that Dumas' 'Novel Factory' had spawned a whole series of works in his name though written by his many assistants and all based on stolen ideas. The story going the rounds was of Dumas meeting his son, also called Alexandre, and asking him, 'Have you read my latest novel?' to which Alexandre replies: 'No, have you?'

Aware that his real source would provoke fresh accusations of plagiarism, in his preface to *The Three Musketeers* Dumas instead supplied an entirely fictitious provenance for his romantic adventure. He claimed to have discovered in the Bibliothèque du Roi an unknown manuscript in folio, numbers 4772 and 4773, entitled *Mémoires du Comte de la Fère.*

Dumas specified the earliest pages of the document, 20, 27 and 31, on which, he said, could be found the first historical references to Musketeers Athos, Porthos and Aramis.

Most readers took Dumas' claim at face value until he made the mistake of alienating a prolific historian and redoubtable bibliophile, Paul Lacroix. In 1850 Dumas brought out another historical novel, **The Black Tulip,** without acknowledging Lacroix's considerable assistance. Lacroix settled the score by disclosing that Dumas' purported source for **The Three Musketeers** could not be found at the Royal Library or indeed anywhere else. Dumas still prevaricated for many years but in 1864 he was cornered in an interview he gave for the journal *Litteraire de la Semaine.* Forced to say whether he believed Athos, Porthos and Aramis to be real people, Dumas could not even then bring himself to admit where he had found their names, instead stating that they 'had never existed and were simply bastards of my imagination'.

Dumas' real source was in fact an obscure work, first published in 1700, *Memoires de Monsieur D'Artagnan* that professed to be the autobiography of the long forgotten Charles d'Artagnan, who really did become Captain of the King's Musketeers. It was in fact written by Gatien de Courtilz de Sandras, and thought by most nineteenth-century historians to be largely apocryphal, Dumas borrowed Courtilz's work from the Marseilles public library, whose records show that he never gave it back.

As Dumas must have noticed, on page eleven of his work Courtilz mentions Athos, Porthos and Aramis as being Musketeers, in the same breath: they are summoned to Paris by Tréville, Captain of the Musketeers, to take on Cardinal Richelieu's guards like professional gunslingers brought in to settle a turf war; and that quite by chance, a hot-headed young Gascon, d'Artagnan, arrives in the capital at the same moment. Here, for Dumas' many enemies, was *prima facie* evidence of plagiarism aplenty.

The irony was that Dumas could safely have stipulated Courtilz as a genuine historical source, for much of Courtilz's so-called autobiography of d'Artagnan was based on fact and, like d'Artagnan himself, the Three Musketeers proved to be real.

They were not from Gascony but Béarn, until 1620 a fiercely independent, pocket-handkerchief state between Gascony and the western Pyrenees. Their antecedents were discovered in the early 1880s when Jean-Baptiste Etienne de Jurgain, a historian eager to preserve the traditions of his native Béarn, began to study its genealogical documents. Jurgain's research, published in the *Revue de Béarn, Navarre et Lannes,* proved the existence of Henri d'Aramitz, Armand de Sillègue d'Athos, and Isaac de Portau. Aramis, Athos and Porthos, as they called themselves, had close family connections. They all moved in the same circle of *bourgeoisie* who had bought their way into the petty nobility but as the younger sons, they saw little prospect of an inheritance. For them, fame and fortune must be earned with a sword.

Although Dumas had d'Artagnan rashly committing himself to fighting successive duels with the Three Musketeers at hourly intervals on his first day in the French capital in May 1640, this had no basis in fact. It was the real-life Porthos who inveigled d'Artagnan into the fight with the Cardinal's Guards, thereby forcing them to rush around looking for a fourth Guardsman sober enough to take part. Far from being a chance encounter, this was a pre-arranged multiple duel to settle old scores. The Musketeers inflicted a humiliating defeat on the Cardinal's men and according to Courtilz, d'Artagnan disposed of his opponent in under a minute, establishing his reputation as a formidable swordsman.

The four friends made powerful enemies and in 1643 were ambushed at the Saint-German fair. In saving d'Artagnan, Athos suffered a fatal sword thrust to his side. When Richelieu's successor, Cardinal Mazarin, disbanded the Musketeers in 1646, his only means of removing Tréville, Aramis and Porthos, fearing further attempts on their lives, returned to Béarn. Aramis married a local heiress, only to die without warning in April 1654. Porthos, found a comfortable *seigneurie* by Tréville, lived to be ninety-five, expiring at Pau from an apoplectic stroke on July 13th, 1712. Although he must have had the constitution of an ox, there is no evidence that Porthos was a particularly strong man. In **The Three Musketeers** Dumas bestowed upon him the prodigious strength of his own father, the Revolutionary general Thomas-Alexandre Dumas, who could allegedly lift barn doors off their hinges with one hand.

Dumas also drew on a work by Antoine-Marie Roederer, *Intrigues politiques and galantes de la cour de France,* (1832) for the main plot of **The Three Musketeers**: the theft of Anne of Austria's diamond studs, her foolish gift to the Duke of Buckingham. Only in Dumas' imagination were the Musketeers involved in this episode (which had actually occurred in 1625) saving the Queen's honour, by replacing the missing diamonds: the real Athos, Aramis and Porthos would have been children, and d'Artagnan still a babe in arms.

Unaware of Athos' true fate, Dumas kept the Three Musketeers and d'Artagnan in robust health until almost the end of the third book in his trilogy, *The Man in the Iron Mask.* For the central figure of that tale (which fictionalizes an essentially true story of a mysterious prisoner of Louis XIV) he followed the most popular current theory of the prisoner's identity, that of an identical twin of the King. In Dumas' version, d'Artagnan, who remains loyal to Louis, escorts the royal twin to the remote Mediterranean island of Sainte-Marguerite and locks him into the mask.

It is unlikely that this theory of the prisoner's identity could be correct. The arrival of an unexpected second child, allegedly nine hours after the first, could surely not have remained undetected in the goldfish bowl of the French court, and infant mortality was so high that the birth of a second son to Anne of Austria would have been more welcomed than feared. Later, Hollywood scriptwriters gave the story a sinister twist by imprisoning Louis himself in the same mask the King had supposedly devised for his innocent brother.

In the novel, the switch of one twin for the other takes place during the spectacular party at Vaux-le-Vicomte in August 1661, held by Nicholas Fouquet, the French finance minister, to celebrate the completion of his extravagant new château. The real event, attended by Louis XIV, proved the catalyst for Fouquet's arrest—by d'Artagnan—on the King's orders almost three weeks later. D'Artagnan had been employed by Mazarin to carry by word of mouth his most private messages. Consequently, d'Artagnan knew better than most the extent to which Mazarin, aided and abetted by finance minister Colbert (1619-83), had also used the state's money as though it were his own, persuasively demonstrated by Daniel Dessert in *Colbert et le serpent venimeux* (2000). The Gascon believed Fouquet was no guiltier than either of them and wanted nothing to do with the hypocrisy of his arrest. D'Artagnan therefore feigned or, at the least, exaggerated illness but Louis had no one else he could trust—even the duc de Gesvres, captain of his palace guard, was in Fouquet's pocket—and simply waited until he had recovered. Nonetheless the arrest was perilously close to being a fiasco, for d'Artagnan missed Fouquet's departure from the royal council and had to pursue him down the street. Acting as Fouquet's jailer for the next three years, d'Artagnan became increasingly partisan in his pris-

oner's interest. Obliged by Colbert to remain within earshot of his charge, d'Artagnan refused point-blank to report on Fouquet's conversations with his lawyers. In 1664, when Fouquet escaped the death penalty, Louis sent him to the remote Alpine prison of Pignerol and as a sign of royal displeasure at his insubordination, d'Artagnan was instructed to lead his escort of a hundred Musketeers across the mountains in savage winter conditions. Olivier Lefèvre d'Ormesson, the only trial judge who had believed Fouquet to be innocent of all the charges, wrote in his journal that d'Artagnan was 'angry at being ordered to travel to Pignerol and would have got out of it if he could'.

Despite now being out of royal favour, d'Artagnan had a stroke of good fortune. For him the post of Captain of the Musketeers, who had been revived under Cardinal Mazarin's nephew, Philippe-Julien Mancini in 1657, remained completely out of reach. Early in 1667, however, Mancini stoked up a row between his sister, Hortense Mancini and her husband, thereby hoping to gain control of Hortense's spectacular inheritance, left by her uncle the cardinal. Louis impulsively decided to make an example of Philippe and early in 1667 forced him to relinquish his company of Musketeers in favour of d'Artagnan—even though in doing so he was giving d'Artagnan a promotion the King did not feel he deserved. Colbert was outraged by Louis' perverse decision as D'Ormesson commented:

> M. de Colbert does not like d'Artagnan . . . the King's decision in this respect is surprising, he knows d'Artagnan is a friend of Fouquet and Colbert's enemy.

Far from becoming subservient to the King, however, in 1671 d'Artagnan repeated his defiance by refusing to arrest a fellow Gascon, the comte de Lauzun, who had dared to court, even possibly to marry in secret, Louis' ageing but wealthy cousin, the Grande Mademoiselle, whose lands the King coveted for his illegitimate offspring. Lauzun was contemptuously dismissive of their mother, Louis' most durable mistress, Athénaïs de Montespan. When the outraged monarch responded by sending Lauzun to Pignerol, once again d'Artagnan was ordered to escort the prisoner there in the depths of winter. What the manipulative Lauzun told d'Artagnan on the journey left the Captain of the Musketeers disillusioned with his king. The two Gascons may have reached the conclusion that Louis was not entitled to sit on the French throne. In his biography, *Louis XIV,* (2000) Anthony Levi offers persuasive evidence that Mazarin, not the homosexual Louis XIII, was the Sun King's real father: perhaps Lauzun was in a position to know the truth.

On his return, d'Artagnan was disrespectful to Louis, and the King decided to remove him from court once more by making him governor of Lille. D'Artagnan lacked the education and guile to make a success of the job, and within a few weeks he had fallen out with the King's favourite, the siege engineer, Vauban. Although recalled in disgrace, at court d'Artagnan automatically returned to the position he held for life as Captain of the Musketeers whose men provided protection for the royal entourage outside the palace walls. They can scarcely have failed to notice when in March 1673 Athénaïs de Montespan, her position as *maitresse en titre* threatened by younger concubines, took part naked in a Black Mass designed to retain the royal favour, at a secluded château south of Paris. It was the most extraordinary incident in what would become known as the Affair of the Poisons, when many of the high and mighty of France were accused of dabbling in black magic and administering lethal substances. Long before the poisons scandal broke, d'Artagnan almost certainly knew what was going on. His reluctance to precipitate a political crisis did not include preserving Athénaïs' reputation and Louis had to take action. In his history of seventeenth-century France, W. H. Lewis concludes that 'Ridicule was perhaps the only thing in the world that Louis feared'.

D'Artagnan, a loose cannon, had to go. In June 1673 an opportunity presented itself when the King personally oversaw the successful siege of the formidable Dutch fortress, Maastricht. The Musketeers, led by d'Artagnan, were ordered prematurely into a night attack and suffered heavy casualties: perhaps Louis was hoping to arrange d'Artagnan's glorious death on the battlefield as a way out of their difficulties. D'Artagnan had a charmed life, and survived unscathed. However, on the following morning, to foil a Dutch counterattack he was drawn into a near-suicidal charge across open ground by the small English contingent on the French side, led by the Duke of Monmouth and John Churchill, the future Duke of Marlborough. While saving Monmouth during 'the bravest and briskest action they had seen in their lives', d'Artagnan was hit in the neck by a stray bullet and reported dead.

Within a few months, a rumour swept Paris of a secret prisoner in the Bastille. He was said to be the playwright Molière, who had challenged the establishment, attacking the hypocrisy and pretentiousness of both the Roman Catholic Church and the court through his comedies. When Molière supposedly died on February 17th, 1673, he did not receive a proper funeral: no burial service took place and the entry in the church register remained unsigned; his body was taken directly to the cemetery of Saint-Joseph late at night. In 1792 his presumed grave would be exhumed and found to be empty and two historians, Anatole Loquin and Marcel Diamant-Berger, writing in 1883 and 1971 respectively were convinced that it was he who became the Man in the Iron Mask. In view of the notoriously poor state of his health, however, it is extremely unlikely that Molière could have survived in prison for more than thirty years. Rather, the Catholic Church may have arranged for him to be buried in unconsecrated ground, as a petty retribution after death for his ridiculing of them in life. The year when the rumour about a mysterious captive began, 1673, and not Molière himself, was the clue.

The state prisoners at Pignerol, Fouquet and Lauzun, were now being guarded by Bénigne de Saint-Mars, d'Artagnan's former quartermaster sergeant, who was forbidden to leave his post for even a single day. In July 1673, however, he sent from Maastricht a coded letter to Louvois about the state of health of a wounded third party, one so important that Saint-Mars himself and some of his men had been sent from Pignerol to the Maastricht battlefield to watch over him.

D'Artagnan was supposed to be dead but none of the purported eyewitness accounts of his demise withstand close scrutiny. One was by a fellow Musketeer who had been injured and missed this part the action; the second by a notorious liar; and the third by a drunken Irish peer. The story of d'Artagnan's Musketeers risking life and limb under withering fire in order to recover the body of their fallen commander was not reported at the time. There would have been no need for such heroics, because frequent truces were declared so that dead and injured combatants could be removed from the battlefield under a white flag. When in 1674 *le Mercure Galant* said that the Musketeers had failed to retrieve d'Artagnan's corpse, the gossip sheet was promptly shut down by the authorities and its editor imprisoned.

In 1873 an army officer, Théodore Iung, published his research into The Man in the Iron Mask, which established that Saint-Mars had been his jailer at four successive prisons. The names of only two of Saint-Mars' prisoners eluded Iung. The first, surely the Mask himself, had arrived at Pignerol from Paris in March 1674 amid extraordinary precautions, 'manacled at night' and 'kept from view' in such a way that he could neither 'shout out or write . . . who he was'. The second, a prisoner in the Bastille at the beginning of 1699, proved to be Gatien de Courtilz de Sandras, the author of the *Mémoires de Monsieur d'Artagnan*.

Courtilz went to such lengths to conceal his identity that the authorities were unsure of his real name. After his military career, he became a writer of pamphlets, political tracts and biographies, more than one hundred works in all, printed outside France to escape censorship. He called Louis XIV 'Le Grand Alcandre', a reference to Corneille's comedy 'L'Illusion Comique', in which the old sorcerer, Alcandre, lives in a cave with his deaf and dumb servants. The Sun King would not have liked the analogy. Courtilz was sent to the Bastille in 1693. He was still a prisoner, although he was given the freedom to go more or less where he liked within its walls, thanks to his influential wife, Louise Pannetier, when Saint-Mars arrived with the Iron Mask in September 1698.

Twenty-five years had elapsed since d'Artagnan's last military campaign, the siege of Maastricht, and outside the senior ranks of the armed forces he was long since forgotten. There is no evidence that Courtilz had ever met d'Artagnan during his military service and Courtilz was never a Musketeer. Courtilz showed no signs of husbanding information on potential subjects for future use, let alone a quarter of a century after the event. Arthur de Boislisle, editor of Saint-Simon's diaries; Jules Lair, author of the definitive biography on Fouquet; and Charles Samaran, who undertook a great deal of original research on the Musketeers, all rejected the cynical view that Courtilz' autobiography of d'Artagnan was pure fiction. Samaran concluded that, 'not only on general events, but on the deeds and actions of individuals, there are amazingly accurate details'. Jurgain determined that Courtilz's collective reference to Aramis, Athos and Porthos, the first mention of them anywhere, was also founded on fact. Courtilz wrote d'Artagnan's biography while in jail, and his wife smuggled out the manuscript. The only rational explanation is that Courtilz had a prime source of information among the prisoners in the Bastille; but none of his nineteen fellow inmates listed in the prison register had the remotest connection with d'Artagnan. That left the sole prisoner not accounted for, the Man in the Iron Mask, confirming, given the wealth of detail he supplied, that he could only be d'Artagnan himself.

In 1687, during his transfer from another Alpine prison, Exiles, to the island of Sainte-Marguerite, off Cannes, a priest at Grasse saw the prisoner in his mask, made not of iron, but steel. His eyewitness account appeared in a newsletter circulated by clerics, which also reported an unguarded remark made by Saint-Mars about the identity of his charge that 'All the people one believes to be dead are not'. This meant that the man in the Mask had to be sufficiently well-known to attract comment, for his supposed death to have been widely reported and for him to be held in the utmost secrecy. D'Artagnan, almost alone of all the credible candidates, meets this criteria.

Just before embarking on his spectacular series of historical novels, Dumas produced **Celebrated Crimes,** a series of eight volumes on dark deeds from history. Volume Six included *The Man in the Iron Mask.* Like much of Dumas's prodigious output, it owed a great deal to the work of others, in this instance his closest collaborator, Auguste Maquet, a former history teacher. As was often the case, Dumas undermined Maquet's meticulous research by some impulsive contributions of his own. Dumas confessed that in writing an earlier play about the Iron Mask, he had been forced to 'choose one view of a dramatic situation to the exclusion of all others . . . and . . . by the inexorable laws of logic to push aside everything that interferes with its development'. He had selected, and would stick with, the notion of an identical twin in the mask, because 'it was incontestably the most dramatic'. How ironic, then, that the qualities of loyalty and honour that d'Artagnan possessed, brilliantly captured by Dumas in fiction, proved the Musketeer's eventual undoing in fact: and that Dumas, in failing to give credit to Courtilz, ensured that an even better story would slip through his fingers, the astonishing secret that d'Artagnan himself was the Man in the Iron Mask.

TITLE COMMENTARY

LES TROIS MOUSQUETAIRES (1844; *THE THREE MUSKETEERS*)

Terrence Rafferty (review date 20 August 2006)

SOURCE: Rafferty, Terrence. "All for One." *New York Times Book Review* (20 August 2006): 13.

[*In the following review, Rafferty offers a positive assessment of a "brisk, agile" new translation of* The Three Musketeers *by Richard Pevear.*]

Words never failed Alexandre Dumas. In his maniacally productive writing career, he pumped out millions and millions of them: some good, some bad and all indifferent to any value other than propelling a story forward at the giddiest possible pace, if not, perhaps, with optimum fuel efficiency. Dumas's novels are shameless word-guzzlers, big and plush and almost sinfully comfortable: ideal vehicles for the long, scenic excursions into French history he regularly conducted for the newspaper readers of mid-19th-century Paris.

He wrote at a speed that pretty much precluded reflection, precision, anything resembling literary refinement, and he famously employed assistants to help out with research, plotting and, some thought, even the writing itself. (The collected works—novels, plays, essays—fill some 300 volumes.) He was accused, in his time, of merely running a "novel factory" and (by no less a personage than Sainte-Beuve) of perpetrating "industrial literature." But if Dumas was a hack, he was a hack with genius. His storytelling never seems the least bit mechanical: no assembly line, then or now, could ever turn out a narrative as joyful, as eccentric, as maddeningly human as *The Three Musketeers.* Originally serialized in *Le Siècle* between March and July of 1844, Dumas's best-known novel has been with us for more than a century and a half and clearly isn't going away any time soon. There's no blueprint for that sort of endurance.

Richard Pevear's brisk, agile new translation succeeds, I think, because it does justice to the pure nuttiness of Dumas's writing: the nonindustrial, nonformulaic, downright peculiar qualities that make a work of popular fiction memorable. *The Three Musketeers* purports to dramatize some significant events from the reign of Louis XIII—the action begins in 1625 and ends three years later—but although many of its characters did actually exist, historical veracity is not (to put it mildly) Dumas's primary concern. History seems too small for him, somehow. Dumas turns the great actors on the world's stage—the king; the queen; her admirer, Lord Buckingham; and Louis's crafty, Dick Cheney-like adviser/puppeteer, Cardinal Richelieu—into bit players, characters whose function is simply to provide opportunities for spectacular displays of bravery, loyalty and wit on the part of the musketeers and their young comrade-in-arms, D'Artagnan.

Lots of historical novels do something similar, of course. What sets Dumas apart is the conscienceless insouciance with which he reduces the mighty to figures in a farce. It would be a stretch, perhaps, to think of him as deliberately subversive, but he has to be credited with an instinctive irreverence toward power

and those who wield it, and this attitude may be the most important reason for his persistent appeal. Every generation since that of the first readers of *The Three Musketeers* has learned, in one way or another, that leaders are on the whole a good deal less noble than those who serve them. Usually—too often—the hard way.

The musketeers—Athos, Porthos and Aramis—and D'Artagnan (who becomes an official musketeer only toward the end of the book) protect their king and queen zealously, even daring at times to sabotage the Machiavellian schemes of the very dangerous Cardinal Richelieu. It's apparent, though, that they perform their prodigious feats not because they believe devoutly in the intrinsic merit of Louis XIII or his queen, Anne of Austria, but because it's their duty to defend the monarchy. This is all the reason they need to risk their lives.

That there's a strong whiff of existential absurdity in their situation is not lost on their creator. Dumas puts his heroes to work at ridiculous-seeming tasks like the recovery of some diamonds, originally presented to the queen by the king, that Anne has imprudently bestowed on the ardent Buckingham. Richelieu, with the aid of his most ruthless agent, the femme extra-fatale known as Milady de Winter, has been trying to get his own pious hands on the gems in order to discredit the queen, so the musketeers' mission isn't inconsequential, and the perils they're exposed to along the way are plenty real. But you remain aware, through all the ambushes and sword fights and breathless escapes, that the queen's predicament is a device better suited to comedy than to the drama of world history.

When *The Three Musketeers* does at last turn its attention to a genuinely significant historical event—the siege of the Protestant stronghold of La Rochelle—Dumas is unable to conceal his irritation at having to deal with it. The siege, he writes, "was one of the great political events of the reign of Louis XIII, and one of the great military undertakings of the cardinal. It is thus worthwhile, and even necessary, for us to say a few words about it. Besides, many details of this siege are bound up in too important a way with the story we have undertaken to tell for us to pass over them in silence"—as he would plainly prefer to do.

Athos, Porthos, Aramis and D'Artagnan are all required to take part in this campaign, but they seem barely present, only marginally more aware of the battle raging around them than Stendhal's young hero Fabrizio is at Waterloo in "The Charterhouse of Parma." As if to emphasize their obliviousness, Dumas gives them an entirely pointless set piece of derring-do: they occupy an abandoned bastion for a quiet conference, over lunch, on strategies to defeat Milady, and calmly finish their meal before finishing off the attackers who have been trying to recapture their refuge. Sang doesn't get more froid than that.

The episode of the St.-Gervais bastion is Dumas at his idiosyncratic best: a heady mix of intrigue, action and laughing-in-the-face-of-death badinage (all superbly rendered in this translation). It's typical of him, too, that the most stirring bit of swashbuckling in this whole rambunctious novel should occur in what is essentially a digression. In a sense, though, *The Three Musketeers* is nothing but digressions. That's the beauty of it—and the reason Dumas was able to continue the musketeers' saga for another several hundred thousand words, first in *Twenty Years After,* serialized in 1845, and then in *The Vicomte de Bragelonne,* which ran in Le Siècle from 1847 to 1850 and is so gargantuan that it's now usually broken up into three hefty volumes (*The Vicomte de Bragelonne, Louise de la Vallière* and *The Man in the Iron Mask*). And it's also the reason, I think, that his work seems so imperishably (if inadvertently) modern.

No novelist since Dumas has been more irreverent of the conventions of well-made fiction or any more determined to tell stories without identifiable centers. There is, finally, something moving about his helpless, logorrheic outpourings of narrative. His historical novels always wind up saying that everything that matters—love, courage, pleasure and, especially, all-for-one-and-one-for-all friendship—exists most vividly not in the supposed centers of power, but elsewhere: in the margins of history, where the musketeers, immortally, live.

LE COMTE DE MONTE-CRISTO (1844-45; THE COUNT OF MONTE-CRISTO)

Andre Maurois (essay date 1957)

SOURCE: Maurois, Andre. "*The Count of Monte-Cristo.*" In *Three Musketeers: A Study of the Dumas Family,* translated by Gerard Hopkins, pp. 219-27. London, England: Jonathan Cape, 1957.

[*In the following essay, Maurois offers background information on Dumas's* The Count of Monte-Cristo, *discussing the origins of the text and the influence of the work on Dumas's life and career.*]

Monte-Cristo is the keyword to Dumas's work and to Dumas's life. It is the title of his best known novel after *The Three Musketeers*: it was the name of the crazy house which was his pride and his ruin. It conjures up, better than anything else could do, his dreams of magnificence and of justice.

The idea of [*The Count of Monte-Cristo*] had been working in his mind by fits and starts over a number of years. He tells, in his *Causeries,* how in 1824, happening to be in Florence, he was asked by Jérome Bonaparte, the ex-king of Westphalia, to accompany his son (the Prince Napoleon) as far as the isle of Elba, which was one of the spots sacred to the Imperial family. Dumas was then thirty-nine, the Prince, nineteen, but, of the two, the novelist was the younger. They reached Elba, explored it from end to end, and then went to join a shooting-party on the near-by island of Pianosa which abounded in rabbits and partridges. Their guide, pointing to a sugar-loaf rock rising straight out to the sea, said:

'That is where Your Excellencies ought to go, if you want good sport.'

'What's the name of the Fortunate Isle?'

'It's called the island of Monte-Cristo.'

The name enchanted Dumas.

'Monseigneur,' said he to the young prince, 'in memory of this trip, I shall call one of the novels I have still to write, Monte-Cristo.'[1]

In the following year, when he was back in France, he signed a contract with MM. Béthune and Plon, for eight volumes to be entitled: *Impressions de Voyage dans Paris.* He intended to make the book a long archaeological and historical ramble, but his publishers explained that that was not at all what they had in mind. They had been struck by the staggering success of *Les Mystères de Paris* which Eugène Sue had recently published. What they wanted was a book of romantic adventure set in Paris.

Dumas was an easy man to convince, and no literary project ever frightened him. He set about looking for a plot. It so happened that, some time before, he had put a marker in volume V of a work by Jacques Peuchet, called *Mémoires tirés des Archives de la Police de Paris.* He had been particularly interested in one chapter, headed *Le Diamant de la Vengeance.* 'What Peuchet made of it', he said in a somewhat ungrateful note, 'was nonsense . . . but it was true, all the same, that deep in that oyster there lay concealed a pearl, a rough pearl, an unshaped pearl, a pearl without any intrinsic value . . . but a pearl awaiting the jeweller's art.'[2]

It was a fact that Peuchet had been the Keeper of the Archives at the Prefecture of Police. From his files he had compiled six volumes which, even today, would be a rich mine for the writers of serial novels. Here is the strange story which had so strongly appealed to Alexandre Dumas.

In 1807 there had been living in Paris a young shoemaker, François Picaud. This poor devil, who was a handsome chap, was engaged to be married. One day, dressed in his Sunday best, he went to the Place Sainte-Opportune to see a friend, the proprietor of a café, who, like himself, came from Nîmes. This man, Mathieu Loupian, had a flourishing business, but other people's successes made him extravagantly jealous. In the café Picaud found three of his compatriots from the Gard Department, who were also friends of the owner. They pulled his leg about his fine clothes, and he then announced his forthcoming marriage to an extremely beautiful orphan, Marguerite Vigoroux, with a fortune of a hundred thousand gold francs, whose affection he had been so fortunate as to engage. The four friends were dumbfounded by what they had heard, and dazzled by the shoemaker's good luck.

'When's the wedding to be?'

'Next Tuesday.'

When he had left, the envious and perfidious Loupian said: 'I'll put a spoke in *that* wheel!'

'How?' asked the others.

'A police inspector's looking in later. I shall tell him that I suspect Picaud of being an English agent . . . He'll be questioned; he'll be very frightened, and the marriage will be postponed.'

Napoleon's police did not take political crimes lightly. One of the three men from Nîmes, Antoine Allut, said: 'I call that a dirty trick.'

But the others thought it a good joke: 'After all, one must have a bit of fun at carnival time!'

Loupian lost no time in putting his plan into action. The inspector turned out to be both imprudent and zealous. He jumped at this chance to distinguish himself and, without making any further investigation sent in a report to the police minister, Savary, duc de Rovigo, who at that time was much worried about certain insurrectionary movements in La Vendée. It's pretty obvious, he thought, that this Picaud is one of Louis XVIII's secret agents. The wretched young man was spirited away during the night, completely vanished, and not a word more was heard of him. His parents and his betrothed set inquiries on foot, but, failing to obtain any satisfaction, resigned themselves to the inevitable. The absent are always in the wrong.

Seven years passed. 1814 came, with the fall of the Empire. A man, prematurely aged by suffering, was released from the castle of Fenestrelle where he had all that time been imprisoned. It was François Picaud. His deeply lined face was barely recognizable, and his body was much weakened. While in captivity, he had, with great devotion, looked after an Italian prelate, who had been imprisoned on a political charge and had not long to live. The dying man had bequeathed to Picaud, by word of mouth, all his goods, and, in particular, a treasure hidden in Milan—diamonds, Lombard ducats, Venetian florins, English guineas, French gold francs and some Spanish currency. No sooner was he released than Picaud searched out this treasure, found it, and moved it to a place of safety. Then, under the name of Joseph Lucher, he went back to Paris, to the district in which he had formerly been living. There he asked what had become of a shoemaker called Pierre-François Picaud who, in 1807, had been going to marry the rich Mademoiselle Vigoroux. He was told that a carnival jest, played on him by four mischievous jokers, had resulted in the young man's disappearance. His betrothed had mourned him for two years, and then, believing him to be dead, had agreed to marry the café-owner Loupian, a widower with two children. Picaud asked the names of the other responsible parties, and was told: 'You can find out about them from a man called Antoine Allut, who lives in Nîmes.'

Picaud, disguised as an Italian priest, and with a quantity of gold and jewels sewn into his clothes, hastened to Nîmes, where he gave himself out to be the abbé Baldini. In return for a fine diamond, Antoine Allut gave him the names of the three other accomplices in the practical joke which had had so tragic a sequel. Some days later, a lemonade-hawker, Prosper by name, got himself a place as a waiter at the Café Loupian. This man, with a ravaged face and threadbare clothes, seemed to be about fifty years old. It was Picaud in yet another disguise. The two men from Nîmes, denounced by Allut, were still regular visitors to the establishment. A day came when one of them, Chambard, failed to turn up at his usual time. It was learned that, at five o'clock that morning, he had been found stabbed on the Pont des Arts. The knife had been left in the wound, and, on the handle, was written: *Number One.*

Loupian had had, by his first wife, a son and a daughter. The girl, then sixteen, was angelically beautiful. A dandy, claiming to be a marquis and a millionaire, seduced her. Finding herself pregnant, she was compelled to confess her fault to Loupian and his wife, and was kindly, even joyfully, forgiven, since the elegant gentleman was prepared to marry the future mother of his child. A civil and a religious ceremony took place, but, between the bestowal of the nuptial blessing and the wedding breakfast, it was discovered that the husband had fled. He turned out to be a liberated convict, and neither a marquis nor a millionaire.

Consternation in the bride's family. On the following Sunday, their house (which combined the functions of home and place of business) was mysteriously burned to the ground. Loupian was ruined. The only persons who stuck by him were his friend Solari (the last surviving member of the group of 'regulars') and Prosper, the former lemonade-hawker, who unknown to Loupian, was the author of all his misfortunes. As was only to be expected, Solari soon died, from poison. On the black drapery which covered his coffin, a piece of paper was found pinned, with, on it in block letters, the words—*Number Two.*

Young Eugène Loupian, the son of the proprietor of the café, a weak-charactered, harum-scarum lad, was led astray by a party of shady strangers from no one knew where. He became involved in an affair of 'breaking and entering' and was sentenced to twenty years imprisonment. The Loupians, husband and wife, penniless and dishonoured, fell lower and lower. They had lost everything—money, reputation, happiness, in this avalanche of disasters. The 'handsome Madame Loupian', the former Marguerite Vigoroux, died of grief, and, since she had borne her husband no children, what remained of her personal fortune went back to the members of her own family, who were her legal heirs.

Prosper, the lemonade-hawker, offered his savings to his destitute employer, but on condition that the haughty Thérèse, Loupian's daughter, should live with him. This the proud beauty agreed to do in order to save her father.

As a result of his misfortunes, Loupian was now half mad. One evening, in a dark alley of the Tuileries Gardens, a masked man appeared before him.

'Loupian, do you remember 1807?'

'Why should I?'

'Because it was the year of your crime.'

'What crime?'

'Have you forgotten that, through jealousy, you had your friend, Picaud, shut away?'

'Ah! God has punished me for it . . . punished me terribly!'

'There you are wrong. It was not God but Picaud who, to slake his vengeance, stabbed Chambard, poisoned Solari, burned your house, brought dishonour on your son, and gave your daughter a convict for husband. . . . See now in Prosper that same Picaud, but in the very moment when he sets his mark upon his *Third Victim*!'

Loupian fell to the ground, murdered. But just as Picaud was about to leave the gardens, he felt himself held in a grip of steel, gagged, and, under cover of the darkness, carried off. In the cellar into which he was thrown, he found himself in the presence of a man whom he did not recognize.

'Well, Picaud, I suppose for you vengeance is no more than a joke, eh? But you are mistaken. It has become a raging mania. . . . You have spent ten years of your life in hunting down three wretches whom you should have spared. . . . You have committed a series of horrible crimes, and in them I have been your accomplice, since it is I who sold you the secret of your misery. . . . I am Antoine Allut! I have followed you at a distance, and seen the way in which you have settled your accounts. Only at the last did I realize who you were. I came to Paris for the purpose of opening Loupian's eyes to your identity, but the Devil gave you a minute's start of me!'

'Where am I now?'

'What does that matter? You are in a place where you can expect neither help nor pity.'[3]

Vengeance for vengeance. Picaud was put to death with the utmost savagery. His murderer escaped to England. In 1828, Allut, who had fallen desperately ill, sent for a Catholic priest to whom he confided a detailed account of these terrible events, and told him to communicate it, after his death, to the French judicial authorities.

Allut's last wishes were scrupulously observed by his confessor, and the precious document found a home in the police archives, where Peuchet must have come across it.

* * *

There, for Dumas, Balzac or Eugène Sue, was a novel ready-made: and not only for them, but for the general public as well. For thousands of years the unhappy human race has found release in cathartic myths. The most popular of their characters have ever been the Magician and the Dispenser of Justice. The humiliated and the injured live with the hope, which no ill-success can weaken, of witnessing the coming, sometimes of the god, sometimes of the hero, who will redress all wrongs, cast down the wicked, and, at long last, give the good man his deserts. For a time, this Dispenser of Justice was physically strong. Dumas, remembering his father, the general, had successfully incarnated in Porthos the myth of Hercules.

In the *Arabian Nights* the Dispenser of Justice is personified as a Magician. His power is no longer physical but occult. He can transport the innocent victim to a place where no persecutor can reach him, and can throw open to the poor great vaults filled with jewels. At the time when Dumas was writing, this enchanter had become confused with the 'nabob' whose wealth permitted him to indulge his every whim, no matter how wild. Dumas dreamed of becoming just such a distributor of earthly happiness. To the extent, now alas much reduced, to which his own financial difficulties allowed him to do so, he delighted in playing this part in the interest of his friends and mistresses. A cup would have held all the gold he had, but this he scattered with a nabob's open-handedness.

He delighted in the idea of creating a character possessed of a fabulous treasure, and scattering far and wide, through an intermediary, sapphires, diamonds, emeralds and rubies and, furthermore, of making that character the Avenger in some great cause. For Dumas, in spite of his happy exuberance, harboured deep within himself many grievances against society at large, and private enemies in particular. His father had been a victim: he himself was harassed by creditors, and slandered by those skilled in the art of blackmail. He shared with many human beings, who have been unjustly treated, that longing for vengeance

which, since the *Oresteia,* has engendered so many masterpieces. He must have been sorely tempted to find compensation in fiction for the iniquities of the real world.

Peuchet gave him the plot for which he was looking. True stories provide an excellent framework, provided the artist can give them the necessary finishing touches. Dumas was already far advanced in his work when he sent out a call for help to Maquet.

> I told him what had been already done, and what remained to do.
>
> 'It seems to me,' he said, 'that you have neglected the most interesting parts of your hero's life. I mean, his love affair with the Catalan woman, the treachery of Danglars and Fernand, and the ten years spent in prison with the abbé Faria.'
>
> 'I shall cover all that,' I replied.
>
> 'But you cannot *narrate* the matter of four or five volumes, and that is what the whole thing will amount to.'
>
> 'You may be right. Come and dine with me tomorrow, and we'll talk about it again.'
>
> All that evening, all that night, and the next morning, I thought over what he had said, and so true did it seem, that I found my original idea completely changed. So, when Maquet next came, he found the work divided into three distinct parts: *Marseille—Rome—Paris.*
>
> Together, that evening, we roughed out the first five volumes. Of these, one should be introductory, three should deal with the period of captivity, and the last should cover the escape and the rewarding of the Morel family. All the rest, though not completely finished, was more or less in draft.
>
> Maquet considered that he had done no more than give me friendly advice. But I insisted on his playing the part of collaborator.[4]

It now remains to see how Dumas adapted Peuchet's material. His hero, Edmond Dantès is, like François Picaud, on the point of marrying the woman he loves, when a series of inexplicable misfortunes come upon him. His Mercédès is stolen from him by Fernand the fisherman as, in Peuchet's story, Marguerite, Picaud's betrothed, is lured into marrying Loupian. But Dumas splits Loupian into two, using him both for Fernand and for the traitor Danglars. The magistrate, Villefort, who sees in the ruin brought upon Dantès a chance of promotion for himself, is modelled on the real police inspector, who was overjoyed to believe Loupian's slanderous denunciation.

The abbé Faria (in the novel, Edmond Dantès's fellow prisoner in the Château d'If) plays the part of the rich Milanese prelate who left his treasure to François Picaud. Dantès, after his escape, assumes a variety of disguises, appearing successively as the abbé Busoni, Sinbad the sailor, Lord Wilmore and the Count of Monte-Cristo, just as Picaud had taken the aliases of Joseph Lucher, the abbé Baldini and the lemonade-hawker, Prosper.

It should not be forgotten that Loupian's daughter, inveigled by an impostor, believed that she was marrying into one of the noblest families in the land, by taking as husband a man who turned out to be a convicted prisoner masquerading as a marquis. This episode was too good to be ignored by the novelist. Dumas introduces under Danglars's roof a certain Benedetto, Villefort's bastard son, a swindler, a thief and a forger, who had once been imprisoned at Toulon and, after escaping, had passed himself off as an Italian prince. The charming Eugénie, Danglars's daughter, accepts his advances, but, on the very day which is to see the signing of the marriage contract in surroundings of the utmost splendour, the bridegroom to be, who is wanted for murder, is arrested.

But normal imagination had not been responsible for the stroke of genius which produced the name *Comte de Monte-Cristo,* which was to become so deeply imbedded in the memories of countless readers. The mysterious chemistry which assists at the birth of great works had been enriched with this precious reagent on the day when Dumas had gone shooting in the islands which lie about Elba.

The real Picaud had pursued his vengeance in too ruthless a manner to become a popular hero. Dantès must be an implacable avenger, but not a savage murderer. Picaud had assassinated his persecutors. He had taken vengeance into his own hands, whereas Dantès *is given* his vengeance. Fernand, after becoming the *général comte de Morceuf* and the husband of Mercédès, commits suicide. Danglars is ruined. Villefort goes mad. But to relieve the hideous darkness of the story, and to recreate the atmosphere of the *Arabian Nights,* Dumas presents Monte-Cristo with an oriental mistress, Haydée, the daughter of the Pasha of Janina. She is the proud and noble slave whom Dumas would so much have liked to possess.

At the end of the book, Edmond Dantès, now sated with vengeance, goes so far as to provide a dowry for Mademoiselle de Villefort, his enemy's child, who marries Morel, his friend's son. But when the young couple wish to thank their benefactor, Monte-Cristo, and ask his sailor: 'Where is the count? Where is Haydée?' the man points towards the horizon:

> They looked in the direction indicated by the sailor and, on the stretch of dark blue water separating the Mediterranean from the sky, saw a white sail no bigger than a seagull's wing. . . .

And so *The Count of Monte-Cristo* finishes like a Charlie Chaplin film, with the back view of a man walking out of the picture.

Notes

1. Alexandre Dumas, *Causeries,* pp. 273-4.

2. Hitherto unpublished. British Museum, 39,672, *Dumas manuscripts,* folios 68-72.

3. See Jacques Peuchet, *Mémoires tirés des archives de la police de Paris,* vol. V, pp. 197-228 (Paris, Levavaseur-Bourmancé, 1838).

4. British Museum, 39,672, *Dumas manuscripts,* folios 68-72 (hitherto unpublished).

Amelita Marinetti (essay date December 1976)

SOURCE: Marinetti, Amelita. "Death, Resurrection, and Fall in Dumas' *Comte de Monte-Cristo.*" *French Review* 50, no. 2 (December 1976): 260-69.

[*In the following essay, Marinetti explores the thematic elements of death and rebirth in* The Count of Monte-Cristo, *arguing that the text exhibits two major mythic cycles—the heroic fall and the myth of the father-seeker/father-slayer.*]

Serious literary criticism has paid little attention to *Le Comte de Monte-Cristo,* apparently concurring with the judgment made on it by Alfred Nettement shortly after its first appearance as a *roman-feuilleton* in the *Journal des Débats.*[1] Nettement's criticism was aimed primarily at what he considered its improbabilities, both historical and psychological, and its immorality. He ignored Dumas' skill in weaving a story full of dramatic incidents into an historical background remarkable for its verisimilitude to anyone other than a scholar looking for inaccuracies of detail. Since his standard of psychological realism required that all a novel's characters exhibit perfect consistency, he found it unbelievable that Monte-Cristo should consider himself a Christian, yet commit destructive acts. He compared *Le Comte de Monte-Cristo,* for its incredibility, to *The Arabian Nights,* yet did not consider that both might contain truth of a different order from that he was seeking.

J.-H. Bornecque, in his preface to the Garnier edition of the work (1962), rehabilitates it and finds justification for its lasting popularity in its expression of the frustrated dreams of its era (for enjoyment, self-expression, and unlimited freedom) and of the deep aspirations of Dumas himself to omniscience, social power, and the conquest of the impossible. In his biography of the three Dumas, André Maurois[2] recognized some of the mythic elements in this expression of dreams as a modern embodiment of the figure of magician and dispenser of justice.

However, the wealth of mythic themes which permeate this novel have not been sufficiently recognized or studied. Particularly important are two myths, those of death and resurrection, which have been briefly noted by Jean Tortel in his "Esquisse d'un univers tragique: le mythe de la toute-puissance,"[3] and that of the fall, an aspect of the novel which has been completely neglected. These two myths inform the entire structure of the book. In these mythic themes, at a deeper level than in that of the omniscient and all-powerful magician, can be discovered the experience, needs, and fears of a revolutionary era. More important as an explanation of the seemingly eternal appeal of *Le Comte de Monte-Cristo* is the fact that these themes have special impact in all ages characterized by social and political instability and rapid change, and therefore have been meaningful to most of the Western world and well beyond it ever since the time of Dumas. We should recognize, moreover, not only the variety of the myths which enter into the work, and the skill with which they are enmeshed in the contemporary setting, but the ways in which all these myths are modified by the psychological and historical forces which were at work within Dumas' world.

There is nothing surprising in the profound influence of myth on the structure and themes of Dumas' novel. The early nineteenth century was a period particularly inspired by myth. Its most powerful writers were mythmakers, gifted at crystallizing popular fantasies and in doing so usually reincarnating the mythic heroes and situations of earlier times. The figure of Satan, for example, became associated in the Romantic period with the aggressive, inventive spirit in man, basis of hubris and heresy, but also of self-reliance. Prometheus came to symbolize man's fight for liberty against oppression, while Faust was transformed into a hero of sensibility and suffering caused by his thirst for absolute experience. Pride and rebellious individualism, always present to some degree in the hero, but considered sins in the earlier centuries of Christianity, became virtues as faith diminished.[4]

Dumas was brought up on sacred history and classical mythology. He learned to read using a magnificent Bible belonging to a family friend and he subsequently found great enjoyment in his own beautiful picture book of mythology. The Bible stories remained so vivid in his mind that he claimed never to have needed to reread it in later life. He also asserted at the time he was writing his memoirs that he still knew every detail of Greek and Roman mythology as thoroughly as he had as a child.[5]

Yet one need not look to classical and Biblical learning or to contemporary literary examples for sources of a myth of resurrection and fall. Dumas' generation had its own fallen and resurrected hero in the person of Napoleon. This man, fallen from extraordinary heights and banished to imprisonment in Elba, had experienced a brief resurrection during the Hundred Days. A few years later, his memory was resurrected by the translation of his remains to France. Once could even see the rise of Napoleon III as a kind of inferior reincarnation.

Le Comte de Monte-Cristo contains two mythic cycles, similar in pattern yet different in development and emphasis. The first begins with the hero in a state of relative innocence, followed by a fall which is far more terrible than a modicum of guilt would seem to justify (and therefore resembles the catastrophe of death in the life of man), which in turn leads to a hard-won but spectacular resurrection into a position of power far beyond any known by ordinary mortals. This cycle, covering Dantès' imprisonment, escape, and discovery of the treasure willed to him by Father Faria, is contained within the first twenty-four chapters of the book, less than a fourth of the whole. The remainder of the novel recounts another cycle, carrying the hero from a position of noble but contaminated omniscience to a second fall, this time clearly justified, and at last to an ambiguous second resurrection. This is the story of Monte-Cristo's revenge on those who put him in prison, his recompense to his loyal employer, his increasing loss of faith in the rightness of his mission, and his return to the world of death through the two young lovers he has chosen as his spiritual descendants, followed by their rebirth and his own disappearance from the known world.

The essential idea of the fall, at least until its reinterpretation in Camus' work, has been that of a basically innocent man or lesser god, of great stature and good intentions, who oversteps the bounds permitted to aspiring humanity, falls into error, and is severely punished. The basic innocence of Dantès is more evident that in most other versions of the myth. Capable sailor, devoted son, faithful lover, totally honest in his relations with the world, he is not without a certain lack of foresight and a too-easy unawareness of the misery and evil lurking in the hearts of his associates. Owing money to the untrustworthy Caderousse, he departed on a long voyage leaving his old father with barely enough money to last until his return. Once back, with the promise of promotion to captain and marriage to the girl he loves, he is oblivious to the enraged jealousy of Fernand and Danglars who covet, respectively, the woman and the job.

Of deeper interest, however, than these slight implications of neglect or indifference on the part of the young hero is the suggestion made by Dantès himself at the height of happiness in his forthcoming marriage and position that innocence alone cannot merit happiness: "Il me semble," he reflects to Danglars, "que l'homme n'est pas fait pour être si facilement heureux! Le bonheur est comme ces palais des îles enchantées dont les dragons gardent les portes. Il faut combattre pour le conquérir" (I, 49).[6]

The form of Dantès' fall is a solitary and interminable confinement which is as close to death as a living man can get. The fallen hero disappears at this point and is transformed into the dead hero who will eventually be resurrected. According to Joseph Campbell,[7] the myth of the resurrected hero is universal in scope, originally concerning a god or the incarnation of one in a human being. When the hero is not divine in nature, the story concerns his leaving the world of everyday existence and going into a strange region where fabulous forces are at work; there a decisive victory is won, and he returns with the power to grant favors to his fellow men. His adventures usually involve instruction, testing, and transmission of power by a father figure of godlike character. Everywhere in mythical thought truly creative acts have their origin in some sort of dying to the world, after which the hero "comes back as one reborn, made great and filled with creative power."[8]

The analogy which Dumas intended between his hero and the Christian version of the resurrection myth is apparent in the title itself, and it is interesting to recall that the element of the novel which first occurred to its author was its title, the island of that name which he happened upon while on a hunting expedition with Prince Napoleon in 1841. Moreover, in describing the coat of arms adopted by the Count to go with his new fortune and title (both derived from the

island), the narrator says that it is a gold-colored mountain on a blue sea, with a red cross at the summit, "ce qui pouvait aussi bien être une allusion à son nom rappelant le Calvaire, que la passion de Notre-Seigneur a fait une montagne plus précieuse que l'or, et la croix infâme que son sang divin a faite sainte, qu'à quelque souvenir personnel de souffrance et de régénération enseveli dans la nuit du passé de cet homme mystérieux" (II, 383).

The extent to which Dumas was inspired by the career of Napoleon, the contemporary embodiment of the myths of fall and resurrection, is most apparent in his efforts to achieve historical realism in the circumstances of Dantès imprisonment. Dantès went to prison in February 1815, a few days before Napoleon's return from Elba; and the Hundred Days, which gave hope to both, turned out to be the last blow for each. Moreover, the subsequent corruption of Dantès' character through his lust for vengeance and the enormity of his power is surely related to a common contemporary view of Napoleon's evolution.

Dumas reiterates throughout the story that Dantès' imprisonment, of fourteen years' duration, was a death for him, and that the Count of Monte-Cristo was a man who had returned from the grave. Dantès' entry into the town jail (even before going to the ominous Château d'If) is rendered fateful by the three resounding knocks on the heavy door, by the young man's fearful hesitation on the threshold, and by a reference to the air on the other side as "other," noxious and heavy (I, 86). Dantès soon comes to look upon himself as dead and to think of the world outside as that of the living. The spiritual equivalent of physical death comes progressively with his loss of pride (he comes to long to be with other prisoners, even the dregs of humanity), his loss of all sense of time, and finally his loss of identity, becoming merely "Number 34."

A preoccupation with death, which is not the morbid quest for sensation present in some Romantic literature, but is closely integrated with the themes of the novel, is evidenced throughout. Monte-Cristo's "death" in prison leaves its mark forever on his skin, which remains pale and cold. When Franz, the Count's first acquaintance among the Parisian aristocracy, and Albert, son of Fernand and Mercédès, are forced by Monte-Cristo to witness a gruesome execution in Rome, they agree with him that death is the only serious preoccupation in life and the only thing that truly reveals character. The supposed death of Villefort's and Mme Danglars' baby, the real death of Franz's father, both of which come back to haunt the living, and finally the simulated death of Valentine, all point to the central conviction of the novel, that death and death alone truly reveals the significance of life.

As was the case in Greek mythology, a journey into the realm of death must involve a descent into an underground place. Dantès' cell is below ground, with only a small shaft of light coming from above, and the place he constructs on the Island of Monte-Cristo after his escape is set deep in an underground cavern. The enormous treasure which is the source of all his future power is found in a grotto. And for the resurrection of Valentine the Count chooses this same underground cavern, into which her lover Maximilien must descend as did Orpheus in search of his lost love.

The process of Dantès' resurrection begins in prison, long before the possibility of actual escape presents itself. As is often the case in myth, it is brought about through the agency of a semidivine creature who comes to the aid of the hero, here the all-wise Faria. It is only at the very threshold of real, physical death, when he has almost succeeded in starving to death, that Dantès first hears the scratching of this other prisoner and finds in the hope of a companion something to live for. But the rebirth that is Faria's gift to Dantès involves far more than release from prison. Through Faria Dantès is completely regenerated into a new man, with all the wisdom, knowledge, wealth, and strength of character to make it possible for him to play the role of a god in the eyes of others. Imprisonment has sharpened and deepened the mind of this learned man in a way that could never have occurred in freedom. Not only does he impart to Dantès his wisdom and knowledge, but also "ce métier patient et sublime du prisonnier, qui de rien sait faire quelque chose" (I, 237). It is he who is able to penetrate the mystery of why Dantès was accused and locked up indefinitely without ever being brought to trial, thus bringing the innocent young man to his first confrontation with real evil. In this way, although Faria is himself angelic in nature, he plays the mythic role of serpent who presents to the hero the knowledge of good and evil. Finally, Faria provides Dantès with the means of using all his acquired knowledge and strength to real advantage by giving him the secret of an immense hidden fortune. Even more important to the mythic aspects of the story is the fact that the escape plans of the two men end in frustration and failure, and that it is ultimately only through Faria's death, and Dantès' sewing himself into the shroud, that the latter is able to escape.

At this point the story incorporates another widespread myth, that of the father-seeker and the father-slayer. Very often the son seeks his father, who has been lost, or who had exiled him (frequently as a threat to the father). The meeting of the two involves a transmission (or violent wrestling) of a precious heritage, sometimes resulting in the death of the father. The story is undoubtedly related to age-old and ever-new difficulties of getting the old to relinquish their powers to the young.

There is no doubt that Faria is a father figure for Dantès. The latter calls upon Faria long after his death as his "second père . . . toi qui m'as donné la liberté, la science, la richesse" (II, 717). Dantès' natural father is seen from the beginning as a helpless old man, incapable of doing anything to aid his son in his hour of need, or even of preventing himself from dying of starvation once deprived of his son's support. Dantès is in desperate need of another father, if he is to be reborn as another man, one capable of rising above and triumphing over the weight of evil which threatens to crush him.[9] Mythic thought requires that a price be paid for such a miracle. The life of the father must be sacrificed, symbolically if not actually. Birth symbolism is very strong in this episode of the novel: the birth canal is represented by the narrow passage dug between the two cells, the womb by the shroud in which Dantès substitutes himself for Faria, the birth cries by the terrible shout uttered by Dantès just before he hits the surface of the sea (of life) when the guards whom he expected to dig him a grave throw him into the ocean instead.

Another theme which is widespread in mythology and closely connected to primitive ritual is that of the testing of the hero. In ritual this involves severe exercises of severance whereby the mind is radically cut away from attitudes appropriate to the old life patterns, in order to prepare the individual for a new state in life, such as puberty or marriage. After the tests there follows an interval of more or less extended retirement, from which the person returns to ordinary life as a new man, as though reborn. In myth, the hero must pass through a series of trials aimed at rendering him worthy of the favor he asks of the gods or the exalted position he is to fill (i.e., the ordeal of Psyche and the labors of Hercules). Basically, this initiation signifies the obedient acceptance of a ruthless and (to man) senseless universe.

The theme of testing plays an important part in the novel of Dumas, both in the prison episode and in the subsequent ten years during which the Count prepares for his revenge. It is repeated at the end of the story as an epilogue. The first test of Dantès' moral fiber comes when Faria is half paralyzed by an attack of apoplexy which puts an end to the two prisoners' hope of escaping together. Although Faria urges his young friend to escape alone, Dantès refuses to leave and vows to stay with him to the end of his life. The reward for this act of loyalty and sacrifice is the secret of Faria's treasure, in the reality of which Dantès refuses for a long time to believe. The crux of the testing within the Château d'If is the withstanding of pain while maintaining hope and moral values. The self-testing to which Monte-Cristo submits after his escape from prison is for the purpose of hardening him to the pain and death of others, essential to one embarked on a spectacular and merciless revenge. Dantès' brief service as a smuggler just after his escape, especially his first taste of gunfire and death, is useful in this regard: "Dantès était sur la voie qu'il voulait parcourir, et marchait au but qu'il voulait atteindre: son cœur était en train de se pétrifier dans sa poitrine" (I, 272-73).

At this point, a lapse of ten years occurs in the narrative. When the resurrected hero reappears, as though from nowhere, it is to rescue the older Morrel from bankruptcy and suicide, to save Albert from Roman bandits, to bedazzle all Paris by his fabulous wealth and apparent omniscience. More than this, the reader sees Dantès as a Protean figure who is able to appear as entirely different people in different places, and within minutes of a prior appearance. Thus, like his mythic predecessors, he is not only reborn, but comes back to the world a totally different person from the Dantès who had entered prison twenty-four years earlier. And again, like the heroes of myth, he is insulated from the world. For example, he appears never to eat. Part of this is a refusal to break bread with his enemies, an eastern custom which he has brought back from his travels in the Orient. Mercédès, who has recognized him and fears for her husband and son, desperately tries to get Monte-Cristo to eat at least a piece of fruit from her garden, as though like Proserpine, the smallest bit of food partaken of would somehow commit him to his host. Yet even when he is host in his cave to Franz, against whom he holds no grudge, he barely touches the magnificent dinner served. Even his voice has a peculiar quality, strident and metallic, as though, visitor from another world, he had not quite succeeded in modulating it to make it sound like that of an ordinary mortal.

Monte-Cristo's apotheosis is the aspect of the novel which aligns it most closely with popular hero litera-

ture of all epochs and is thus of less concern to this study of the novel as a variation of the myths of death, resurrection, and fall. However, the resurrection experience is repeated several times during the period of apotheosis in a way that links it closely to the early nineteenth-century fascination with the search for a new identity. Monte-Cristo's identity, unknown to all but Mercédès, is revealed to each enemy in turn, but only when the latter is on the brink of death, madness, or utter ruin, and is no longer in a position to retaliate. Each revelation of the name of Dantès is a moment of such intense drama, is so devastating to the enemy who learns it, and so exhilarating to Monte-Cristo, that one is reminded of the importance in myth and religion of the very name of the deity. The magic power given by earlier peoples to a name had reappeared in Romantic literature as an intense preoccupation with the quest for identity. In a rapidly shifting social and political environment, the status and role of the individual, therefore his identity, are a matter of doubt for him.[10] Small wonder that for Dumas and his contemporaries who had grown up in the post-Revolutionary era, there was untold satisfaction in the fact that the pronouncing of one's name alone could produce utter despair in one's enemies, and hope out of despair in those who merited one's gratitude.

Unfortunately, Monte-Cristo's apotheosis, splendid as it is, contains within it the seeds of a new fall. Dantès' state of relative innocence had lasted only until the gift of power and knowledge bestowed on him by Faria offered the possibility of taking action to free himself. It appears that when man defends himself against evil he inevitably becomes to some extent corrupted by it. A basic implication of the myth of the fall is that perfect happiness is necessarily accompanied by perfect innocence and trust, i.e., man before the fall. Knowledge is equated with the temptation to evil. Ambition and inventiveness, which demonstrate an aggressive and analytic attitude toward the universe, are associated with rebellion against God. The children of Cain were both wicked and inventive (inventing the harp, the organ, metal work, planning cities) as was Prometheus (who brought not only fire and light, but the sciences, city building, agriculture, transportation, and music, to man). Thus competence is idealized, but it is also suspect, and man through the ages has striven for competence and longed for innocence.[11]

Dumas clearly shows in his novel that the truly innocent—Dantès' father, both Morrels, Victorine, Haydée—are doomed to poverty, humiliation, and a wretched death without the aid of the Count's somewhat contaminated competence. The contrast is most striking when we consider the character of Faria, a genius who yet helplessly languishes in prison because of his angelic purity. He cannot envisage the use of power except in the cause of good. He will assent to the possibility of killing a guard to effect their escape only if utterly unavoidable, while Dantès does not understand such scruples. Faria's last days are brightened by thoughts of all the good Dantès will be able to do his friends with the fortune he has bequeathed him, while Dantès can think only of revenge on his enemies.

Monte-Cristo was warned very early, at the brink of his discovery of Faria's treasure, that evil lurks in this new power. A poisonous snake lay coiled at the entrance of the cave like a guardian of the treasure. Yet he clings to the belief that he has been chosen as an agent of Providence for the punishment of the wicked: "Je me sentais poussé comme le nuage de feu passant dans le ciel pour aller brûler les villes maudites" (II, 703). He receives each of his early successes as confirmations of his calling. His pride goes to greater extremes when he boasts of finding pleasure unknown to other men in struggling "contre la nature qui est Dieu, et contre le monde qui peut bien passer pour le diable" (II, 341). Nowhere is the exaggerated pride of Monte-Cristo more evident than in the scene following his promise to Mercédès to spare her son in the duel between them, a forbearance which must necessarily entail his own death. More unbearable to him than the idea of death or of giving up his great project is the fear of being thought defeated, the victim rather than the agent of Providence. Above all else, he is anxious to let the world know in some way that he has stopped the course of Providence *by his own will alone.* The thought that the self that he has forged with such long efforts will be obliterated is also unbearable to him: "Ce moi que je croyais quelque chose, ce moi dont j'étais si fier, ce moi que j'avais vu si petit dans les cachots du château d'If, et que j'avais su rendre si grand, sera demain un peu de poussière!" (II, 434).

This immoderate pride is vanquished when the Count perceives that the pursuit of his revenge entails harming the innocent. The discovery that Villefort's daughter Valentine, about to be poisoned by her stepmother, is loved by his beloved protégé Maximilien, and even more the discovery of the death of Villefort's son, only a child, both of which situations he brought about himself, are the events that truly shake his faith in his mission. He can no longer number

himself among the gods because they have the power to limit the results of their actions—chance is not stronger than they. Symbolic of this problem is the red elixir, the recipe for which Monte-Cristo gives to the ambitious poisoner, Mme de Villefort. On the exact dosage depends whether it cures, injures, or kills. Man can control the dosage of a drug, but once he has attained supreme knowledge and power he cannot control the dosage so as to do only justice and no evil.

This impasse which Monte-Cristo must confront between the legitimate aspirations of man for a social order closer to his conception of justice, and his inability to control the power unleashed by his new freedom to act, is an echo of the central ambivalence of the age. Men of all shades of political opinion were convinced that the forces released by the two revolutions, the French and the industrial, would inevitably bring tremendous changes. But some felt that these changes would be in the direction of greater social justice through scientific rationality, while others were filled with dread of coming chaos and horror. As Jacob Talman has expressed it: "The progressives of all hues spoke of the rights of man: the reactionaries countered with the malignant fickleness of man and the omnipotent, benevolent wisdom of God."[12] Dumas himself was basically republican and liberal in spirit. But he felt horror for the excesses of the Revolution, and he blamed Napoleon for what he had cost in the blood of Frenchmen.

The last chapters of the novel are devoted to Monte-Cristo's attempt to resolve this problem. The resolution involves, on the one hand, his own efforts to do good deeds in order to add to the "poids jeté dans la balance en regard du plateau ou j'ai laissé tomber le mal" (II, 761), and on the other hand, an attempt to relive, through the agency of Maximilien, who is as a son to him, the whole experience of death and rebirth through testing and the sacrifice of the father. This time the goal is not revenge or even justice, but love alone, and Maximilien is reborn not as a monster of power and knowledge but as a purely good man.

Monte-Cristo pardons Danglars, the last of his enemies, while he still has his life, his sanity, and the dregs of his fortune, because he himself needs to be pardoned. He does what he can to protect the wife and son of Fernand from the worst effects of the latter's ruin and suicide. He has already saved Valentine from death by poison. But it is not enough simply to reunite the young lovers. Maximilien must believe Valentine dead, must be ready to die himself, not just immediately in the first throes of grief, but after a period of time which would dull the pain of a less devoted lover and give him hope of finding solace elsewhere. Like Dantès many years earlier, he must go to the very door of death in order to be born again into the perfect bliss of love. Only thus will he become worthy of possessing Valentine, "un bonheur infini, immense, inconnu, un bonheur trop grand, trop complet, drop divin pour ce monde" (II, 617).

The temptation motif, less prominent in Dantès' ordeal, is very clearly analogous to that of Christ when it is Morrel's turn to be tested. Monte-Cristo offers him his entire fortune, reminding him of all the power and pleasure it provides, if only he consent to go on living without Valentine. When Maximilien withstands this temptation, Monte-Cristo chooses for the scene of resurrection (of both Morrel and Valentine) the underground cavern that is his palace and has Morrel enter the realm of death through taking hashish, which the latter thinks is a fatal drug. As Morrel is recovering consciousness Monte-Cristo says to Valentine: "Désormais vous ne devez plus vous séparer sur la terre; car pour vous retrouver il se précipitait dans la tombe" (II, 765). Even the theme of the sacrifice of the father reappears, for Monte-Cristo, after leaving them wealth in the form of all his European property, disappears into some mysterious realm, probably never to be seen again. His final message to Morrel is, "Attendre et espérer!" This is the essence of faith and trust in God, and the opposite of the implacable force and omniscient wisdom of the self he had spent most of his adult life to construct and unleash upon the world.

The overall theme of **Le Comte de Monte-Cristo** is a deeply ambivalent one. Although human independence and competence, in the person of Monte-Cristo, have been shown imperfect and even dangerous, they have brought about a much closer approximation of justice than this particular society offered before his coming. Therefore, despite the shedding of a little innocent (though shown to be potentially guilty) blood in the death of Villefort's young son, it cannot be said that Dantès would have done better to wait and hope. On the contrary, only because a Monte-Cristo has taken on man's guilt, can a Morrel live in innocence and follow his admonition to "attendre et espérer."

Notes

1. *Etudes critiques sur le feuilleton-roman* (Paris: Lagny Frères, 1947), II, 291-412.

2. *The Titans: A Three-Generation Biography of the Dumas,* trans. Gerard Hopkins (Westport, Conn.: Greenwood Press, 1957), p. 224.

3. *Cahiers du Sud,* special issue: *Quelques Aspects d'une mythologie moderne,* 1951.

4. Peter L. Thorslev, *The Byronic Hero: Types and Prototypes* (Minneapolis: Univ. of Minnesota Press, 1962), pp. 85-87 and 108-11.

5. *Mes Mémoires* (Paris: Gallimard, 1954), I, 196-98.

6. References are to Alexandre Dumas, *Le Comte de Monte-Cristo,* ed. J.-H. Bornecque, 2 vols. (Paris: Garnier, 1962).

7. "The Historical Development of Mythology," in *Myth and Mythmaking,* ed. Henry A. Murray (1960, rpt. Boston: Beacon, 1968), p. 19.

8. Joseph Campbell, *The Hero with a Thousand Faces,* (Princeton: Princeton Univ. Press, 1968), pp. 35-36.

9. One is reminded here of the importance of the theme of father-seeking and the father substitute in Stendhal's works. Other points of similarity in theme between Dumas and Stendhal are the importance of death as the true key to character and of imprisonment as a source of self-discovery.

10. S. B. John, "Violence and Identity in Romantic Drama," in *French Literature and its Background,* vol. 4: *The Early Nineteenth Century,* ed. John Cruickshank (London: Oxford Univ. Press, 1969), pp. 137-38.

11. Thorslev, pp. 94 and 113. See also Jerome S. Bruner, "Myth and Identity," in *Myth and Mythmaking,* op. cit., pp. 276-86.

12. *Romanticism and Revolt: Europe 1815-1848* (New York: Harcourt, Brace and World, 1967), p. 24.

Richard S. Stowe (essay date 1976)

SOURCE: Stowe, Richard S. "The Chronicler of Romance: *Le Comte de Monte-Cristo.*" In *Alexandre Dumas (père),* pp. 116-26. Boston, Mass.: Twayne, 1976.

[*In the following essay, Stowe expounds on the elements of realism in* Le Comte de Monte-Cristo, *noting that, "almost as soon as the novel was published readers everywhere began seeking or inventing traces of the characters in the locales it described."*]

During a visit to Marseille in 1841[1] Dumas borrowed from the city library a copy—never returned—of Courtilz de Sandras' *Mémoires de Monsieur d'Artagnan.* In all probability this fortuitous happening planted the seed that ultimately produced *Les Trois Mousquetaires.* Another such casual, unplanned occurrence lies at the beginning of *Le Comte de Monte-Cristo,* the only book of Dumas's to challenge, if not to surpass, that novel in popularity. Dumas tells the story in one of his *causeries* written many years later, "*État civil du* Comte de Monte-Cristo" ("Vital Statistics on *The Count of Monte-Cristo*").[2]

Early in 1842 Dumas, who was then living in Florence, took the young Prince Napoleon to visit the island of Elba at the request of the prince's father, Jerome Bonaparte. After touring Elba they decided to go hunting on the nearby island of Pianosa. The peasant who carried their game bag assured them that the hunting would be better on yet another island, just visible on the horizon—the island of Monte-Cristo. Off they sailed the next morning to Monte-Cristo, but neither to land nor to hunt. Their rowers informed them as they were about to jump ashore that, the island being deserted, boats could not stop there without all who landed subsequently being quarantined for five or six days. The prince and Dumas debated the risks, then Dumas suggested:

> . . . if Monseigneur is willing. . . . —What?—We will simply go around the island.—What for?—To fix its geographical position. After that we will go back to Pianosa.—It will be fine to pinpoint the location of the island of Monte-Cristo, but what good will that do?—It will enable me, in memory of this trip I have the honor of making with you, to give the name of the island of Monte-Cristo to a novel I shall write someday.—Then let's go around the island of Monte-Cristo, said the Prince, and send me the first copy of your book.

The novel remained no more than a name in the back of Dumas's mind for a year at least. In 1843 he contracted to write eight volumes of *Impressions de voyage dans Paris* for the publishers Béthune and Plon, but before he began writing M. Béthune came to inform him that they did not want a "historical and archaeological stroll through Caesar's *Lutèce* and Philippe Auguste's Paris." What the publishers now envisioned was a novel to compete with Eugène Sue's overwhelmingly successful serial *Les Mystères de Paris,* in which the Parisian "travel impressions" would be merely incidental.

The change was an easy one for Dumas to make. Searching for a plot, he recalled an anecdote from the police files that had intrigued him for several years and decided to use it as a starting point. Called *The Diamond and the Vengeance,*[3] it told the story of a low trick—a false denunciation—played on a poor shoemaker, François Picaud, as a consequence of which he was imprisoned for seven years. During his imprisonment Picaud served an Italian ecclesiastic who was also a political prisoner, then fell heir to an enormous fortune upon the Italian's death. The second part of the story recounts Picaud's systematic search, after his release from prison, for vengeance on those who had wronged him.

Dumas began his story in Rome, where a rich nobleman named the Count of Monte-Cristo did a great favor for a young French traveller. His recompense was to have the Frenchman serve as his guide when he in turn visited Paris. The trip to Paris, ostensibly to see the city (and to provide Dumas with the pretext for his *impressions*) was in reality to track down and punish enemies who had had the count imprisoned for ten years. When Dumas had written what now constitutes, with some alterations, Chapter 31-40—the Italian portion of the novel—he spoke of his work to Maquet. Maquet suggested that Dumas was skipping over the most interesting part of his hero's life by starting where he did and he pointed out the awkwardness of trying to fill in that much background material by flashbacks and narration. Dumas continues:

> "You may be right," I said. "Come back for dinner tomorrow and we'll talk it over."
>
> That evening, night, and next morning I had thought over his observation and it had seemed so right to me that it prevailed over my original idea. So when Maquet arrived the next day he found the work divided into three distinct parts: Marseille, Rome, Paris. That very evening we worked out together the outline for the first five volumes. . . .
>
> The rest, without being completely finished, was almost all roughed out. Maquet thought he had just done me the favor a friend would do. I insisted that he had done a collaborator's job.
>
> That is how *The Count of Monte-Cristo,* begun by me as travel impressions, turned gradually into a novel and ended up a collaboration between Maquet and me.

Fragments of the outline in Maquet's writing and letters exchanged between the two men illuminate their continuing active collaboration as they refined and elaborated characters, motivations, and details of action to produce the enormous structure of the completed novel. It was published serially over a year and a half, with several long interruptions for which Dumas invented impressive but vague excuses. In reality the delays were inevitable. During the entire time of composition and publication Dumas and Maquet were engaged in writing plays and other novels—sometimes three at once—together, while Dumas was writing and publishing still more alone, suing Eugène de Mirecourt, and planning his own Château de Monte-Cristo to be built at Port-Marly.

I. MARSEILLE, ROME, PARIS

The three sections into which Dumas divided his novel are unequal, but appropriately so. Part one, *Marseille,* contains thirty chapters; part two, *Italie,* which is really a bridge between the captivity and the vengeance, has nine noticeably longer chapters; the accomplishment of Monte-Cristo's vengeance in part three fills the remaining seventy-nine chapters (1040 pages in the Garnier edition).

Each of the three sections opens on a precise date— part one on February 24, 1815, as the three-master *Pharaon* sails into the port of Marseille under the command of Edmond Dantès, the nineteen-year-old first mate who had taken charge when the captain died at sea. Upon the orders of the dying captain Dantès had stopped at the island of Elba where he had delivered a letter to Murat, seen Napoleon, and been given a letter to deliver personally to the Bonapartist group in Paris. The owner of the ship, M. Morrel, welcomes Dantès warmly and promises that his captaincy will be made permanent before the ship sails again. By thus performing his duty and earning the respect of both shipmates and superiors Dantès sets up his happiness: he pays his elderly father's debts to a grasping neighbor, Caderousse, and plans an immediate wedding with his fiancée Mercédès. Unknowingly, by the same deeds he has prepared his downfall. His rival for Mercédès, Fernand, and the envious ship's accountant, Danglars, with the knowledge but not the active help of Caderousse, send a letter to the King's Prosecutor denouncing Dantès as a Bonapartist conspirator. Seized by the authorities in the midst of his prewedding party, Dantès is questioned by M. Noirtier de Villefort, the assistant prosecutor, who had been called away from his own engagement party to conduct the interrogation. At first sympathetic to Dantès, the ambitious and ultraroyalist Villefort is stunned to discover that the letter given Dantès to deliver in Paris is addressed to his own father—a *girondin* and Bonapartist whose political

views Villefort finds intolerable. Fearful for his own position if word should leak out, Villefort reads and destroys the letter, swears Dantès to secrecy, then sends him off to solitary confinement in the Château d'If. There Dantès remains for fourteen years.

The rest of part one details Dantès' imprisonment, the tortures of his loneliness and ignorance of why he is there; his friendship with the abbé Faria[4] who not only tells him the secret of the treasure on the island of Monte-Cristo but gives him the incalculable wealth of learning; his near-miraculous escape, and his return to Marseille a transformed man. Now free and endowed with apparently inexhaustible riches and power, Dantès seeks to unravel the mysteries of his years of imprisonment. His father is dead; Mercédès has disappeared. In disguise he tracks down Caderousse and bribes him into revealing the story of the false denunciation, thus confirming his suspicions. In another disguise he intervenes to right the financial affairs of his former employer and friend Morrel, who had been driven near suicide by a series of disastrous reverses. At the end of part one a new *Pharaon* sails into the port—a duplicate to the last detail of the old vessel once captained by Dantès and recently reported down in a storm. His friends thus rewarded, Dantès is now ready to punish his enemies.

Part two takes place during the pre-Lenten carnival season in Italy in 1838. Before joining his friend Albert de Mortcerf in Rome for Mardi Gras, the young baron Franz d'Épinay decides to take a trip to Elba. From there he goes to Pianosa to hunt, but is disappointed and, like Dumas and Prince Napoleon, accepts his guide's suggestion to push on to the island of Monte-Cristo. They approach the island at night, see the campfires of presumed smugglers, but ascertain that they are friendly and—unlike Dumas and the prince—go ashore. Franz is invited to dine with the leader of the bandits and is escorted blindfolded into the sumptuously appointed caves of the Count of Monte-Cristo, who identifies himself as Sinbad the Sailor. (Franz in turn introduces himself as Aladdin.) Not only the names but the entire episode seem drawn from the *Arabian Nights*; the description of the interior of the cave, the meal served by the mute slave Ali—everything is unreal, mysterious, and luxuriously exotic. After the meal Franz is given one of his host's hashish tablets and experiences a sort of opium dream, also described in vivid detail. When he awakes Franz is again on the shore and only "Sinbad's" boat on the horizon offers confirmation of the reality of what has happened.

In Rome, Franz and Albert become acquainted with the enigmatic Count of Monte-Cristo who occupies a suite in their hotel. Franz recognizes him as his host on the island but says nothing. The count shows the young men every kindness and it is to him that Franz turns for help when Albert is kidnapped by the notorious bandit Luigi Vampa. Instead of lending the ransom money that Franz asks for, Monte-Cristo goes with him to Vampa's hideout in the catacombs of San Sebastian and secures Albert's immediate release. Before leaving for Paris the next day Albert extracts a promise from the count that he will come to visit him at his home in Paris exactly three months hence, at 10:30 A.M. on May 21st.

Early in the third part it becomes apparent that not only are the sins of the fathers visited on their sons, but the sons are often the instruments of their fathers' punishment. Twenty-three years have elapsed since Dantès was sent off to prison and a new generation has matured, the lives of the young people entangled by threads from a past of which they are often unaware. Maximilien Morrel, son of Dantès' benefactor, is in love with Valentine, daughter of his enemy Villefort by his first marriage. Danglars has a daughter, and Albert de Mortcerf is the son of Mercédès and Fernand. The intricacy of the plot in this long section defies analysis, but a résumé would serve little purpose in any event. Suffice it to say that through all the web of often sordid relationships and family skeletons, Dantès relentlessly pursues his vengeance. Inexorably he prods fate, exposing past crimes or forcing their exposure, precipitating latent crises and catastrophes until again the innocent fall victim to the guilty and he wonders if he has gone too far. A final meeting with Mercédès ends in a final farewell. Dantès revisits the Château d'If. And at the novel's end Maximilien Morrel and Valentine de Villefort stand side by side on the island of Monte-Cristo, watching the count's ship as it disappears beyond the horizon.

II. ART IMITATES LIFE

Le Comte de Monte-Cristo, we are frequently reminded, is not a historical novel but a *roman de moeurs*—a novel of manners. The story Dumas tells here was not remote from the first audience to which it was addressed; quite the contrary, the bulk of its action was placed squarely in contemporary times and in the city where most of its first readers lived. A fundamental concern, then, for Dumas and Maquet, was reconciling reality and fantasy so as to be convincing—and satisfying—on both levels. Let us look first at the realistic elements, those which

justify calling this *Arabian Nights* adventure a novel of contemporary manners.

The most immediately obvious realism is in settings. From the opening scene on, especially in parts one and three, places are identified and identifiable. All the landmarks of the harbor at Marseille are named as the *Pharaon* approaches the port and passes them one by one, then streets and squares of the city as Dantès hastens first to see his father, then to the Catalan village to find Mercédès. The engagement dinner of Villefort and Mlle de Saint-Méran is located precisely "on the rue du Grand-Cours, opposite the fountain of the Méduses, in one of those aristocratic old houses built by Puget. . . ." As Dantès is escorted to prison, he recognizes with horror the Château d'If looming up from its rock in front of the boat. Descriptions are brief but, like references to places, concretely real. The same geographic precision, the same concreteness of detail and allusion characterize the description of Caderousse's Auberge du Pont du Gard (Chapter XXVI) and the *quartiers* and houses of Paris among which characters and action move in part three. Dumas rarely fails to specify not only the part of the city but street names and house numbers. Even the eerie, semihallucinatory episodes of the Italian section of the novel take place in manifestly real locations, be they the hotel of *maître* Pastrini on the Piazza di Spagna in Rome (both hotel and proprietor were personally known to Dumas), the carnival-filled streets, the moonlit Colosseum, or the island of Monte-Cristo itself.

Dumas's realism goes beyond geography, however; it extends to characters, events, and milieux as well. Other real persons besides *maître* Pastrini figure in the novel in imagined roles or by way of allusion: the imaginary Haydée, for example, is the daughter of the real Ali Pasha of Janina and is received in the Luxembourg palace by a real *Président de la Chambre des Pairs*. The text is filled with references to fashionable clubs and restaurants, to real newspapers, to artists and writers of the day, to operas and plays that were being performed. From all this, as from the parallel engagement parties on different levels of society, the balls and dinners of the rich, the financial struggles of the poor, the honest bourgeois life of the Morrels, the social-climbing of Villefort, the unsavory dealings of Caderousse and Cavalcanti, the politics and commerce, there emerges a rich and accurate picture of a society, a picture at once authentic and minutely familiar to the book's first public.

Maquet's notes reveal with what meticulous care the relationships and psychology of the characters were prepared so that this aspect of the book too would be convincing. Behavior is always believable without always being predictable. The avarice of Caderousse is established before he succumbs to the temptation of the false abbé Busoni's diamond. Fernand's role in the tragedy at Janina is consistent with the weakness of character he had demonstrated in 1815, just as the courage and force of character displayed by old Noirtier at the end are in keeping with all prior impressions of him. Danglars's cupidity motivates his participation in the plot against Dantès, dominates his family relationships, and produces both his financial success and his ultimate ruin. The shift of the opening action from 1807—the year of Picaud's imprisonment—to 1815 makes the denunciation of Dantès more immediately believable because it is political. Villefort's motivation is strengthened by the same change.

A final realistic element—though it may not at first seem to be one—is the plot, which is drawn, as we have seen, from a true story. Though Dumas has expanded the simple tale at every point, elaborated the characterizations and profoundly altered the outcome, the core of truth—as fantastic as any fiction—remains. We may suspect that it was to emphasize this aspect of the work that he had Peuchet's anecdote appended to his text in the second reprinting of 1846.

The realism of *Le Comte de Monte-Cristo,* far from making its fabulous elements seem less believable, makes them more so. They are firmly rooted in a reality so familiar as to be almost tangible. If the reader believes in this reality of setting and situations, if he finds the characters and motives human and credible, then he will be much more ready to accept the impossible as possible. At every point it is clear that Dumas is working from this assumption.

The fantastic is not only rooted in reality; it grows from it also. Dumas's procedure in adapting his source is quite consistently to magnify or exaggerate the ordinary in order to arrive at the extraordinary. The imprisonment of Picaud lasted seven years; Dantès is in the Château d'If for fourteen. The fortune to which Picaud fell heir—admittedly already more than ordinary—amounted to about eleven million francs in property, diamonds and cash, and was located in Milan; Dantès found at least ten times as much buried in the cave on the deserted island of Monte-Cristo. The rich Italian whom Picaud served in prison "less as a servant than as a son" became the abbé Faria, who not only possessed the secret of

Monte-Cristo but was in every way an exceptional man, qualified to enrich Dantès intellectually and spiritually as well as materially. The disguises employed by Dantès are more numerous and varied than those used by Picaud in tracking down his enemies. Most striking of all, the humble shoemaker who devoted his life to avenging a wrong becomes a young man of promise transformed by his experience into a Promethean superman.

But the magnification occurs not only in such transformations; it is inherent in Dumas's manner of telling the story as well. One needs only to reread Chapter XXIV—in which Dantès finds the treasure—to see how a relatively simple narration, by its pacing and building up of detail, amplifies the action to a dimension consistent with the spectacular discovery at its end. Dantès himself cannot believe that he will find a treasure there, but step by step as the abbé Faria's words prove true, the reader—like Dantès—is forced to accept first the probability and then the reality.

Not all the fantasy in the novel, of course, thus grows from its factual source or from the realistic fictional context. The most conspicuously fabulous elements spring from Dumas's imagination and temperament. Dantès's remarkable escape from the Château d'If was Dumas's invention—at least it did not come from Peuchet—and it is worth noting that the part of the novel written by Dumas alone is the most heavily charged with romantic exoticism. In that section, starting from his personal experience—which he assigns to Franz d'Épinay—Dumas turns his imagination loose, revelling in the color of the Roman carnival, the mystery of moonlit ruins, the terror of bandits who strike by night. All this is, at bottom, quite conventional and in the vein of Hugo's *Orientales* and a whole body of literature of fifteen to twenty years before. But the barren rock of Monte-Cristo calls up more remote and personal memories, and he creates inside it a fabulous cavern from the *Arabian Nights* and a hero who, like the heroes of those tales, blends in his person power, wealth, and mystery.

In his introduction to the Garnier edition of the novel J.-H. Bornecque suggests that Dantès is a projection of Dumas's dreams, frustrations, and nature.[5] Relating him to the heroes of *Pauline* (1838) and *Georges* (1843), whom he finds to be less complete versions of the type fully embodied in Monte-Cristo, Bornecque argues that the personal qualities of Dumas that Monte-Cristo shares—for example, his love of the sea, his combination of humble origins and exceptional accomplishments—are only the starting point of the resemblance. Monte-Cristo realizes all his dreams, including the final affirmation of his rights and his superiority, in vengeance on his enemies and humiliation of his detractors; through Monte-Cristo, says Bornecque, Dumas vicariously shares this achievement. "Monte-Cristo, determined to conquer the impossible by force of will, is absolutely Alexandre Dumas as he sees himself or as he wishes himself to be."[6]

Bornecque's arguments are persuasive and his idea is both illuminating and suggestive. There are other comparisons to be made, however, which avoid the fascinating but tricky psychological identification of author and hero. Dantès may be examined in relation to others among Dumas's heroes such as Antony and Kean. Like them he is an *homme supérieur* who is a victim of society and the laws, prejudices, and hostility of lesser men than himself. Unlike Antony and Kean, Dantès is enabled to move above and beyond the limitations others would impose on him. Where both Antony and Kean ultimately have no choice but to yield to society as it exists, Edmond Dantès, Count of Monte-Cristo, successfully turns the forces of society to his own ends, against those individuals who have been its instruments in his life. For all the differences between them and between the authors, one can see a parallel as well between Monte-Cristo and Balzac's Vautrin, another superman. But where Vautrin's hostility, like Antony's, is directed against society as a whole, Monte-Cristo's is more specific. Where Vautrin does not hesitate at direct intervention to change the course of events (e.g., having Frédéric Taillefer killed in *Le Père Goriot*), Monte-Cristo operates more indirectly: his victims are made to become victims of themselves—of their own weaknesses of character; their own misdeeds. As Sigaux has pointed out in comparing Dantès and Picaud of *Le Diamant et la Vengeance*,[7] it is not insignificant that while Picaud—like Vautrin, we add—*takes* vengeance, Dantès *is avenged*. At the end justice is achieved and virtue is rewarded because good is ultimately stronger than evil, not merely because of Monte-Cristo's power. This optimistic conviction persists, overriding Monte-Cristo's doubts about his right to take unto himself the prerogatives of God and ringing forth in his final admonition to young Morrel and Valentine: "Wait and hope."

III. LIFE IMITATES ART

Such a view of the world could only add to the appeal of a work already so attractive in its excitement, its surprises, and its value as sheer entertainment. If

Monte-Cristo was a projection of Dumas's own dreams, he was surely even more the embodiment of the aspirations of a whole generation, just as the novel was an expression of the visible reality that generation knew. But the aspirations of that generation proved to be universal also. The success of *Le Comte de Monte-Cristo* was instantaneous, phenomenal, and enduring. Like *Les Trois Mousquetaires,* this novel has known no period of eclipse in popularity, still appearing in new editions with astonishing frequency and ageing scarcely at all. Its hold on the public imagination is as firm as ever and its hero has assumed a degree of reality for readers at least the equal of d'Artagnan's.

Indeed, if the historical d'Artagnan has become indissolubly merged with the fictional one, the fictional Monte-Cristo has become correspondingly "historical." Dumas transmuted something of the magical world of his novel into reality with his Château de Monte-Cristo at Port-Marly, though this dream was realized only briefly.[8] But almost as soon as the novel was published readers everywhere began seeking or inventing traces of the characters in the locales it described. Dumas wrote of this phenomenon in 1857, in the introduction to *Les Compagnons de Jéhu*; what he says there would be almost as true had he written it yesterday. Speaking of the importance he attaches to visiting the actual sites of events he writes about, he observes:

> That gives such a quality of truth to what I write that the characters I plant sometimes grow where I have planted them, to the extent that some people end up believing they actually existed.

> There are even people who claim to have known them.

> So now I am going to tell you something in confidence, dear readers, but do not repeat it. I don't want to wrong the honest *pères de famille* who live by this little industry; but if you go to Marseille they will show you Morrel's house on the *Cours,* the home of Mercédès in the Catalan village, and the cells of Dantès and Faria in the Château d'If.

> When I staged *Monte-Cristo* at the Théâtre-Historique I wrote to Marseille to have a drawing of the Château d'If made and sent to me. The drawing was intended for the stage designer.

> The artist to whom I wrote sent the drawing I had requested, but he went further than I had dared to ask. Under the drawing he wrote: "View of the Château d'If showing the place from which

Dantès was thrown." I have learned since that a good man attached to the staff of the Château d'If was selling fish-bone pens made by the abbé Faria himself.

The only problem is that Dantès and the abbé Faria never lived except in my imagination and that, consequently, Dantès could never have been thrown down from the Château d'If nor could the abbé Faria have made any pens.

But that is what comes of visiting localities.

Notes

1. The date is probable, not verified. Cf. C. Samaran, introduction to *Les Trois Mousquetaires* (Paris: Garnier, 1956), p. xii (note 1). J.-H. Bornecque in his edition of *Le Comte de Monte-Cristo* (Paris: Garnier, 1962) places the incident in 1843 (see pp. iv and lxxii).

2. *Causeries* (Paris: Michel Lévy, 1860), vol. I, pp. 263 ff.

3. *Le Diamant et la Vengeance,* by Jacques Peuchet, was published in 1838 as part of a six-volume work called *Mémoires tirés des archives de la police de Paris.* In his *causerie* Dumas refers to it as *La Police dévoilée.* He printed Peuchet's tale with *Le Comte de Monte-Cristo* in the second printing of the edition published "*Au Bureau de l'Écho des Feuilletons*" in 1846.

4. The abbé Faria was not merely Dumas's equivalent in the novel of the Italian prelate imprisoned with François Picaud; a real abbé Faria existed and almost certainly provided Dumas with some characteristics as well as a name. Cf. Sigaux, preface to *Le Comte de Monte-Cristo* (Editions Rencontre), pp. 15-16; Clouard, p. 301; Bornecque, preface to *Le Comte de Monte-Cristo* (Garnier).

5. Bornecque, pp. xlii-li.

6. *Ibid.,* p. xliii.

7. Sigaux, preface to *Monte-Cristo* (Editions Rencontre), p. 15.

8. Completed in 1847, the "château" was a house as extravagant and fantastic in its appointments as anything in the *Arabian Nights*; its architect was one of Dumas's stage designers at the Théâtre-Historique. Maurois and Clouard, along with many others, describe the house and grounds as well as the celebrated party that opened Dumas's residence there. Dumas himself reminisces about Monte-Cristo and its me-

nagerie of exotic pets in *Histoire de mes Bêtes.* Barely a year after he occupied it Dumas was forced to move out and eventually sold it for less than a tenth of its cost in order to pay off debts. The building still stands, externally at least in woefully dilapidated condition.

Timothy Unwin (review date July 1992)

SOURCE: Unwin, Timothy. Review of *The Count of Monte-Cristo,* by Alexandre Dumas, edited by David Coward. *Modern Language Review* 87, no. 3 (July 1992): 754.

In his famous article on *Madame Bovary,* Baudelaire observes that the final years of the reign of Louis-Phillippe are synonymous with 'les dernières explosions d'un esprit encore excitable par les jeux de l'imagination'. If excitement was what the reading public craved, then excitement was most certainly what it got with Dumas's famous novel, serialization of which began in the *Journal des débats* in 1844. This cloak-and-dagger masterpiece is, however, interesting in many ways, not least because it gives quintessential expression to the nineteenth-century myth of the protean and omnipotent manipulator (deliciously caricatured by Gide in *Les Caves du Vatican*). The present edition makes available in one inexpensive volume the complete text of the anonymous 1846 translation. This translation, which has been the basis of most subsequent ones, reads so well that one is almost tempted to forgive those who thought that **The Count of Monte Cristo** was an English novel! Together with the text, the editor provides a bibliography, a chronology of the life of Dumas, a useful series of explanatory notes, and a brisk and readable introduction which covers a wide range of subjects: the literary methods of the author, sources and composition of the novel, historical background, and critical reception. The judgement on Dumas's text is favourable but balanced, and constitutes a compelling invitation to read or to reread this classic tale of retribution and vengeance.

LE VICOMTE DE BRAGELONNE (1848-50; THE MAN IN THE IRON MASK)

Richard E. Goodkin (essay date 1999)

SOURCE: Goodkin, Richard E. "Separated at Birth: *The Man in the Iron Mask*; or, A Louis XIV for the Nineties." *Papers on French Seventeenth-Century Literature* 26, no. 51 (1999): 319-26.

[*In the following essay, Goodkin compares and contrasts Dumas's original text for* The Man in the Iron Mask *with its 1998 film adaptation.*]

The nineties have not always been kind to the age of Louis XIV, which, with its endless obsessions with rank and privilege, has at times been labeled as elitist and exclusionary. It is true that the literature associated with Louis XIV may be more resistant to popularization than some, if only because its intended public was so unembarrassedly a social elite. And there are probably some aficionados of the classical period who exult in the untouchable status that the very notion of classicism seems to confer on a body of work that may be thought immune to the ups and downs of literary taste across the centuries. I personally think that those ups and downs are part of the fascination of literature; the world of books would be a more boring place if every era did not have its own particular versions of Racine and Molière and its own distinct visions of historical figures like Elizabeth I, currently being embodied onscreen by Cate Blanchett, and Louis XIV, who to 1998 moviegoers turns out to bear a remarkable resemblance to Leonardo DiCaprio.

To get down to specifics, I have chosen to analyze the 1998 film, *The Man in the Iron Mask,* not because I find it to be a masterpiece; although parts of the film are compelling, it is not a great film by any stretch of the imagination.[1] Rather, I believe that studying a film about Louis XIV made for an American audience in 1998 can be an instructive way to reflect upon a place that all students of the French classical period inhabit: the intersection between a courtly culture distanced from us temporally, geographically and politically, and our own culture, from whose standpoint we inevitably view Louis XIV and his contemporaries. My premise is that however much we attempt to contextualize the literature of this period in reading and analyzing it, we are still inevitably influenced by our own culture, with all its implicit beliefs; needless to say, this tends to be even more true of our students. In spite of our best efforts, our students bring to seventeenth-century French courtly literature the same kinds of culturally-conditioned questions they bring to contemporary American literature and film, and it may be instructive and enriching to examine those questions, as well as our own cultural prejudices.

So, to put all this in terms of a simple question: what can the 1998 version of *The Man in the Iron Mask* tell us about the *Zeitgeist*? If Hollywood's current take on Louis XIV turns Louis into a figure relevant to the presumably youngish audience targeted by the film, it may be able to teach us about some of the cultural baggage that our own youngish audiences bring to the reading of the texts of this period.

The film, set in Paris in 1662, is very loosely based on Alexandre Dumas' *Le Vicomte de Bragelonne,* the third book in Dumas' trilogy about the three musketeers, Athos, Porthos, and Aramis, played in the film by John Malkovich, Gérard Depardieu and Jeremy Irons, respectively, and their sidekick d'Artagnan, personified by Gabriel Byrne. The story of the man in the iron mask is not the main subject of *Le Vicomte de Bragelonne,*[2] but the story does provide the novel's climactic episode. The legend of the man in the iron mask, a prisoner forced to wear a metal contraption on his face so that he could not be identified by his captors, already had a long history by the time Dumas became interested in it in the 1840s; the legend sprang from the historical incident of a prisoner who was apparently wearing a black silk mask when he was transferred to the Bastille in 1698. Dumas knew of at least nine versions of the story, which mainly date from the second half of the eighteenth century and which identify the masked prisoner as anyone from a bastard son of Louis XIV and Mademoiselle de la Vallière to Fouquet.[3] The version Dumas adopts is taken from a late eighteenth-century work attributed to Jean-Louis Soulavie (1752-1813), secretary to the maréchal de Richelieu, the cardinal's great-nephew. According to this work, the man in the iron mask was the twin brother of Louis XIV, born about eight hours after Louis and spirited away to be raised in obscurity. Louis' twin was purportedly imprisoned and forced to wear the iron mask from the age of nineteen, when he accidentally discovered his true identity, until his death.

How does this unlikely tale fare in the hands of Randall Wallace, who both directed *The Man in the Iron Mask* and wrote the screenplay? Wallace follows Dumas in making his hero Louis XIV's younger twin,[4] a man unaware of his identity until he is rescued by the musketeers, who intend to use him in a plot to replace the corrupt, autocratic Louis with his malleable, humane brother. Much of the first half of the film serves to establish the image of Louis XIV as a heartless, debauched ruler, a latter-day Nero who fiddles with nubile young women while Paris burns with the famine brought on by Louis' warmongering. One of the main components of Dumas' novel, the love affair between Louise de la Vallière, mistress of the Vicomte de Bragelonne, and the king, in the film becomes the simple story of a virtuous young couple split apart by an evil king with a roving eye. Louise de la Vallière is rebaptised Christine Belfort, and when Louis becomes infatuated with Christine, he treacherously sends her fiancé, named Raoul as in the novel but now transformed into the son of the musketeer Athos, back to the front, where he is killed. The grieving Christine gives in to Louis' advances so that he might agree to help her destitute family, but she eventually learns that Louis sent Raoul back to the front in order to get her in bed, and she commits suicide by hanging herself in front of his bedroom window.

Once the image of Louis XIV as a tyrannical monster has been established, the existence of his younger twin becomes the only way to save the day. The twin, who, like Louis XIV's historically attested younger brother, is called Philippe,[5] is kept in isolation by the musketeers and secretly trained to conduct himself not only like a king, but like the unfeeling autocrat that is his brother. The substitution of Philippe for Louis is carried off at a masked ball, with the aid of the twins' mother, Anne of Austria, who has been transformed from the sixty-something matron that history says she should have been in 1662 into a passionate figure of unfulfilled desire incarnated by the actress Anne Parillaud, who incongruously looks like a more conservatively dressed but equally nubile version of "la femme Nikita," a role she played in 1991. The second-biggest invention of Randall Wallace (I will discuss the biggest one subsequently) is the romance between Anne of Austria and d'Artagnan, which has been going on in great secrecy for many years.

Anne, who had been told the younger of her twin sons had died in childbirth, is now eager to make it up to him by bringing him to power, thereby killing two birds with one stone, since he would presumably be a better ruler than Louis. After the substitution of Philippe for Louis has taken place, the newly-reunited mother and younger son preside regally over the masked ball, but after Anne withdraws to her chambers, Philippe cannot carry it off: he is simply not imperious enough to be convincing. D'Artagnan is not in on the plot, because unlike the three musketeers he has mysteriously remained loyal to the king in spite of Louis' tyrannical ways, but d'Artagnan suspects what has happened when he observes Philippe's kindly manner at the masked ball. He manages to take Philippe prisoner and free Louis, thus leaving Philippe in the clutches of the restituted Louis and putting the three musketeers to flight. D'Artagnan finally withdraws his allegiance from Louis when the latter sadistically returns his brother to the iron mask in spite of Philippe's request to die rather than spend another hour in the iron mask.

The climax of the film is the battle waged against the king and his guard, a younger generation of muske-

teers, by d'Artagnan and the three musketeers attempting to liberate Philippe from the Bastille. The real eye-opener in an otherwise predictable scene that sees the victory of the good twin over the bad one is a revelation that marks the film's greatest invention. After Philippe and the four musketeers have been cornered, Philippe offers himself up as a hostage in order to save his four friends. D'Artagnan, tearful with paternal pride, confesses that he himself is the father of Louis and Philippe.[6] Philippe's willingness to sacrifice himself to save his four allies marks the first moment that d'Artagnan has ever felt pride as a father—his stubborn lifelong allegiance to Louis is now understandable.

In the final battle in the Bastille, d'Artagnan is killed when Louis tries to stab Philippe and d'Artagnan intercedes to take the blow. The young captain of the present generation of musketeers is won over to Philippe's cause, and without the knowledge of anyone besides him, the three surviving musketeers, and Anne of Austria, Philippe is substituted for Louis. The cruel despot is sent to prison to live out his life in the iron mask he had intended for his brother, and as the music swells and the audience gathers together its belongings to exit the theater, the weary but contented voice of Jeremy Irons intones, "The king known as Louis XIV brought to his people food, prosperity and peace, and is remembered as the greatest ruler in the history of his nation." Perhaps this is in fact the greatest invention of the entire film.

What are we to make of this turn-of-the-millennium American version of Louis XIV? The evil image projected by Louis XIV is not in itself all that surprising. One of the founding myths of the United States is the belief in the accountability of those who govern, and Louis is portrayed in this film as purely a law unto himself. One might object that given the various alliances and power struggles that were the underlying reality of Louis XIV's absolutist rule, he most certainly was never anything as simple as a law unto himself, but then historical complexity has never been Hollywood's strong suit. Whereas Dumas' novel is chockablock with political intrigue, particularly the ongoing battle between Colbert and Fouquet, Randall Wallace has freed us from such annoying complications.[7] In the absence of any serious attempt at portraying the politics of the period, we must conclude that the film simply reflects the deep-seated American mistrust of monarchy and all other forms of inherited privilege. Louis XIV really is portrayed as having no redeeming features: he is a nefarious, utterly unscrupulous ruler, a man incapable of any human emotions other than triumphant arrogance when he dominates and controls those around him and destructive fury on those few occasions when he cannot.[8]

Given this vision of Louis XIV that goes quickly from bad to worse, the basic problem of the film might be read as this: how can Louis XIV be made palatable to a late-twentieth- century North American audience? How can we reconcile Louis's annoying, stubborn reputation as a glorious king—a reputation that even Hollywood would probably think twice before dispensing with altogether, if only because without it Louis would lose the prestige that makes him fascinating to the general public—with our suspicions that anyone born to that much privilege cannot be the hero of the piece?[9] The distrust of inherited privilege is one of the most basic themes of the film, and it requires a kind of rehabilitation of Louis not from above, say, by reconciling him with his God, but from below, in typical Capraesque—or perhaps I should say, DiCaprioesque—fashion. I do not think the casting of Leonardo DiCaprio as the titan of French kings is completely unrelated to his recent role in *Titanic* as the archetypal American good guy with nothing but heart. The Franco-American confection resulting from DiCaprio's casting as Louis might be termed a grassroots Louis XIV who owes his appeal to the following two conceits: 1) *The Man in the Iron Mask* makes Louis XIV not the son of a king, but the son of a worthy, hard-working fighting man, d'Artagnan; and 2) the film turns Louis XIV, that is to say, the man who under the name of Louis XIV ruled over France for more than half a century, into his own long-suffering younger brother.

Randall Wallace's transformation of d'Artagnan into the true father of Louis XIV goes a long way toward giving him that thing we love to believe in this country, accountability. Even though d'Artagnan's paternity is not revealed until the last scene of the movie, the earlier sizzling scenes between him and Anne of Austria, as well as rather ponderous pronouncements by d'Artagnan like "Fatherhood is a blessing"—significant pause—"I can only imagine," give us a fairly clear idea of the revelation that is in store for us. The film goes out of its way to make d'Artagnan into not only a faithful father but a vigilant one with high expectations of his son. Early on d'Artagnan piously intones, "I have not yet lost faith that he may become the king we may all wish him to be," and in a later scene he says to Louis, "I have prayed every day for you to become better than your office, better than the law." If d'Artagnan does not give up on

Louis until he has seen indisputable evidence that his son is a monster, he is essentially playing a role borrowed from a long history of socially-engaged Hollywood films, the role of the vigilant, caring adult who refuses to give up on the troubled youth, whether a concerned teacher, a social worker, a psychiatrist, or even a parole officer—I know of no earlier cases in which this role is played by a musketeer. How ironic when one considers that the role of the unrepentant hood in this film is played not by the abused twin, Philippe, but rather by Louis XIV himself.

Since accountability proves to be an ineffective strategy in the case of Louis XIV, who can be neither spanked nor sent to his room, the film must come up with an alternate solution, which comes in the oh-so-nineties form of twins separated at birth. What a simple, elegant way out of the dilemma of inherited privilege: Louis XIV doesn't have an evil twin, he *is* the evil twin! Now it is true that the story of Louis' identical twin, unlike that of d'Artagnan's paternity, is already in Dumas, but Wallace takes it a step further than Dumas. In Dumas' novel, the substitution of Philippe does take place, briefly, but it fails miserably, and Philippe is sent back to prison and life in his iron mask.[10] In Wallace's film, Philippe is the perfect solution for the dilemma of how the American public can live with the idea of Louis: after the final substitution, Philippe will live the same life of privilege that Louis would have lived, but he will presumably not be corrupted by power, for he knows first-hand what it is like to suffer a tyrant's whims. Equally importantly from the point of view of the *Zeitgeist,* the audience files out of the cinema thinking, that poor man has *earned* the right to lead a charmed life from now on. We have no problem with rags-to-riches stories; in fact, they reinforce our national myth that people have the power to make their own good fortune come to pass. A wretch who has been tortured for many years, imprisoned for who he is, and more specifically for the way he looks: put in those terms, the story of Philippe sounds like a tale of the persecution of a pariah who through no fault of his own just does not fit in, and such a tale is quick to raise our sympathies.

Philippe's suffering has given him the very quality lacking in Louis: sensitivity to others. Philippe's inability to pass as the egotistical, impulsive Louis during the scene of the masked ball points to the very thing that gives him the American public's stamp of approval: his refusal or inability ever to be a law unto himself. The mask then becomes a metaphor for deference to others and for the need to play various roles that take into account factors other than one's own wishes and desires. Although he does ultimately become king, Philippe is never completely unmasked in the sense of becoming the kind of pure narcissist that anyone with absolute power might reveal himself to be, and this is precisely what marks his difference from his brother. In one of the film's most poignant scenes soon after Philippe has been freed from prison and the iron mask, he is seen at the window putting the mask back on of his own free will. He confesses to Aramis, "I've worn this mask so long I don't feel safe without it." Philippe never completely sheds his mask: in exchange for the iron mask, he dons the mask of someone playing the role of a king. He can learn to make his facial expression imitate his brother's, but he feels he will always be a fake at playing a king. When Aramis says to him, "We're offering you the chance to be king," he replies "You're offering me the chance to pretend to be king." Presumably, from the point of view of American moviegoers, that is to his credit.

In conclusion, one of the reasons that it behooves us to pay heed to popular representations of the seventeenth century in the media, whether film, television, or the worldwide web, is that it will help us to renew and replenish the questions we bring to the study of the texts of this period. If a film like *The Man in the Iron Mask* helps us to realize yet again to what extent our students are apt to be resistant to the idea of inherited privilege so central to Corneille, Racine, Lafayette and many others, we would do well not to avoid but rather to confront this issue head-on. There are many ways we might respond to students' uneasiness with some of the values set forth by courtly literature. We might point out that we have our own forms of inherited privilege in this country, which are deeply woven into our social fabric even if they are not always easily perceptible. We might suggest that the courtly literature of the period itself questions the status quo in various ways, by staging irresolvable conflicts between duty and personal happiness, for example. Or we might observe that even culturally circumscribed literary texts—which all literary texts are, in the final analysis—can and should be studied in terms that go beyond their cultural specificity. Even that most elitist of forms, classical tragedy, raises issues that transcend the social conditions in which it is produced, for example questions of sibling rivalry; seniority vs. merit; duty vs. individual happiness; fidelity to the past vs. openness to the present. I am not recommending trying to make all courtly literature into blockbusters. But I do believe that a film like *The Man in the Iron Mask* can teach us something quite useful about what it means to study the literature of another time and place that, in spite of our own attempts to immerse ourselves in them, remain very different from our own.

Notes

1. A number of films have been made about the story of the man in the iron mask; a history of these versions is beyond the scope of this study. Rather, I aim simply to investigate how the most recent film version of a tale that takes place in the France of the seventeenth century reflects certain cultural prejudices of the present decade toward that period of French history.

2. In fact the incident does not take center stage until chapter 207, about three-quarters of the way through the novel, although the existence of an "alternative" king is hinted at as early as chapter 134.

3. See Alexandre Dumas, *Le Vicomte de Bragelonne,* 2 vol. (Paris: Robert Laffont, 1991), 2: 916-924.

4. By contrast Mike Newell's 1977 version—which is, by the way, quite an excellent film—makes the prisoner into the older twin and rightful heir to the throne. Newell makes the story into a miniature seventeenth-century-style tragedy about the choice between love and duty, as the prisoner is ultimately forced to choose between leading a life of obscurity with the woman he loves and assuming the identity of the king and losing her, since the king is already married.

5. This is all the more peculiar in *Le Vicomte de Bragelonne,* since the "other" Philippe, Monsieur, is also a character in the novel.

6. Randall Wallace may not have done much research into this question, but it is actually true that Louis XIII's bisexuality, his disinterest in his wife, and the couple's twenty-year history of infertility have long made doubts about the paternity of Louis XIV a staple of *la petite histoire.*

7. Mike Newell's version, which was made for a British audience, preserves this aspect of Dumas' novel.

8. The only hint of a more vulnerable side of Louis in the film comes in his relationship with Christine Belfort. In a plot development faintly reminiscent of Racine's explorations of the relations

of love and power and the ways the latter constantly contaminates the former, it is only when Christine reveals that she does not love the king but is simply submitting to his power and authority that Louis abandons all attempts to control his vicious impulses.

9. An interesting point of comparison is Shekhar Kapur's *Elizabeth,* a film about the early years of the reign of Elizabeth I of England. Kapur portrays Elizabeth as sympathetic precisely insofar as her power is tentative and her reign in danger. Once her power base has been established, she is vindicated from the point of view of a late-twentieth-century audience because the film dwells on the personal sacrifice Elizabeth purportedly makes—her substitution of herself as "Virgin Queen" to take the place of the image of the Virgin Mary tarnished in the popular imagination by the Reformation—for the benefit of her people.

10. See *Le Vicomte de Bragelonne,* chapter 230.

📖 *CAPTAIN PAMPHILE'S ADVENTURES* (1971)

Spectator (review date 13 November 1971)

SOURCE: Review of *Captain Pamphile's Adventures,* by Alexandre Dumas, translated and adapted by Douglas Munro. *Spectator,* no. 7481 (13 November 1971): 695.

Captain Pamphile's Adventures by Alexandre Dumas will make a superb present for anyone of about eleven on; the book is most attractively produced with a fine illustration by William Papas of the rascally Captain on the cover, and the translation, by Douglas Munro, reads well. The story is absorbing, and covers the history of the American Indian, the flora and fauna of tropical jungles, the operation of the slave trade, the whaling industry and international finance.

The world is Captain Pamphile's oyster and he invariably sails off with the pearl. He is a most gentlemanly swindler whose final triumph is, as His Highness the Cazique Don Guzman y Pamphilos. to bamboozle Samuel, a London banker, out of a sum not unadjacent to 12 million pounds. Alexandre Dumas and Captain Pamphile both know well how to tell a tall story and how to tell it with style.

📖 *THE NUTCRACKER* (1977)

Bulletin of the Center for Children's Books (review date May 1979)

SOURCE: Review of *The Nutcracker,* by Alexandre Dumas, translated and adapted by Douglas Munro, illustrated by Phillida Gili. *Bulletin of the Center for Children's Books* 32, no. 9 (May 1979): 153.

Based on Hoffmann's *The Nutcracker and the Mouse King,* [*The Nutcracker*] is the adaptation used by Tchaikovsky for the ballet version, although it is not identical; one episode (the story of Princess Pirlipatine) is omitted, Marie becomes Clara in the ballet, and there are other minor changes. The translation of the Dumas version is excellent; the narrative flows smoothly, and the humor is preserved. The sophistication of the writing style and the vocabulary demand readers older than those who are the usual audience for spun-sugar magic, but the book should be of interest to children familiar with the ballet or to those readers who can appreciate the style of Dumas *père.*

FURTHER READING

Bibliography

Munro, Douglas. *Alexandre Dumas Père: A Secondary Bibliography of French and English Sources to 1983.* New York, N.Y.: Garland, 1985, 173 p.
   A bibliography of critical writings on Dumas.

Biography

Ross, Michael. *Alexandre Dumas.* London: David & Charles, 1981, 293 p.
   A biography of Dumas.

Schopp, Claude. *Alexandre Dumas: Genius of Life,* translated by A. J. Koch. New York, N.Y.: Franklin Watts, 1988, 506 p.
   A comprehensive biography of Dumas.

Criticism

Bell, A. Craig. *Alexandre Dumas: Le Vicomte de Bragelonne (The Man in the Iron Mask): A Critical Study.* Devon, England: Merlin Books, 1995, 136 p.
   Book-length critical analysis of *The Man in the Iron Mask.*

Hemmings, F. W. J. "The Novelist." In *Alexandre Dumas: The King of Romance,* pp. 114-30. New York, N.Y.: Charles Scribner's Sons, 1979.

Discusses Dumas' writing process and provides an overview of his career as a novelist.

Maurois, Andre. "*The Three Musketeers.*" In *Alexandre Dumas: A Great Life in Brief,* translated by Jack Palmer White, pp. 113-35. New York, N.Y.: Alfred A. Knopf, 1955.

Presents a detailed analysis of the influence of the theatre on Dumas's career.

———. "Dumas and Co., Manufacturers of Novels." In *Alexandre Dumas: A Great Life in Brief,* translated by Jack Palmer White, pp. 123-35. New York, N.Y.: Alfred A. Knopf, 1955.

Explores questions surrounding the nature and extent of Dumas' collaborative writing process.

Sharpe, Kevin. "Queen and Martyr." *Times Literary Supplement,* no. 3864 (2 April 1976): 393.

Offers a positive assessment of *Marie Stuart,* by Dumas, translated by Douglas Munro.

"Flannel and Steel." *Times Literary Supplement,* no. 3634 (22 October 1971): 1332.

Evaluates the strengths and weaknesses of *Captain Pamphile's Adventures,* by Dumas, translated and adapted by Douglas Munro.

Additional coverage of Dumas's life and career is contained in the following sources published by Gale: *Authors and Artists for Young Adults,* Vol. 22; *Beacham's Guide to Literature for Young Adults,* Vol. 3; *Dictionary of Literary Biography,* Vols. 119, 192; *DISCovering Authors; DISCovering Authors: British Edition; DISCovering Authors: Canadian Edition; DISCovering Authors Modules: Most-studied Authors, Novelists; DISCovering Authors 3.0; European Writers,* Vol. 6; *Guide to French Literature, 1789 to Present; Literature and Its Times,* Vols. 1, 2; *Literature Resource Center; Nineteenth-Century Literature Criticism,* Vols. 11, 71; *Novels for Students,* Vols. 14, 19; *Reference Guide to World Literature,* Eds. 2, 3; *Something about the Author,* Vol. 18; *Twayne's World Authors; World Literature Criticism,* Ed. 2; and *Writers for Children.*

Marissa Moss
1959-

American illustrator and author of picture books, activity books, and juvenile fiction.

The following entry presents an overview of Moss's career through 2004.

INTRODUCTION

Author and illustrator Moss has produced several popular picture books, as well as a series of beginning readers featuring a young writer named Amelia. Beginning with *Amelia's Notebook* (1995), Moss follows her eponymous heroine through her daily adventures in the fourth grade, as the young protagonist changes schools, makes new friends, and copes with an annoying older sister. Hand-lettered and bound in a manner that resembles a black-and-white school composition book, *Amelia's Notebook* and its companion volumes—*Amelia Writes Again* (1996) and *Amelia Hits the Road* (1997)—laid the foundation of Moss' best-selling "Amelia's Notebook" series, which has spawned several spin-off series, activity books, and a selection of animated videos. In addition to her "Amelia" books, Moss has illustrated works for other authors, her own picture books, and two additional juvenile series—the "Young American Voices" series and "Max's Logbook" series—which follow the journal format that she employed in *Amelia's Notebook*.

BIOGRAPHICAL INFORMATION

Moss was born on September 29, 1959, the second daughter of Robert and Harriet Moss. During her adolescence, Moss was an avid reader and kept a journal about her life, experiences, and family. She originally attended San Jose University for an education in fine arts, but transferred to the University of California at Berkeley where she earned a B.A. in art history. Moss later decided to specialize in illustration and enrolled in the California College of Arts and Crafts. Her first published work was *One, Two, Three, and Four—No More?* (1988) by Catherine Gray, a picture book that Moss illustrated. Less than one year later, Moss published *Who Was It?* (1989), a picture book that she both wrote and illustrated. She has now authored over thirty-five books for children, including her popular "Amelia's Notebook" series. Moss resides in Berkeley, California, with her husband and their three children.

MAJOR WORKS

Moss's earliest publications are traditional picture books, which she either illustrated for another author or wrote and illustrated herself. Her first self-authored work, *What Was It?*, examines a child's decision to tell the truth about a misdeed rather than lie. *Knick Knack Paddywack* (1992) presents a unique rendition of the popular children's rhyme, and *But Not Kate* (1992) focuses on a young girl who feels like she has nothing she excels at, until she is asked to help a magician onstage. *In America* (1994) tells the story of a young boy whose grandfather describes his own immigration from Lithuania years earlier. Moss's later picture books continue this trend of highlighting historical events. For example, *True Heart* (1999), illustrated by C. F. Payne, centers on the story of Bee, who, in the late nineteenth century, works her way to the position of train engineer. Moss presents the stories of other historical women who overcame overwhelming odds in the picture books *Brave Harriet: The First Woman to Fly the English Channel* (2001) and *Mighty Jackie: The Strike-Out Queen* (2002), both illustrated by C. F. Payne.

Moss is best known for her various journal series, most notably, the "Amelia's Notebook" series, which is written from the perspective of a spunky introspective girl. The books are formatted like normal school composition books and are filled with handwritten text, child-like illustrations, and drawings that simulate photographs a young girl might tape inside her journal. In her journals, Amelia discusses school, her annoying big sister, having to move away from friends, boys, her parents' divorce, and other normative topics associated with a child's adolescence and maturation. The series began with *Amelia's Notebook* and *Amelia Writes Again* and now includes over fifteen titles, including *Amelia Hits the Road,* which discusses an incredibly long road trip Amelia undergoes with her mother and big sister; *Amelia Takes Command* (1998), which pits Amelia against the school bully; and *Amelia's Family Ties* (2000), in which Amelia is reunited with her father, meets his new family, and discerns her place in his new life. Moss' "Young American Voices" series features journals of young girls from America's past and focuses on the difficulties and rewards of their eras. The series is comprised of *Rachel's Journal: The Story of a Pioneer Girl* (1998), *Emma's Journal: The Story of a Colonial Girl* (1999), *Hannah's Journal: The Story of an Immigrant Girl* (2000), and *Rose's Journal: The Story of a Girl in the Great Depression* (2001). Though she most commonly employs female protagonists, Moss also writes from the male perspective in her "Max's Logbook" series and the journal *Galen: My Life in Imperial Rome: An Ancient World Journal* (2002). *Galen*, the first in a new series, is narrated by a twelve-year-old Greek slave in the palace of Caesar Augustus. Galen explains both Roman and Greek customs and provides historical information to readers. *Max's Logbook* (2003) and *Max's Mystical Logbook* (2004) are more contemporary journals featuring young Max, a mechanically inclined boy whose inventions occasionally go awry. In *Max's Logbook*, Max must come to terms with his parents' dissolving marriage. In *Max's Mystical Logbook*, Max and his friend try to create a love potion to reunite Max's parents, but his older brother accidentally drinks it first. Like Amelia, Max must deal with the normal pressures of growing up and, in addition, his parents are on the verge of divorce. Max's logbooks include handwritten text and are filled with drawings of new inventions and boyish comic strips.

CRITICAL RECEPTION

Reviewers have applauded Moss' non-traditional use of journal format in her "Amelia's Notebook," "Young American Voices," and "Max's Logbook" picture books. Critics have noted that through her use of the journal-style writing, Moss encourages her young readers to become journal keepers and writers. While reviewing *Amelia Takes Command*, Carolyn Phelan has commented that, "The freshness of Amelia's voice is reflected in the small ink-and-watercolor illustrations of drawings, pictures, and souvenirs that brighten every page. Capturing the ups and downs of a child's life with sympathy and wisdom as well as humor, this entertaining book makes journal writing look like fun." Some have argued that the handwritten script in Moss' journals is more difficult to read

than standard type—suggesting that the format might actually be discouraging to struggling young readers—but, on a whole, critics have praised the look and originality of Moss's handwritten journals and sketches.

PRINCIPAL WORKS

Picture Books

One, Two, Three, and Four—No More? [illustrator; written by Catherine Gray] (picture book) 1988

Who Was It? (picture book) 1989

Mother Goose and More: Classic Rhymes and Added Lines [illustrator; adapted by Dr. Hickey] (picture book) 1990

Regina's Big Mistake (picture book) 1990

Want to Play? (picture book) 1990

But Not Kate (picture book) 1992

Knick Knack Paddywack (picture book) 1992

After-School Monster (picture book) 1993

In America (picture book) 1994

Mel's Diner (picture book) 1994

The Ugly Menorah (picture book) 1996

The Lapsnatcher [illustrator; written by Bruce Coville] (picture book) 1997

G Is for Googol: A Math Alphabet Book [illustrator; written by David M. Schwartz] (picture book) 1998

True Heart [illustrations by C. F. Payne] (picture book) 1999

Brave Harriet: The First Woman to Fly the English Channel [illustrations by C. F. Payne] (picture book) 2001

Mighty Jackie: The Strike-Out Queen [illustrations by C. F. Payne] (picture book) 2002

"Young American Voices" Historical Journal Series

Rachel's Journal: The Story of a Pioneer Girl (juvenile fiction) 1998

Emma's Journal: The Story of a Colonial Girl (juvenile fiction) 1999

Hannah's Journal: The Story of an Immigrant Girl (juvenile fiction) 2000

Rose's Journal: The Story of a Girl in the Great Depression (juvenile fiction) 2001

Amelia's Notebook—Elementary School Journal Series

Amelia's Notebook (juvenile fiction) 1995

Amelia Writes Again (juvenile fiction) 1996

Amelia's Are We There Yet, Longest Ever Car Trip (juvenile fiction) 1997

Amelia's Bully Survival Guide (juvenile fiction) 1998

The All-New Amelia (juvenile fiction) 1999; revised edition, 2007

Dr. Amelia's Boredom Survival Guide: First Aid for Rainy Days, Boring Errands, Waiting Rooms, Whatever! (activity book) 1999

Amelia's Family Ties (juvenile fiction) 2000

Madame Amelia Tells All (juvenile fiction) 2001

Amelia's 5th-Grade Notebook (juvenile fiction) 2006

Amelia's School Survival Guide (juvenile fiction) 2006

Amelia's Notebook—Middle School Journal Series

Amelia's Most Unforgettable Embarrassing Moments (juvenile fiction) 2005

Amelia's 6th-Grade Notebook (juvenile fiction) 2005

Amelia's Book of Notes and Note Passing: A Note Notebook (juvenile fiction) 2006

Amelia's Guide to Gossip: The Good, the Bad, and the Ugly (juvenile fiction) 2006

Amelia's Longest Biggest Most-Fights-Ever Family Reunion (juvenile fiction) 2006

Amelia's Must-Keep Resolutions for the Best Year Ever! (juvenile fiction) 2006

Amelia's 7th-Grade Notebook (juvenile fiction) 2007

Vote 4 Amelia (juvenile fiction) 2007

Other Amelia Titles

Amelia Hits the Road (juvenile fiction) 1997

Amelia Takes Command (juvenile fiction) 1998

Luv, Amelia Luv, Nadia (juvenile fiction) 1999

Amelia's Easy-as-Pie Drawing Guide (activity book) 2000

Amelia Works It Out (juvenile fiction) 2000

Oh Boy, Amelia! (juvenile fiction) 2001

Amelia Lends a Hand (juvenile fiction) 2002

Amelia's Best Year Ever: Favorite Amelia Stories from American Girl Magazine (juvenile short stories) 2003

Other Works

Galen: My Life in Imperial Rome: An Ancient World Journal (juvenile fiction) 2002

Max's Logbook (juvenile fiction) 2003

Max's Mystical Logbook (juvenile fiction) 2004

AUTHOR COMMENTARY

Marissa Moss and Sally Lodge (interview date 31 August 1998)

SOURCE: Moss, Marissa, and Sally Lodge. "Journaling Back through Time with Marissa Moss." *Publishers Weekly* 245, no. 35 (31 August 1998): 20.

[*In the following interview, Moss discusses the success of her "Amelia's Notebook" series of fictional journals and offers details on her new "Young American Voices" series of historical fiction for children.*]

The process of recording one's thoughts and daily experiences in a diary has become a popular activity for middle-grade girls, and it seems that the opportunity to read the secrets a peer records in her journal is even more enticing. So one might conclude from the brisk sales reported by Tricycle Press, as well as a handful of retailers polled, for Marissa Moss's series of hand-lettered, playfully illustrated journals penned by a girl named Amelia. Moss followed up the original 1995 title, **Amelia's Notebook,** with three additional hardcover releases, **Amelia Writes Again, Amelia Hits the Road** and the just-released **Amelia Takes Command,** as well as a paperback fill-in book, **My Notebook (with Help from Amelia).**

Together, the books have sold close to one million copies and recently, according to industry sources, Pleasant Company agreed to buy rights to the series for an eye-opening $3 million (though no one queried would confirm the dollar amount). Now, Moss has given her diary format a historical twist in her latest series, Young American Voices, which Harcourt Brace's Silver Whistle imprint launches in September with **Rachel's Journal: The Story of a Pioneer Girl.**

Moss said that her own childhood inspired her choice of format, characters and subject matter. "I always kept a notebook as a girl and loved to read those of others," she explained. "My memories of being nine or 10 years old are especially vivid, since this is a time when you have a real sense of who you are— before the self-conscious preteen years start. Before I began writing the first Amelia book, I bought a composition book at the drug store and wrote down as much as I could remember about my life at that time. Amelia is very much based on me, and my sister is the model for her older sister, Cleo."

Though a number of publishers turned down the initial draft of **Amelia's Notebook,** after several reworkings she showed it to her friend Mollie Katzen.

Katzen, author of the book for children published by Tricycle in 1994. She encouraged Moss to show the manuscript to Tricycle's publisher, Nicole Geiger. As Geiger recalled, "Mollie told me that her own son had taken *Amelia's Notebook* into his bedroom and wouldn't give it back, which struck me as quite a recommendation. And then I, too, instantly fell in love with Amelia's incredibly true voice."

RECREATING THE PAST

"Marissa has an uncanny ability to be an eight- to 12-year-old girl," concurred Paula Wiseman, editorial director of Silver Whistle. Explaining how her company came to publish Young American Voices, Wiseman said, "I was very fond of the Amelia books and I had already signed up a picture book by Marissa, called *True Heart.* And my eight-year-old daughter was keeping a journal that she was passionate about."

Tackling *Rachel's Journal* presented Moss with new challenges. Obviously, she had to call on more than childhood memories to shape this heroine, who in 1850 travels with her family along the Oregon Trail from Illinois to California. "I had to make this voice as real, yet I clearly couldn't rely on my life here," Moss said. "Though I began my research by reading some general history on this period, I soon narrowed my focus to reading firsthand accounts written by pioneers at this time—mostly women and children." The author characterized writing historical fiction as "a great deal more intense" than writing the Amelia books, since, in her words, "I didn't want to lose Rachel's voice or the sense of her era. I carried this character around in my head all day long. When I wasn't writing, I had an almost obsessive need to get back to her."

With an initial printing of 25,000 copies, *Rachel's Journal* has obviously sparked enthusiasm from the publisher. Booksellers, too, noting healthy—and growing—sales for Moss's Amelia notebooks, expressed high expectations for her new series. Among them was Michele Cromer-Poire of Red Balloon Bookstore in St. Paul, Minn. The combination of diary format and historical fiction, she commented, has also helped make Scholastic's Dear America series a hit in her store and others. According to Cromer-Poire, "The diary format grabs the kids and the history angle appeals to parents and teachers."

This is exactly what Moss hopes Young American Voices will achieve. The writer and artist—who receives (and personally answers) an enormous volume of mail from readers who enthusiastically declare "Amelia is me!"—doesn't expect the audience for her new series will identify as completely with her historical heroines as they do with Amelia. "But what I do want them to get from Rachel and the other characters," she said, "is a firsthand sense of another time period, and to discover that learning about history can be cool. Where Amelia has encouraged a lot of kids to write themselves, I hope Rachel makes kids want to learn more about her era."

Marissa Moss and Lynne T. Burke (interview date January-February 2004)

SOURCE: Moss, Marissa, and Lynne T. Burke. "*Instructor* Interviews: Author/Illustrators: Marissa Moss." *Instructor* 113, no. 5 (January-February 2004): 29.

[*In the following interview, Moss discusses her "Amelia's Notebook" series and the importance of journal writing for children.*]

[*Burke*]: *Where did you get the idea of shaping a picture book around Amelia's notebook?*

[Moss]: Notebooks allow for all kinds of record-keeping, and I kept one myself as a kid. I was attracted to mixing up words and pictures freely, since that's how I think. It seems like a natural way for a lot of kids to work, especially boys.

You write different kinds of books. How do you approach different projects?

When I'm working on historical books, I'm much more organized. I usually read about 100 books to get the depth of knowledge I need. As I read, I think about the kind of story I want to write and keep copious notes on index cards.

What do you hope kids will learn from Amelia?

I hope that Amelia shows them how easy it is to keep a journal. They can take anything in their lives and turn it into a story, just like she does. Amelia shows that it's not what happens in life that counts, but rather how you frame it, how you talk about it. Every kid has a story to tell!

GENERAL COMMENTARY

Lynne T. Burke (review date April-May 2001)

SOURCE: Burke, Lynne T. Review of the *Amelia's Notebook* and *Young American Voices* series, by Marissa Moss. *Reading Today* 18, no. 5 (April-May 2001): 32.

[*In the following review, Burke offers a brief overview of the format of Moss's "Amelia's Notebook" series and*]

"Young American Voices" series and provides a positive assessment of both series.]

THE AMELIA SERIES

This series single-handedly revived the interest in salt and pepper notebooks worldwide! Each of the 11 books in the series contains the musings, rants, and mementos of young Amelia, who suffers, survives, and celebrates everything childhood has to offer, including an older sister. In her latest escapade, **Amelia Works It Out,** this spunky girl learns about earning money when she has to come up with cash for something she really wants.

Fans who want to start their own black and white library should grab a copy of **My Notebook (with Help from Amelia),** a guided journal with lots of lined space, color graphics, and ideas to get those brain cells working.

YOUNG AMERICAN VOICES SERIES

These journals are written by the author of the Amelia series and bear Marissa Moss's unmistakable trademark style: notebook format and detailed color illustrations. The biggest difference is that each of the three titles in this series is the diary of a girl from a different historic period: a pioneer, a colonist, and a turn-of-the-century immigrant (so far).

TITLE COMMENTARY

BUT NOT KATE (1992)

Ilene Cooper (review date 1 March 1992)

SOURCE: Cooper, Ilene. Review of *But Not Kate,* by Marissa Moss. *Booklist* 88, no. 13 (1 March 1992): 1287.

[In **But Not Kate,** e]veryone has something special, except Kate. Alfred can draw, Sara writes the neatest, and everyone brings interesting lunchtime desserts. Kate doesn't feel very good about herself, and when a magician comes to the school, the last thing she wants to do is volunteer to be his assistant on stage. But the magician chooses her, and as Kate makes flowers appear and pulls rabbits out of a hat, she feels magical for the first time in her life. Moss' simple story will have meaning for children who need a little work on the self-esteem front, and her message is

nicely tucked into an appealing vehicle. Though the mice children of Kate's class look more like bats, the lively watercolors still have a spontaneity that buoys the tale.

Heide Piehler (review date June 1992)

SOURCE: Piehler, Heide. Review of *But Not Kate,* by Marissa Moss. *School Library Journal* 38, no. 6 (June 1992): 100.

PreS-Gr. 1—[In **But Not Kate,** l]ittle mouse Kate doesn't feel she's the best at anything or special in any way. She's so ordinary and so unspectacular— until the school magic show. Then, a reluctant Kate is chosen to be the magician's assistant. Suddenly, ordinary Kate can make flowers appear, pull rabbits out of a hat, and turn a plain old scarf into a star-spangled streamer. The story, like Kate herself, seems slight and unspectacular at first glance. But like her, it offers hidden charms. Most children will relate to Kate's shrinking-violet feelings and cheer when she finally discovers her own unique talents. Unfortunately, the illustrations don't quite match Kate's blossoming talents. The pencil-and-wash paintings are colorful and animated, but the depiction of the main character and her rodent classmates are of mass-market cartoon quality. Henkes's coterie of mouse characters are a much more attractive and appealing group. This title is similar in theme to his *Chrysanthemum* (Greenwillow, 1991), but is for a slightly younger audience. Not a must purchase, but a useful and entertaining addition.

KNICK KNACK PADDYWACK (1992)

Publishers Weekly (review date 24 February 1992)

SOURCE: Review of *Knick Knack Paddywack,* by Marissa Moss. *Publishers Weekly* 239, no. 11 (24 February 1992): 53.

Cheerful, action-filled pictures and alliterative, tongue-twisting word creations distinguish Moss's (**Who Was It?**; **Want to Play?**) lighthearted variation on this song favorite [**Knick Knack Paddywack**]. An overall-clad, smiling old man—obviously a devoted recycler—collects a variety of materials (one fish in a bowl, two windows, three trash barrels, four rubber tires and so on). Moss's zippy verse playfully ties in with the item in hand: carrying seven flyswatters, "he played slip slap whap and then / With a slip slap rat-tatap, give a dog a bone." With each spread this resourceful fellow's entourage of dogs (and bones) grows as he uses his recycled goods to create a rocket ship. Like the canine onlookers, readers' spirits will be sky-high when—after counting down, of course—"This old man goes soaring off." *Ages 2-8.*

Jody McCoy (review date May 1992)

SOURCE: McCoy, Jody. Review of *Knick Knack Paddywack,* by Marissa Moss. *School Library Journal* 38, no. 5 (May 1992): 92.

PreS-Gr. 2—This new old man has a wonderful time playing with language, building a spaceship, and feeding a hilarious collection of dogs [in **Knick Knack Paddywack**]. With toes-a-tappin' and eyes-a-twinklin' he "bip bops," "jig jugs," and "splish splashes" from one to ten, and then counts down to blast off and flies to the moon. Pleasant watercolor washes within playful pen-and-ink sketches create such a lively little man and pack of pups that one suspects they might dance right off the page. The use of language will tickle all but the tongue tied. Practice before a read-aloud or a sing-along is recommended for this classic counting song refurbished to win the hearts and tangle the tongues of yet another generation. Unfortunately, the music is not included.

📖 *IN AMERICA* (1994)

Hazel Rochman (review date 15 May 1994)

SOURCE: Rochman, Hazel. Review of *In America,* by Marissa Moss. *Booklist* 90, no. 18 (15 May 1994): 1683-84.

Ages 5-8—While Grandfather and Walter walk through the busy city streets to the post office, Grandfather talks about why he came to the U.S. from Lithuania as a boy of 10. He tells about the anti-Semitism that made him leave the shtetl, how hard the journey was, and what he left behind. He also celebrates this country as a nation of immigrants. The pictures of Eastern Europe and the immigrant journey [in **In America**] are like photographs in an album, pale and slightly blurry. In contrast, the view of the contemporary bright and sharp, a bustling multiethnic community, sunlit with possibility. A good book to use with Say's Caldecott Medal winner *Grandfather's Journey* (1993), this shows that Grandfather left behind forever the old familiar ways of doing things, even as he found the courage to make his way alone across the sea.

Publishers Weekly (review date 16 May 1994)

SOURCE: Review of *In America,* by Marissa Moss. *Publishers Weekly* 241, no. 20 (16 May 1994): 63-4.

Looking at an album of photos taken when his grandfather was a child in Lithuania [in **In America**], Walter asks why the elderly man came to America. "I wanted to have the same freedom as everyone else, without anybody bothering me," responds Grandpa, who explains that, as his family was Jewish, "we were bothered a lot, because people thought we were different." As the two walk to the post office, Grandpa tells how he made the long sea journey to America alone at the age of 10. Pondering whether *he* would be brave enough to make such a trip, Walter asserts himself by insisting that he cross a busy street by himself (after the light changes). Though a small step, this feat gives the boy a sense of accomplishment, and enables Moss to tuck yet another worthwhile message into her resonant tale. Her art alternates between rather routine depictions of the walk to the post office and arresting, softly colored simulated photographs of life in a Lithuania of the past. Laced with engaging anecdotes (Grandpa tells Walter that the first time he had a banana—a food unknown in the old country—he ate the peel and threw away the fruit inside), this story has a quiet power. *Ages 4-8.*

Diane S. Marton (review date June 1994)

SOURCE: Marton, Diane S. Review of *In America,* by Marissa Moss. *School Library Journal* 40, no. 6 (June 1994): 112.

K-Gr. 3—As Grandpa and Walter take a long walk to the post office, the elderly man tells his grandson why he left his home in Pikeli, Lithuania, to come to the U.S. alone. America offered opportunity, but more importantly, freedom, which Grandpa, a Jew, did not have in his homeland. He tried to persuade his brother to join him, but the younger boy was afraid to leave his familiar life. Strangely enough, [in **In America,**] parents are never mentioned, nor whether any relatives were waiting in the New World; a 10-year-old motivated to emigrate primarily by a desire for freedom seems odd. Line-and-watercolor cartoonlike illustrations alternate with paintings set to look like photos in an old album. The whole recalls Judith Caseley's *Apple Pie and Onions* (Greenwillow, 1987), although more of that story is devoted to life in the old country.

📖 *MEL'S DINER* (1994)

Hazel Rochman (review date 1 October 1994)

SOURCE: Rochman, Hazel. Review of *Mel's Diner*, by Marissa Moss. *Booklist* 91, no. 3 (1 October 1994): 333-34.

Ages 4-8—Like Loomis' *In the Diner* [*BKL* Ap 15 94], [*Mel's Diner*] is a warm, lively picture book about an informal neighborhood eating place. Mabel is an African American child who loves helping Mama and Pop in their diner. During early morning breakfast preparations and throughout the day, Mabel welcomes the regular customers, brings menus, serves food, and fills sugar bowls. After school, she and her friend do homework at one of the tables, then dance to the jukebox. And of course, they love to eat. Moss' full-color illustrations show a great diversity of people enjoying themselves in a brightly lit art-deco diner. From ketchup and coffee to Jell-O and french fries, the food is great, and so is the company.

John Peters (review date December 1994)

SOURCE: Peters, John. Review of *Mel's Diner*, by Marissa Moss. *School Library Journal* 40, no. 12 (December 1994): 79.

K-Gr. 2—Young Mable outlines a comfortable routine as she helps her parents run their diner—setting up, serving, visiting with the regulars, and hanging out after school with a friend, dreaming of the diner she'll have when she grows up. The narrator and her parents are African Americans, but there really isn't much difference between this story [*Mel's Diner*] and Melanie Greenberg's *My Father's Luncheonette* (Dutton, 1991), in that both show an affectionate, rather generic family working in a clean, well-lit space decorated with ketchup bottles, napkin holders, and other familiar details for readers to pick out. The illustrations lack the intimacy of those found in Anne Shelby's *We Keep a Store* (Orchard, 1990) or the comic bustle of Christine Loomis's *In the Diner* (Scholastic, 1994), and Mable uses none of the lingo that makes Alexandra Day's *Frank and Ernest* (Scholastic, 1988) such a hoot. A conventional supplementary purchase.

📖 *AMELIA'S NOTEBOOK* (1995)

Publishers Weekly (review date 20 March 1995)

SOURCE: Review of *Amelia's Notebook*, by Marissa Moss. *Publishers Weekly* 242, no. 12 (20 March 1995): 61.

Moss (*Mel's Diner*) designs [*Amelia's Notebook*,] this upbeat, first-person story to resemble a real diary; the cover bears the familiar black-and-white abstract design of a composition book, decorated with color cartoons by Amelia, the book's nine-year-old "author." Inside, on lined pages, Amelia writes about her recent move to a new town, doodles pictures of people she meets and saves such mementos as postage stamps and a birthday candle. She misses her best friend, Nadia, but her moments of sadness are balanced by optimism—she distracts herself by drawing and by writing short stories. In appropriately conversational terms, Amelia complains that her big sister invades her privacy ("So Cleo if you are reading this right now—BUG OFF and STAY OUT"); gripes about cafeteria food ("Henna says they use dog food. I believe it!"); and jokes in classic elementary-school gross-out fashion. Readers will understand Amelia's wish to put her "top secret" thoughts on paper, and they'll notice that even though she's uneasy about attending a different school, she's starting over successfully. An on-target presentation. Ages 7-up.

Carolyn Noah (review date July 1995)

SOURCE: Noah, Carolyn. Review of *Amelia's Notebook*, by Marissa Moss. *School Library Journal* 41, no. 7 (July 1995): 79.

Gr. 3-5—Nine-year-old Amelia keeps a lively, funny journal, recording her family's move (a three-day trip) and her feelings about her older sister, her new house and school, and the best friend she's left behind. [*Amelia's Notebook*] looks like an unusually well-bound, black-and-white-covered, lined elementary school notebook, and it's chock-full of personal asides and tiny spot drawings. Amelia adorns its pages with artistic experiments (studies of noses and perspective), as well as all kinds of astute observations. Entirely hand-lettered, the narrative rings true with third-grade authenticity. The lettering is black, but the drawings make full use of the 24 color markers that Amelia's friend Nadia has given her as a farewell gift. Moss offers the same immediacy and vividness as Vera Williams's *Stringbean's Trip to the Shining Sea* (Greenwillow, 1988), though composition is much more informal and less premeditated. In fact, Moss becomes entirely invisible and lets Amelia shine through. Her notebook will be relished especially by young girls who will empathize with many of her emotions, but also by those teaching writing skills, journal-keeping, or helping children adapt to transitions.

📖 *THE UGLY MENORAH* (1996)

Publishers Weekly (review date 30 September 1996)

SOURCE: Review of *The Ugly Menorah,* by Marissa Moss. *Publishers Weekly* 243, no. 40 (30 September 1996): 87.

This wan effort [*The Ugly Menorah*] uses the holiday setting to drive home familiar lessons from the beauty-is-in-the-eyes-of-the-beholder school. Spending Hanukkah with her recently widowed grandmother, Rachel thinks her grandmother's menorah is ugly, even after she is told how her grandfather lovingly fashioned it from scraps years ago when he could not afford to buy a fancy one. But after it's lit, Rachel has an (unconvincing) epiphany: "For the first time since Grandpa died, she felt he was with her again." As if to underscore the point about appearances, Moss's illustrations are almost aggressively plain, with stiff, almost gauche figures peopling ill-lit settings. *Ages 5-8.*

📖 *AMELIA HITS THE ROAD* (1997)

Jackie Hechtkopf (review date November 1997)

SOURCE: Hechtkopf, Jackie. Review of *Amelia Hits the Road,* by Marissa Moss. *School Library Journal* 43, no. 11 (November 1997): 95-6.

Gr. 2-5—Amelia creates a travel notebook [in *Amelia Hits the Road*] about a family car trip back to California to see Nadia, her best friend since kindergarten, stopping at the Grand Canyon and Yosemite on the way. Amid complaints about big sister, Cleo, Amelia ponders how much her friend has changed in the last year by drawing one picture of Nadia as she remembers her, and one picture of a bald Nadia, labeled with handwritten questions regarding her current hair length. As in the previous books about Amelia, the adorable diagrams that illustrate the child's witty observations will be pored over by readers. The diapers she draws for a mule as a means of keeping the Grand Canyon trails clean are a riot. Her descriptions of the scenery create a sense of being there. When the family stops at the site of Manzanar, the girl draws a barbed-wire fence with a speech bubble saying simply, "I'm mad." The story climaxes with the long-awaited reunion with Nadia. Sweet reminiscences of *Amelia's Notebook* (Tricycle, 1995) show the girls wearing matching friendship necklaces and doing the experiments from a science kit Nadia promised to save until Amelia's first visit. This book will delight long-time fans and draw new ones. Once again, Moss proves that journal writing is great fun.

Carolyn Phelan (review date 15 November 1997)

SOURCE: Phelan, Carolyn. Review of *Amelia Hits the Road,* by Marissa Moss. *Booklist* 96, no. 6 (15 November 1997): 561.

Gr. 3-4, younger for reading aloud—In [*Amelia Hits the Road,*] the sequel to *Amelia's Notebook* (1995) and *Amelia Writes Again* (1996), Moss sends spunky journal-keeper Amelia and her old-fashioned black-and-white-speckled composition book on a car trip through the Southwest with her mother and older sister. Amelia's mother insists that they "should enjoy the togetherness," but even her patience wears thin after hundreds of miles of listening to backseat bickering and off-key camp songs. The book is a facsimile of Amelia's notebook, in which she records her impressions of the Grand Canyon and Death Valley, as well as her disgust with her sister and her longing to see her old friend Nadia. There's more than enough toilet and car-sickness humor, but Amelia sensitively describes the scenic vistas and new experiences as well. Amelia's drawings brighten every page of this lively journal, which readers will find just as readable and entertaining as the previous two.

📖 *AMELIA TAKES COMMAND* (1998)

Carolyn Phelan (review date 1 September 1998)

SOURCE: Phelan, Carolyn. Review of *Amelia Takes Command,* by Marissa Moss. *Booklist* 95, no. 1 (1 September 1998): 120.

Gr. 3-5—Amelia's many fans will welcome [*Amelia Takes Command,*] the latest in the series of fictional journals, in her own handwriting, including *Amelia's Notebook* (1995), *Amelia Writes Again* (1996), and *Amelia Hits the Road* (1997). As fifth grade begins, Amelia struggles with two unexpected problems, an inconstant friend and a constant bully. Spending winter break at Space Camp with her old friend Nadia, Amelia works hard, learns a lot, and develops her skills as a leader. The confidence she gains as commander of a mock shuttle mission gives her the boost she needs to meet the more down-to-earth challenges back at school. The freshness of Amelia's voice is reflected in the small ink-and-watercolor illustrations of drawings, pictures, and souvenirs that brighten every page. Capturing the ups and downs of a child's life with sympathy and wisdom as well as humor, this entertaining book makes journal writing look like fun.

Faith Brautigam (review date October 1998)

SOURCE: Brautigam, Faith. Review of *Amelia Takes Command,* by Marissa Moss. *School Library Journal* 44, no. 10 (October 1998): 108-09.

Gr. 3-5—Amelia's latest journal [*Amelia Takes Command*] provides another winning glimpse into the life of a funny and likable contemporary child. In this fourth title in the series, the girl is beginning fifth grade and is the target of the class bully. Through candid notebook entries and lively, captioned drawings, readers share Amelia's frustration and anger at being ostracized and cheer when she gains the necessary confidence at Space Camp to stand up to her intimidator back home. The engaging format resembles a hand-written, blue-lined composition book filled with full-color childlike drawings. Amelia's comments range from typical elementary school humor ("Just pretend Hilary is a giant booger. Then you won't care what she says or does") to the whimsical (fashion rating: "Bad socks, D-") to the more serious. With its hook for the voyeur in us all, a format that keeps the pages turning, and an "every girl" who vanquishes the ubiquitous bully, this satisfying read is right on target.

RACHEL'S JOURNAL: THE STORY OF A PIONEER GIRL (1998)

Publishers Weekly (review date 3 August 1998)

SOURCE: Review of *Rachel's Journal: The Story of a Pioneer Girl,* by Marissa Moss. *Publishers Weekly* 245, no. 31 (3 August 1998): 86.

Moss extends the format she perfected in *Amelia's Notebook* and *Amelia Writes Again* to cover historical fiction in [*Rachel's Journal: The Story of a Pioneer Girl,*] this solidly researched and wholly captivating illustrated diary "by" a 10-year-old girl who travels with her family along the Oregon Trail in 1850. The excitements and hardships of the seven-month journey spring vividly to life, whether Rachel is crossing the eerie, skeleton-strewn Nevada desert by moonlight, trading her long red braids for an Indian pony, eating flour soup when provisions get low, or awakening one morning to greet a new baby sister.

Character sketches—of the shiftless Mr. Bridger; the oh-so-perfect Prudence Elias, bane of tomboy Rachel's days; sourpuss Mr. Henry Sunshine, whose wife, Louisa, providentially drops her dentures during a tense encounter with the Pawnee, frightening them away—are a sheer delight, adding depth, texture and, of course, humor. The language is equally colorful. One of the smaller children in Rachel's wagon party, for example, is "no bigger than a bar of soap after a week's wash." Moss shoehorns in an amazing amount of information, giving readers an excellent understanding of life on the trail. Lined sepia-toned pages give the book the look of an antique diary; and, in the style of the Amelia books, hand-lettered text and cleverly captioned thumbnail illustrations with a childlike sensibility add to the authentic feel. This engrossing glimpse of the westward movement is as good a choice for pleasure reading as it is a valuable classroom resource. Ages 8-12.

Robin L. Gibson (review date September 1998)

SOURCE: Gibson, Robin L. Review of *Rachel's Journal: The Story of a Pioneer Girl,* by Marissa Moss. *School Library Journal* 44, no. 9 (September 1998): 177.

Gr. 3-5—Ten-year-old Rachel records her family's trip west from Illinois to California in 1850 [in *Rachel's Journal: The Story of a Pioneer Girl*]. The girl's voice is fresh and enthusiastic; for her, the journey is filled with exciting new experiences. She learns to drive the wagon and crack the whip, climbs Courthouse Rock and views the sunset, and even cuts off her long red braids and trades them for an Indian pony. She does have occasional moments of contemplation, thinking about faraway relatives and friends. Overall, however, her journal paints a rosy picture of this dangerous voyage: there are some injuries but no serious illnesses or deaths, encounters with different Native Americans are all friendly, and Rachel's new baby sister arrives safely at the end. An author's note explains that the narrative is based on numerous children's diaries from the period, and that many of the writers viewed the trek as "one long adventure." The hand-lettered script and yellowed, lined-paper background create the look of a diary. Watercolor illustrations and notes in the margins add to the personal look of the book and often provide helpful supplementary information. *Rachel's Journal* is a good choice for those readers not quite ready to tackle the "Dear America" series (Scholastic) and for Laura Ingalls Wilder fans who want to read more about pioneer life.

EMMA'S JOURNAL: THE STORY OF A COLONIAL GIRL (1999)

Carolyn Phelan (review date 15 September 1999)

SOURCE: Phelan, Carolyn. Review of *Emma's Journal: The Story of a Colonial Girl,* by Marissa Moss. *Booklist* 96, no. 2 (15 September 1999): 261.

Gr. 3-5—Like Moss' popular Amelia series, these books in the Young American Voices series are first-person handwritten accounts told in journal form through words and childlike illustrations. The difference is Amelia is modern day, whereas the American Voices are historical. *Emma's Journal* records events in Boston from 1774 to 1776 from the point of view of 10-year-old Emma, who has been sent away from the family farm to help her Aunt Harmony and ends up helping the Revolutionary cause. Fresh and readable, the text offers a simple introduction to the times, while colorful, informal little drawings add visual appeal to the hand-lettered pages. The Young American Voices series, which includes *Rachel's Journal* (1998), will attract Amelia's fans as well children who have read the American Girl books. A prelude to longer, more challenging historical fiction.

Susan Hepler (review date December 1999)

SOURCE: Hepler, Susan. Review of *Emma's Journal: The Story of a Colonial Girl,* by Marissa Moss. *School Library Journal* 45, no. 12 (December 1999): 108.

Gr. 3-5—Caught in the British blockade of Boston from 1774 to 1776 and separated from her family, young Emma describes the events she witnesses or overhears [in *Emma's Journal: The Story of a Colonial Girl*]. While she works at her elderly aunt's boarding house, she meets or hears about such famous figures as Paul Revere, Benjamin Franklin, Patrick Henry, George Washington, and Dr. Joseph Warren, as well as British General Burgoyne, Governor Gage, and others. The story unfolds with secret messages, spying, snippets of rude songs printed in the margins that are sure to provoke giggles, and Emma's trials with the vain young Tory boarder, Thankful, who is in love with a British soldier. Emma's final entries tell of the reunion with her family and of the stirring reading of the "Proclamation of Independence" in July of 1776. As in Moss's "Amelia" journals (Tricycle) and her *Rachel's Journal* (Harcourt, 1998), information appears in tiny drawings or souvenir bits "pasted" in the margins. The handwritten

text is eye-catching and printed on aged, lined yellow paper. An author's note separates fact from fiction, provides extra information on women spies in the Revolution, and reveals the author's sources. All in all, a seductive introduction to the period, especially for readers who remain neutral to textbook accounts.

TRUE HEART (1999)

Publishers Weekly (review date 1 March 1999)

SOURCE: Review of *True Heart,* by Marissa Moss, illustrated by C. F. Payne. *Publishers Weekly* 246, no. 9 (1 March 1999): 69.

Moss (*Rachel's Journal: The Story of a Pioneer Girl; Amelia's Notebook*) uses her flair for capturing girls' voices to tell a remarkable and exhilarating story [in *True Heart*]. A turn-of-the-century photograph of an all-women work crew for a railroad inspired this tale of a teenager's first time driving a train, an experience that launches her career as an engineer. Newly orphaned in 1893, 16-year-old Bee takes a job loading freight on the railways to support her eight siblings. Moss evokes the love of trains that keeps Bee in the engineer's cab every spare moment, watching and asking questions, and her joy at driving for the first time, when an injured engineer and a train full of impatient passengers pressure the station manager to give her a chance. On the final spread, Bee recalls that inaugural experience: "I felt so free and strong, galloping across whole states in my iron horse, blowing my whistle for all the sky to hear." For his first children's book, Payne uses mixed media in a crisp, realistic style. He so meticulously defines the action that the illustrations seem frozen in time, oddly tranquil: unexpected angles and tight close-ups create arresting compositions. This book will be welcomed by a wide audience: train lovers, frontier buffs, all girls—and any adult who, like Bee, can "remember wanting something so much you can't think of anything else." *Ages 5-9.*

Nina Lindsay (review date April 1999)

SOURCE: Lindsay, Nina. Review of *True Heart,* by Marissa Moss, illustrated by C. F. Payne. *School Library Journal* 45, no. 4 (April 1999): 106.

Gr. 2-4—[In *True Heart,* a]n engineer for the Union Pacific at the turn of the century reminisces about the event that made the dream of driving trains become a reality. As a freight loader, Bee took every opportunity to sit in the cab and watch the engineers work, and was occasionally offered a chance to drive from one station to the next. One day on a run from San Francisco to Chicago, a group of bandits shot and injured the engineer at the controls. Bee volunteered to complete the run and the station manager agreed, marking that day as the start of a new career for Bee. This comfortably paced story has a familiar feel to it and a secret that will disclose itself to attentive readers: Bee is a woman. The use of nicknames throughout and an avoidance of gender pronouns draw the attention to the heart of the story—Bee's dream—rather than her sex. Accompanying the author's note at the end of the book is a black-and-white photograph of a group of female freight loaders that inspired this book. The mixed-media illustrations are realistic but softened with sepia tones, as if with age; and except for a couple of double-page spreads, full-page illustrations on the right face text on faux-stained parchment backgrounds. Visually and textually, this quiet story is a treasure.

Hazel Rochman (review date 1 April 1999)

SOURCE: Rochman, Hazel. Review of *True Heart,* by Marissa Moss, illustrated by C. F. Payne. *Booklist* 95, no. 15 (1 April 1999): 106.

Gr. 2-4, younger for reading aloud—A young girl takes over the wheel, proves herself a hero, and saves the day in two stories set a century ago. [. . .]

Moss' hero [in *True Heart*], Bee, tells her own story of working on the railroad since she was 16 in 1893, loading freight with her buddies for the Union Pacific in Cheyenne, Wyoming, always dreaming of being an engineer. She watches the drivers closely, asks lots of questions, badgers them to let her drive—and then one day she gets her chance when the engineer is wounded by bandits, and the station manager allows Bee to drive the train. Since then she has driven trains across the continent, "joining together the two ends of this great nation." Bee's first-person narrative expresses the rhythm and excitement of the railroad, how she loves to hear the clatter and roar of the trains. With extraordinary depth, Payne's brown-tone, full-page paintings combine realism and romance, showing long views of the trains steaming through the prairie, close-ups of the amazing machinery, pictures of Bee and her grinning crew, and then the triumphant scene of Bee proud and strong when at last she climbs into the cab in an engineer's cap. In an

afterword, Moss says her story was inspired by a museum show, Women and the American Railroad, and by women's journals of the time.

AMELIA'S FAMILY TIES (2000)

Carolyn Phelan (review date 15 February 2000)

SOURCE: Phelan, Carolyn. Review of *Amelia's Family Ties,* by Marissa Moss. *Booklist* 96, no. 12 (15 February 2000): 1113.

Gr. 3-5—In the latest volume of the Amelia's Notebook series [*Amelia's Family Ties*], Amelia records her experiences and feelings when she receives a letter from her father (who divorced her mother and left when she was a baby) and visits him in Chicago. Amelia's adjustment to her father and stepmother is realistically portrayed, with the good intentions, false starts, and awkwardness inherent in the situation. Toward the end of the visit, Amelia is able to ask her father the questions she's been asking herself for years and hear answers that begin to heal the hurt that her father's absence and silence caused. Jaunty ink-and-watercolor illustrations, purportedly Amelia's work, decorate every page of this highly readable book. The voice is consistently Amelia's, but the points of view of other characters, from her sister to her stepmother, come through as well. A fine addition to a popular series.

BRAVE HARRIET: THE FIRST WOMAN TO FLY THE ENGLISH CHANNEL (2001)

Publishers Weekly (review date 16 July 2001)

SOURCE: Review of *Brave Harriet: The First Woman to Fly the English Channel,* by Marissa Moss, illustrated by C. F. Payne. *Publishers Weekly* 248, no. 29 (16 July 2001): 180.

The creators of *True Heart* once again laud a historical heroine with gentle restraint [in *Brave Harriet: The First Woman to Fly the English Channel*]. Here they give pilot Harriet Quimby just the right note of quiet confidence: "I hadn't grown up wishing to be a pilot, because there were no planes when I was a girl, but once I saw one, I knew where I belonged—there, at the controls, with blue sky all around me." Harriet wins her license from a skeptical board ("No woman has ever received a license to fly," a licensing official says), works as a barnstormer, then conceives the idea of crossing the English Channel. Her pilot friend Gustav Hamel tries to dissuade her, offering to fly for her in disguise; Harriet refuses. She completes her mission, but the sinking of the *Titanic* on the same day overshadows news of her success. "But it didn't matter, because I knew I had done it," she says. Payne's spreads resemble period photographs—stop-action shots of wood-framed airplanes taken from striking angles, a newsboy reading the headlines about the *Titanic* and Harriet looking wistfully across the Channel, her skirt billowing in the wind. Pair this with Julie Cummins's *Tomboy of the Air* (Children's Forecasts, July 2) for a complete picture of the first women pilots. Ages 6-9.

Elizabeth Bush (review date January 2002)

SOURCE: Bush, Elizabeth. Review of *Brave Harriet: The First Woman to Fly the English Channel,* by Marissa Moss, illustrated by C. F. Payne. *Bulletin of the Center for Children's Books* 55, no. 5 (January 2002): 179-80.

In this imagined narrative, [*Brave Harriet: The First Woman to Fly the English Channel,*] early twentieth century pilot Harriet Quimby tells of her love-at-first-sight affair with aviation and her daring flight from England to France, guided only by a compass, intuition, and intense determination to be the first woman to complete the journey. Opening pages focus on Quimby's mastery of the "rattletrap, gum-and-spit contraption" and on her defiance of social norms to earn the license and backing to become a professional aviatrix. Her channel crossing is, of course, the signal event here, and although the journey is relatively brief, it packs its share of adventure: "The plane was tilting sharply, and the steep pitch caused the engine to misfire. The motor began to sputter. There was no time to think, only time to act." Obviously her mission ends in success, but the triumph she hoped for never materialized, because "it was April 16, 1912, and for that day—and for days afterward—there was other news that eclipsed mine." In the penultimate spread, a newsboy hawks the London *Times* whose headline blares "TITANIC DISASTER." Whether the often dreamy tone of this fictionalized Quimby accurately reflects the pilot's real expression is impossible to ascertain from the appended notes, and with the narrow focus on Quimby's Channel flight, exciting details of her barnstorming career and tragic death never emerge. The mixed-media art is sometimes too earthbound, but there's enough dramatic use of sweeping perspective and swooping aircraft to evoke sympathy for Quimby's fascination with the air. Chil-

dren who'd prefer wings to feet will delight in the story, and teachers planning a unit on flight can encourage comparisons with Blériot's crossing in Provensen's *The Glorious Flight.*

OH BOY, AMELIA! (2001)

Carolyn Phelan (review date 1-15 January 2002)

SOURCE: Phelan, Carolyn. Review of *Oh Boy, Amelia!,* by Marissa Moss. *Booklist* 98, nos. 9-10 (1-15 January 2002): 859.

Gr. 2-5—[In **Oh Boy, Amelia!,**] Amelia is intrigued, but not entirely pleased, when older sister Cleo, who has a crush on a boy and actually invites him over to work on a science project. At school, Amelia's new life-skills class, teaching sewing, carpentry, cooking, and bicycle repairs, brings up issues of gender expectations. As she copes with Cleo's newfound femininity and her preference for woodwork over needlework, Amelia expresses her thoughts and feelings in her own inimitable way, in her diary-like notebook. Childlike drawings with colorful washes brighten every blue-lined page of the book. The light, but sympathetic treatment of Amelia's concerns will appeal to many girls. An entertaining addition to a popular series.

GALEN: MY LIFE IN IMPERIAL ROME: AN ANCIENT WORLD JOURNAL (2002)

***Publishers Weekly* (review date 21 October 2002)**

SOURCE: Review of *Galen: My Life in Imperial Rome: An Ancient World Journal,* by Marissa Moss. *Publishers Weekly* 249, no. 42 (21 October 2002): 76.

Ably balancing fact and fiction, Moss (the Amelia's Notebook and Young American Voices series) uses her signature notebook-style jottings and drawings to launch the Ancient World Journal series [with *Galen: My Life in Imperial Rome*]. The fresh, diverting first-person account of fictitious 12-year-old Galen, an aspiring artist, describes life as a slave in the palace of Emperor Augustus. As the tale opens, Galen is living with his artist father and brother as slaves of Pollio, a pompous equestrian who bought Galen's father to have him decorate his villa. A dramatic incident occurs while the emperor Augustus visits the villa on his way home to Rome: Pollio threatens to kill Galen's brother when the boy accidentally breaks a treasured wine cup. Augustus, outraged by Pollio's cruelty, buys the family and takes them to Rome with him. The chatty narrator recounts the goings-on in the busy household (which includes Augustus's cold wife, Livia, and his scheming, bullying grandson, Agrippa) while providing a clear, intriguing portrait of ancient Roman life, with such customs as gladiator fights, chariot races and celebrations of the Saturnalia and the feast of Liberalia. Moss's marginal notes in Galen's engaging voice plus his sketches offer insight about food, dress ("Togas are impossible to drape by yourself") and hairstyles. Moss caps this account with Galen's climactic discovery of a plot to poison Augustus so that Tullus Antonius can become emperor. Youngsters will be so drawn into the story that they might not realize how much history they're learning along the way. *Ages 8-12.*

Deborah Stevenson (review date December 2002)

SOURCE: Stevenson, Deborah. Review of *Galen: My Life in Imperial Rome: An Ancient World Journal,* by Marissa Moss. *Bulletin of the Center for Children's Books* 56, no. 4 (December 2002): 168.

In [*Galen: My Life in Imperial Rome,*] this new addition to the burgeoning genre of historical faux-journals, a young Greek slave describes his life at the palace of Augustus, where he, his brother, and his artist father moved after Augustus bought them all from a provincial knight. There Galen broadens his worldview as he learns the wonders of Rome, makes friends, and hopes eventually to free himself and become a Roman citizen. En route, however, he must evade the anger of bullying young Postumus Agrippa, Augustus' grandson, and alert Augustus to a plot against his life. There are definitely some glitches in the book, both in usage (four years past 2 B.C. isn't actually "the second century A.D.") and in history (the text wrongly states that Caligula killed his own mother), but there's also a lot of accurate detail; Moss is particularly good at conveying the Greek/Roman cultural divide and the way Roman slavery functioned. Though there's some meandering in the text (and the framework of Galen's grandson's discovery of this narrative is unnecessary), Galen's drive to please Augustus and to become a man in Roman style are sufficient to drive the story, and there's nothing like a good old murder plot (especially a fact-based one) for narrative impact. The hand-lettered font is a little harder going than type, but the plethora of interpolated thumbnail sketches and sidebar notes makes the square cream pages inviting and more accessible. An author's note provides information on sources; some additional historical background, a glossary, and some useful period maps are included.

MAX'S LOGBOOK (2003)

Publishers Weekly (review date 14 July 2003)

SOURCE: Review of *Max's Logbook,* by Marissa Moss. *Publishers Weekly* 250, no. 28 (14 July 2003): 76.

Hand-lettered on graph paper, infused with childlike drawings and collages, Moss's (the Amelia's Notebook series) paper-over-board facsimile of a boy's journal [*Max's Logbook*] ostensibly spotlights his experiments and inventions (these range from classroom exercises to microwaving marshmallows in order to create "Godzilla Puff" in his kitchen and devising an alarm that will sound when someone enters his bedroom). But the underpinnings of Max's musings are more emotional than scientific (despite the periodic table of elements on the inside front cover). Upset by his parents' frequent arguments, Max fears they are headed toward divorce. He imagines inventing such solutions as a "Prevent-a-Divorce Machine," an "Instant Happiness Robot" and "Hypnodisks" that will force his mother and father to behave as he wishes. There are some silly, irrelevant asides here, e.g., Max's comic strips featuring "Alien Eraser," which imagine the exploits of a pencil-top eraser confiscated by Max's teacher, and Moss doesn't always trust readers to interpret Max's behavior ("I can make my army and alien erasers do whatever I want, but not my parents," Max explains). Even so, the boy's anguish and anxiety will resonate with kids who have faced similar situations, and his gradual acceptance of his parents' eventual separation may well provide solace. *Ages 7-10.*

MIGHTY JACKIE: THE STRIKE-OUT QUEEN (2004)

Publishers Weekly (review date 19 January 2004)

SOURCE: Review of *Mighty Jackie: The Strike-Out Queen,* by Marissa Moss, illustrated by C. F. Payne. *Publishers Weekly* 251, no. 3 (19 January 2004): 76.

Delivered with the force of a hard fastball, [*Mighty Jackie: The Strike-Out Queen,*] the true story of athlete Jackie Mitchell makes a strong addition to Moss's (*Amelia's Notebook*) library of brave girl tales. Payne (*Casey at the Bat*) sets the stage with photo-real, fish-eye-distorted spreads of Jackie as a child, hurling baseballs long after nightfall and getting tips from Dodgers pitcher Dazzy Vance. Moss relays the details of then-17-year-old Jackie's April 2, 1931, game against the two best hitters of the day—Babe Ruth and Lou Gehrig—with the blow-by-blow breathlessness of a sportscaster and the confidence of a seasoned storyteller: "Jackie held that ball like it was part of her arm, and when she threw it, she knew exactly where it would go." Payne's pictures mirror the text's immediacy. Close-ups show Ruth's face as he awaits Jackie's first pitch, then later his expression of dismay and outrage as the umpire calls "*Strrrrike three!*" Jackie disposes of Gehrig even more expeditiously, and the story ends as she basks in the cheers of fans who had jeered her only moments before. The wind seeps out of this jubilant moment when readers old enough to understand the end note discover that Jackie was immediately removed from her team and banned from baseball (the commissioner claimed his decision was for her own protection, as baseball was "too strenuous" for women, according to an author's note). Yet the drama of her two memorable strike-outs has a mythic dimension, and girls with sporting aspirations will be thrilled by Jackie's legacy. Ages 5-8.

Elizabeth Bush (review date March 2004)

SOURCE: Bush, Elizabeth. Review of *Mighty Jackie: The Strike-Out Queen,* by Marissa Moss, illustrated by C. F. Payne. *Bulletin of the Center for Children's Books* 57, no. 7 (March 2004): 289.

Power pitcher Jackie Mitchell may have been short-changed by the major leagues, but she's getting her due in children's books. The chapter-book crowd was introduced in Jean L. S. Patrick's *The Girl Who Struck Out Babe Ruth* (*BCCB* 6/00), and now the picture-book audience makes Jackie's acquaintance with an account that delves further back into her childhood [in ***Mighty Jackie: The Strike-Out Queen***], depicting her practicing tirelessly with her father and a bull's-eye painted on the siding, learning some tricks from Dazzy Vance, and advancing her dream of "playing in the World Series." As Moss points out in her concluding note, Jackie never made it that far. After one triumphant game in which the young woman struck out both the Babe and Lou Gehrig,

she was banned from major and minor league ball and only played on the sly for small teams. There are some important questions left unanswered, such as how an eight-year-old came to be coached by a star pitcher and how she made her break in signing with the Chattanooga Lookouts in the first place. The focus here, however, as in Patrick's work, is on Mitchell's day of fame, and Payne's heroic mixed-media illustrations do their subject full justice. Payne, who's worked the diamond in Bildner's *Shoeless Joe & Black Betsy* (*BCCB* 2/02) and Thayer's *Casey at the Bat* (2/03), knows just how to zero in on a player's attitude. Jackie, with the slightly elongated shoes that root her to the mound and delicately detailed fingers caressing the ball, glares determinedly into the distance in a pose that begs to be cast in bronze, while a close-up of Babe Ruth, equally determined, presents a man who, in that moment, believes himself to be incapable of defeat. This is a tale worth telling, and there's every reason to acquire another angle on the story.

FURTHER READING

Criticism

O'Hara, Sheilamae. Review of *Knick Knack Paddywack,* by Marissa Moss. *Booklist* 88, no. 21 (July 1992): 1941.
    Compliments Moss's verse and illustrations in *Knick Knack Paddywack.*

Phelan, Carolyn. Review of *The All-New Amelia* and *Luv, Amelia Luv, Nadia,* by Marissa Moss. *Booklist* 96, no. 5 (1 November 1999): 530.
    Offers a positive assessment of two additions to Moss's "Amelia" series—*The All-New Amelia* and *Luv, Amelia Luv, Nadia.*

Weisman, Kay. Review of *Rachel's Journal: The Story of a Pioneer Girl,* by Marissa Moss. *Booklist* 95, no. 3 (1 October 1998): 330.
    Evaluates the strengths and weaknesses of *Rachel's Journal: The Story of a Pioneer Girl.*

Additional coverage of Moss's life and career is contained in the following sources published by Gale: *Contemporary Authors,* Vol. 171; *Contemporary Authors New Revision Series,* Vol. 130; *Literature Resource Center*; and *Something about the Author,* Vols. 71, 104, 163.

Charles Perrault
1628-1703

French author of nonfiction, verse, verse tales, and fairy tales.

The following entry presents an overview of Perrault's career through 2006. For further information on his life and career, see *CLR,* Volume 79.

INTRODUCTION

Writing in seventeenth-century France during the reign of King Louis XIV, Perrault is best remembered as the creator of the modern fairy tale. His greatest legacy is his collection *Histoires, ou Contes du temps passé, avec des moralitez,* (1697; *Histories or Tales of Past Times;* also published as *Fairy Tales or Histories of Past Times, with Morals,*) which contains some of the most enduring and widely recognized stories in all of Western literature, including "La Belle au bois dormant" ("Sleeping Beauty in the Woods"), "Cendrillon ou la petite pantoufle de verre" ("Cinderella, or the Little Glass Slipper"), "Le Maître chat ou le chat botté" ("The Master Cat, or Puss in Boots"), and "Le Petit chaperon rouge" ("Little Red Riding Hood"), among others. Translated into numerous languages and adapted by authors and artists of every medium, Perrault's fairy tales are considered among the most influential works in children's literature, having played an integral role in European folk culture for over three hundred years.

BIOGRAPHICAL INFORMATION

The youngest of five boys, Perrault was born on January 12, 1628, in Paris, France, to Pierre Perrault, a member of the Paris Parliament, and Pâquette Leclerc Perrault. He briefly attended the Collège de Beauvoir before dropping out, preferring to study poetry and philosophy on his own. In 1651 Perrault received a law degree and passed the bar, but soon grew disillusioned with the French legal system. He took a job as a clerk under his brother—a tax collector—in 1654, and began publishing poems in 1660. His work drew the attention of Jean-Baptiste Colbert, an aide to King Louis XIV, and Perrault was appointed artis-

tic advisor to the royal court. After working for Colbert at the office of Royal Buildings, Perrault became a member of the Académie française, the official authority on French language and literature. He married Marie Guichon in 1672 and was promoted that same year to Controller of His Majesty's Buildings. When his wife died in 1678, Perrault was left with the task of raising and educating their four children. In 1687 Perrault caused an uproar within the Académie française with his poem *Le Siècle de Louis le Grand,* which argued that modern French culture was superior to classical antiquity. This controversial notion formed the central argument for what became known as the Quarrel of the Ancients and Moderns, the cultural debate over whether classical or contemporary works should serve as literary models. Perrault's first verse tale, "La Marquise de Salusses ou la patience de Griselidis," based on a tale in Giovanni Boccaccio's *Decameron,* was published in 1691. Perrault compiled five new tales in "Contes de ma mère l'oye" ("Tales of Mother Goose"), a manuscript which he presented to Louis XIV's nineteen-year-old niece Elisabeth-Charlotte d'Orléans in 1695. In 1697 he published *Histoires, ou Contes du temps passé, avec des moralitez,* which collected eight tales, including the five originally presented in his 1695 manuscript. Perrault died on May 15, 1703, while composing his memoirs.

MAJOR WORKS

Contes de fée, or fairy tales, became highly fashionable within the aristocratic salons of late seventeenth-century France. Finding the light verse which characterized the fairy tale well-suited to his talents as a poet, Perrault also saw the genre as a vehicle for his modern social and moral concerns. Thus, many of the story elements he created for the tales in *Histoires, ou Contes du temps passé, avec des moralitez* serve a didactic purpose, emphasizing the values of wisdom, virtue, and obedience. Each of the tales in the collection follows a similar structure, presenting a story in prose followed by a moral in verse form. Perrault borrowed basic motifs and plot elements from other documented folktales, including such works as *The Arabian Nights* and Giambattista

Basile's *Pentamerone* to supplement his unique vision for the fairy tales. For example, the framework for the Cinderella story existed in multiple versions prior to 1697, but Perrault's "Cendrillon ou la petite pantoufle de verre" marks the first appearance of the fairy godmother, the pumpkin carriage, the midnight curfew, and the glass slipper. In earlier versions of "La belle au bois dormant," the princess is awakened after being raped by the prince, but Perrault's tale presents a morally sound prince who takes Sleeping Beauty as his wife. Other tales, such as "Le Petit chaperon rouge," "Le Maître chat ou le chat botté," and "Le Petite poucet" ("Little Thumb"), had been part of oral tradition and folklore before being recorded and adapted into their widely recognized forms by Perrault. Published in 1729, Robert Samber's English translation of *Histoires, ou Contes du temps passé, avec des moralitez, Histories or Tales of Past Times*, increased the popularity of Perrault's work throughout Europe and featured a reproduction of Perrault's original frontispiece to the 1697 edition. An illustration of a peasant woman reading to a group of children, this page introduced the image of "Mother Goose"—already familiar to the French audience—to English and American readers. Attesting to Perrault's significant contribution to the European folktale tradition, the Brothers Grimm selected Perrault's stories for inclusion in their landmark compilation of fairy tales, *Kinder- und Hausmärchen*, which was originally published in several volumes between 1812 and 1815.

CRITICAL RECEPTION

The works which comprise Perrault's seminal volume of fairy tales have been embraced by—and thoroughly ingrained in—Western culture. Critical studies of his work have focused on his indispensable contribution to children's literature and the universal appeal of the fairy tale form. Scholars have examined the illustrations which accompanied early editions of Perrault's collection to explore notions of oral storytelling and the role of women within the folktale tradition. Additionally, critics have underscored themes and subtexts in Perrault's tales, identifying undercurrents of sexual desire, gender identity, and voyeurism in his stories despite their connotations of innocence and simplicity. While acknowledging that Perrault was but one of many authors publishing fairy tales during his lifetime, several scholars have credited the endurance of Perrault's tales to their adaptability to the popular pantomime stages of nineteenth-century England. Though his name may be unfamiliar

to the generations of readers which have appreciated his stories, Perrault has left a lasting impression on the fairy tale genre. His work has been cited as the earliest example of children's literature and remains a source of critical interpretation and discovery.

PRINCIPAL WORKS

Le Siècle de Louis le Grand (verse) 1687

Parallèle des anciens et des modernes, en ce qui regarde les arts et les sciences. 4 vols. (nonfiction) 1688-1697

L'Apologie des femmes (verse) 1694

Griselidis, nouvelle, avec le conte de Peau d'Ane et celui des Souhaits ridicules (verse tales) 1694

Histoires, ou Contes du temps passé, avec des moralitez (fairy tales) 1697; translated by Robert Samber as *Histories or Tales of Past Times*, 1729; revised as *Fairy Tales or Histories of Past Times, with Morals*, 1794

Contes de Ma Mère l'Oye, Histoires ou Contes du Temps Passé (Par le Fils de Monsieur Perreault) (fairy tales) 1698

Perrault's Popular Tales [edited by Andrew Lang] (fairy tales) 1888

Perrault's Tales of Mother Goose: The Dedication Manuscript of 1695 Reproduced in Collotype Facsimile. 2 vols. [edited by Jacques Barchillon] (fairy tales) 1956

Contes [edited by Gilbert Rouger] (fairy tales) 1967

Contes de Perrault: Fac-similé de l'édition originale de 1695-1697 (fairy tales) 1980

Contes [edited by Roger Zuber] (fairy tales) 1987

Contes [edited by Marc Soriano] (fairy tales) 1989

Cinderella: And Other Tales from Perrault [illustrations by Michael Hague] (fairy tales) 1989

Cinderella, Puss in Boots, and Other Favorite Tales [translated by A. E. Johnson] (fairy tales) 2000

Cinderella [retold and illustrated by Barbara McClintock] (fairy tales) 2005

GENERAL COMMENTARY

Jacques Barchilon and Peter Flinders (essay date 1981)

SOURCE: Barchilon, Jacques, and Peter Flinders. "Perrault's Fairy Tales as Literature." In *Charles Perrault*, pp. 63-100. Boston, Mass.: Twayne Publishers, 1981.

[*In the following essay, Barchilon and Flinders offer a critical overview of Perrault's most famous fairy tales from* Histoires ou Contes du temps passé, *discussing the status of the fairy tale genre in seventeenth-century France and the elements of the supernatural in each tale.*]

I. Which Are the Fairy Tales of Perrault?

We have now reached the moment to present Perrault's most important contribution to world literature, his fairy tales, which have only been mentioned incidentally up to now. Let us first list them in the order of their publication. The list is impressive, if not large; and the reader will immediately recognize the familiar titles. There are eleven of them: *Griselidis* [*Patient Griselda*], published in 1691 for the first time, not really a fairy tale; *Les Souhaits ridicules* [*The Ridiculous Wishes, or The Three Wishes*], published in 1693; *Peau d'Ane* [*Donkey-Skin*], published in 1694; these three first works are known as the verse tales. They were followed in 1697 by the more famous prose tales, the *Histoires ou Contes du temps passé* [*Histories or Tales of Past Times*], familiar in both French and English as *Contes de Ma Mère l'Oye* [*Tales of Mother Goose*].

Such a popular title is generally associated in English-speaking countries with nursery rhymes rather than with fairy tales; nevertheless, the English expression is simply a translation of the French and did not cross the Channel until the first translation of Perrault's tales appeared in England in 1729.

The prose fairy tales are: **"La Belle au bois dormant"** [**"Sleeping Beauty"**], **"Le Petit Chaperon rouge"** [**"Little Red Riding Hood"**], **"Barbe bleue"** [**"Bluebeard"**], **"Le Maître Chat ou le Chat botté"** [**"The Master Cat or Puss in Boots"**], **"Les Fées"** [**"The Fairies"**], **"Cendrillon ou la petite pantouffle de verre"** [**"Cinderella or The Little Glass Slipper"**], **"Riquet à la houppe"** [**"Rickey with the Tuft"**], **"La Petit Poucet"** [**"Tom Thumb, or Hop O' My Thumb"**].

These stories were cast in enduring form by Charles Perrault long before the Brothers Grimm, in 1812, published their celebrated collection of folktales, in which most of the tales of Perrault appeared in German. They had crossed the Rhine through the first German translation of 1745, and through other oral channels.[1] This chapter and the next will treat of the fairy tales of Perrault at length, as their importance warrants. There will be presentations of the stories in a literary as well as in a sociohistorical context. Most importantly, we will also account for the special circumstances in which fairy tales became popular in seventeenth-century France.[2]

II. What Are the Fairy Tales of Perrault?

It will be useful to have for handy reference simple summaries of each of Perrault's tales. We have tried to write these summaries in a style that neither repeats the stories lifelessly nor reduces them to mere skeletal outlines. We added no extraneous commentaries. A remark is necessary on the subject of *Griselidis*; the story has no magical element. Nevertheless, Perrault included it in his collection of verse tales, considering it a *Nouvelle* (novella), a tale seemingly based on reality. But he considers the patience of Griselidis as so unusual in his time and day that he wrote in the dedication of the story, "That a Lady as patient / As the one I am praising here, / Would cause quite a surprise anywhere, / But in Paris would be considered a prodigy." Clearly, in his mind such a story tells of something long gone, a tale of passed times, as the very title of his collection of prose tales emphatically spells out.

We have added to our summaries a brief statement about each of the morals of the prose and verse tales, as they are rarely discussed in the criticism of Perrault published in English; furthermore, ignorance of their content amounts to a neglect of Perrault's own concept of his *Contes*. Our main intent in this section is to facilitate discussion by making our author's tales familiar. Of course, nothing replaces direct contact with the texts themselves. The salt, the wit of the language, in French or in English, cannot be savored in our summaries. And we should emphasize that these tales are among the shortest of fairy tales, a brevity they share with those of the Grimm Brothers.

A. Griselidis

A certain prince who believed that women were faithless and deceitful vowed that he would never marry. His subjects, however, wished for an heir and urged him to wed. He replied that he would, only on the condition that his future wife be without pride or vanity, patient and obedient, and with no will of her own.

One day while hunting the prince strayed from the main hunting party and came upon the most beautiful young lady he had ever seen, a shepherdess watching over her sheep by the edge of a stream. He learned that she lived alone with her father and that Griselda was her name. At the palace he called his council and announced that he would not choose a wife from a foreign country but from among his own people and that he would not give her name until the day of the wedding.

Great was the excitement among the ladies of the land. Knowing that he was looking for a chaste and modest wife, they all took to styles more suitable to his taste, softening their voices, letting their hair fall loosely around them, and putting on high-necked dresses with long sleeves, so that only their little fingers showed. Great preparations were made for the wedding, and when the day arrived, the prince rode off on the path he usually took to go hunting, his courtiers following behind. At length he came to Griselda's hut where he asked her to marry him. She consented, but not before he made her swear that she would never go against his wishes.

Griselda was the perfect queen, and she gave birth to a beautiful daughter, whom she loved dearly. But the prince suspected her behavior and put her to the test. He ordered that her child be taken from her and brought up apart. He sent the child to a convent to be brought up by nuns. Fifteen years passed and she grew into a beautiful young lady, and fell in love with a great nobleman and wished to marry him. The prince, however, told Griselda that her daughter had died. Griselda was greatly grieved but her only thought was to comfort her husband. The prince was pleased with her but yet put her to the test once again by announcing publicly that he must remarry in order to provide an heir to the throne. He had chosen for wife the girl he had brought up in the convent. Griselda returned, in rags, to her hut, but shortly thereafter the prince called her back again to the palace to make ready the rooms for his new bride.

When the wedding guests arrived, the prince announced that he had only been putting his wife to the test. He then freed his daughter to marry the nobleman and promised to think only of his wife's happiness and to proclaim her virtues to the world. The marriage was celebrated and all eyes were on Griselda, whose praises were sung above all others.

And the people had great admiration for the prince, forgiving him his cruelty to his wife, for it had given rise to such a model of patience. Perrault did not publish a separate moral at the end of this story. Instead he expounded on a few ideas in the introductory dedicatory letter to an unknown and unnamed "Mademoiselle." He ironically insisted that patience "Is not a virtue of Parisian wives, / But through a long experience they have acquired the Knack / Of teaching it to their husbands."

B. "PEAU D'ANE"

There once lived a king who was the happiest of monarchs and dearly loved by his people. The queen was a most beautiful and virtuous princess. The daughter was lovely and full of charm, so much so that having more children did not matter to them.

One of the king's most prized and most unusual possessions was a donkey who had the place of honor in his magnificent stables; for this donkey, instead of dropping manure onto the straw, deposited gold coins which were collected each morning. One day the queen took ill and died. The king was overcome with grief. Before she died, the queen had made the king promise that, should he wish to remarry, he would marry only a princess more beautiful than she. The king vowed he would never marry again, but time, and his councillors, convinced him that he must remarry in order to provide a male heir to the throne. He searched and searched throughout the kingdom but could not find a princess more beautiful than the queen to whom he had been married. He began to think that there was no more ravishing beauty than his own daughter, who was even more talented and delightful than her mother, and he decided to marry her. The young princess recoiled in horror at this thought and begged her father to reconsider. But the king was persistent and ordered her to make ready for the marriage.

For assistance the princess called upon her fairy godmother who suggested that she marry the king only if he could make for her a gown which was the color of the sky. The king, much flattered at her request, promptly produced a gown more beautiful even than the blue of the sky. A second gown was suggested by the fairy godmother, a gown the color of the moon, and a third, a gown as brilliant as the color of the sun. But the king had his tailors produce them as quickly as the first. So the fairy godmother proposed to put the king to the most terrible test of all: that he should sacrifice the skin of his gold-producing donkey if he truly wished to marry his daughter. To her dismay, the king dispatched the donkey in no time at all and delivered its skin to the princess. In desperation, she fled, with the donkey skin upon her back, as a disguise to a farm where she became a scullery maid. And so she became known as Donkey-Skin.

The only pleasure she had at the farm was on Sundays, when opening the trunk which her fairy godmother had magically transported for her, she would put on her beautiful gowns, one after the other, and admire herself in the mirror. One day a prince happened by and, having seen her through the keyhole of her cabin, fell madly in love with her, returned home to his palace, and stopped showing any interest in food or entertainment. He told his mother, the queen, that he would eat only a cake baked by Donkey-Skin, the ugly maid who looked after turkeys on a farm. The queen, thinking that her son's every whim, however irrational, must be satisfied, ordered that Donkey-Skin make a cake for the prince.

Donkey-Skin baked the cake, most willingly, as ordered, but in it hid her ring, hoping that the prince might discover it. The cake was brought back to the prince, who ate it most greedily, and almost choked on the ring. So delighted was he to find the ring that he kept it under his pillow. The prince did not want to displease his mother and father by marrying a peasant girl but, upon examining carefully the ring, they all agreed that it must surely fit the finger of a high-born lady. The king and queen acquiesced in the prince's request that he be allowed to marry the girl whose finger fitted the ring.

Throngs of princesses, duchesses, marquises, and baronesses arrived at the palace to try on the ring, but it would not fit the finger of any of them. The prince asked that Donkey-Skin be fetched so that she too might try on the ring. With shouts of ridicule the prince's men led her to the palace, covered in her donkey skin, underneath which, however, she had the foresight to put on one of her beautiful gowns. The ring fit perfectly and Donkey-Skin shed her ugly clothes to reveal a princess in all her beauty.

The king and queen were delighted about the marriage of their son to this beautiful princess. Great potentates from distant countries were invited, including Donkey-Skin's father, who, fortunately, had forgotten his misguided love for his daughter and was now very glad to be a happy parent at the wedding.

This story appeared framed by a dedication and by a statement or moral of twenty-four lines of verse at the end. The dedication to the marquise de Lambert contains the familiar defense of the fairy tale: "Why marvel / If the most rational of men, / Often tiring of insomnia, / Take pleasure in entertainment / Of ingeniously contrived day dreams / Tales of Ogres and fairies." As for the final moral it was a reminder that the purpose of the story is to:

> Teach children
> That they should suffer the worse of troubles
> Rather than fail in accomplishing their moral duties;
> That the righteous path can bring about much misfortune
> But eventually it crowns the virtuous with success.

The last verses of the moral have become well known in France. "Donkey-Skin is difficult to believe, / But so long as our world will bring forth children, / Mothers and grandmothers, / Her story will be remembered."

C. "LES SOUHAITS RIDICULES"

A woodcutter who wished to die because his life was so miserable was overheard by Jupiter, who took pity on him and promised to grant him any three wishes he made, whatever they might be. Overjoyed, he went home to his wife Fanchon and told her the good news. She told her husband they must think things over carefully and wait until morning to make their wishes. The husband, whose name was Blaise, agreed, had a good drink, stretched his legs in front of the fire and said, "I wish I had a nice big sausage to cook over this nice fire." A sausage appeared, snaking its way toward his wife. In anger Fanchon declared that only a stupid oaf could have made a wish like that. Her husband flew into a rage, saying, "To hell with this sausage! I wish it would stick to your nose!" And so it did.

Thinking of all the wondrous things he could wish in using his last wish, he asked Fanchon if she would prefer being a grand princess with a horrible nose, or whether she would rather remain a woodcutter's wife with the nose she had before. She preferred to be as she had been rather than an ugly queen.

And the woodcutter was, after all, only too glad to use his last wish to turn his wife back into her old self, which is what he did.

D. "LA BELLE AU BOIS DORMANT"

There was once a king and queen who, grateful for finally giving birth to their first child, a girl, celebrated with a magnificent christening ceremony. As was customary, all the fairies in the realm attended, including one, who through an oversight, had not been invited. Feeling deliberately slighted, she cast an evil spell on the young princess: that she would die by pricking her finger on a spindle. One of the good fairies, however, counteracted this spell and decreed that the princess, instead of dying, would fall into a deep slumber lasting one hundred years.

As predicted by the fairies, the princess grew into a beautiful and talented young lady. But one day, high in a garret at the top of the tower, she met an old lady spinning at her wheel. The evil fairy's wish came true, in part: she pricked her finger on the spindle but, instead of dying, she fell into a hundred years' sleep, as did the entire castle. At the end of a hundred years, a young prince, adventurous and wishing for love and glory, arrived at the castle as the trees and bushes parted magically for him. As he approached the bed of the sleeping princess, she awoke, the spell having been broken, and declared, "Is it you, dear prince? You have been long in coming!" The entire castle awoke too and the young couple were married in the castle chapel. Two children were born of this union, Dawn, a girl, and Day, a boy.

The prince, however, kept his marriage a secret from his mother and father, who were king and queen of the realm in which he lived, and especially from his mother, who was descended from a race of ogres who loved to eat little children. The king died shortly and the prince ascended to the throne, whereupon he proclaimed publicly his marriage to Sleeping Beauty. Consequently, Sleeping Beauty and her two children came to reside at the palace of the queen mother. A few months later the prince was obliged to go off to war. In his absence, ever jealous of Sleeping Beauty, the queen mother asked her chief steward to serve Dawn, her granddaughter, for dinner. The chief steward, who loved little Dawn dearly, slaughtered a young lamb in her place. The queen mother, pleased nevertheless with her dinner, ordered the same fate for her grandson, Day, but was tricked again in the same manner by her chief steward. She soon discovered the ruse, however, and ordered a huge vat filled with vipers, toads, and snakes of all sorts to be brought into the courtyard. Sleeping Beauty, her children, the chief steward, his wife, and their servant girl were all to be thrown into it. At the last moment, the king rode into the courtyard and the queen mother at once threw herself into the vat and was devoured forthwith. The prince, naturally grieved at the death of his mother, in time found ample consolation in his beautiful wife and children.

"La Belle au bois dormant" appeared in its final version with two morals. The first stressed with a touch of erotic humor the "modern" unlikelihood of a hundred years' sleep: "Now at this time of day, / Not one of the Sex we see / To sleep with such profound tranquillity." In the second moral Perrault characteristically expands on the same message, insisting on the "female sex's ardor in seeking marriage."

E. "Le Petit chaperon rouge"

Little Red Riding Hood, so called because of the red hood she wore everywhere, went off to visit her sick grandmother, bringing her flat cakes and a pot of butter. On the way she met the wolf, who wanted to eat her but dared not, because of woodcutters nearby. Instead, he asked her where she was going and suggested they see who could get there first. He took the shorter route, ran as fast as he could to grandmother's house and, having been let in, gobbled her up in no time at all. Little Red Riding Hood, chasing butterflies and gathering hazelnuts on the way, arrived later, and was let in by the wolf, who had gotten into grandmother's bed. The wolf told her to get undressed and get into bed too, which Little Red Riding Hood did, much amazed at the undressed state of her grandmother. When Little Red Riding Hood exclaimed to the wolf, "What big teeth you have!" the wolf replied, "They're to eat you up with!" And with those words he pounced upon Little Red Riding Hood and ate her up.

Perrault's moral clearly indicates the allegorical nature of his story; it is a tale symbolically recounting the seduction of a young child or woman, and he equates wolves with seducers: "I say the wolf, since not all wolves are of the same kind." The popularity of this tale and its erotic innuendoes probably account for the widespread use of the expression "wolf" as synonymous with seducer.

F. "La Barbe bleue"

Bluebeard was a wealthy man but so ugly and frightful that he terrified women. No one wanted to marry him because he had already married several wives and nobody knew what had become of them. In time, one lady, eyeing eagerly his magnificent possessions, decided that his beard was not so blue after all and agreed to marry him. The marriage took place and soon thereafter Bluebeard was obliged to go away on a business venture. He instructed his wife to enjoy herself and to invite her friends over to his sumptuous castle but, at the same time, cautioned her never to open the door of the little room at the end of the long passage on the lower floor. Having given her the key, he departed. No sooner had he left than she invited her friends over to see her wonderful surroundings, but she was so curious about the little room that she left her guests and rushed to the forbidden door.

Upon entering she discovered a floor entirely covered with clotted blood and in this were mirrored the dead bodies of several women that hung along the walls: all of Bluebeard's wives, whom he had slain, one by one. The key to the little room was stained with blood but, try as she would, she could not wash it off. Bluebeard returned, asked for his keys, and noticed that the key to the little room was missing.

When his wife finally produced the key, Bluebeard realized her transgression and informed her she would be killed like his other wives. He made ready to behead her, but at the last moment her two soldier-brothers arrived and dispatched him with their swords. Bluebeard's wife subsequently inherited her former husband's wealth and married a worthy man who banished from her mind all memory of the evil days she had spent with Bluebeard.

There are two morals, the first blandly blaming curiosity as the cause of much trouble in the world, the second alluding to **"Bluebeard"** as a tale of past times and a story presenting a cruel husband, the like of which had disappeared.

G. "Le Maître chat ou le chat botté"

A certain miller died and bequeathed to his three sons all the earthly possessions he had. The youngest son received only a cat. Puss, overhearing his master's remarks of disappointment, assured his master of a comfortable life if only he would get him a pair of boots so that he could walk in the woods. Puss, being very clever, caught many a fine rabbit or partridge with his trap and presented these to the king as a gift from his master, the marquis de Carabas (a title he had invented for his master).

He laid further plans for his master by contriving an encounter of the king and his daughter with the marquis de Carabas while he was swimming in a nearby river. Robbers (said the cat) had stolen his master's clothes and he had nothing to wear. The king immediately provided him with a magnificent wardrobe and invited him to travel with him and his daughter in the royal carriage. They soon came upon peasants mowing in the fields who had been forced by Puss to declare that all the surrounding lands belonged to his master. The king was duly impressed by the great wealth of the marquis de Carabas.

Finally, Puss, preceding the royal carriage, came upon a rich ogre whom he tricked into a fateful metamorphosis, for the ogre could change himself into any kind of animal. He changed first into a lion and almost frightened Puss to death. And then, bullied into changing into a mouse, the ogre was promptly devoured by Puss. At that moment, the king's coach arrived at the ogre's castle, which Puss declared now as the property of his master, the marquis de Carabas.

At the king's request, his daughter and the marquis were married that same day. As for Puss, he never chased mice again except for amusement.

Perrault's two morals cynically extol opportunism and good looks as inestimable assets for a young man's progress in the world: "Youth, a good face, a good air and good mien / . . . ways to win / The hearts of the fair, and gently inspire the flames of sweet passion, and tender desire."

H. "Les Fées"

A widow with two daughters, one beautiful and kindly, the other arrogant and disagreeable, preferred the latter, for she was of the same temperament. The beautiful daughter was made to work in the kitchen from morning to night. One day when she was at the spring fetching water, an old lady of the village (in truth, a fairy) asked her for a drink, which the beautiful daughter promptly and cheerfully gave her. Grateful, the fairy bestowed a gift on his daughter: that with every word she uttered, there would fall from her mouth either a flower or a precious stone.

At home, when she spoke, she scattered diamonds right and left, and the mother was truly amazed. Greedily she urged the arrogant daughter, Fanchon, to do the same and sent her to the spring also. When the fairy, this time disguised as a princess, asked for a drink of water, the haughty Fanchon refused rudely and told the fairy to get the drink herself. Displeased, the fairy decreed that when Fanchon spoke, a snake or a toad would fall from her mouth. At home the mother was greatly angered at this and banished the good daughter from their home. Later, in the woods, she met the king's son, who fell in love with her, and they were married.

As for the other sister, she became so unbearable at home that her mother drove her out into the forest where, no one being of a mind to take her in, she lay down and died.

The two morals of the tale praise the youngsters who display good manners and *honnêteté* (a French word whose meaning was then roughly synonymous with courtesy).

I. "Cendrillon ou La Petite pantoufle de verre"

A widower who had a beautiful and kindly daughter married for a second time a proud and haughty woman with two daughters who were as ill-tempered as their mother. They treated their stepsister most cruelly, making her do all the chores and forcing her to sleep in a garret at the top of the house while they lived in luxurious rooms. She was forced to sit among the cinders in the corner of the hearth and thus acquired the name of Cinderella.

The king's son decided to give a ball and invited persons of high state, including Cinderella's two stepsisters. For days they talked about nothing but the ball and made Cinderella assist them in their toilette and in their choice of dresses, which she did good-naturedly and with exquisite taste. When the two sisters left for the ball, Cinderella began to cry. She was soon comforted by her fairy godmother, who with her magic wand fashioned for her a coach from a pumpkin, horses from mice, a coachman from a whiskered rat, and six lackeys from six lizards. Her gown was of gold and silver, bedecked with jewels, and she had a pair of tiny slippers made of glass. Her fairy godmother imposed one condition: that she leave the ball before midnight.

At the ball everyone was awed by the beauty of the unknown princess, and the king's son fell in love with her. On the third night of the ball, he retrieved one of her glass slippers which, in her haste to leave before midnight, she had dropped. She arrived home late, and all the fine finery had disappeared except for the one glass slipper, which she kept.

A few days later, the king's son issued the proclamation that he would take for wife the woman whose foot fitted into the glass slipper which he had in his possession. All the ladies of the court tried to fit into the glass slipper, including Cinderella's step-sisters, who squeezed and squeezed, but could not make it fit. Then Cinderella, laughing gaily, cried out: "Let me see if it will not fit me." The sisters shrieked in ridicule, but the equerry who was trying on the slipper saw that she was very beautiful and let her try it on. The slipper fitted perfectly and all were astonished, but even more so when Cinderella drew out of her pocket the matching slipper and put it on, too.

At this the sisters fell down upon their knees before Cinderella and begged forgiveness for the ill-treatment they had given her. She pardoned them with all her heart. Cinderella and the prince were married and, for her sisters, she set aside apartments in the palace and married them to two fine gentlemen of the court.

"Cinderella"'s two morals mention *grâce*—in its French connotation of innate elegance and graciousness—reinforced by propitious godmothers' upbringing. The importance of godfathers is also emphasized.

J. "RIQUET À LA HOUPPE"

A queen once gave birth to a most misshapen and ugly son. A fairy who was present at the birth consoled the mother by promising that her son would possess great intelligence and that he would be able one day to impart the same degree of intelligence to the one he loved best. His name was Rickey with the Tuft, because of the tuft of hair on his head.

Some years later there were born to a queen in a nearby kingdom two daughters, one very beautiful but stupid, the other intelligent but ugly. She became well-known for her wit and, gradually, became more popular than her beautiful sister. This deeply chagrined the beautiful princess, who went off into the wood one day to bemoan her misfortune. There she met Rickey with the Tuft, who had seen her portrait and was on his way to visit her from his father's kingdom. He proposed to ease her distress by telling her that he had the power of imparting his intelligence to the one he loved best and that she was, indeed, the one he loved best. The only condition was that she should marry him. She would have a year to decide. But she accepted immediately, promising to marry him a year from that day. At once she felt a change come over her and found that she was able to speak brilliantly on many subjects. She engaged in a lengthy argument with Rickey and, holding forth quite well, caused Rickey to fear that he had given her a greater part of his intelligence than he had retained for himself.

At court she amazed all with her newfound wit, overshadowing even her sister, who became quite saddened. Her father found her so intelligent that he consulted her on affairs of state and often held council in her apartments. Many asked for her hand in marriage, and she agreed to consider seriously a man who was extremely powerful, rich, witty, and handsome. To ponder her decision before giving it, she went for a walk in the wood, the very one in which she had met Rickey with the Tuft. There she came upon a kitchen full of cooks and scullions making ready for a great banquet, the marriage feast of Rickey of the Tuft. In a flash the princess remembered that it was a year to the very day since she had promised Rickey with the Tuft to marry him.

Rickey then appeared to claim her hand in marriage, but the princess replied that she had not yet made up her mind. A lively but erudite lovers' discussion ensued, most intelligently stated by both parties. Rickey won over the princess's hand by informing her that the same fairy who had bestowed upon him his wit also gave to the woman of his choice the power to bestow beauty upon the man she loved. The princess agreed to the marriage and instantly Rickey with the Tuft appeared to her as the most handsome, attractive, and graceful man she had ever laid eyes upon. As Rickey with the Tuft had foreseen, the royal marriage took place, as planned, the next day.

Love's "magical" power is once again extolled in the two morals: "Everything is beautiful in the object of our love. / Everyone we love has wit, intelligence, and great spirit."

K. "LE PETIT POUCET"

A woodcutter and his wife had seven children, the littlest of whom was called Tom Thumb, because at birth he was no bigger than a person's thumb. During a bad year of famine, the mother and father decided they could no longer support their children and resolved to lead them into the forest to die. Tom Thumb, who was the cleverest of the seven children, overheard their conversation from under his father's stool. In the morning, he rose early, went to the edge of a brook, and filled his pockets with stones. The mother and father and their seven children arrived the next day deep into the forest and, while the children were busy, the parents abandoned them and ran away home. Tom Thumb led his brothers safely back home by the trail of stones he had left to show the way. The parents, who had received some money meanwhile, were overjoyed beyond words to see their children again.

But when poverty struck a second time, the mother and father once again resolved to lose their children in the forest. Tom Thumb resolved also to get his stones by the brook in the morning but found the door of the house doubly locked. It occurred to him then to use bread crumbs in place of stones. The children were led away again and this time truly did get lost because the trail of bread crumbs which Tom Thumb had left had been eaten by the birds.

In the midst of fierce winds, heavy rain, and the howling of wolves, the children made their way to a house in the forest inhabited by an ogre who loved to eat little children. The ogre's wife took pity on them and decided to hide them from her husband till morning. But the ogre smelled fresh flesh and discovered the children under the bed. He ordered his wife to fatten them up, put them to bed, and he would have them for supper the next day. Pleased with himself, the ogre proceeded to drink a dozen more cups of wine than usual and it went somewhat to his head.

The ogre had seven daughters who had all gone to bed early, each wearing a golden crown on her head. On a separate bed slept Tom Thumb and his brothers. Tom Thumb, fearful that the ogre might change his mind and eat them earlier than expected, took the golden crowns from the heads of the seven daughters and put them on his own and his brothers' heads. Then he took his own and his brothers' sleeping caps and put them on the heads of the ogre's daughters.

The ogre did change his mind and went upstairs to the children's room to cut the throats of Tom Thumb and his brothers; but he cut the throats of his daugh-ters instead. Tom Thumb and his brothers left the house and fled through the forest while the ogre slept. When the ogre discovered his dreadful mistake in the morning, he ordered his wife to fetch his seven-league boots so that he might overtake Tom Thumb and his brothers. In his pursuit, the ogre became weary and fell asleep on the very rock which was hiding Tom Thumb and his brothers. Tom Thumb took off the magical seven-league boots of the ogre and put them on and raced back to the ogre's house, where he tricked the ogre's wife into giving him all that the ogre possessed. Laden with all the ogre's wealth, Tom Thumb repaired to his father's house where he was received with great joy.

Another account—given by Perrault himself as another ending—denies that Tom Thumb committed the theft from the ogre: he went to work in the service of a nearby king, became very wealthy, and returned to his father's house, where he was received with the greatest joy imaginable.

The one moral of seven lines expands on one topic: the hidden talents and the sudden benefits that might accrue to a family from its youngest, shortest, and most unnoticed child.

III. THE CLIMATE OF THE FAIRY TALE

In seventeenth-century France, there was much interest in the allegorical, the mythological, the emblematic, and, of course, the fairy tale. Much evidence survives concerning the telling of fairy tales in courtly circles. Here is an intimate sidelight into the youth of Louis XIV, from Pierre de La Porte, his personal valet since childhood: " . . . I was among the first entrusted with sleeping in the room of his majesty . . . what caused him the most chagrin was that I could not regale him with the telling of fairy tales, which up to now had been told to him before going to sleep by the ladies in charge of him."[3] Just as interesting is this statement about the great minister of state: "Monsieur Colbert, in his leisure hours, invited people to tell him fairy tales, especially stories like that of Donkey-Skin. What a pity that in those days Mesdames d'Aulnoy and Murat [women authors of fairy tales] were not then occupied with their fairies. He would have often received them."[4] Similarly, Mme. de Sévigné, the celebrated letter writer, in a letter to her daughter Madame de Grignan, writes on August 6, 1677: "Mme. de Coulanges [a relative] . . . was kind enough to retell us some of the tales with which ladies at Versailles are entertained . . . she told us of a green island in which a princess, the fairest of all, more beautiful than the day, was growing up; the fairies were showering their favors on her continuously . . . the tale lasts a good hour."[5] The impressive point of these examples is the emphasis on the *oral* telling of fairy tales, before any author, Perrault included, showed any inclination to commit them into print.

According to Gilbert Rouger, "long after his youth Louis XIV was still interested in listening to fairy tales, Versailles had its Mother Goose [teller of tales], wife of a state councillor, Mme. Le Camus de Melsons, a friend of Mlle L'Héritier [niece of Perrault]," who wrote the following lines to praise the woman who could entertain a king: "You whose lifelike tones / Found the way to entertain so many times / With your enchanting tales the most powerful of kings / Inimitable Mme Le Camus."[6] These lines can be dated 1695, through the date of publication of the work in which they appear. In that year, Perrault had already published three stories in verse, of which one was certainly a fairy tale, *Peau d'Ane,* that typical folktale, which he rewrote so delightfully. It was about that fairy tale that La Fontaine, Perrault's model as a writer, had written (in 1675): "If *Donkey-Skin* were told to me / I would enjoy it extremely, / They say the world is old: I believe it; nevertheless / We must still amuse it like a child."[7]

In the immediate vicinity of the king, Fénelon, the appointed teacher of the royal heir, thought of fairy tales in terms of their enjoyment and educational value. For him the animal fable, with its talking animals, and the fairy tale were kindred genres. In this respect there is a meeting of minds between Fénelon, La Fontaine, and Perrault. Fénelon had, in fact, written some twenty-seven stories (many of them fairy tales), around 1690. In that year there appeared the first literary fairy tale in French literature, the tale of "l'Isle de la Félicité" [The Island of Happiness] by Mme d'Aulnoy. The story, a rewriting of a very well known folktale, the "Land Where No One Dies," is to be found inside a novel entitled *Hypolite.*[8]

With all these "signs" of a taste for that peculiar art form, appealing at once to children and adults, partaking of mythology and popular traditions, it would have been surprising if Perrault, throughout his life a man ready to be "in the wind" or "at the scene" of all trends, had not picked up the scent, and had not started to produce his own fairy tales. And he had an imperative incentive, the education of his children, for whom he felt that entertainment and instruction went hand in hand.

IV. PERRAULT, BOILEAU, AND THE FAIRY TALES

In one of his earlier works, the allegorical *Dialogue de l'Amour et de l'Amitié* (1661), Perrault had foreshadowed, by his delicate evocation of the "magical" power of love, the tone and the subject of his fairy tale **"Riquet à la houppe."** Similarly, in his **"Labyrinthe de Versailles,"** he had created a structural anticipation of his fairy tales—little illustrated prose narratives or "fables" accompanied by verse commentaries or morals, some of which are curious foretellings of the morals in the tales. The following lines form a kind of introduction to the **"Labyrinthe"**:

> Any wise man who knowingly enters
> The labyrinthine paths of love
> And wishes to travel through the whole of it,
> Must be cautious and sweet in his language,
> Gallant, clean in his appearance,
> And especially not behave like a wolf.
> Otherwise all the beauties of the fair sex
> Young, old, plain, or fair,
> Blond, brunettes, sweet, cruel
> Would throw themselves on him and
> Would gobble him up like owls.[9]

Another versified statement uses the same rhymes as the moral of the tale of **"Little Red Riding Hood"** to express the same message: "Beware of these sweet-talking young men [*doucereux*], / They are a hundred times more dangerous [*dangereux*]."

Furthermore, Perrault alluded frequently to fairy tales in the text of his *Parallèle.* He felt that the popular but "modern" French fairy tales of Mother Goose were superior to the tales of antiquity, such as those of Apuleius (*The Golden Ass*) and many others. He found that French popular tales were "cleaner" than such stories from antiquity. He reproved their eroticism with his typical "Victorian" prudishness (2:126).

It is obvious that during those years of the writing of the *Parallèle* (1688-1697) his mind was occupied with the fairy tales, as well as with the Quarrel of the Ancients and the Moderns. For a man like Perrault, the hyperboles of Homer referring to Fate having her head in the clouds, or the horses of the gods making gigantic leaps, seemed somewhat more nonsensical than the "modern" imagination of the seven-league boots, which he praises in terms that sound somewhat Cartesian to the modern mind: "There is quite a bit of sense in that invention [of the seven-league boots], for children conceive of these as some kind of big stilts which ogres can use to cross long distances in less than no time" (3:120). Since the third *Parallèle* was published in 1692, this reference to the seven-league boots and ogres, practically the essential themes of **"Le Petit Poucet,"** attests that this story was either known by Perrault or already in manuscript form at that date, fully five years before its publication in the famous collection of 1697. Interestingly enough, Perrault, in the same passage, felt the need to define the term "ogre," as if the expression was not too familiar at that date: "those cruel men, which are called Ogres, who smell fresh meat, and who eat little children. . . ."

But the most suggestive references to fairy tales are those in which Perrault writes of poetry and of the opera as imaginative expressions which partake of the supernatural, like the fairy tales. One of the passages deserves full quotation:

> In an opera, everything must be extraordinary and supernatural. Nothing can be too fabulous in this kind of poetry; the old wives tales, like those of Cupid and Psyche, provide the most beautiful subjects and give more pleasure than the most complicated theater plots. . . . These kinds of fables . . . have a way of delighting all sorts of people, the greatest minds as well as those of the lower classes, the older men and women as well as children: these wonderful fictions, when they are artistically handled, entertain and put to sleep the powers of reason, even though they may be contradictory to it, and they can charm this reasoning mind far more than the most true-to-life works of art.
>
> (3:283)

What Perrault is developing here is an aesthetic theory of the fairy tale. He is stating, adroitly and convincingly, that there is a kind of aesthetic seduction in the enjoyment of the supernatural. He anticipates by three centuries notions that are quite familiar to men of our era. Wish-fulfillment seems to be the name of the game. But he is also stating that verisimilitude has little to do with reality. The fairy tale, even though it may be apparently nonsensical, has its own inner logic. He develops his ideas further when he states that the fairy tale need not be versified to be poetic, just as tragedies need not be written in verse to be tragic. There can be poems or fairy tales in prose, just as there can be tragedies or comedies in prose: "Since comedies written in prose are no less dramatic poems than comedies in verse, why could not the fantastic stories written in prose be poems like those written in verse? Verse is but an ornament in poetry, a great ornament which is not essential" (3:148). All of these references to the art of the fairy tale, or the poetry of the fabulous, once again suggest that Perrault had already begun to write fairy tales. However, the story now becomes murkily delicate:

Perrault, as we have earlier noted, had an enemy in the person of Boileau, who thought that writing fairy tales was ridiculous.

Perrault first published *Griselidis* in 1691. This versified tale is close in tone and style to the sort of story La Fontaine could have written. The versified tale of *Les Souhaits ridicules* [*The Ridiculous Wishes*, 1693], is not very original either; it is but a flat adaptation of a fable La Fontaine had already treated, *Les Souhaits* [*The Wishes*]. The third verse narrative, *Peau d'Ane* (1694), is truly the first fairy tale Perrault ever published. Here we have the whole fairy tale paraphernalia of wonders: an all-powerful fairy godmother, a magical chest which follows Donkey-Skin wherever she goes, and a donkey whose litter is not manure but pure minted gold pieces (not an original invention by Perrault). This extraordinary tale was put on sale by the distinguished bookseller-printer Jérome Coignard at a time when both Perrault and Boileau were not on the best of terms. After the publication of *Peau d'Ane,* Boileau circulated the following satirical poem, which we translate and quote only in part:

> If you want to find the perfect model
> For the most boring of works
> Don't search the Heavens for it. . . .
> At the printer's Coignard, eaten through
> With worms, here is the incomparable
> Poet [Perrault]
> The inimitable author
> Of *Donkey-Skin* versified.[10]

In June, 1694, Boileau wrote to the great theologian Arnauld, who had agreed to mediate the quarrel between the two academicians, scathingly referring to "the tale of Donkey-Skin and the story of the woman with the sausage nose, put into verse by M. Perrault of the French Academy."[11]

It is true that in *The Ridiculous Wishes* the unfortunate peasant wife Fanchon has had wished upon her, magically and unfortunately, a sausage for a nose by her irate husband. To Boileau that kind of popular tale, fable, or fairy tale had no literary value whatsoever. he had not the slightest interest in popular tradition of any kind. The intellectual divorce between his type of mind and that of Perrault was almost absolute.

We can well understand why Perrault felt defensive about publishing his first volume of collected verse tales (1695) with a preface that took pains to explain that fairy tales were "legitimate." The next volume of eight prose tales appeared under the "authorship" of his son, Pierre Perrault d'Armancour, whose initials P. P. (Pierre Perrault) appear both in the manuscript of 1695 and in the first edition of 1697 at the end of the dedicatory letter to Elisabeth Charlotte d'Orleans, Louis XVI's niece. Gilbert Rouger is correct in stressing that Perrault took all possible precautions to ensure that the real author could deny he ever wrote the book.[12] After all, he must have said to himself, "this is child's play, nothing that Boileau could blame on the father. . . ."

V. Who Wrote the Mother Goose Tales of Perrault?

Stated in such terms the question seems absurd. For the answer can only be: "Perrault wrote the tales of Perrault." The question is more subtle: yes, it is Perrault, but which one? The son or the father? While it is understood that the father may have thought it unwise to claim authorship for himself, and thus was glad to pretend that his son was the author, quite a few scholars have discussed seriously the possibility that the son may have been the author. Here is the case for the son.

Mlle L'Héritier, we recall, had printed a dedicatory letter of sorts to Mlle Perrault mentioning the good upbringing which Charles Perrault was bestowing on his children, who were all so intelligent and full of spirit. In that letter she mentioned the "tales which one of his young students has just put down on paper with such successful expression . . . please offer this story to your worthy brother . . . to be added to his pleasant collection of tales."[13] Such a statement seems to indicate clearly that Perrault's son had just written a collection of tales, in 1695, when Mlle L'Héritier's book was published. It may have been the very manuscript which the Pierpont Morgan Library acquired in 1953. However, since this manuscript is the work of a professional scribe, and therefore not in the hand of either the father or the son, we cannot find confirmation of authorship by its existence.

There is, however, another statement, in the story, "Marquise-Marquis de Banneville" (anonymous, *Mercure Galant,* September, 1696) which attributes without equivocation the text of **"Sleeping Beauty"** (published in that same magazine in February, 1696) to the son: "the Author . . . is the son of a Master [Perrault]. . . ." There does not seem to be anything ambiguous in these phrases. And the evidence so clearly points to the son that there seems to be no point in discussing the subject any further. But not all contemporaries were agreed that Pierre was the author, or the sole author.

The following dialogue from a book published in 1699, two years after the appearance in print of Perrault's tales, is suggestive:

> . . . the best tales . . . are those which imitate most closely the style and simplicity of Nurses; and it is precisely for that reason that you seem fairly satisfied with those attributed to the son of a celebrated member of the Academy. . . . [Answers the other interlocutor] . . . one has to be an experienced writer to imitate convincingly their plain ignorance, and that is not anyone's gift; and no matter how much I admire the son of that member of the Academy, I find it hardly believable that the father did not have a hand in the writing of his book.[14]

The words "attributed to the son" seem to imply that at the time there was doubt or discussion about the question of authorship. The last words of the quotation suggest a collaboration; contemporaries found it quite plausible that the tales could have been written by the son, provided the father had helped him. Some critics have gone to great length to try to discern and unravel what might have been written by the father, and what by the son. Sainte-Beuve found the morals disruptive, because their refined and gallant tone differed so strikingly from the tales themselves. The conclusion was that only the father could have written them.[15] According to another critic, the father added many of the little digressions on love, the little parodies of manners, the remarks on feminine psychology, and the descriptions of interiors; other elements of the tales, such as the witty remarks, the love of the countryside, and the simplicity of the style would point to the son.[16]

The authorship question is not a puzzle that is easy to solve; quite a case can be made for the father as the author. Besides, the tales give the impression of an organic whole, a finished work of art, which rather suggests the product of but one mind, or the result of a very harmonious integration of many parts.

The son may well have helped the father, or vice versa. What we do know about the son did not, until recent years, amount to very much: the testimony of his collaboration, the date of birth (1678), and of his death (1700). When he died he was in the army. His death notice mentions that he had been a "lieutenant in the Regiment Dauphin. He was the son of Mr. Perrault . . . of whom we have many very esteemed works of poetry and erudition."[17]

Why was there no mention of the fairy tales in that death notice? The tales had already achieved quite a success, gone through many editions in France and

Holland, and there was quite a vogue for published fairy tales at the time. The case could rest on these last shreds of evidence.

Since the recent publication of hitherto unknown documents from seventeenth-century archives new light has been shed on both the father and the son. We have already mentioned briefly the tragic affair of the involuntary homicide in which Pierre killed a young neighbor with his sword. Who started the quarrel, Pierre or the neighbor? We only know what a friend of Perrault wrote in a letter, "that his youngest son, who is only sixteen or seventeen years old, having drawn his sword against one of his neighbors of the same age, an only son, whom he killed while defending himself."[18]

The young man who was killed was the son of a woman named Marie Fourré, widow Caulle. There were many confrontations and actions in the courts between the father Perrault and the mother of the victim. Finally the affair was more or less settled (the documents available are not quite clear or conclusive) with the payment of an indemnity of two thousand seventy-nine French *livres* ("pounds") on April 15, 1698.

The reader may wonder what all this has to do with the question of authorship of the tales. According to the French critic Marc Soriano, this event had a profound significance in the life of Charles Perrault. He believes Pierre Perrault was a child prodigy, a fact which explains that he could have written the fairy tales. The father and the son became fast friends and collaborators. At this moment of his life the elder man was past the age of sixty-five. In his gifted son he had found an unconscious resonance going all the way back to the circumstances of his twin birth. His son became for him the substance (and no longer the unconscious and repressed shadow) of his long lost brother François who had come into the world a few hours before him and died at six months of age. The happiness of creation in a "twin situation" was then one sunny moment in the life of Charles Perrault. He had practically "fallen in love" with his son (at the time between seventeen and nineteen) whom he unconsciously confused with his lost twin. Suddenly, the "dream" was shattered by this tragic affair of involuntary homicide.[19]

Whether we accept the theory that Pierre Perrault was a child prodigy (or rather at seventeen an adolescent prodigy), or not, there is no doubt that the event must have been very painful, very disappointing for

Charles Perrault. Three hundred years ago, as now, it is a tragic affair for a father to "rescue" a son involved in a homicide.

This twin situation is discovered practically everywhere in the fairy tales and other works of Perrault. Apparently our author was obsessed with the number two. It was part and parcel of his unconscious. It is impossible to discuss the son without being faced with the problems of the father. When all is said and done, the father is more important than anyone in the elaboration of the tales, even if we admit that the son played his part in the initial composition of the work.

There are quite a few contemporary statements pointing to Charles Perrault as the sole author. The Abbé Dubos regularly sent reports about the Paris literary scene to a common friend, the historian-critic Pierre Bayle, then exiled in Holland. The following extracts are in chronological order:

> [September 23, 1696] The publisher [Barbin] is also printing the Tales of Mother Goose by Mr. Perrault. They are trifles with which he did amuse himself in the past in order to entertain his children. . . .

> [March 1, 1697]. . . . Madame Daunoy [d'Aulnoy] is adding a second volume to the tales of Mother Goose of Monsieur Perrault. Our age has become quite childish concerning its taste in books; we need tales, fables, novels, and little stories. . . . Their authors are those who enrich booksellers and which are reprinted in Holland.

> [August 19, 1697]. Monsieur Perrault sends his greetings, but he does not believe you. He says that you are wrong to think that he could believe your kind compliment because he was simple and naive enough to have written fairy tales.[20]

The three previous passages were not intended for publication: they were private letters in which one could feel free to say most anything. From the first one, dated September, 1696, it appears clearly that the Abbé Dubos unequivocally identified the elder Perrault as the author of the tales, almost as if he had just spoken to him and were reporting his own words: " . . . trifles with which he entertained his children. . . ." The second passage again attributes the tales to Charles, a few weeks after they had appeared in print (in January, 1697). As for the third passage, it is even more explicit in reporting the very words of our author: " . . . he does not believe you, . . . because . . . he wrote fairy tales. . . ."

The French word used in the third passage, which we translated by two words "simple and naive," was *bonhomme*. There could well be a touch of humor in the use of that word (practically untranslatable in English); it denoted something like peasantlike simplicity, a certain naive credulity, and perhaps a little dose of senility, depending on the context in which it was used.

In the periodical *Mercure galant* (January, 1697) there is a long passage giving news of Perrault's forthcoming publications, the fourth volume of the **Parallèle,** the first of the **Hommes illustres,** and then, without transition, as if it was understood only too well that Perrault was the author, mention of the story of **"Sleeping Beauty"** (which had been published separately the year before), then the following paragraph concerning the fairy tales.

> . . . a collection of tales which contains seven new ones, with that one [**"Sleeping Beauty"**]. Those who produce that kind of work are usually rather pleased if it is believed that they have invented them. As for him, he insists that one should know that he did nothing else than record them naively the way he heard them told in his childhood. The connoisseurs maintain that they are all the more worthy for that fact and they must be considered as having for authors an infinite number of fathers, mothers, grandmothers, governesses, and great-grandfriends, who for more than a thousand years probably have added of their own, always piling up more agreeable circumstances, which did remain in the narrative, while anything that was not of a good inspiration fell into oblivion. They say that these are all original tales, genuine as old mountains, easy to remember, and whose moral is very clear, the two strongest signs of the goodness of a tale. Be that as if may, I am quite certain that they will greatly entertain you, and that you will find in them all the merits that such trifles can possess. To be found at Barbin's [the bookseller].

No name is mentioned, to be sure; however, who would not think of Charles Perrault? This long commentary on the antiquity of fairy tales is almost a modern definition of folklore, with its insistence on the "informants" as authentic sources. And yet there is this other insistence on the element of elaboration from each individual storyteller. The editor of the magazine could not have written such a passage: the ideas are Perrault's. Like a leitmotiv we find again the insistence on the pedagogical value of fairy tales told by parents, nurses, or relatives—as in the **Parallèle,** as in the preface to the verse tales edition of 1695—and again mention of the valuable morals in the fairy tales, while still maintaining that they are *bagatelles* ("trifles"). Such ideas will be repeated almost verbatim in the dedicatory letter of the 1697

edition. In that edition the issuance of the *privilège* to the son can easily be interpreted as a warning that the father would resent the tales being definitely attributed to him.

For nearly three hundred years scholars have debated the question: "father or son?" In our opinion, it is a vain question that can be answered: "both," but we will never accurately know what proportion each of the collaborators contributed the most. We tend to believe, on the strength of the numerous references in other works which we have already mentioned, that it must have been mostly Perrault. The well-known and respected twentieth-century novelist (and writer of tales) Marcel Aymé wrote an introduction to Perrault's tales in which he favors the father as author. Concerning the son, he writes: "I am not of that opinion. If you ask a boy—like this one certainly must have been—to write a story which he has heard told by his nurse, you will find not naiveté, but preciosities, affected expressions which will spoil the simplicity of the original narrative. I believe that it is more probable that the young Perrault, well trained and well formed by his father, tried to report faithfully. . . ."[21] To this opinion of Marcel Aymé we add our feeling that it must have been the father who revised both the text of the 1695 manuscript and that of the first edition of 1697. A further element of "proof" can be adduced from the death notice of the father. Perrault's obituary in the *Mercure galant* issue of May, 1703, is fairly explicit, although still allusive in implying authorship of the famous work: "The felicitous fiction in which Dawn and the little Day [names of the two children in **"Sleeping Beauty"**] are so ingeniously presented, and which appeared nine or ten years ago, has subsequently brought to birth all the fairy tales which have been published since that time."

Thus, when such an important writer as Perrault dies, the *Mercure galant* editor did state that he was talking about the author of **"Sleeping Beauty"** (and other tales), the author who had inspired the vogue of the fairy tale in the final years of the century. In our next chapter we will again discuss more evidence in favor of Charles Perrault.

Marcel Aymé referred to an oft-quoted passage of Mark Twain concerning the authorship of Shakespeare's plays, a statement which is fully applicable to the problem of authorship of Perrault's tales. In that spirit, we could say that the fairy tales of Perrault are not the work of the Perrault we may believe, but they are still the tales of Perrault, just as

Mark Twain concluded that the theater of Shakespeare is not Shakespeare's, but the work of another author by the same name.[22]

VI. The Sources of Perrault's Tales

The phrase "Mother Goose," is a direct translation of the French *Ma Mère l'Oye*. In designating fairy tales in the seventeenth century, it was common practice to say or write *Contes de Ma Mère l'Oye* [*Tales of Mother Goose*]. Mother Goose came to England—and thus into the English language—through the first translation of Perrault's *Tales* in 1729. The English edition reproduced the archetypal frontispiece of the first French edition of 1697, showing a peasant woman spinning and entertaining a group of three enthralled children sitting by the fireplace. On the wall a placard reads, for the first time in the language of Shakespeare, the translated title, *Mother Goose's Tales*.[23] Through that English translation, Mother Goose was beginning its diffusion outside of France: first German translation, 1746; first Dutch translation, 1747; first Italian translation, 1752; first Russian translation, 1768. Insofar as French editions are concerned, they number somewhere between five hundred and one thousand, and continue to appear regularly. The first American edition appeared in Haverhill, Massachusetts in 1794, followed by that of J. Rivington (1795), a bilingual, luxuriously illustrated edition.[24]

There are stories somewhat similar to those of Perrault which existed in Latin, German, Catalan, Italian, and French literature before 1697. They constitute the tradition of the *Mother Goose Tales* before Perrault.[25]

It is currently assumed that all of Perrault's tales came from folklore or popular tradition, and that all he had to do was to transcribe them from some peasant woman (presumably Mother Goose) and publish them. The usual sources of popular tales are the chapbooks, which the French call *livres de colportage*, or *Bibliothèque bleue*.[26]

Of the eleven stories that Perrault wrote, only one, *Griselidis,* can be found in chapbooks which were published before his stories.[27] Extensive research has not yet produced any other such trace. While it is true that many of these volumes of chapbooks contain Perrault's fairy tales, they are all *subsequent* to the publication of his stories, and are mere reprints of his text.

Even if we do not have earlier texts from popular tradition, we can be reasonably confident that most of the basic elements of what the folklorists call motifs existed long before his renditions of them. A motif is "the smallest element in a tale having a power to persist in tradition. In order to have this power it must have something unusual and striking about it."[28] As we examine these sources or analogues we will become more familiar with Perrault's tales.

Griselidis is not a fairy tale, but he included it in his collection of verse tales, in 1695, along with *Peau d'Ane* and *Les Souhaits ridicules*. *Griselidis* is not at all of Perrault's invention. It is a *nouvelle* (short story with a basis in reality) about a forlorn wife finally rewarded and exalted for her exemplary patience, almost a female Job. Boccaccio was the first to tell the story (*Decameron,* X, 10) in the mid-fourteenth century, to be followed in 1374 by Petrarch who wrote a Latin version, which probably inspired Chaucer's "The Clerk's Tale" in the *Canterbury Tales*. These versions were translated into French, and there were many versions throughout the centuries, eventually many chapbook versions. Thus, "the story of Griselda, abandoned by lettered men, comes down into the petty middle classes, even the lowly people. . . ."[29] Perrault knew Boccaccio's story and he researched other versions of the story before he wrote his own rendition. He carefully "pruned" whatever he did not consider proper in popular versions, for he found that "Griselda had been somewhat soiled [become a bit indecent] through the hands of the people."[30]

The tale of *Peau d'Ane* is also present in popular tradition long before Perrault. One of the essential motifs of this story is the flight of the heroine. She is trying to escape from the incestuous pursuit of her father, eventually hiding from him under the skin of a donkey (hence the name of the tale). Like the expression "Mother Goose Tales," the phrase "Donkey-Skin Stories" (*Contes de Peau d'Ane*) was synonymous with fairy tales. It is quite probable that Perrault knew many of the previous analogues of this story: the episode of Nerones in the anonymous fourteenth-century French novel *Perceforest* in which a princess hides under a goatskin; the "Doralice" story from the Italian Straparola (*Piacevoli Notti,* I, 4) many times translated into French; or "l'Orza" in the Neopolitan Giambattista Basile's *Cunto de li cunti overo Pentamerone* [The Tale of Tales, or Pentamerone, 1634-1636].[31]

Insofar as the last verse tale, *The Ridiculous Wishes,* is concerned, this story of the ill-spent first two wishes only corrected by the third wish reestablishing the initial poverty of the "wisher" goes back to the Middle Ages. It was even present in Oriental tradition.[32]

As we now turn to the more famous prose fairy tales, we can pursue their sources closely and in more detail, as we assume the reader knows most of these stories quite well from his youngest years.

In **"Sleeping Beauty,"** the magical sleep motif is very old. The Greek Epimenides slept for fifty-seven years, and the Seven Sleepers of Ephesus were dormant for two hundred years. And there are many other examples. From Indian mythology comes the story of Surya Bai, whose finger was pricked by an ogre's claw, causing her to fall asleep and be awakened by a king. Similarly, in the *Volsunga Saga,* the German hero Sigurd discovers the Valkyrie Brunhilde asleep, surrounded by a wall of fire, and he frees her. However, Perrault's **"Sleeping Beauty"** seems closer to the following stories: the anonymous fourteenth-century Catalan versified narrative of "Frayre de Joy e Sor de Placer" [Brother of Joy and Sister of Pleasure];[33] the adventure of Troylus and Zellandine in the sixteenth-century novel *Perceforest*; the tale "Sun Moon and Talia" in Basile's *Pentamerone.*

The impressive difference between these stories and that of Perrault consists in his treatment of Sleeping Beauty's discovery by the prince. In each of these previous versions, the enchanted princess is raped during her sleep by her discoverer, becomes pregnant, and only after having delivered one or two of her offspring does she awaken. We find none of this in Perrault. We recall how he had decided that *Griselidis* had become somewhat "soiled" through popular tradition. He would "clean it up" according to the French classical tradition of *bienséances* ("decorum"). And he did the same for **"Sleeping Beauty."** He could not tell such a violent tale to either a courtly audience or a group of children. It is impossible to assume that he was ignorant of the earlier, coarser versions. The censoring, editing, and pen of the author are everywhere present in the *Tales of Mother Goose.*

The next story in the collection, **"Le Petit Chaperon rouge"** ["Little Red Riding Hood"], does seem to come from oral tradition, and we know of no literary version of this narrative before Perrault. Readers will no doubt compare the stark ending of Perrault's version with the happier final fate of the rescued Little Red Riding Hood in the Brothers Grimm's *Rotkäppchen.*

After **"Le Petit chaperon rouge"** comes **"Barbe bleue."** Perhaps Perrault intended the two most fearful stories of his collection to follow one another. We tend to believe that the tale of the cruel husband may well be an original invention of Perrault. However, two elements come from earlier popular tradition: the motif of the forbidden chamber, and the magical key with the indelible spot of blood.

The last five stories of the collection all seem to owe something to earlier literary models. **"Le Chat botté,"** the story of an animal providentially helpful to his master, is present in the tradition of many countries. The closest literary model Perrault may have known is that of the story of "Constantino Fortunato," from Staparola's *Piacevoli Notti.* The absence of the character of the ogre and a few differences in the plot notwithstanding, both stories seem patterned from one another. Basile, in "Gagliuso" (*Pentamerone,* II, 4) also retells **"Le Chat botté,"** with one interesting plot difference at the end of the tale: the cat hurriedly leaves the house of his ungrateful master who wants to kill him. In Perrault, it will be recalled (in the last sentence of the story), the cat sits in the home of the master he helped to become a king, and "hunts mice only for pleasure and not out of necessity."

The story of **"Cendrillon"** ["Cinderella"] has a long tradition that antedates Perrault all the way back to Egyptian antiquity, if we consider the story of Queen Rhodopis losing her slipper as one of the earliest prototypes. Yet the name of the heroine dates from Basile's "Gatta Cenerentola" [The Cat Cinderella] as found in his *Pentamerone* (I, 6). The very word "Cenerentola" already evokes the sound of **"Cendrillon"** and **"Cinderella."** The word has an interesting etymology. It incorporates the two Latin words for "ashes" (*cinis*), and for "carry" or "remove" (*tollere*). Cinderella, sitting close to the ashes in the hearth, is thus the ash carrier or remover. Perrault in his text exploits the idea: when the persecuting sisters refer to Cinderella they call her "Cucendron" (Ash-ass, or Ash-bottom). The first English translation of 1729 also plays upon the analogies: the persecuted heroine is called "Cinder-breech."

The subtitle of the story refers to the celebrated glass slipper. Nonsensical and fragile as it may seem or sound, glass slipper it is in the first edition; and this is what Perrault meant. In the magic realm a glass slipper can certainly be unbreakable. The idea of it is unmistakably Perrault's, like the invention of the elegant boots for his master cat.

The last story of the *Contes,* **"Le Petit Poucet"** is sometimes confused with another tale of a diminutive hero, *Tom Thumbe* (1621). While it is true that this earlier story is close to Perrault's because of that similar motif, there are notable differences in plot and incidents. In particular, the seven-league boots so prominent in Perrault seem to be invented by our author. English and American readers of this book will appreciate that the different tale of *Tom Thumbe* is the only one somewhat close to Perrault's that can be traced with certainty in previous English tradition. Here is the full title of that tale: *The History of Tom Thumbe, the Little, for his Small Stature Surnamed, King Arthur's Dwarfe*.[34]

In **"Les Fées"** [**"The Fairies"**] and **"Riquet à la houppe"** [**"Rickey with the Tuft"**] we have two stories already printed before Perrault by two women authors he knew: his niece, Mlle L'Héritier, and Mlle Bernard. Mlle L'Heritier prefaced her collection of stories, *Oeuvres meslées* (1695), with a letter to Mlle Perrault, the daughter of our author, and offered her a story to be included in the *recueil* ("collection") which her brother Pierre was supposedly writing. That story was not accepted because it was too long, but another one, "Les Enchantements de l'Éloquence" [The Enchantments of Eloquence], although still too long, might have inspired Perrault.[35] It is the same typical fairy tale known to English and American children as that of **"Diamonds and Toads,"** in which the fairies bestow on a civil young girl the gift of uttering a precious stone or flower with every word, and, on a rude girl, the curse of spewing out frogs or serpents. The main difference between the two stories is in their length: one hundred and thirty-one pages for Mlle L'Héritier, a mere eleven pages for Perrault. Here our author proves himself a master of concision.

VII. The Supernatural in Perrault

Perrault wrote fairy tales in which, by definition, supernatural events occur; but this "supernaturalness" is not what is really supernatural. The supernatural in Perrault is the mood evoked by the magic of language. Because he was so influential, and therefore so imitated, much of what we can say about him also applies to many other authors. But we must remember that he was among the very first to articulate the language of the supernatural in literature.

There is a sort of logic of the supernatural: in fairy tales, by convention, the *tragic is abolished*. Thus the miller's son in **"Puss in Boots"** receives the lowest portion of his father's estate; by all odds of normal life, he should be a loser. Yet he comes out a winner against all these adverse odds: a contradiction to the conditions of real life. In **"Hop O' My Thumb,"** a diminutive hero is confronted by the most frightening

situations, yet he will come out on top, save his brothers, and make his parents rich. In **"Cinderella,"** according to the timeless rule of the fairy tale, the poorest girl gets the prince. By our acceptance of the world of the fairy tale we enter a new realm where "wicked" every day reality is considered not only invalid but unjust and therefore immoral. Let our heroes and heroines win all the time. Perrault certainly understood this, as we have already mentioned in our discussion of his preface to the verse tales.

Consequently, no adventure of Perrault resembles those of reality. André Jolles is right to write that the veritable basis of the fairy tale is that in its unfolding "the wonderful is not wonderful but is natural."[36] In legends, which differ from fairy tales, the miracle, in terms of divine intervention, is the agent which makes everything plausible and natural. In the fairy tale the wonderful element, in a similar way, ensures not only its plausibility, but also its verisimilitude, if within a psychological realm of artistic or oneiric make-believe (wherein lies the difference from legends). What we wish is what we believe for the moment, according to the time-honored principle of wishfulfillment. Thus we find it natural that the brothers of Blue Beard's wife arrive just in the nick of time to rescue her from death; similarly, it is only natural that the rags of Cinderella become princely clothes. In a word, it happens because we *expect* it. Anything which happens is not logical if it does not happen through the wonderful agency of the magical.

How Perrault articulates this principle shows that he understands the naturalness expected of the genre. He does not bother to give too many explanations, but those he gives contribute to make the fantastic acceptable in a typically logical and French way. When the whole palace awakens with Sleeping Beauty, *chacun songeait à faire sa charge* (each character was thinking about fulfilling his appointed office), as if everyone—after a hundred years' sleep—was carrying his or her genetic code to do this or that job (perhaps like ants or bees). But how could it be otherwise? The whole world of Sleeping Beauty would collapse like a castle of cards without all the palace's attendants. It is once again poetic suspension of disbelief which carries so strongly our conviction. Strangely enough, even the element of humor, which some critics interpret as a disruption, can also function to increase the convincingness of the narrative. So, "since [the palace officers] were not all in love, they were dying of hunger. . . ." Once again, how could it be otherwise? Significantly, Perrault suppressed a sentence from the first two versions of the story: "it had been quite a long time since they had eaten."

The "reality principle" of Perrault and of the fairy tale in general consists of removing that reality from the world of today, so that it happens "long ago and far away" in a dreamlike realm where we can become children again, and believe anything and everything. We are asked to suspend our own incredulity in accepting the supernatural: a subtle game of aesthetic complicity in which adult and child commune in the pleasure of the irrational made rational or natural. We have seen already how Perrault "rationalized" the invention of the seven-league boots by stating that children conceive of them as "big stilts."[37] He understood that an aesthetic principle was at work: "these well handled chimera [fairy tales] have a way of pleasing. . . ."[38] The realism of many descriptions is one of the facets of his art of the supernatural. For the realistic details of the supernatural adventure help seduce us into believing it. There are many passages in the *Mother Goose Tales* that "root" them in the sociotemporal context of the age of Louis XIV. Time and again critics have noticed a striking resemblance between the palace of Sleeping Beauty and that of the Sun King: courtyards paved with marble, huge halls of mirrors, concerts of violins and oboes, menageries of animals, entourage of officers for the service of the royal family. It seems nothing is missing. The fairy tales of Perrault are complete worlds in themselves.

Yet the actualization of the supernatural is still dependent on other factors, notably the evocation of feelings and the liveliness of dialogues. It is not true that fairy tale heroes are "cold as shadows,"[39] at least in the case of Perrault. Any reader of his **"Sleeping Beauty"** can recall the trembling and admiration of the young prince upon the discovery of his enchanted princess, the fear and horror of Bluebeard's wife, not to say anything of the many moments of sadness throughout practically every story. A particularly felicitous expression of feelings is to be found in **"Cinderella."** After her sisters go to the ball and leave her behind: "She followed them with her eyes as long as she could, and when she had lost sight of them she began to cry. Her godmother who saw her all in tears asked her what was the matter. 'I wish I could, I wish I could.' . . . She was crying so much that she could not finish. Her godmother, who was a fairy, said to her: 'You wish you could go to the Ball, is that it?'"[40] This is a clear evocation of childhood, with warm and tender attention to the speech of a child.

The Cinderella of Perrault is vividly real and different from other Cinderellas, which makes us think that perhaps she was patterned after one of Perrault's children. She leaps out of the page again, when having caught the excitement of the magical game, she says to her godmother: "I'll go and see if there be never a rat in the rattrap, we'll make a coachman out of him."[41] The child playing with her godmother, finally provided with the famous pumpkin carriage, has now become a regal person; yet she had almost gone to the ball in rags: "Yes, but am I to go like this in my ugly clothes?"[42] We do not need to summarize the story; we know how the godmother's wand changed her clothes into royal garments of gold and silver.

What captivates us in this rendition of an immortal story is how suddenly the transformation of the crying waif into a princess was effected: a case of sudden adolescence, or adulthood, for Cinderella did not have the education which had been lavished on her sisters. How did she find time to learn how to dance? The real magic of Cinderella is the magic of growth, not the pumpkin coach. That pumpkin coach, so basic to the story, so well-known, is a pure invention of Perrault—a fact not clearly understood by one of the greatest interpreters of fairy tales, Bruno Bettelheim. He writes ironically: "Perrault's Cinderella, who goes to the ball in a carriage driven by six horses and attended by six footmen—as if the ball would take place at Louis XIV's Versailles."[43] But Bettelheim does not seem to realize that in the France of 1697 it is perfectly normal for a young lady to dream of going to the ball at Louis XIV's court. Indeed, why not? And where else? Critics and psychologists of German background, like Bettelheim, often tend to have an idealized version of the fairy tale as a "pure" folk form that must not be embellished by "literary" elaborations; as if it could be a literary elaboration, even for a peasant girl, to dream of being invited to the royal court.

In any case, the realism of Perrault's tales is rooted in the evocation of the royal surroundings of the period he himself knew, because this is how the drabness of his present day was compensated for in dreams of the splendor with which he had been associated. This dream clothed in reality partakes of the wonderful, just as in dreams or fantasies we need the realistic touches in order to make pass for plausible the odd, the strange, or the supernatural.

To come back to our subject: the evocation of the feelings of fairy tale characters. The feelings of fairy-tale characters correspond to the feelings of readers or listeners first within a given cultural context (France) and then outside of France, provided the tales are successfully transmitted abroad. The dialogues are ways in which characters "come alive" in various ways. Here is fear in Bluebeard: "Why is there blood on this key?" "I do not know at all," replied the poor woman, paler than death. "You do not know at all?" exclaimed Bluebeard; "I know well enough. You did enter the little room! Well, madam, enter you shall—you shall go and take your place among the ladies you have seen there."[44]

Everyone knows the dialogue between Little Red Riding and the wolf, and appreciates its atmosphere of mock-tragedy or mock-drama, with the questions leading, in crescendo levels of expectation, to the dreadful end. However, it is little known that this celebrated dialogue was first printed in Perrault's collection and may well be his own invention, an invention that has become a tradition, the property of the world. That Perrault was aware of the dramatically pleasant impact of this dialogue is obvious from a very interesting marginal note in the manuscript text of **"Little Red Riding Hood."** The note refers to the key words of the wolf's last reply: "It is to eat you with." The marginal note reads: "One says those words in a loud voice to frighten the child as if the wolf was going to eat her."[45] The words of this note should be interpreted as a playful, humorous aside from the adult Perrault himself. Such humor and playful drama is overinterpreted by Marc Soriano who writes that these words are an ethnographical indication.[46] Perhaps, but we prefer to believe that in his family Perrault used to say those words in such tones as a game, just as we remember that our own parents, on telling us this story, would instinctively raise their voices, and then burst out laughing, telling us that "there was no wolf, and it was all a game, a story. . . ."

Notes and References

1. See Harry Velten, "The Influence of Charles Perrault's *Contes de Ma Mère l'Oye* on German Folklore," *Germanic Review* 5 (1930): 4-18.

2. See Mary Elisabeth Storer, *La Mode des contes de fées* (Paris, 1928), for the period 1685-1700. For the period 1700-1790 see Jacques Barchilon, *Le Conte merveilleux français de 1690 à 1790* (Paris, 1975).

3. Pierre de La Porte, *Mémoires* (Paris: Foucault, 1872), p. 411.

4. Ibid., p. 412.

5. Mme. de Sévigné, *Lettres* (Paris: Gallimard, 1955), 2:320.

6. Rouger, *Contes*, p. xxii, n. 5.

7. La Fontaine, *Oeuvres Complètes* (Paris: Gallimard, 1965), "Le Pouvoir des fables," in *Fables*, VII, iv., 128-29.

8. Mme. d'Aulnoy, *Histoire d'Hypolite* (Paris: Sevestre, 1690), pp. 143-81.

9. *Recueil*, p. 239.

10. Nicolas Boileau, "Parodie burlesque de la première Ode de Pindare à la louange de M. P[errault]," in *Oeuvres Complètes* (Paris, 1966), p. 264.

11. Ibid., p. 793.

12. Rouger, *Contes*, p. xxxi.

13. *Oeuvres meslées*, pp. 5-6.

14. Pierre de Villiers, *Entretien sur les contes de fées* (Paris: Collombat, 1699), p. 109.

15. *Nouveaux Lundis* (Paris: Garnier, 1861), 1:296-314.

16. Charles Marty-Laveaux, "Quelle est la véritable part de Charles Perrault dans les contes qui portent son nom?" *Revue d'Histoire Littéraire de la France* 7 (1900): 221-38.

17. *Mercure Galant* (March, 1700), p. 105.

18. Quoted from Yvonne Bezard, *Fonctionnaire maritimes et coloniaux sous Louis XIV* (Paris: Albin-Michel, 1932), p. 200.

19. Soriano, *Contes de Perrault*, pp. 340-64.

20. Emile Gigas, ed., *Choix de la Correspondance inédite de Pierre Bayle, 1670-1706* (Copenhagen: Gad, 1890), pp. 276, 294, 304.

21. *Contes de Perrault*, introduction by Marcel Aymé (Paris, 1964), p. 10.

22. Ibid., p. 8.

23. While it has been established that John Newbery, the celebrated first London publisher and bookseller of children's books, did prepare an edition of nursery rhymes with the title *Mother Goose's Melody, or Sonnets for the Cradle*, no copy of that first issue of 1781 has survived. The earliest extant edition is that of 1791, published in London. It has been published in facsimile, with introduction, by Jacques Barchilon and Henry Pettit, *The Authentic Mother Goose Fairy Tales and Nursery Rhymes* (Denver, 1960).

24. A unique copy of the second American edition of Perrault is at the Houghton Library, Harvard University.

25. The best book on the subject is still Charles Deulin's *Les Contes de Ma Mère l'Oye avant Perrault* (Paris, 1878).

26. See Pierre Brochon, *Le Livre de colportage en France depuis le XVIᵉ siècle* (Paris: Gründ, 1954).

27. Rouger, *Contes,* pp. 11-14.

28. Stith Thompson, *The Folktale* (New York, 1946), p. 145.

29. Rouger, *Contes,* p. 12.

30. Ibid.

31. The standard English edition of Basile is that of Norman Moseley Penzer, *The Pentamerone of Giambattista Basile* (London: Dutton, 1932). The English text is not translated directly from the Neapolitan of Basile, but from the Italian translation of Benedetto Croce.

32. Rouger, *Contes,* pp. 79-80.

33. This story is still not published in its entirety. A partial text published by Paul Meyer appeared in *Romania* 13 (1884): 264-84. A complete edition, based on the extant manuscripts, is being prepared by Professor Ester Zago, Department of French and Italian, University of Colorado.

34. A unique copy of the oldest surviving edition of *Tom Thumb* is at the Pierpont Morgan Library.

35. This story of Mlle L'Héritier is reprinted in Rouger's edition of Perrault's *Contes,* pp. 235-65.

36. André Jolles, *Formes Simples* (Paris, 1972), p. 192. This is a French translation of the original German, *Einfache Formen* (Tübingen, 1930).

37. *Parallèle,* 3:120.

38. Ibid., p. 284.

39. Raymond Christinger, *Le Voyage dans l'imaginaire* (Geneva: Mont Blanc, 1971), p. 134.

40. Rouger, *Contes,* p. 159.

41. Ibid.

42. Ibid., p. 160.

43. *Uses of Enchantment: The Meaning and Importance of Fairy Tales* (New York, 1976), p. 263.

44. Rouger, *Contes,* p. 126.

45. Jacques Barchilon, ed., *Perrault's Tales of Mother Goose: The Dedication Manuscript of 1695* (New York, 1956), 1:133.

46. Soriano, *Contes de Perrault,* p. 153.

Jacques Barchilon and Peter Flinders (essay date 1981)

SOURCE: Barchilon, Jacques, and Peter Flinders. "Formal and Nonformal Elements in the Fairy Tales." In *Charles Perrault,* pp. 101-26. Boston, Mass.: Twayne Publishers, 1981.

[*In the following essay, Barchilon and Flinders explore stylistic elements of Perrault's fairy tales and comment that, "Were Perrault alive now he would probably be simultaneously pleased and surprised to read all of the criticism and thought lavished upon stories which he did not even clearly acknowledge as his own."*]

I. OF STYLE AND SUBSTANCE

Nothing is more difficult to define than style. We can use the following workable definition: a writer's choice and use of words in a definite sociocultural context in order to express his intent. Opinions concerning Perrault's style are contradictory: he is either "one of the greatest writers of the seventeenth century,"[1] a statement we fully endorse, or he is the collector of popular stories told in plain language by plain people,[2] a mere transcriber, not a creator.

The contradiction we have just sketched seems inescapable and we shall attempt to resolve it as best we can. In this chapter we will compare the manuscript and the final printed text of the tales, show how computer-aided analysis of Perrault's vocabulary has yielded interesting results; attempt to show how characteristic Perrault's style can be; and how his particular genius was translated into the English language. In the remainder of the chapter we will consider such aspects of Perrault's tales as their connection with folklore, and, finally, their profound moral and psychological significance. Were Perrault alive now he would probably be simultaneously pleased and surprised to read all of the criticism and thought lavished upon stories which he did not even clearly acknowledge as his own.

II. THE MANUSCRIPT AND THE FINAL TEXT OF THE MOTHER GOOSE TALES

The comparison between a manuscript and its final printed text is no mere inconsequential trifle of scholarly fussiness. It can be a fascinating exercise in precision and an invaluable key to the inner mind of a writer as he wrote and revised his work. For well-known and influential texts, such as *Alice in Wonderland* and Perrault's stories, this exercise can be both revealing and entertaining.

All of Perrault's corrections show a stylist at work, aware of the significance of the right word in the right place. This is obvious from the very first pages, those of the dedicatory letter. This letter was important for the career of Perrault's son, Pierre, who was nineteen years old at the time. The dedication of a book to a royal personage by the son of an academician is not without ulterior motive, for "Mademoiselle" could, in return for a flattering one, bestow some important official favor on the young man. Luxurious leather binding decorated with the royal arms of the house of Orléans, careful scribal handwriting throughout, and especially beautifully colored gouache illustrations make this "publication" unusually rich.

As we glance at both texts—the manuscript and the printed text in the first edition—we find differences of vocabulary which suggest rewriting by the more experienced father. Thus in the manuscript dedicatory letter we read that these stories reveal a very sensible moral "for those who listen to them." In the printed text we find the same words with only one exception: "those who *read* them." This is indeed the passage from the "oral text" to literature, the realm of reading. A few other additions elaborate on the personality of Mademoiselle, which could only have been thought of by Perrault—the father, an accomplished courtier—and not by his young son. While the manuscript simply praises Mademoiselle for a mind "which has the power to rise to great things and to stoop to small ones," the first edition adds another sentence: "one will not be surprised if the same princess, whom nature and education have familiarized with the loftiest subjects, should deign to find pleasure in trifles such as these [fairy tales]."[3]

In both **"Barbe Bleue"** and **"Le Chat botté"** we find additions to the manuscript text which again show the hand of a stylist at work. Everyone knows the passage in which the unfortunate wife finds the bodies of women killed by her husband when she opens the forbidden chamber. The manuscript simply tells us of "several dead women standing up and attached along the walls. She almost fainted with terror."[4] The printed text is much more explicit: "dead women hanging along the walls. (They were all the previous women which Bluebeard had married be-

fore and whose throats he had cut one after the other.) She nearly fainted with terror."[5]

Time and again we find more of those finishing touches. In **"Le Petit Chaperon rouge"** the young child is described as unaware "that it is not good to stop and listen to a wolf," but the final printed version reads: "she did not know that it is dangerous to stop and listen to a wolf."[6] The addition of "dangerous" reasserts the meaning much more effectively and contributes to the familiar suspense we ourselves may well remember from childhood.

A number of additions bring out humorous or gently satirical "pokes" at the characters. At the end of **"Le Chat botté,"** although we are first told simply that the king's daughter "fell in love" with the handsome miller's son, we now find in the printed text: "the daughter of the king found him quite handsome and agreeable, and the count of Carabas only had to glance at her two or three times in a respectful and somewhat tender way to cause her to fall in love madly."[7]

Thanks to the manuscript, it is possible to observe the technique of Perrault at close range. Every generation has experienced a feeling of direct communication in reading or hearing the tales. They seem to have been always with us, as if we had dreamed them into existence. These stories, however, are the result of a writer's careful craftsmanship.

III. Of the Computer and Mother Goose

The computer is one of the most modern techniques that can be used by critics for vocabulary analysis. The first thing that must be said is that the computer is essentially an adding machine that sorts out and counts words in a prodigiously rapid way, but it does *not* think. Man must do the thinking and evaluate the results "printed out" by the computer. A question lurks in the mind of every scholar attempting a statistical evaluation by computer: "Will I ever find the word or words most frequently used by this author? Will this or that expression finally reveal or betray his or her secret obsession?"

It would be gratifying for us to say that we have found the secret obsessions of Perrault through the statistical analysis of his vocabulary. But the simple truth is that we are not sure that whatever revelations there are will be of a spectacular nature. However, some statistical findings from our computer-aided research are suggestive.[8]

While the total number of words used to write the eight prose tales is 18,320, the corresponding total for the three verse tales is 14,100. In *proportional* terms it would seem that for only three verse tales does Perrault's vocabulary seem quite as rich as that of the eight prose tales. In terms of different alphabetized vocabulary entries—what in computer jargon is called "word-types"—Perrault's prose language amounts to 2,676 headings, against 2,611 headings for the poetic entries. In other words, Perrault's vocabulary for prose comprises sixty-five more words than were used for poetry.

As we compare these statistics with those available for Perrault's contemporary, Racine, we find that the author of *Phèdre* and eleven other plays needed a total of five thousand words. Perrault's vocabulary—considering his much more modest output of only eleven tales—is roughly one half that of either Racine or Corneille. If we compare Perrault's poetic vocabulary to that of La Fontaine—a more logical choice for comparison than Racine—we find that Perrault's total of different terms (2,611) is once again roughly one half of the 6,354 words of the celebrated French writer of the *Fables.*[9]

Perrault's language, like that of La Fontaine, Corneille, Racine, or Molière, is striking in its economy of words, once again, classical. But the vocabulary of fairy tales—imaginative as it may be—cannot quite compare with that of tragedies written in verse form. What we can, and must, say is that the vocabulary of Perrault is not overly rich, like that of his fellow writers of the age of Louis XIV.

Now what about the frequencies and the obsessions? Let us first state that in all languages the most frequently used words are the "tool words"—"of," "to," "at," "he," "she," "that," "what"—which are necessary to construct sentences and which we give here in their English garb. The enormous frequency of these words does not in itself prove anything. The frequencies we are seeking are those of other words.

Some interesting conglomerations or constellations of frequencies of substantive words struck us. These we print in parentheses after each item in English and in French. The words "king," *roi* (69), "princess," *princesse* (53), "beautiful," *belle* (34), "queen," *reine* (34), certainly suggest an aristocratic climate. The fairy tale almost always evokes the life of those "happy few" at the top of the social scale of the Old Regime before the French Revolution. There is nothing "abnormal" in this finding of the computer: after all, why should the lower classes not dream of the life of kings and queens? The dream of the fairy tale is the dream of the higher social order of wealth and power where everything is possible. The concordance reveals that family words are rather frequent: "children," *enfants* (46), "mother," *mère* (30), "sister," *soeur* (32), "father," *père* (22), "brother," *frère* (20); one could consider as family-related two additional entries: "woman," *femme* (56) and "little," *petit* (53).

The constellations of frequencies in the verse tales are also interesting. The words "prince" (51), "love," *amour* (30), "heart," *coeur* (27), "day," *jour* (26), "young," *jeune* (21), "beautiful," *beau* (19), "sky" or "heaven," *ciel* (19), "spouse," *époux* (19), "time," *temps* (19), "all," *toute* (19), "at last" or "finally," *enfin* (18), "great" or "tall," *grand* (17), "gold," *or* (17), "eyes," *yeux* (17), "to speak," *dire* (16), "king," *roi* (16), "lord," *seigneur* (16), "beautiful," *belle* (15), "pain," *peine* (15) seem to suggest or hum some kind of poetic phrase or some passionate aria from a familiar opera.

Similarly, the verbs most frequently used in the prose tales can be suggestive. The forms "had" or "had been," *avait* (150), "was" or "there was," *était* (157), "he went" or "she went," *alla* (42), "they went," *allèrent* (20) can only suggest two ideas: first, the emphasis on the *past* tense, and second, the emphasis on *movement,* through the use of the verb *aller* ("to go") conjugated in so many forms.

The computer is a tool of research to be used judiciously. Overly anxious about the possibilities of spectacular revelations through a "scientific" method of investigation, a scholar might in his maze of figures and statistics miss the forest while looking for the lone tree. Insofar as we are concerned, we are glad that the statistically revealed vocabulary of Perrault has proved to be so basically simple. Were Perrault alive right now, and looking at our computer printout of his vocabulary, he might well agree with our observations. He would not be surprised to learn that his fairy tales tell of adventures of kings, queens, princes, and princesses, families of parents and children as they happened long ago in a fast-paced world filled with characters often on the run.

IV. A Sense of Classical Style

All the features commonly associated with French classicism are present in Perrault's stories: concision, precision, economy of words, and multifaceted and powerful suggestiveness. What we praise in Pascal, Racine, La Fontaine, or La Bruyère is also present in Perrault's most famous work. Nearly everything he wrote in prose during the last ten most productive years of his life tends toward concision and simplicity.

While he was publishing the fairy tales, he was also putting to press his *Hommes illustres* (discussed above in chapter 3), in which he was summarizing in neat, elegantly penned notices of one or two pages the lives and works of a hundred distinguished Frenchmen of his age. That style is also present with its often concise sense of efficient formulation in the *Parallèle,* in the *Mémoire de ma vie,* and in the **"Pensées chrétiennes."** All these works have a stylistic kinship with the *Contes.*

As we turn to the tales we notice how rarely they are encumbered by too many details or descriptions. We often find a tendency toward condensation and concision, especially when we find two states of a given text. In **"La Belle au bois dormant"** Perrault deliberately eliminated the dialogues and digressions so apparent in the first text of 1695 (published in the *Mercure Galant*). While in the first (*Mercure* edition) there are two pages of conversation between Sleeping Beauty and her prince after he discovered her, we have nothing in the final text save this transition: "They had been talking for four hours and yet they had not succeeded in uttering one half of the things they had to say to each other. Meanwhile the whole palace had awakened."[10] The two pages of dialogue suppressed were printed in the first version between the words "each other" and "Meanwhile the whole palace." We surmise that very few readers ever felt they "missed" the suppressed dialogue upon reading in French or in English the story of **"Sleeping Beauty."**

And we do find numerous remarks on style in the *Parallèle*; the following, in particular, we consider rather suggestive because of its analogy between literature and architecture: "It is true that, on the one hand, architects dishonor their buildings by a grand abundance of superfluous ornaments; it is the same in eloquence [literature] where an excess of brilliant turns of phrase and excessive affectation will mar its grandeur and majesty (2:165).

Let us glance back at the statement just quoted from the *Parallèle*: "mar the grandeur and majesty. . . ." What has this to do with the style of fairy tales? Simply the notion that a certain sense of grandeur, pomp and circumstance, formalness, logic, and appropriateness reigned supreme in the minds of Perrault and his contemporaries. There was a sense of style in everything they did and thought. It was then, as it is still now, a dominant cultural trait of the French. So much so that one English critic even wrote a book called *The Formal French*,[11] in which the bulk of his

examples come from the age of Louis XIV. A beautiful, and today very relevant, example of this preoccupation with form and logic is Arnauld and Nicole's *Logique ou l'Art de penser,* which ran through five editions in three years. It was read and admired by Perrault, and, we believe, echoed with unconsciously harmonic resonances. When we read in the *Logique* this example illustrating a syllogism:

Divine law orders men to honor kings:

Louis XIV is King;

Divine law therefore orders us to honor Louis XIV,[12]

we cannot help thinking that this is precisely the kind of example Perrault would have thought of to illustrate a syllogism in "modern" terms. To our twentieth-century eyes this example for a syllogism might seem jarring. It is probably superfluous to state that it did not *then* seem jarring but natural: it was part and parcel of the divine and secular world view taken for granted in which logic, grammar, style, and belief were much more "integrated" than our own beliefs and our own much more complex institutions.

The connections all this has with the fairy stories is their inner logic and coherence. We must not forget that Perrault was trained as a lawyer, as May Hill Arbuthnot justly reminds us. It means that the stories were written with "outstanding logic without any loose ends unaccounted for, with every detail worked out to completion with legal precision . . . the kind of work one would expect from a legal mind."[13] The endings of some of the tales are good examples. In **"Bluebeard"** we are informed that the deceased husband had no heir, and thus his wife inherited his castle and his wealth. Perrault then explains that she used one share of the inheritance to enable her sister to get married to a nobleman who had been in love with her for many years, another share to purchase officers' commissions for her two brothers, and the last share, or "the remainder"—to use Perrault's expression—she used to get married, that is, we assume, to locate a husband in order to join her wealth with his, as was the custom of the bourgeoisie of those days. The endings of **"Le Chat botté," "Cendrillon,"** and **"Le Petit Poucet"** also have the same legalistic precision. Such carefully thought endings point obviously to the mature mind of the sexagenarian father Perrault, rather than to that of the seventeen-year-old son Pierre as the author of the stories.

For Perrault, anything which is not necessary to the action or movement of the story should be cut out. He expressed this clearly in this striking statement:

"one must compose as a painter and finish as a sculptor, that is to say, when one writes, first jot down many ideas on paper and then finish up by removing as much as possible. I sketch as a painter and I finish as a sculptor."[14] The best "show" of Perrault's mind at work is the comparison between the first and final state of **"La Belle au bois dormant."** This process of condensation or concision often results in a style full of understatements, ellipsis, and wit.

Such characteristics link his style with that of other classical authors of his age, particularly La Fontaine, Racine, and Pascal. The resemblance with La Fontaine has often been noted. One could say that Perrault's three first tales in verse sound like works of La Fontaine. In *Les Souhaits ridicules* we find the suggestion that the "magical" misfortune of the peasant's wife, who could not talk very easily because she was afflicted with a long sausage welded to her nose, can be a boon to her husband who thought her too talkative anyway. All these ideas are expressed by us, but only inferred by Perrault.

> Cet ornement en cette place
> Ne faisait pas bon effet;
> Si ce n'est qu'en pendant sur le bas du visage
> Il l'empêchait de parler aisément,
> Pour un Epoux merveilleux avantage.[15]
> This decoration in such a spot
> Did not look very good;
> And in hanging in front of her mouth
> Prevented her from talking very easily,
> For a husband what a wonderful boon.

It is in the last two lines that we find a significant ellipsis, because the sentence would be more grammatically correct if it were stated thus: "prevented her from talking easily / Which for a husband is a wonderful boon."

This is the time, once again, to say: "Brevity is the soul of wit." Our explanation is already too long. In our translation of Perrault's key line, we should have left out the word "what" and the line should have read: "For a husband a wonderful boon." Poetry is a language in which affect is elicited by a mysterious relationship between context, meaning, and sound. And when it is felicitous, poetry, whether in verse or in prose, is characterized by its concinnity. That harmony between the parts, that melody of sound and meaning, that inner coherence of the work of art— such is the definition of concinnity. Not a word could be suppressed from the narratives we know as **"Little Red Riding Hood," "Puss in Boots," "Cinderella,"** or **"Hop O' My Thumb."** Who could, who would dare change the perfect dialogue between the wolf

and Red Riding Hood? Marcel Aymé, in his introduction to Perrault's **Contes,** is certainly right in writing that he would shudder at the thought of what **"Bluebeard"** or **"Puss in Boots"** might have become at the hands of either Boileau or a twentieth-century "arranger" or "adaptator."

V. PERRAULT IN ENGLISH

The stories of Perrault came into the English language, we recall, with the 1729 translation of Robert Samber. There will be no attempt here to repeat what has been said in other publications concerning that little known edition.[16] In the text we will look for the ways in which the first translator dealt with a material which was first very new, from across the Channel (or across the Atlantic), but then became very familiar.

The first English translation has something debonair and attractive about it: the print is large and clear and the illustrations of the original French edition are carefully reproduced; the text is prefaced by an interesting letter of dedication to the countess of Granville, which may well be the first criticism in English of Perrault's tales. A crucial passage deserves to be quoted in its entirety:

> The Author of the following stories has happily succeeded . . . and perhaps nothing yet extant can equal them in their admirable Design and Execution. It was however observed that some of them were very low and childish, especially the first, Little Red Riding Hood. It is very true, and therein consists their Excellency. They therefore who made this an Objection, did not seem very well to understand what they said; they should have reflected that they are designed for Children; and yet the Author hath so ingeniously and masterly contrived them, that they insensibly grow up, gradually one after another, in Strength and Beauty, both as to their Narration and Moral, and are told with such a Naiveté, and natural innocent Simplicity, that not only Children, but those of Maturity, will also find in them uncommon Pleasure and Delight.[17]

In this statement we encounter, for the first time, praise for the "admirable Design and Execution" of the fairy tales. The way in which Perrault had "contrived" them, however, does not correspond to Perrault's original order of publication. The first story of the original manuscript and first edition was **"Sleeping Beauty,"** not **"Little Red Riding Hood."** The sequence followed is that of the French edition of 1721, and the practice was often adopted in subsequent reprints, probably in order to suggest a sort of gradation. **"Little Red Riding Hood"** must have seemed the most childish tale, followed by **"The Fairies," "Bluebeard," "Sleeping Beauty,"** and **"Puss in Boots"**; afterward, the last three tales follow in the original order.

Samber ends his dedicatory letter with a witty criticism of English "Fabulists" who wrote for children at the time, the better to extol, by implied contrast, the virtues of Perrault: "they content themselves in venting some poor insipid trifling Tale in a little tingling jingle, adding some pretty Witticisms, or insignificant useless Reflection, which they call a Moral, and think they have done the Business."[18] What he found in Perrault's text must have seemed to him the kind of narratives which adults and children of England had needed, as he wrote: "Strength and Beauty . . . uncommon Pleasure and Delight.[19]

As we read the English text we find amusing renditions of the original French. In **"Little Red Riding Hood"** the cakes of Perrault become custard pie, the woodcutters (*bûcherons*) become faggot-makers, and instead of using the expression "knock-knock at the door," Samber reproduces the French words used by Perrault: "Toc Toc." Whatever may have been his reasons for thus changing the text, the translator cannot be blamed for not using the word "woodcutter," which seems not only the most natural word to use, but also the most accurate translation: "woodcutter" probably did not then exist in the English language. Its first recorded use dates from 1774, in the *Pennsylvania Gazette*. In truth the word is an Americanism. In most English or American editions published since the beginning of the nineteenth century, the word "woodcutter" is used.

Other differences from the French text fall into three categories: they are either obvious mistakes in translation, examples of picturesque speech, or expressions of eighteenth-century English. Some mistakes are interesting. To translate the expression "elle ne se sentait pas de joie" (referring to Cinderella)—which means she was beside herself with joy—Samber wrote: "she appeared indifferent."[20] Most mistranslations are not worth signaling, but an extraordinary one occurs in **"Bluebeard"** and refers to the terrifying moment when the unfortunate woman discovers the bodies of the previous wives. The passage in Samber's text reads: " . . . after some moments she began to observe that the floor was all covered over with clotted blood, on *which lay the bodies of several dead women ranged against the walls*"[21] (our italics). Obviously the dead women could not at the same time "lay" on the floor and be "ranged" against the wall. This logical impossibility is the result of a careless translation. What the French text says is that the floor was covered with clotted blood in which were reflected (*se miraient*) the bodies of several women attached (or hanging) along the walls. The bizarre translation quoted above was reproduced in the first American edition (1794) and thus proves that the American publisher simply reprinted Samber's translation.

Some samples of picturesque speech, even footnotes to the translation by the translator, are significant. The wolf in **"Little Red Riding Hood,"** "compère le Loup," becomes "Gossop Wolf," which is more accurate—a term certainly closer to the French meaning of the text than "Father Wolf," which we find in a 1912 English and American edition; it is certainly a more suggestive translation. In **"Bluebeard"** there is an oddly colloquial and modern question: "How comes this blood upon the key?"[22] In the same tale, we find it quaint that the wife and her sister address each other with the archaic "thee" and "thou." The famous question—"Anne, ma soeur Anne, ne vois-tu rien venir?"—concerning the hoped-for arrival of the rescuing brothers, becomes: "Anne, sister Anne, dost thou see nothing coming?"[23]

In **"Sleeping Beauty"** and **"Cinderella,"** the two tales which contain so many realistic details, the translator was at a loss to find expressions which would correspond to the original French and therefore nicely anglicized his text. The enchanted palace is guarded by Beefeaters and not by the traditional *Suisses,* the mercenary soldiers used by French kings for their personal protection. What we traditionally recognize as the famous "Hall of Mirrors," or the "Galerie des Glaces," then not too familiar in England, becomes the "Hall of looking glasses." There were occasions when the translator had to give explanations concerning items probably not yet familiar to his English readers. In 1729 this statement was added to the original text: "Now an Ogre is a giant that has long teeth and claws, with a raw head and bloody bones, that runs away with naughty little boys and girls and eats them up."[24] Probably the most amusing extrapolation is a culinary note—the recipe for *Sauce Robert*—which the wicked mother-in-law orders for her dinner of Sleeping Beauty's daughter, Dawn (served as a royal stew): "*Sauce Robert* is a French sauce, made with minced onions, and boiled tender in butter, to which is added vinegar, mustard, salt, pepper, and a little wine."[25] A few translations stand out like commentaries on the text of Perrault and with one more quote—without by any means having exhausted the subject—we will end our treatment of the first appearance of Perrault in English. After Sleeping Beauty and her prince charming were married—a few hours after her awakening—they went to bed. The French text simply says that "they slept little, the princess had no great need of it."[26] The manifest meaning of the language used is clear: she did not sleep much, because she had slept already for one hundred years. The English translation, however, is more Gallic than the original, in that it suggests a latent or erotic meaning: "they slept very little; the Princess *had no occasion*"[27] (our italics).

If we have dwelt at length on this first translation, it is because we know that what we are discussing is largely unfamiliar to the majority of our readers; our main intent is to show that there was a beginning to the tradition of Sleeping Beauty and Cinderella in the English language: it started with a literary translation of Perrault. What happened afterward in England and in the United States is a story of constant change and adaptation, including bowdlerized versions—theater performances and film adaptations at all levels—adult or "childish." In this respect we should mention the Walt Disney film versions of **"Cinderella"** and **"Sleeping Beauty,"** which have achieved world-wide diffusion without any acknowledgment of Perrault's authorship. In France the 1967 Jacques Demy film adaptation of **Peau d'Ane** with Jean Marais and Catherine Deneuve has been a great success.

Among the many translations which have appeared in this century, four stand out. The first is that of A. E. Johnson (1912), which has had a widespread "revival"[28] through the attractive reprint (1969) reproducing the large, beautiful, and suggestive illustrations of Gustave Doré, which first appeared in 1867. The second translation of note, partial though it is—only **"Puss in Boots," "Sleeping Beauty"** and **"Cinderella"**—is the work of the American poet Marianne Moore.[29] The quality of her translation is such that it lends plausibility even to her mistakes. She confuses the verb *plaire* ("to please") with the verb *pleurer* ("to weep"), with the interesting result that Sleeping Beauty and her prince "shed some tears" (after all, why not?), while all Perrault wrote was that the words of the prince-discoverer pleased (*plurent*) his paramour. This error is also present in the 1729 translation, and Marianne Moore may have made use of it. In general her text is imaginative and poetic: an "American" flavor pervades her versions. A magistrate becomes a "man with a great seal," and Puss wears his boots "like a general."

The translation of the English scholar of French literature, Geoffrey Brereton,[30] is certainly the most accurate. At least there are no mistakes due to his misunderstanding of the French language. The morals are also included; they were omitted in the Marianne Moore translation.

But the best and probably most *complete* translation of Perrault is that of Anne Carter,[31] who included the three verse tales. Her text is at least as careful as that of Geoffrey Brereton, and it is a pleasure to read Perrault's **Donkey-Skin** and **Griselda** in English. The illustrations are pleasant, but at times erroneous: Cinderella was not driven to the court ball in a carriage driven by *mice*.

The bibliography of translations of very popular works is not the kind of work frequently undertaken by literary scholars. However, for two stories of Perrault, **"Puss in Boots"** and **"Cinderella,"** the bibliographical information can be found in the works of Denise Escarpit[32] and Anna Birgitta Rooth.[33] These books tell a tale of wide diffusion since the eighteenth century. Literature and popular traditions intermingle throughout the centuries.

VI. PERRAULT'S TALES AND FOLKLORE AND LITERATURE

One of the most common misconceptions about fairy tales is that the majority of them are folktales, merely collected from oral traditions and rarely the work of authors. It is true that many fairy tales are also folktales with a long oral history: there is quite a flowering of fairy tales in Russia where they, as well as folktales, are still told and read today. This is apparently also the situation in French Canada. There is a lively oral tradition in both countries.

The narratives of Perrault have been so enormously popular in the English language that they have become accepted as native English stories, perhaps replacing similar ones in oral tradition. We do not, however, have examples of Perrault's tales in either English or French popular tradition recorded *before* the publication of Perrault's **Contes de Ma Mère l'Oye.** We could—for a moment—accept the notion that he simply jotted tales down upon hearing some peasant woman telling the stories to his children. In that case we would agree with Iona and Peter Opie that: "If only it had occurred to him to state where he had obtained each tale, and when, and under what circumstances, he would today probably be revered as the father of folklore."[34] It is not Perrault who is revered as the father of folklore today but Jacob and

Wilhelm Grimm who published their *Kinder und Hausmärchen* [*Household Stories*] in 1812-1815. They had bothered to state their "where and when and under what circumstances," even though they did not transcribe faithfully what they collected, but "improved" the style of folk informants.[35]

Perrault was, nevertheless, quite conscious of popular tradition. He referred to the success and wide distribution of chapbooks published in Troyes in the preface of his *Apologie des femmes*. In the *Correspondance* of the exiled Protestant writer Pierre Bayle, there is an interesting letter of the Abbé Jean-Baptiste Dubos concerning Perrault's research for *Griselidis*. He had read Boccaccio's version of the story (but apparently not that of Chaucer), and he also knew chapbook versions of *Griselidis*.[36] He mentions these as being printed on *papier bleu* ("blue paper"), the traditional color for chapbooks until the French Revolution. He was conscious of the tradition of the story before him, but we must not think of him in terms of a twentieth-century folklorist anxious to recapture the "soul" of the people. His chief source was Boccaccio, and not any specific folklore version. As was the custom of the time, he used the text of Boccaccio as a source of inspiration, and he wrote freely. One major difference of treatment in Perrault's text is that the daughter of Griselidis has a fiancé—a new character not found in Boccaccio.

For the other tales, notably the famous prose tales, Perrault has provided posterity with a long acknowledgment of his "popular" sources. The salient points of that statement were: the insistence of having "recorded naively [stories] the way he had heard them told in his childhood," the antiquity of the tales, and their moral value. Very few scholars have disputed that Perrault did not tell anything but the truth in these affirmations. It is possible, however, that such a statement reflects more a literary convention than it does the truth about the folk origin of the Mother Goose tales. Three hundred years ago nobody would readily admit authorship of children's stories such as fairy tales. They had to come, therefore, from some "infinite number of fathers, mothers, grandmothers, governesses and greatgrandfriends . . ." (Perrault's own words in the *Mercure Galant,* January 1697). Perrault, however, had also admitted having written these fairy tales in order to amuse his children.

The contradictory assumption—whether Perrault was the recorder of the tales or the writer of the tales—need not be defended: Perrault is both. There is no reason why he could not have used material from popular tradition—indeed, also from literary tradition before him—but he made all this material his own. Two examples from the realm of music will perhaps clarify this argument. Were not Chopin and Bartok inspired by Polish and Hungarian folksongs? And yet, all we know is their music, and there is a chance that the original folksongs they used as sources of inspiration may have become completely lost or forgotten. What we have is their music. And what we have are Perrault's stories.

Perrault's tales were so often reprinted and translated that they became very well-known not only in France but in the rest of Europe as well, and exerted a great influence on oral tradition. When the Grimm Brothers began gathering their German folktales for the publication of their famous collection, they found examples of all of the stories of Perrault in the German language. Some stories even had titles which were close translations from the French, such as "Rotkäppchen" [Red Riding Hood], "Blaubart" [Bluebeard], or "Aschenputtel" [Cinderella]. In the case of "Blaubart," the Brothers Grimm must have felt somewhat disturbed. The story, which was in fact printed in the first edition of 1812, disappears from all subsequent editions. That version of **"Bluebeard"** was in all respects similar to that of Perrault. According to Gilbert Rouger, "fearing that [it] could be nothing but a mere translation of Perrault's tale, they removed it"[37] and used another similar story of German origin, "Fitschers Vogel."

Thus, even in stories collected from German oral tradition, a story of Perrault's literary text reappears almost verbatim. There could be no clearer example of the influence, or diffusion, of a literary text into the stream of oral tradition. What happened was that the stories of Perrault were told *in French* and retold by French governesses entrusted with the education of German children during the eighteenth century, a period during which practically all Europe was affecting French manners and worshiping French culture and institutions. The diffusion of Perrault's tales in Germany has been well documented in the article of Harry Velten.[38] What is true of German tradition is even truer of English and American tradition, in which the stories of Perrault have achieved universal recognition while Perrault as their author is not very well known. Everyone has heard of **"Sleeping Beauty"** and **"Cinderella,"** but who has heard of Perrault?

After the Brothers Grimm passed on, the science of folklore continued to flourish, culminating in the monumental *Motif-Index of Folk-Literature*,[39] in which the very titles of Perrault's tales were found to be so universal that they reappear as subtitles in the basic folklore nomenclature. The oral stories collected by folklorists in this and the last century still reflect the influence of Perrault. Specialists of folklore have fully acknowledged the importance of Perrault in this respect: "Largely because of the influence of Perrault's collection of fairy tales, one of the best known of all stories of helpful animals is **"Puss in Boots"**. . . . Perrault's French version . . . has been of primary influence on the traditions of this tale."[40] Another authority on folklore goes even further: "Perrault's version . . . has been taken as *the* version almost everywhere and has altered the detail of the older folk form everywhere that it has penetrated."[41]

The simple truth about Perrault is not that he was a collector of folklore material: he was a great inventor and artist, certainly inspired by popular tradition, but above all one of the greatest influences on the folklore of the western world. His contribution has resulted in the crystallization of a few images and types that have for some reason stuck in our "collective" imagination. The mention of Cinderella immediately elicits a few images: the persecuted stepchild, the kitchen maid, the fairy godmother, the ball, the pumpkin carriage, the glass slipper. Of all these images, the carriage, the slipper, and the idea of midnight "curfew" are probably the best known. We all too easily forget that the simplest, clearest, and most effective version was that of Perrault, and that it appeared over a hundred years before the version of the Brothers Grimm. Both versions have become immensely popular, at least in the United States, through numerous editions (accurate and "vulgarized"), including the famous film version of Walt Disney: the tale has become ubiquitous, truly part of the oral tradition of our century. Everyone knows, or thinks he knows, the story of Cinderella. But usually one confuses unknowingly Perrault and Grimm. Thus the carriage of Perrault's version is frequently remembered (as well as the pumpkin from which it was made), but it does not appear at all in the Grimms' text. But who really cares? It is characteristic of commonly accepted images that very few of those who use them know their origins. If an American adolescent says "after midnight I turn into a pumpkin," does she realize that she is inaccurately echoing Perrault's text?

To clarify the connection between Perrault and folklore, we will list below a few reference works (cited also in the bibliography). There is, first of all, Stith Thompson's *The Folktale* (1946), which suggests that

much research needs to be done on the "stylistic interaction between the literary and the oral folktale,"[42] while admitting the enormous influence of Perrault.

In France itself the central work is the comprehensive two-volume *Catalogue du Conte merveilleux français* [Catalogue of the French Wonder Tale, 1957-1964] by the late Paul Delarue and Marie-Louise Tenèze, in which we find Perrault's tales classified according to the international nomenclature of Aarne-Thompson's *Motif-Index,* as well as some interesting remarks on the influence of Perrault. Paul Delarue was a folklorist first and foremost. He believed that the oral "pure" folktale was superior to the literary fairy tale. Consequently, anything in Perrault which seems too refined and too widely imitated by other authors, he does not consider the authentic voice of the people. Delarue could not fully admire Perrault, and lamented his influence on the score of women fairy tale authors who published in the last ten years of the seventeenth century. He decried as well the enormous flowering of the fairy tale in the eighteenth century, resulting in the forty-one volumes of the *Cabinet des Fées,*[43] published just before the French Revolution (1785-1789). But these authors and their collections belong to literature and not to folklore—even though it is sometimes difficult to distinguish one from the other.

We have ample evidence of the diffusion of Perrault in the "popular" stream through numerous reprints in chapbooks during the eighteenth and nineteenth centuries. In our century, the French scholars Pierre Brochon, Geneviève Bollème,[44] and Robert Mandrou[45] have published well-documented volumes which attest once again to the influence of Perrault and the ubiquity of the fairy tale in all chapbook collections.

VII. The Moral and Psychological Import of Perrault

In previous pages we have mentioned the morals of Perrault's tales. The simple truth is that the moral message of the Mother Goose stories is rather pedestrian, utilitarian, and at times rather cynical. We see no profound ethical lesson in what happens in **"Puss in Boots," "Bluebeard,"** or **"Hop O' My Thumb."** We do not find much inspiration either in the versified morals of these stories.

Yet Perrault, like La Fontaine, professed to be moral and offered his stories as educational tales for the betterment of the young. It is possible that both La Fontaine and Perrault believed that their fables and tales possessed an educational value. It is also possible that in their days a lesson of opportunism might pass for a moral lesson. We profess a much broader ethical conception. For us there is ethical value in any narrative that becomes a classic. Such a narrative gives an impression of order and beauty, rhythm and elegance. Children, and *a fortiori* adults, become better human beings through the experience of beautiful narratives. Paul Hazard stated in *Books, Children, and Men,* one of the most suggestive books ever written about children's literature, that nursery rhymes do not seem "unconscious of the fact that by placing rhythm at the beginning of life they are conforming to the general order of the universe."[46] The statement applies to the tales of Perrault, if we paraphrase it thus: fairy tales, by their recital of immemorial adventures told at the beginning of youth, tell the child that he belongs to the same universal order as that of heroes and heroines in the supernatural world.

The child perceives that fairy tales are symbolic narratives even if he does not understand them fully. For a child, **"Little Red Riding Hood"** is a story about the danger of wolves, a warning tale that has been well analyzed in semiological terms.[47] But for an adult the story can be ironic because he reads the narrative as an allegory of sexual seduction. The "obscure" way in which the child may still have an awareness of the symbolic import of any kind of narrative is of enormous educational importance. For, if the child accepts a fairy tale at face value, there must be something wrong with his emotional makeup. It is through the fairy tale that he may first learn the difference between fiction and reality. He learns to accept fairy tales as beautiful fictions which enrich his innermost mind. Perrault understood this very well when he wrote that fairy tales are like "seeds that one throws, which first bring forth the emotions of joy and sadness, but which will inevitably bloom later in the form of worthy feelings."[48]

Furthermore, since fairy tales are first told or read aloud to children by parents or friends, they act as an emotional bridge between adult and young. Each enjoys the tale in his own way: the adult pretending to become young again and a believer of fairies, the child dreaming of supernatural powers like those of the wonder-tale heroes. But that emotional bridge is also an aesthetic bridge. When both an adult and a child pretend to believe in a fairy tale, not because it is absolutely convincing, but because it is beautifully expressed, they become "aesthetic accomplices?

In that large ethical and aesthetic sense, Perrault's fairy tales acquire a new dimension. They have been told and retold so often that they seem immortal:

Sleeping Beauty, Puss in Boots, Cinderella are reborn with each new generation of children. Such characters have become legendary in our Western culture (and probably outside of it, in China or Japan as well). We fully agree with the statement of Mircea Eliade that the fairy tale has an initiatory function in our civilization: "Without realizing it, and thinking he is merely entertaining himself or escaping, modern man still enjoys the imaginary initiation which fairy tales bring to him."[49]

Eliade is here comparing the fairy tale to the legends and myths told the young in "primitive" societies. In the context of these cultures it is through the recital of the deeds of heroic ancestors that the young learn of their forefathers—whom they are urged to imitate. It might be argued that insofar as the fairy tales are concerned they do not contain any adventures or feats as heroic as those that can be found in such epics as the *Iliad* or the *Odyssey*. We do not agree. The characters of Perrault, because of their interesting combination of stylization and psychological appeal, are the kind of heroes whom the young—consciously or unconsciously—want to imitate. A young girl readily daydreams about the fate of Cinderella, a young boy might easily dream of owning such a wonderful "gadget" as the seven-league boots.

In those dreams reside the fulfillment of life, as Joseph Campbell beautifully expressed it: " . . . they are the heroes and villains who have built the world for us. The debutante combing her hair before the glass, the mother pondering the future of a son, the laborer in the mines, the merchant vessel full of cargo, the ambassador with portfolio, the soldier in the field of war—all are working in order that the ungainsayable specifications of effective fantasy, the permanent patterns of the tale of wonder, shall be clothed in flesh and known as life."[50] In another passage, Campbell emphasizes the symbolic content of fairy tales: "The function of the craft of the tale . . . was not simply to fill the vacant hour, but to fill it with symbolic fare. And since symbolization is the characteristic pleasure of the human mind, the fascination of the tale increased in proportion to the richness of its symbolic content."[51]

The psychological import of Perrault's tales derives from their symbolic content. Each symbol has its corresponding psychological resonance. The recent book of Bruno Bettelheim provides explanations or rather a psychoanalysis of about fifteen fairy tales, most from the Grimms' collection, a few from Perrault's. Since his work has achieved a great popularity—and been translated into French—no analytical discussion of Perrault's fairy tales is now possible without referring to it. In many ways Bettelheim seems to have interpreted Perrault's stories in a thoroughly definitive way, as only a psychoanalyist and a child psychiatrist could. We will give an account of his interpretations. But we do not wish to suggest that we entirely agree with him.

To discern a symbol is to explain how we think, or vibrate inwardly with its message. In **"Sleeping Beauty,"** Perrault articulated the idea of sleep as a symbol for the passive, introspective period of puberty: "This is how the symbolic language of the fairy tale states that after having gathered strength in solitude the young have now become themselves."[52] Perrault emphasized the value of "sleep" as a period of learning when he told his audience not to be amazed if the princess was perfectly alert, pert, and articulate after her century of sleep: "she had plenty of time to think and learn through the many pleasant dreams her fairy had inspired in her."[53] This remark of Perrault—which some may dislike or dismiss as an extraneous interpolation—is peculiar to his version.

"Bluebeard" is a story of sexual transgression. In her husband's absence the wife has been unfaithful. It is a terrifying story suggesting that on a "preconscious level the child understands from the indelible blood on the key and from other details that Bluebeard's wife has committed a sexual indiscretion."[54] But he was wrong in seeking such a cruel revenge (death by beheading). The tale teaches deep down a higher morality, which Bettelheim finds expressed by Perrault himself in the second moral: "One can well see that this is a story of times past; / There are no longer such terrible husbands who demand the impossible / Even when they are dissatisfied or jealous, / They act gently toward their wives."[55]

We have no difficult in accepting Perrault's point of view as expressed above. But the explanation of Bettelheim that the key and the forbidden room symbolize sexual infidelity can be open to question. There is no doubt that the two motifs do suggest sex—as many dreams and stories have confirmed—but there is not the slightest reference within the story as told by Perrault that another man was present in any form in the life or the thoughts of Bluebeard's wife. Fairy tales are usually very explicit narratives, even though they may be highly symbolic. What disturbs us in Bettelheim's explanations is that he does not seem to grant the possibility that any story or element of a story can be interpreted in more ways than one (his

own). Perhaps the story as told by Perrault is also valid as an allegory of infant curiosity and adult cruelty, including the possibility of sexual curiosity, but not excluding either Perrault's plainly manifest content and interpretation.

The tale which has been the most elaborately interpreted by Bettelheim is **"Cinderella."** We will not repeat all he wrote concerning the interpretation of Cinderella's slipper as a symbol for the vagina. We are, in fact, quite ready to agree with him. A ring or a slipper are common motifs in fairy tales, and easy to interpret as such. We disagree with him concerning the character of Perrault's heroine. He feels that she is passively "sugar sweet and insipidly good . . . and completely lacks initiative."[56] No, the Cinderella of Perrault is, on the contrary, very alive, very spirited, and full of initiative. Any reader of this tale (in French or in an English translation) can see for himself: all he has to do is read the dialogues between Cinderella and her fairy godmother, or her conversations with her sisters, or the account of the ball at the royal palace, or the reference to the laughter of Cinderella pulling out of her pocket the other slipper which she had kept all along.

Another instance where we feel Bettelheim has failed to understand something essential—in fact, thoroughly missing a plausible interpretation—is the case of the famous carriage. The idea of the carriage itself he finds a useless addition to the story, as we have already shown. He explains at great length how the fairy scoops the pumpkin and transforms it into a beautiful carriage; then, following the opinion of Marc Soriano, he considers that in this episode Perrault treats the magical in an ironic way (he may well be right) which detracts from the beauty and wonder of the story (an opinion which can be debated).

Applying Bettelheim's own method of interpretation and analysis, we suggest the following. The carriage is *essential* for Cinderella. Dressed as she was in regal clothes, she could not—in her own social context of 1697—go to the ball on foot. Furthermore, she needed its *protection* and *comfort*. The thoughtful fairy wanted her ward to have some kind of parental protection, be it in the form of a carriage, to go "out in the world alone." We recall the act of scooping the inside of the pumpkin, transforming it into the golden carriage, and finally placing Cinderella inside of it and sending her along. This sequence begs for interpretation. Cinderella was a stepchild without a mother. What the fairy did was to create symbolically a womb (the pumpkin) in which she placed Cinderella, who was reborn again inside of it, as a full blown woman ready to mate, ready to meet her prince. This obvious analysis seems to have escaped our analyst.

There is one other point about this tale we wish to make. Bettelheim insists that Perrault is too interested in clothes as an outward symbol of wealth, and that he does not pay enough attention to the *character* of Cinderella, where clothes are unimportant. We beg to differ. Here is a reference to the beauty "without clothes" of Cinderella: "Cinderella, notwithstanding her raggedy clothes, was a hundred times more beautiful than her sisters who were so luxuriously dressed."[57] As to the fact that the prince or his entourage ought to have been able to recognize Cinderella after the ball when she was dressed in her usual ugly clothes (as is the fact in the Grimm version), we will simply recall that when the nobleman in charge of trying the slipper comes face to face with Cinderella, he disregards the sarcasms of the wicked sisters, and "having looked intently at Cinderella, and having found her quite beautiful,"[58] proceeds with the famous slipper test.

We do not wish to "overargue" our case concerning Cinderella, but it so happens that, in preparing the Perrault *Concordance*, we have *copied* with our own hands the text of Perrault, and know almost by heart all the fairy tales. We have practically total recall of the text of our author.

In general the book of Bruno Bettelheim gives the impression of a "grammar of symbols," a sort of closed world in which symbols are explained once and for all. We feel that context is of the essence in the explanation of symbols. True, they may be a universal language, but only in a kind of dynamic dialectic sense, in the exchange that takes place between the story (or producer of the story) and its listeners or readers. It is all a question of psychic resonance within a given sociocultural context.

We will only briefly deal with **"Puss in Boots."** We agree that it is an amoral story. The hero's success is arranged through shameless deceit and effrontery. The same can be said about **"Tom Thumb."** In both these tales the youngest child, the most underprivileged, finally prevails, thanks to his resourcefulness. The function of such tales is not to give a choice between good and bad, but to give a child hope that even someone as small and as disinherited as he may be, can, like the peasant boy of **"Puss in Boots," "Tom Thumb,"** or **"Jack the Giant Killer,"** suc-

ceed in life.[59] There is also in **"Puss in Boots"** a totemic element: the animal is here the protector-provider of his master, just as in American Indian tribal legend a certain animal is the totem or protector of the clan.

"Beauty and the Beast" is the last story which Bettelheim interprets. Perrault's variation of that theme is **"Riquet à la houppe."** Everything that Bettelheim writes on the subject seems quite relevant and correct. The beast as a sexual symbol is quite obvious, quite easy to discern from the various narratives he analyzes. **"Riquet à la houppe"** is not treated at length; it is the object of a long footnote.[60] The story of Perrault can only be understood as a version of "Beauty and the Beast," within a tradition of tales originating with the myth of Cupid and Psyche. We presented (in 1960 and in 1975)—prior to Bettelheim—our analyses of both the myth and the fairy tale,[61] and Bettelheim's interpretation coincides with our own.

Furthermore, on the question of **"Riquet à la houppe,"** we feel that a fuller analysis is necessary. There are two stories by that name, that of Mlle Bernard, which appeared before Perrault's in 1696, and that of our author, published the following year. The main difference between the two stories consists in the fact that in Mlle Bernard's version Riquet marries his princess before the end of the tale; she tires of him and manages to have an affair with a friend she hides in the palace. Riquet punishes his wife in an unusual way: he transforms the handsome lover into his twin brother, with the result that the princess is condemned to live with two husbands, not knowing which of the two she should hate.

Perrault's version is much simpler. As we know, the princess has no lover. We recall that when she agreed to marry Riquet, he seemed immediately to be transformed into a handsome man. The clever explanation that it was love that made the princess find the ugly Riquet suddenly handsome is Perrault's refined way of suggesting discreetly that his story is a symbolic account of the power of sexual attraction. It is also clear that Perrault knew the previous version of his story, and saw fit to eliminate the lover. In his story the lover and the husband coincide. The moment Riquet is accepted as a sexual person he becomes attractive. But this acceptance of Riquet as a sexual companion is an expression of maturity: his wife welcomes him as he really is, and as adult wisdom demands according to psychological truth and custom.

In conclusion we must say that not all of Perrault's stories have been completely interpreted to our satisfaction. On the story of **Donkey-Skin,** with its obvious incestuous element of a father seeking to marry his daughter, we have not found any analytical criticism. We are also surprised that the Grimm Brothers' version of that tale (*Allerleirauh,* or Skin of all Animals), in which the father finally *marries* his daughter, is not even mentioned.[62]

A major work of synthesis remains to be written on the interpretation of all fairy tales, not only those of Perrault. This work would show that after myths, which are the easiest to interpret, the fairy tales offer the simplest structures and styles. Like dreams, myths and fairy tales are the royal road to the unconscious. Among authors of fairy tales Perrault seems to us one of the best, because of a style which is at once simple, or naive, and yet very refined in its gentle humor and irony. That combination of refinement and naiveté is not unique to Perrault. It is present in all the great authors of fairy tales: Mme. d'Aulnoy, Mme Leprince de Beaumont, Andersen and Lewis Carroll, to name but a few. Their literary charm enhances our world and constantly elicits interpretations wherein we find images of our complex psychic selves.[63]

Notes and References

1. Louis Marin, "*Puss in Boots*: Power of Signs—Signs of Power," *Diacritics* 7 (1977): 54.

2. Paul Delarue, *Le Conte populaire français, Catalogue raisonné . . .* (Paris, 1957), p. 30. The second volume (published by Marie-Louise Tenèze after Paul Delarue's death) appeared in 1964.

3. Mademoiselle, niece of Louis XIV, was the daughter of his brother Philippe d'Orléans and of his second wife, Elisabeth Charlotte de Bavière, known as the "princesse Palatine." The brother of Mademoiselle became regent after the death of Louis XIV. Mademoiselle (Elisabeth Charlotte d'Orléans) was nineteen years old and a person of some importance at the court. It was natural that a work of literature should be dedicated to her. In 1698 she married Leopold, duke of Lorraine. She became a widow in 1729. One of her thirteen children married Maria Theresa of Austria, whose daughter, Marie-Antoinette, became Louis XVI's unfortunate wife and queen of France. Mademoiselle died in 1744. There are many allusions to her and her family in the *Mémoires* of Saint Simon, attesting that she was rather vivacious, and greatly beloved at the court of the Sun King.

4. Barchilon, *Tales of Mother Goose,* p. 140.

5. Rouger, p. 125.

6. Ibid., p. 113.

7. Ibid., p. 139.

8. Jacques Barchilon (with E. E. Flinders, Jr., and Jeanne Anne Foreman), *A Concordance to Charles Perrault's Tales,* vol. 1, *Contes de Ma Mère l'Oye*; vol. 2, *The Verse Tales, Griselidis, Peau d'Ane and Les Souhaits Ridicules* (Darby, Penn., 1977-1979).

9. See *A Concordance to the Fables and Tales of Jean de La Fontaine* (Ithaca: Cornell University Press, 1974).

10. Rouger, *Contes,* p. 103.

11. William Lewis Wiley, *The Formal French* (Cambridge: Harvard University Press, 1967).

12. Antoine Arnauld and Pierre Nicole, *La Logique ou l'art de penser* (Paris: Flammarion, 1662; reprint ed. 1978), introduction by Louis Marin, p. 263.

13. Quoted in d'Alté A. Welch, *A Bibliography of American Children's Books Printed Prior to 1821* (Worcester, 1967), p. 59.

14. Paul Bonnefon, "Pensées . . . de Charles Perrault," p. 535.

15. Rouger, *Contes,* p. 184.

16. Barchilon and Pettit, *The Authentic Mother Goose* (Denver, 1960).

17. Ibid., pp. 54-55.

18. Ibid., p. 56.

19. In further pages of this book we will again refer to this aesthetic principle in the fairy tale, which Robert Samber formulated so simply and effectively.

20. *Authentic Mother Goose,* p. 84.

21. Ibid., p. 23.

22. Ibid., p. 25.

23. Ibid., p. 26.

24. Ibid., p. 43.

25. Ibid., p. 51.

26. Rouger, *Contes,* p. 103.

27. *Authentic Mother Goose,* p. 48.

28. *Perrault's Fairy Tales,* with thirty-four full-page illustrations by Gustave Doré (New York, 1969).

29. Marianne Moore, *Puss in Boots, the Sleeping Beauty, and Cinderella* (New York: Macmillan, 1963).

30. Geoffrey Brereton, *The Fairy Tales of Charles Perrault* (Edinburgh, 1957).

31. Anne Carter, *Perrault's Fairy Tales* (London, 1967).

32. *Histoire d'un conte, Le Chat botté en France et en Angleterre.* Ph.D. dissertation (Aix: Université de Provence, 1979).

33. Anna B. Rooth, *The Cinderella Cycle* (Lund: Gleerund, 1951).

34. Iona and Peter Opie, *The Classic Fairy Tales* (London, 1974), p. 22.

35. André Jolles, *Formes simples,* pp. 175-79.

36. Rouger, *Contes,* p. 13.

37. Ibid., p. 120.

38. In his article Harry Velten prints side by side the French of Perrault and the text of Grimm for selected stories, showing how the German is seemingly a translation of the French.

39. Bloomington (1932-1936).

40. Thompson, *The Folktale,* pp. 58-59.

41. *Funk and Wagnalls Standard Dictionary of Folklore* (New York, 1950), 2: 913.

42. Thompson, *The Folktale,* pp. 459-60.

43. Reprinted partially (less the Oriental tales) under the title *Nouveau Cabinet des Fées,* 18 vols., introduction by Jacques Barchilon (Geneva: Slatkine, 1975).

44. *La Bibliothèque bleue, littérature populaire en France* (Paris: Juillard, 1971).

45. *De la Culture populaire aux XVIIIᵉ siècle* (Paris: Stock, 1964).

46. Paul Hazard, *Books, Children, and Men* (Boston, 1947), p. 81.

47. Victor Laruccia, "Little Red Riding Hood's Metacommentary," *Modern Language Notes* 90 (1975): 517-34.

48. Rouger, *Contes,* p. 6.

49. *Aspect du mythe* (Paris, 1963), p. 244.

50. Joseph Campbell, "Folkloristic Commentary," in *Grimm's Fairy Tales* (New York: Pantheon Books, 1944), p. 864.

51. Ibid., p. 862.

52. Bettelheim, *Uses of Enchantment,* p. 226.

53. Rouger, *Contes,* p. 102.

54. Bettelheim, *Uses of Enchantment,* p. 302.

55. Rouger, *Contes,* p. 129.

56. Bettelheim, *Uses of Enchantment,* p. 251.

57. Rouger, *Contes,* p. 158.

58. Ibid., p. 163.

59. Bettelheim, *Uses of Enchantment,* p. 10.

60. Ibid., p. 304.

61. "*Beauty and the Beast,* from Myth to Fairy Tale," *Psychoanalytic Review* 46 (1960). See also, *Le Conte merveilleux* (1975), chap. 1.

62. This is the sixty-fifth story in the Brothers Grimm's collection.

63. This chapter has been enriched and inspired by many discussions with Dr. José Barchilon, clinical professor of psychiatry at Cornell University; among Dr. Barchilon's publications, his studies of Twain's *Huckleberry Finn* and Camus's *The Fall* (*Journal of the American Psychoanalytic Association,* 1966, 1971) have been most useful.

Ségolène Le Men (essay date spring 1992)

SOURCE: Le Men, Ségolène. "Mother Goose Illustrated: From Perrault to Doré." *Poetics Today* 13, no. 1 (spring 1992): 17-39.

[*In the following essay, Le Men examines various illustrated editions of the Mother Goose fables, including Perrault's* Contes.]

"Once or twice she had peeped into the book her sister was reading, but it had no pictures or conversations in it, 'and what is the use of a book,' thought Alice, 'without pictures or conversations?'" Lewis Carroll's famous sentence captures the need for a specific kind of book devoted to children, and it points to the importance of visual and verbal expressions in the child's perception of a book. Illustration, as a reading of the text, helps adapt a literary work to the child. In addition to fables, tales are one of the principal genres of children's literature, and ever since Charles Perrault's tales were first issued in 1697, a plethora of editions, often illustrated, has been published. This text is therefore an apposite case for examining the historical semiotics of illustrated children's books. Although a considerable amount of excellent criticism has addressed Perrault's tales, it is surprising to note that the issue of their illustrations has usually been neglected. Marie-Louise Teneze, who referred to the illustrations in her article "Si Peau d'Ane m'était conté . . . A propos de trois illustrations des Contes de Perrault" (Teneze 1957), is exceptional in this regard. For the most part, researchers have occupied themselves with myriad other questions: the authorship of the **Contes** (Bonnefon 1904); the sources of the tales and the question of popular versus high culture (Soriano 1968); the structural organization of narration (Escarpit 1985); the psychological function of tales in a child's development (Bettelheim 1976); the relevance of the tales to history and to rural everyday life in seventeenth-century France (Darnton 1984); and the integration of the tales into children's fairy-tale literature (Zipes 1983; Shavit 1986). All of these questions, starting with the authorship riddle, could also be addressed apropos of the illustrations which appeared in the first edition of the tales. That edition, published in Paris by Barbin in 1697, deserves attention because its illustrations have become visual archetypes. Indeed, it is possible to trace the evolution of the illustration process up to the end of the nineteenth century by means of one particular picture, the frontispiece of Mother Goose telling her tale. (Various versions of this illustration are reprinted in Escarpit [1985].)

In a brilliant article, Catherine Velay-Vallantin (1987) shows how Perrault's **Contes** were integrated into French chapbooks; she views the illustrations as part of a general process of adaptation implied in the "*bibliothèque bleue*" editions. Although the questions she raises, arising out of Roger Chartier's seminar at the Ecole Pratique des Hautes Etudes, are close to the ones we wish to address, the corpus we analyze is oriented toward children's literature, which achieved its autonomy in French literary history mostly during the nineteenth century. The famous Gumuchian Catalogue (1931) has been very helpful in attempting to trace the illustrated versions of Perrault's **Contes,** as has a recent article by Laura Noesser (1986) on the evolution of illustrations of tales over two centuries. Finally, this survey would not be complete without citing Louis Marin's seminal study of the Mother

Goose frontispiece and of the illustrations for **Les Fées.** Originally a 1984 lecture in Chartier's seminar "Socio-histoire des pratiques culturelles," Marin's study, "La Trajectoire d'une illustration: Un conte de Perrault," has given rise to various articles, the latest one appearing in a special issue on Perrault of *Europe* (Marin 1990 [1984]).

As a series of pictures, illustrations may be considered from two perspectives: one may study the sequence of images in a single edition (e.g., Perrault 1697); or one may investigate iconographic transformations in successive versions of the same episode (Hop o' My Thumb pulling on the ogre's boots, for instance; see Le Men and Renonciat 1989; Renonciat 1990) or in one key illustration (such as the scene of Mother Goose telling her tale). This last approach reveals changes in the reading and intended reception of the text. In fact, the ideal method is to combine the two, using both the syntagmatic and the paradigmatic axes in order to detect illustrative archetypes and trace their derivations as stereotypes. At the same time, this method reveals the role of the artist, who lends a new orientation to the illustrative chain as he transforms and recreates the standard iconography. The present article aims to examine in detail the illustrations of the original, Barbin edition of Perrault's tales, then to focus on the paradigm of the frontispiece—the scene of Mother Goose telling her tale—and to survey its transformations in succeeding children's books up to Doré's masterly interpretation of 1862.

THE 1697 EDITION

In searching for visual archetypes, the first step is to return to the original illustrated edition of a text, where the prototypes are often found. The art of illustration is extremely conservative and almost always alludes to earlier illustrated versions, which are sometimes made into vague, but strong, visual-image memories. This is also true of Perrault's tales. But the first illustrated edition of those tales also happened to be the original edition, despite the fact that for various reasons, business and financial, technical and editorial, one would have expected the original edition to appear without illustrations. Why?

In the late seventeenth century illustrated books were still unusual because the trade rules did not allow a typographer to issue prints, nor a print engraver a typographical text longer than a caption of a few lines (see Duportal 1914). Large books, which were more like portfolios of plates, and luxury editions with engraved frontispieces were almost the sole forms of the illustrated book. The only other exceptions were books on fortifications, architecture, geography, or botany, which relied mainly on figures and were, once the ten-year privilege was granted, under the protection of a well-placed person at court. One of the finest examples of a French seventeenth-century illustrated book is *Les Hommes illustrés* by Claude Perrault, adorned with 104 portraits engraved mainly by Edelinck, and released in 1696, one year before the ***Histoires, ou Contes du temps passé*** (1697). Apart from special traditions, such as emblems or some devotion books, intaglio techniques (engraving in relief), which entailed a printing separate from that of the typographical text, were used only in plates. The "pocketsize" duodecimo format of the latter was common to that period and usually had no illustrations or, at most, ornamental woodcuts. An edition of the tales in verse, printed in 1695, followed this standard; its only pictorial elements were ornamental woodcuts, such as the publisher's monogram on the title page and the headpiece and rubric of the preface. *Peau d'Ane* appeared without illustrations in that collection of tales and its first readers reproved it for this lack of visual impact.

> Je n'ai aucune idée de ***Peau d'Ane*** dans son déguisement à quoi je puisse me fixer. Tantôt je me la représente barbouillée et noire comme une bohémienne avec sa peau d'âne qui lui sert d'écharpe, tantôt je m'imagine que la peau d'âne est comme un masque sur son visage et qu'elle y est tellement jointe que les spectateurs la prennent pour sa peau naturelle; quelquefois pour lui changer les traits et pour la rendre aussi dégoûtante que le veut l'auteur, je conçois qu'elle s'est fait un fard de laideur avec de la vieille graisse et de la suie de cheminée . . . le poète qui n'a pas pris soin de m'apprendre en quoi consistait le déguisement, détruit lui-même par quelques mots en passant tout ce que je tâche d'imaginer là-dessous.
>
> *(Lettres de Monsieur de* * * *à Mademoiselle* * * * sur les pièces de Griselidis et Peau d'Ane* [anonymous text published in the 1964 edition of the Moetghens collection of tales])

No such reproach was ever addressed to the subsequent collection of tales. Although introduced by Sébastien Le Clerc in the last quarter of the seventeenth century, the fashion of small-format books with vignettes only came into its own in the eighteenth century.

All these facts demonstrate that in Perrault's tales there was a special requirement for illustrations, which needs to be taken into account. The material reason is simple: not very long ago, it was discovered that the 1697 edition had been based on an illuminated manuscript dated 1695. The earlier manuscript, unexpectedly rediscovered in Nice in 1953 and acquired by the Pierpont Morgan Library in New York, was edited by Jacques Barchilon (1956). The purpose of this manuscript seems to have been twofold: it was a deluxe dedication copy intended for nineteen-year-old Mademoiselle Elisabeth Charlotte d'Orléans (niece of Louis XIV and daughter of his brother Philippe), and it was also the model, or mock-up ("maquette"), for publication. In this copy all the illustrations are placed just as they are in the subsequent 1697 edition. Here, too, they are pen and ink sepia drawings colored with gouache and include the frontispiece, the vignette for the opening page of the dedication, and the five vignettes for the opening pages of the following tales: ***La Belle au bois dormant*** (***Sleeping Beauty***), ***Le Petit Chaperon rouge*** (***Little Red Riding Hood***), ***La Barbe bleue*** (***Bluebeard***), ***Le Maistre Chat, ou le Chat botté*** (***Puss-in-Boots***), ***Les Fées*** (***The Fairies, or Diamonds and Toads***). The last three tales—***Cendrillon, ou la Petite Pantoufle de verre*** (***Cinderella***), ***Riquet à la Houppe*** (***Riquet with the Tuft***), ***Le Petit Pouçet*** (***Hop o' My Thumb***)—do not appear in the manuscript. Probably, they were not yet written.

The manuscript and the edition differ primarily in style, a function of the change to printed reproduction: the calligraphy became typographical letterpress, the gouaches black and white linear engravings, all in reverse, as required by the printing process. Except for the frontispiece and the vignette for ***Bluebeard,*** the design of each opening page in the manuscript and the edition is similar, with a superposition for the headpiece, title (completed by the word "conte" except for ***Bluebeard***), and the first lines of the text. The printed edition added only an ornamental rubric—usually an "I"—which draws attention to the recurrent opening phrase, "Il était une fois" ("Once upon a time"). Even the size of the drawings (4.2 × 6.2 cm) is identical to the size of the prints except for the frontispiece, which is slightly larger in the manuscript, in spatial proportion to the larger dimensions of the manuscript page. The three pictures added to the printed edition maintained that pattern.

The organization of the illustrated page shared by the manuscript and the edition may suggest the reason why Perrault's tales were illustrated in the first place. Tales belong to an emblematic tradition, as do fables. It is very likely that the visual strategy of the Barbin edition of Perrault's ***Contes*** was based on the earlier example of La Fontaine's *Fables* (also issued by

Claude Barbin, in 1668), which included 118 engraved vignettes by François Chauveau placed between the title and the beginning of the text of each fable (see Bassy 1986, 1974). In his two articles, Alain-Marie Bassy uses the term "emblem" differently, in a strict sense (1986) and in a broader sense (1974). Here, we deal with the more general sense, as applied to the emblematic page setting. It is clear that the strict definition of the emblematic image, as used in emblem books, indicates a quasi-hieroglyphic image based on symbols and allegories that would not be appropriate to the illustrations of fables and tales. Emblems are a mixed medium rooted in the interplay between the concrete and the abstract, involving both text and image. They were invented by Alciati in 1531 and were in fashion for over two centuries (Praz 1939-1947; Klein 1970). The image appeals to the senses and emphasizes the concreteness of the text, that is, the story. The rhymed epigram, or "morality," belongs to the emblem's abstract aspect, its moral lesson. The motto is used to link image and text, and it has a double meaning: the first is related to the picture preceding the tale; the second is discovered with the "morality" at the end, which becomes integrated only upon a second reading. This format is indicative of how involved illustrations are in the reading and rereading process.

There is some evidence that Perrault was interested in emblematic language before 1697. His **Recueil de divers ouvrages en prose et en vers, Le Labyrinthe de Versailles** (Perrault 1675) is an important work related to the art of illustration (Wilhelm 1936; Bassy 1976). It was based on the Versailles maze, designed by Le Notre in 1664 and decorated between 1672 and 1674 with thirty-nine fountains inspired by Aesop's fables and their traditional iconography. Like a guide book, the text relies on external objects; like an emblem book, the title, or motto, on each page is used to connect the icon and the text. The Versailles maze took a literary subject, Aesop's fables, for its theme. Perrault reversed the illustration process, deriving a collection of textual emblems from the sculpture garden. (These were reproduced in the *Imprimérie royale* edition [Perrault 1677-1679] in the plates by Sébastien Le Clerc.) **Le Labyrinthe de Versailles** is testimony to Perrault's interest in mixed-media expressions, intersemiotic transpositions, and emblematic effects. The contrast between the prose "tale" and the "morality" in verse is already present.

Perrault's headpieces work as "shifters" or mediators between the title and the text, the story and its moral. For example, in **Sleeping Beauty,** the illustration of the princess asleep and about to be awakened by the prince is appropriate to the title and echoes the first epigram:

> Attendre quelque temps pour avoir un Epoux,
> Riche, bien fait, galant et doux,
> La chose est assez naturelle,
> Mais l'attendre cent ans, et toujours en dormant,
> On ne trouve plus de femelle,
> Qui dormit si tranquillement.
>
> (Perrault 1697)

An emblem usually fits on a single page; a fable may cover two pages. Tales are longer, but Perrault's share the same binary verbal composition whereby the story is separated from the "morality." La Fontaine explained this structure with an image referring to the duality of human nature: a fable has a "soul" as well as a "body." In his 1668 preface La Fontaine insisted on the moral impact of fables, and, under the latter's influence, so did Perrault in the 1695 preface to his rhymed tales.

> [Les gens de bon goût] ont été bien aises de remarquer que ces bagatelles n'étaient pas de pures bagatelles, qu'elles renfermaient une morale utile et que le récit enjoué dont elles avaient été enveloppées n'avait été choisi que pour les faire entrer plus agréablement dans l'esprit et d'une manière qui instruisît et divertît tout ensemble; dans les contes que nos aïeux ont inventés pour leurs Enfants, ils ont toujours eu un très grand soin que leurs contes renfermassent une moralité louable et instructive. Partout la vertu y est récompensée, et partout le vice y est puni. Ils tendent tous à faire voir l'avantage qu'il y a d'être honnête, patient, avisé, laborieux, obéissant, et le mal arrive à ceux qui ne le sont pas. N'est-il pas louable à des Pères et à des Mères, lorsque leurs Enfants ne sont pas capables de goûter des vérités solides et dénuées de tous agréments, de les leur faire aimer, et si cela se peut dire, les leur faire avaler, en les enveloppant dans des récits agréables et proportionnés à la faiblesse de leur âge.
>
> (Barchilon 1956)

The editions of La Fontaine's fables have exactly the same kind of page format as those of Perrault's tales, intertwining text and image. The emblematic device, based on pictorial pedagogy, had already been used by the Jesuits. In spite of this pedagogical and moralistic intent, though, it is clear that children are interested only in the story. They forget about the moral in the case of the fable just as readily as in the tale. To use Perrault's own metaphor, they take just "the honey" and reject "the medicine!" Their attention is drawn to the pictures, and they ignore the concluding morals, which are often not read to them, and in Perrault's tales, not even addressed to them. Jean-Jacques Rousseau's complaint in *L'Emile* about the lack of morality in La Fontaine's fables was therefore irrelevant, even though it was repeated by authors such as Ratisbonne in *La Comédie enfantine.* In the last quarter of the eighteenth century, tales were criticized mainly for their lack of moral pedagogy, a requirement of the new children's literature of Berquin and Madame de Genlis. By the nineteenth century, however, children's editions of Perrault's tales had begun to be published without the morals, which, supposedly, were not intended for children.

Thus, there was a reason for the presence of illustrations with Perrault's text, that is, one linked to its inner nature. Even though Perrault was probably not responsible for the illustrations, they were part of the bookmaking ("mise en livre") of an emblematic text in both the 1695 manuscript and the 1697 edition.

HOW PERRAULT'S TALES WERE ILLUSTRATED

There are essentially two kinds of pictures in the original edition, the frontispiece and the in-text illustrations. (A third kind—the headpiece cartouche which adorns the dedication—I would like to set aside for the purposes of this discussion. It belongs to the motto genre, also a mixed-media expression based on the combination of one textual motto and a visual allegory.) The frontispiece played a commercial role comparable to that of a poster: it conveyed a picture to a selected audience. The in-text illustrations, namely, the headpieces, focused on the major scenes of the tales and were related to the narrative process. In subsequent editions the headpieces were used as visual equivalents of the titles and as visual signs of the tales. The distinction between the frontispiece and the headpieces also marked a way of organizing the tales within the book: the in-text illustrations emphasized the opening of each tale and played a role in the subdivision of the book, which is presented as a whole by the frontispiece.

The frontispiece depicts a night scene illuminated by a candle: an old woman with a cat is spinning close to a fireplace. She is telling a tale to three people. On the door behind her is a sign which reads "Contes de ma Mère l'Oye," following the title of the 1695 manuscript, later adopted by the English tradition (although it was replaced in the 1697 edition by *Histoires, ou Contes du temps passé* and shortened, in the French tradition, to *Contes de Perrault*). This sign immediately raises the question of authorship, as does the transposition of folktales into written literature, symbolized by the book-poster. Facing the

anonymous title page, the frontispiece attributes the tales to Mother Goose. Folklore scholars have interpreted the term "Mother Goose" as personifying the old storyteller associated with "contes de vieille," "contes bleus," and "contes de nourrice." She is linked to the oral transmission of popular culture from generation to generation in the rural setting of fireside evenings. The first description of the traditional "veillée" appeared in the *Propos rustiques* by Noël du Fail (1956 [1547]; Darnton 1984: 251). If the old spinning woman is Mother Goose, then why should she appear at the opening of *Histories,* or *Tales from Times Past*? And who is represented in her audience?

The gouache depicts three figures listening to the old woman. These may represent the Perrault children, according to Soriano (1968): two sons, twenty-one and nineteen years old, and a twenty-three year-old daughter. Seated in front, as a kind of foil, is one of the young men, probably Pierre Perrault, the son to whom Charles Perrault attributed the authorship of the tales. He acts as the scribe, or witness, who records the old woman's oral legacy. In the picture plane, he appears between the storyteller scene and the reader. Charles Perrault himself is not mentioned on the title page of the original edition, nor does he appear in the picture. There is no author writing a text, only a chain of transmission from the popular storyteller to the cultural intermediary, who may be compared to a folklorist in his role.

In print, the subtle chiaroscuro of the manuscript's gouache drawings is transformed into a very precise linear style. One detail is changed: the youngest boy standing near Mother Goose becomes instead a man kneeling in front of the storyteller. Other changes are the result of the publication process. The manuscript had a semiprivate circulation, so its readers would have been able to recognize whoever might have been represented in the gouache. Such identifications were lost on the wider audience of the printed version. The only remaining clue to the identities of the figures is the contrast between the elegant clothes of the three listeners and the rural costume of the spinner. The frontispiece thus highlights the confrontation between popular and high culture. From the drawing to the printed illustration there is a considerable shift implied in the subject matter, that is, from the fabrication to the reception of the text.

A frontispiece is usually meant to announce the content of a book. In the case of Perrault's tales, the frontispiece defines its own content as a literary genre: the tale—symbolized by the spindle, which represents the thread of oral discourse—comes into confrontation with the printed word, stressed by the book-poster. But the picture also includes a series of details from the tales themselves: The carefully closed door and its visible keyhole recall Bluebeard's cabinet; the kneeling posture belongs to the prince awakening Sleeping Beauty; the beautiful young woman represents all the beauties and princesses, just as the old woman is reminiscent of Little Red Riding-Hood's grandmother and the fairy, or "bonne femme." The old spinning woman heralds *Sleeping Beauty*—a tale in which the spindle is an important narrative feature. (This is treated as such in one tailpiece of the 1843 Curmer edition and is paralleled in the frontispiece scene of the 1862 edition illustrated by Gustave Doré.) Once the search for such details is started, even themes of the three tales absent from the manuscript but present in the printed version may be discovered in the picture. This proves the extent to which popular tales base their fantasy elements on everyday life: The fireplace conjures up the house of Hop o' My Thumb's parents as well as Cinderella, whose nickname "Cucendron" literally means "ass in cinders." The candle on the mantelpiece is similar to that held by the ogre's wife when Hop o' My Thumb and his brothers arrive at her house. The cat portends *Puss-in-Boots.* The kneeling boy's strange hat and the curl of his hair signal Riquet. Only the listener in the foreground, with whom the reader identifies, remains outside this preview of the tales. Consciously or not, the frontispiece is constructed exactly like a memory image, according to the rhetorical tradition, and it works as a visual summary of the collection of tales; its hidden complexity is quite different from the simple imagery of the headpieces.

All the headpieces stress the narrative nature of the tales and portray scenes, never portraits, landscapes, or still lifes. Each presents the main characters, either human or animal, including the hero of the tale. (This exemplifies the difference between conventional emblems, where the human figure was forbidden, and the illustration of tales, even though the latter belong to an "emblematic" text and image tradition.) The figures are linked by a single action, a major episode of the tale, which also often happens to be climactic: the prince kneels in front of Sleeping Beauty and the princess wakes up; the wolf lunges to devour its victim; Bluebeard raises his big knife over his wife as the two brothers/horsemen arrive; the cat speaks to the peasant holding his scythe; the younger daughter serves water to the fairy; Cinderella runs away as the prince picks up the slipper; Riquet presents himself

to the princess and bows in front of her; and Hop o' My Thumb carefully pulls on the ogre's boots. These illustrations use the text as a sequence of scenic indicators for establishing their theatrical images; the figures, roughly sketched, are viewed from a distance, and textual indications of attitude, gesture, and setting are precisely adhered to: For example, in *Sleeping Beauty,* "il vit sur un lit, dont les rideaux étaient ouverts de tous côtés, . . . une Princesse . . . se mit à genoux auprès d'elle. . . . La Princesse s'éveilla." In *Bluebeard,* "puis la prenant d'une main par les cheveux, et de l'autre levant le coutelas en l'air, il allait lui abbattre la tête."

Although the pictures do use theatrical conventions in many ways, they also transgress the codes of classical drama. They depict events which, with respect to the three unities of time, action, and place, as well as the code of propriety, would never be represented on the stage. For instance, the illustrations for *Little Red Riding Hood* and *Bluebeard* both portray moments prior to murder and death. In each case it is the imminent danger and not the crime itself which is pictured, as baroque pictorial conventions would dictate. As Lessing later explained in his 1766 work, *Laokoon,* which draws parallels between literature and the visual arts, the climactic effect is better achieved when not the climax itself, but the instant before it, is represented, leaving the imagination to remain free. Four of the headpieces (*Bluebeard, Puss-in-Boots, Cinderella,* and *Riquet with the Tuft*) are based upon the conjunction of different actions, whose hierarchy is conveyed through oppositions in size. In *Bluebeard,* the picture is evenly split into two parts in order to show two settings and actions simultaneously: Bluebeard and his wife vis-à-vis the galloping horsemen; the inside vis-à-vis the outside of the castle. This dual vision is typical of children's drawings. Other features of the illustrations also recall children's drawings: there are no individual characterizations (which makes it difficult to distinguish Little Red Riding-Hood from her grandmother), and the relative sizes of pictorial elements are determined by their importance, not by perspective. This conceptual composition of an image is common to both children's drawings and medieval representations (Shapiro 1973). Even when there is an attempt at spatial perspective through the representation of a path (*Puss-in-Boots*), a forest (*Diamonds and Toads* and *Riquet with the Tuft*), or a ballroom (*Sleeping Beauty*), the space is flat and the motifs look like cutouts placed in front of the picture plane. This is particularly true of the first headpieces, *Sleeping Beauty, Little Red Riding Hood,* and *Bluebeard.* The engraved version of *Sleeping Beauty* shows the bed curtains floating in the air, in a manner which is absent from the drawing. There is, in general, more subtlety in the drawings than in the engraved illustrations, a difference obvious in the backdrop for *Puss-in-Boots.* However, the last three pictures (those which do not appear in the manuscript) have a less "naive" composition, and in the frontispiece the spatial composition is well mastered. On the other hand, the violent scenes of *Bluebeard* and *Little Red Riding Hood,* expressed with simple gestures, are close to the style of popular broadsheet imagery.

The manuscript has other features in common with medieval art and children's drawings. Illuminated manuscripts are a relic of the Middle Ages. Colorful illustrations, elsewhere restricted to a court audience, were an important ingredient in children's art and children's books. The cheerful, bright colors of Perrault's manuscript disappeared from the engraved version and did not reappear until the tales were again colored according to children's taste, first in popular imagery and only later in book form. Meanwhile, children sometimes colored the black and white prints in the engraved version themselves. All this suggests that the "naiveté" described by Perrault in his 1695 preface is as much a property of the illustrations as the text, as Sainte-Beuve later acknowledged:

> Le Conte de Peau d'Ane est ici raconté
> Avec tant de naiveté,
> Qu'il ne m'a pas moins divertie,
> Que quand auprès du feu ma Nourrice ou ma Mie
> Tenaient en le faisant mon esprit enchanté.

The folkloric quest is paralleled by the semi-popular, semi-childlike style of the illustrations.

The illustrations transcend theatrical conventions, entering the realm of fantasy with scenes of strong emotional impact. In the drawing for *Little Red Riding Hood,* the nocturnal apparition of the wolf between the bed curtains recalls the popular etymology of the word "nightmare"—the mare of the night. (The pre-Romantic artist Fuseli followed exactly the same archetypal iconography in a famous painting called *The Nightmare.*) And Hop o' My Thumb's pulling on the ogre's boots symbolizes the child's changing into an adult, in a confrontation resembling the iconography of David and Goliath often presented in children's Bibles. This image also prefigures the picture of Gulliver tied up by the Lilliputians. The structure of the illustrated book further accentuates the link between illustration and dream imagery: this connection has already been introduced by the night scene of the frontispiece; it then recurs in the "sleeping"

frame provided by the bed motif and by the theme of sleep in the book's opening and closing tales and their illustrations. The first tale, *Sleeping Beauty,* uses both the bed motif and the theme of sleep; the following tale, *Little Red Riding Hood,* presents the bed in a nightmare context, while the last tale shows the ogre asleep.

Each tale is illustrated by a single picture. But four of the tales have pictures based on a recurring situation in the text. Repetition is known to be an important narrative feature of oral literature, both lending rhythm and effecting a crescendo-like expression of the transformations in the stories. The simple imagery of each tale's opening illustration remains with the reader, who may visualize it at various stages of his reading. The illustrated episodes may be easily identified by their specific details, but they deserve a second look (and a second reading!). In *Cinderella,* where the ball scene occurs twice, the illustration depicts the second night, when Cinderella loses her slipper. In *Riquet with the Tuft* the meeting between hero and princess both opens the tale and is repeated one year later. The setting of the banquet in a forest makes it clear that the illustration is of the second meeting. In *Diamonds and Toads* as well, the illustrated scene occurs twice in the text, but the illustration describes the first meeting, with the younger daughter. The fairy appears as a "bonne femme," not as a "Dame magnifiquement vêtue"; the daughter holds a "cruche," and not "le plus beau Flacon d'argent qui fût dans le logis." In each of these instances, the illustrated scene is the most important one in the tale. Only once is the illustration ambiguous, in *Little Red Riding Hood.* Who is the wolf going to eat, the grandmother or Little Red Riding-Hood? The wolf is not yet dressed in the grandmother's clothes, so perhaps it means to devour her; however, it seems to jump out of the sheets and, therefore, to have been already waiting in bed for Little Red Riding-Hood. The final choice is the reader's. Referring to the preparatory drawing, though, makes it clear that this ambiguity resulted from a misunderstanding on the part of the engraver. Perhaps he considered it impossible not to portray the hero, who gave her name to the tale, in the opening picture. The manuscript drawing shows the costume of a woman, with the wolf seeming to jump out of nowhere, from the darkness of the background through the picture itself. This extraordinary apparition has been pictorially clarified in the engraved version of the picture, which added the sheets, showing the wolf in bed. But this also made the meaning uncertain. Only much later, in the 1781 edition, was the picture's meaning clarified.

No one knows who drew these illustrations, even though the frontispiece was signed by an engraver named Clouzier. He was probably someone close to Perrault, as was the scribe of the manuscript. And, presumably, Perrault himself approved the illustrator's interpretations since he gave the illuminated manuscript to "Mademoiselle." The illustrations reflect the style of the tales, in both their naiveté and their maturity, their popular and their sophisticated nature. This dualism is also contained in the father/son collaboration and in the conjunction of the names Mother Goose and Charles Perrault, the Academist. The particular appropriateness of the illustrations to the tonality of the text may explain their long success.

THE TRANSFORMATIONS OF MOTHER GOOSE

Beginning with Perrault's tales, the evolution of the frontispiece takes on a special interest, as it implies transformations in the status of the tales. Just as the headpieces became individual pictorial emblems, the frontispiece, which began as an emblem for Perrault's tales in their entirety, later came to be a generic emblem for any collection of tales. The engraving for the first edition was reproduced in later editions of Perrault's tales. In the 1700 edition it was reversed and then reversed again in the plate of the 1742 edition, which was still in use forty years later, in the 1781 edition. This plate, however, includes an important change: the "witness," seated in front, has disappeared. The theme of collecting and recording tales has been completely eliminated. Otherwise, the general pattern of the plate remained unchanged.

But early in the nineteenth century, editions of Perrault's tales began to be produced exclusively for an audience of children. The frontispiece records this shift, allowing us to date and locate this phenomenon. It may be traced to England, circa 1803, in the juvenile edition produced by one of the first publishers of juvenile literature, Harris, Newbery's successor. In the quaint woodcut of this frontispiece, there are still three listeners, but now they have become children. Five years later, in 1808, this changed audience appeared in a French edition published by Duprat-Duverger, within a new compositional format: the scene has been placed on the title page and has been changed from the painterly frontispiece to the title-page vignette, showing silhouette figures in no specific setting. The only feature remaining from the fireside setting is Mother Goose's spindle. An audience of small children stands gathered around her, including one still dressed as a baby. The perspective is new, with the old woman no longer seen in profile. She faces both her audience and the reader, who implicitly becomes part of the audience.

Around 1815, in France, the title-page vignette registered another crucial change: the spindle was replaced by a book. The tales no longer belonged to an oral tradition but to the written language. Nevertheless, this caption still quoted the traditional opening of a tale—"Once upon a time there was a king"—in recognition of the written tales' oral origins. The scene itself depicts the oral mediation of the written page by an adult for an audience of children. Mother Goose is turned into a pedagogical figure, a governess or grandmother wearing eye glasses, which imply the advanced age of the storyteller. The scene evokes the study corner shown in many contemporary frontispieces of the French "libraires d'éducation." The picture also indicates for whom the book is intended. Various ages are represented, from the young boy and the little girl to the baby; the gender differentiation of role models is made clear by the early representation of the doll in the arms of the little girl, right in the center of the composition. The girl-and-doll group echoes the adult-and-child group on a smaller scale. The ability to read is shown as the distinguishing feature of being grown up. And the book is placed in the center of the title page, carefully highlighted in a void within the pictorial composition.

Publishers of the French Romantic period generally followed the new scheme, but with variations: the Langlumé and Peltier edition of 1830 returned to popular culture with a daytime, outdoor village scene. The nocturnal fantasies associated with the fireside have been replaced by a reassuring picture without any darkness. The image of the book remains a focal element in the composition, but the semi-written/semi-oral genre of the tales is now conveyed by the two positions of the village woman's hands. One hand holds the book open on her knees, but she is not reading it; the other hand is positioned to recall the medieval code of gesture. The woman's index finger points in the digital gesture for the opening of discourse—a pictorial equivalent of the earlier caption, "Once upon a time."

Originally an exclusive feature of Perrault's tales, the iconography of the old woman telling a story became a generic pictorial reference for tales. In 1850, it appeared on the cover of Madame d'Aulnoy's *Selected Tales*. It was also used as a familiar device in adapting foreign tales to a French audience. Although *Tom Thumb* had its own specific title-page imagery in British chapbooks dating back to the seventeenth century, the juvenile publisher Blanchard preferred to employ the familiar French pictorial archetype in adapting the story for a French audience. The frontispiece resembles the British one only in its caption, "La bonne femme racontant l'histoire de Tom Pouce." (The phrase "bonne femme" is borrowed from the beginning of Perrault's *Diamonds and Toads.*) In contrast, the first French publisher of Grimm's tales did not hesitate in 1826 to issue a copy by the French engraver Ambroise Tardieu that was illustrated with etchings by the Englishman George Cruikshank, probably because that remarkable artist had, in 1823, created a witty version of the Perrault frontispiece, based on the fireside-corner iconography, and had already transferred it to Grimm's tales.

The frontispieces also record changes in the nature of children's books during the nineteenth century. During the Romantic period the notion of picture books as "toy books" arose. The traditional duodecimo format of the children's book evolved into an album to be placed on a corner of the drawing room table and flipped through by mother and child. (Here are the roots of the coffee-table book!) The picture equates reading with other nursery activities, such as building a castle with cards or playing with a doll. Children's literature then began to illustrate games. The little theater designed to be used by the family circle was depicted on top of the box containing it, in a vignette which serves as the pictorial equivalent of an explanatory notice. Mother Goose has now been replaced with the mother in the domestic space of the nursery.

Like Cruikshank, all major book illustrators were challenged by Perrault's frontispiece. The Art Nouveau designer Mucha created a symbolist version of it to illustrate Xavier Marmier's *Contes des grandsmères.* Reclining in an armchair, the grandmother tells her two grandchildren a story: one of them, long-haired and lying in bed, is attracted by the fantastic creatures in the tale and nightmarish figures emerge from the background, as in Goya's famous *Capriccio 43, el Sueño de la razón produce monstruos.* This rendering is also derived from the intersection of two prototypes from earlier illustrated books: for the background, the Romantic vignettes after Tony Johannot's (1843) *Le Voyage où il vous plaira*; for the foreground, the frontispiece by Doré to *Contes de Perrault* (Perrault 1862), both published by Hetzel.

Doré's interpretation was a brilliant synthesis of traditional motifs and new ones. Mother Goose became a grandmother with spectacles, sitting in a cozy armchair with children of various ages sprawled around her or sitting on her knees. Even the mother, positioned behind her like a guardian angel, is listening. The foreground is strewn with toys typical of a contemporary nursery: the theater is a metaphor of the illustration process, traditionally associated with the frontispiece iconography. But the importance of illustrations is underlined primarily by the painting on the back wall. It recalls the emblematic archetype of *Hop o' My Thumb,* picturing the scene where the hero pulls on the ogre's boots, which is also treated inside the book. The painting's ornamental gilt frame is a sign that, for Doré, illustrations are similar to paintings, individual works of art which do not need to rely on an accompanying text because their subject matter is accessible to anyone—the tales are universally known. Children look at picture books; they do not read them. Toy books and albums from the second half of the nineteenth century were based on that fact. These were the luxury books, published as New Year's gifts and designed as beautiful "frames" for the illustrators' visions. Doré's interpretation of Perrault's tales was the culmination of a slow process leading to the text's transformation into a classic of children's literature, on the one hand, and to the establishment of the tales as masterpieces of universal literature, on the other. During the second half of the century, the tales became the subject matter of Salon paintings: *Cinderella* and *Riquet with the Tuft* were painted by Gaston La Touche (1854-1913) in such works as *Le Mariage de Riquet à la houppe* (Musée d'Orsay); *Hop o' My Thumb* was the subject of a Gobelin tapestry (Abbeville Town Hall) by Luc-Olivier Merson (1846-1920). Millet illustrated the tales in two series of drawings for his children and grandchildren (Département des arts graphiques, Louvre). Perrault's tales had become so famous that the text was, paradoxically, no longer a necessary component of picture books. Each period added new pictures to the original group of single illustrations. In Doré's interpretation, some striking images of Little Red Riding-Hood and Hop o' My Thumb are placed in the preface, well ahead of the stories' positions. And within the body of the tales, his illustrations—which had so much impact on young readers, as George Sand later recalled—are displayed on independent plates grouped in pictorial suites. Doré's conception was consistent with the new definition of the picture book as a kind of armchair fantasy-film show.

The illustration of Perrault's tales provides an interesting case where the image is permanently present, from the manuscript to the printed edition and from edition to edition. The first edition was affiliated with the emblematic tradition, in which the vignette appeared between title and text. Within the familiar context of the fireside evening, the Mother Goose frontispiece included many details drawn from the tales (e.g., the keyhole, the candle, and the cat). The plate acquired the force of a kind of memory image, connected to the content of the tales but simultaneously stressing the issue of oral versus written culture. The transformations of the frontispiece mark the introduction of Perrault's tales into children's literature and register several changes in the culture of reading which evolved during the nineteenth century. Most surprising of all is a factor highlighted by Doré's version—the number and power of the images that finally evicted Perrault's text, replacing it with oral commentary suggested to child and adult by the images themselves. The picture ultimately restored the book to the oral culture initially displaced by the printed word, just as the poster of the frontispiece engraved by Clouzier revealed.

References

Barchilon, Jacques, ed. 1956. *Perrault's Tales of Mother Goose: The Dedication Manuscript of 1695 Reproduced in Collotype Facsimile with Introduction and Critical Text* (New York: Pierpont Morgan Library).

Bassy, Alain-Marie. 1974. "Du texte à l'illustration: Pour une sémiologie des étapes," *Semiotica* 2(4): 297-334.

1976. "Les Fables de La Fontaine et le labyrinthe de Versailles," *Revue française d'histoire du livre* (Fall).

1986. *Les Fables de La Fontaine: Quatre siècles d'illustration* (Paris: Promodis).

Bettelheim, Bruno. 1976. *The Uses of Enchantment* (New York: Alfred A. Knopf).

Bonnefon, Paul. 1904. "Charles Perrault. Essai sur sa vie et ses ouvrages," *Revue d'Histoire littéraire de la France* 11: 365-420.

Darnton, Robert. 1984. *The Great Cat Massacre* (New York: Basic Books).

Du Fail, Noël. 1956. [1547] "Propos rustiques de maître Léon Ladulfi Champenois," in *Conteurs français du XVIè siècle,* 620-21 (Paris: Pierre Jourda).

Duportal, Jeanne. 1914. *Etude sur les livres à figures édités en France de 1601 à 1660* (Paris: H. Champion).

Escarpit, Denise. 1985. *Histoire d'un conte, le "Chat botté" en France et en Angleterre* (Paris: Didier-Erudition, s.d.).

Gumuchian Catalogue. 1931. *Les Livres de l'enfance du XVè au XIXè siècle* (Paris: Librairie Gumuchian).

Johannot, Tony. 1843. *Le Voyage où il vous plaira* (Paris: Hetzel).

Klein, Robert 1970. *La Forme et l'intelligible* (Paris: Gallimard).

Le Men, Ségolène, and Annie Renonciat. 1989. *Livres d'enfants, livres d'images* (Paris: Réunion des Musées Nationaux).

Marin, Louis. 1990. [1984] "La Trajectoire d'une illustration: Un conte de Perrault," *Europe* (November-December).

Noesser, Laura. 1986. "L'Illustration dans le conte merveilleux (1700-1940)," *La Revue des livres pour enfants* 107-8: 75-84.

Perrault, Charles. 1675. *Recueil de divers ouvrages en prose et en vers, Le Labyrinthe de Versailles* (Paris: Jean-Baptiste Coignard).

1677-1679. *Imprimérie royale* edition. Plates by Sébastien Le Clere.

1697. *Histoires, ou Contes du temps passé* (Paris: Barbin).

1862. *Contes de Perrault.* Frontispiece by Gustave Doré (Paris: Hetzel).

Praz, Mario. 1939-1947. *Studies in Seventeenth-Century Imagery,* edited by Fritz Saxl (London: Warburg Institute).

Renonciat, Annie. 1990. "Petit Poucet dans la jonchée des feuilles," *Le Vieux papier* (April): 205-18.

Shapiro, Meyer. 1973. *Words and Pictures: On the Literal and the Symbolic in the Illustration of a Text* (Paris and The Hague: Mouton).

Shavit, Zohar. 1986. *Poetics of Children's Literature* (Athens: University of Georgia Press).

Soriano, Marc. 1968. *Les Contes de Perrault: Culture savante et Traditions populaires* (Paris: Gallimard).

Teneze, Marie-Louise. 1957. "Si Peau d'Ane m'était conte . . . A propos de trois illustrations des Contes de Perrault," *Arts et traditions populaires* (April-December): 313-16.

Velay-Vallantin, Catherine. 1987. "Le Miroir des contes. Perrault dans les bibliothèques bleues," in *Les Usages de l'imprimé,* edited by R. Chartier, 129-85 (Paris: Fayard).

Wilhelm, Jacques. 1936. "Le Labyrinthe de Versailles," *Revue de l'histoire de Versailles et de Seine-et-Oise* (January-March).

Zipes, Jack. 1983. *Fairy Tales and the Art of Subversion: The Technical Genre for Children and the Process of Civilization* (London: Heinemann).

Elizabeth W. Harries (essay date June 1996)

SOURCE: Harries, Elizabeth W. "Simulating Oralities: French Fairy Tales of the 1690s." *College Literature* 23, no. 2 (June 1996): 100-15.

[*In the following essay, Harries evaluates Perrault's fairy tale collections and those of other seventeenth-century authors as they relate to the role of women writers in oral storytelling.*]

> . . . we must give up the fiction that collects these sounds under the sign of a 'Voice,' of a 'Culture' of its own—or of the great Other's. Rather, orality insinuates itself . . . into the network—an endless tapestry—of a scriptural economy.
>
> Michel de Certeau, *The Practice of Everyday Life,* 132

Fairy tales and orality seem intimately connected. We think of written tales as transcribing stories handed down orally for hundreds of years, as simply "putting into print" the traces of that long-standing tradition. Most writers of fairy tales have done their best to reinforce that impression: Charles Perrault's alternative title, *Tales of Mother Goose,* suggests a traditional, spoken origin; the Grimm brothers work hard to create a simple and naive narrative voice: Hans Christian Andersen's stories often begin with formulae like "now then, here's where we begin" that imitate oral story-telling. I don't mean to deny that many fairy tales had been (and continue to be) part of an ongoing oral, popular culture, but I do want to show that our sense of access to that culture through reading fairy tales is an illusion—an illusion carefully and deliberately created by many fairy tale collectors, editors, and writers.

We can become conscious of that illusion by looking at another strand in the history of written fairy tales—the tales written by women in the 1690s in France. Unlike Perrault, their contemporary, these women only occasionally appealed to the oral, popular tradition and never attempted to imitate an illiterate or uneducated voice. Rather, they simulated a different kind of orality—the conversation that animated the salons of the later seventeenth century. Most of the long, elaborate tales they wrote are set within a conversational frame, a frame that reproduces the milieu and the carefully formulated repartee that was part of salon culture.[1]

The frontispiece of the 1697 edition of Perrault's *Contes* [*Histoires ou Contes du temps passé, avec des moralitez*]—a frontispiece that has become so familiar to us that we no longer see its full implications—defines one conception of the oral story-telling situation. Let's look at it again: the frontispiece gives us, in miniature, a version of what the traditional story-telling situation is traditionally thought to be. The frontispiece shows a fireside scene: three fashionably-dressed children seated by a fireplace, listening to a simply-dressed older woman, perhaps a nurse, tell a story.[2] The fire and the candle suggest that the story-telling is taking place in the evening, as in the traditional *viellée*; the lock on the door and the cat by the fireplace underscore the intimacy and the comforting domesticity of the scene. The older title of the collection, the title that Perrault had used for an earlier manuscript edition of the *Contes* in 1695, appears as a placard affixed to the door in the background, just above the spindle that is traditionally associated with women's story-telling: *Contes de ma Mere Loye* [*Stories of Mother Goose*].[3] The writing on the placard is rather irregular and clumsy, compared to the elegance of the type used on the title-page, just as the title on the placard contrasts with the more elaborate and distanced formal title: *Histoires ou Contes du temps passé, avec des Moralitez* [*Stories of Times Past, with Morals*]. In the physical set-up of the first edition, there is a subterranean tension between appeals to the aristocratic audience Perrault hoped to reach (as in the dedication to Louis XIV's niece, with its elaborate coat of arms) and appeals to a peasant story-telling tradition.

As Catherine Velay-Vallantin has pointed out, the frontispiece suggests the fictive reading situation that Perrault and his publisher wanted to prescribe, a simulation of oral tale-telling, or what she calls "factitious orality" (130).[4] In his prose tales, Perrault mimes the voice of the peasant story-teller, always elegantly walking the line between the practices of writing and the supposed "oral" transmission "within a culturally more aristocratic mode of reading" (132). The frontispiece also suggests that the voice that Perrault is simulating is female. Women are often supposed to be tellers of tales: those anonymous, lower-class nurses and grandmothers who taught and entertained children by telling them stories. The murky legend of "Mother Goose" is an instance of this belief; Madame de Sévigné's letter of October

30, 1656, refers to it casually, as if this were part of the well-known lore about fairy tales:

> Et si, Mademoiselle, afin que vous le sachiez, ce n'est pas un conte de ma mère l'oie,
>
> Mais de la cane de Montfort
>
> Qui, ma foi, lui resemble fort.
>
> [And if, Mademoiselle, you must know, this is not a tale of Mother Goose, but of the drake of Montfort, there are strong resemblances between them.]

Perrault's frontispiece confirms the prevailing myth about the appropriate role for women in the transmission of fairy tales: as patient, nurturing conduits of oral culture or spinners of tales.

This belief has not really faded. As Trinh Minh-ha says, "The world's earliest archives were the memories of women. Patiently transmitted from mouth to ear, body to body, hand to hand. . . . Every woman partakes in the chain of guardianship and of transmission" (121).[5] Trinh still imagines oral culture as literally handed down by women, in a particularly physical, intimate way ("from mouth to ear, body to body, hand to hand"). Women are still said to be the guardians of tradition, passing on to their children and grandchildren the stories of their culture. But, as folklorists like Linda Dégh have shown, women are and were not the only, or even the primary, story tellers in most oral cultures.[6] The myth of the anonymous female teller of tales, particularly strong in the legend of Mother Goose, is just that: a myth—but a myth that has several important functions and corollaries. If women are the tellers of tales, story-telling remains a motherly (or grand-motherly) function, tied (to use the language of the French feminist critics) to the body and nature, as we see in the quotation from Trinh. Stories are supposed to flow from women like milk and blood. And if women are thought of as *tellers* of tales, it follows that they are not imagined as the collectors or writers of tales. As fairy tales moved from oral tales to "book tales" (*Buchmärchen,* or tales that have been written down) to written, invented tales (*Kunstmärchen*), women were subtly relegated to the most "primitive" stage. Perrault's frontispiece may have been an attempt to etch his female writing competitors out of existence.

The frontispieces of volumes of tales the women wrote in the 1690s tales often seem to be designed to contest the ideological force of Perrault's. In the frontispiece of early editions (1698 and 1711) of Marie-Catherine le Jumel de Barneville, Baronne d'Aulnoy's

Contes nouveaux (reproduced in Gabrielle Verdier's recent article about the *conteuses*), a woman dressed as a sibyl is writing the title of one of Aulnoy's tales, "Gracieuse et Percinet," in a large folio or book, again with children as her audience, but children dressed in rather the same way and probably of the same class as the story-teller. The story-teller is *not* represented with a spindle, but rather with the flowing robes and turban-like headpiece usually associated with a sibyl. There's a fireplace, but the fire is out. Instead of the locked door, there is a window opening out on a summer country scene. Instead of the domestic cat, there is an exotic monkey—again perhaps a reference to one of Aulnoy's tales, "Babiole"). This mirror effect—the reflection of some of the tales in the introductory picture—heightens the conscious articiality of the scene and of the tales that follow.

The frontispieces of a 1725 Amsterdam edition of Aulnoy's *Nouveaux contes des fées* also work against the image of the woman as lower-class story-teller. The frontispiece of Volume I shows a fashionably dressed women seated on an elevated dais, gesticulating as she speaks to an audience, similarly dressed, that seems to be primarily adult. Far from an enclosed, domestic, fireside scene, this is a large room with classical columns and an open window that looks out on a faintly classical landscape with obelisks and a tower. The decorative *rocaille* around the title at the top of the page underscores the aristocratic milieu of this story-teller. The frontispiece of Volume II again represents a woman writing: we see a woman with a helmet on her head—probably Pallas Athena, since she is accompanied by an owl—writing on a large tablet with a quill and apparently speaking at the same time. In the foreground there is an audience of fashionably dressed adults, in the background a scene that might represent, in miniature, the plot of one of Aulnoy's tales. The frontispieces used for the *conteuses*' tales, then, usually represent them as sibyls, or aristocratic story-tellers, or as Greek goddesses, not as spinning peasant women.[7] In another paradoxical illustration of the interweaving of the oral and the written, they often are represented as "writing to an audience," inscribing words on a tablet or folio in front of a listening group.

Because women have been perennially associated with the telling of tales—in nurseries, in spinning and weaving circles, in quilting bees, by the fireside—it has been difficult for them to think of themselves, and to be thought of, as fairy-tale writers. As Joan DeJean points out in *Tender Geographies,*

France was the only country where "the written transcription of fairy tales was not totally controlled by men" (233n), at least until the nineteenth century. It was not primarily the traditional passivity of most female protagonists of fairy tales that made it difficult for women to take the active step of writing them down and inventing them, but rather the pervasive notion that women were the designated oral transmitters of those tales. But the women who wrote tales in the 1690s chose frontispieces and created narrative structures that contested this limiting prescription. The tales the women wrote—again in contrast to Perrault's—are full of references to a feminine, aristocratic, listening audience: "Perhaps you are going to think, Madame . . ."; "Isn't it true, Countess, that . . ."; "I'm sure you have heard, Madame. . . ." The typographical forms in which their tales were printed rarely reflect any interest in suggesting popular origins for the tales; rather they tend to be identical to those forms in which the many novels and "nouvelles" of the late 1600s were printed. Perrault's tales in his 1697 volume always have a crude illustrative engraving on the first page; the tales in the women's collections usually have only the same decorative stylized headpieces that they use for their other writing. The tales embedded in the women's novels are sometimes not set off from the rest of the text at all, as in Aulnoy's "Ile de la félicité" (usually considered to be the first written fairy tale in France, included in her 1690 novel *Hipolyte, Comte du Duglas*); sometimes they are separated by a chaste and simple border of florets. The *conteuse*'s words do not appear "in costume" to delight children or to simulate popular orality;[8] their fairy-tales are primarily documents of an ongoing (though perhaps fading) salon practice.[9]

II

To trace the tales written in the 1690s by women, then, is to trace a practice based on a very different conception of the "oral" from Perrault's dominant model. The *conteuses* do sometimes write stories based on traditional material; they also occasionally echo traditional formulae that seem to define women as the oral conduits of popular culture. For example, both Perrault, in his verse tale **"Peau de l'âne"** (1694), and his niece Marie-Jeanne L'Héritier, in her tale "Les enchantemens de l'éloquence" (1696), include almost identical verses:

> Ils ne sont pas aisez à croire:
> Mais tant que dans le monde on verra des enfants.
> Des meres & des mere-grands,
> On en gardera la memoire.

[These stories are not easy to believe, but as long as there are children, mothers, and grandmothers in the world, they will be remembered.][10]

These lines, and other similar ones, occur once in a while in the women's tales, linking the written stories to an ongoing tradition of story-telling and marking that tradition as transmitted by women to children. But, much more often, and usually simultaneously, the *conteuses* place their tales in the complex and playful ambience of salon conversation. The "oral" for them is not primarily naive and primitive, but rather a highly-charged, high-cultural event.

We still tend to identify the oral with peasant, illiterate, or "folk" culture; like the Grimms, we tend to think of the oral as coming before the written, or as part of the origins of culture. But, as Alan Dundes has pointed out, there are many different kinds of "folk" and illiteracy is not a requirement.[11] Walter J. Ong has pointed to a different kind of orality: the residues of ancient rhetorical practices that continued to be taught in schools for boys throughout the seventeenth century.[12] In his book *Orality and Literacy,* Ong makes an interesting guess about women's leading role in the invention of the novel:

> A great gap in our understanding of the influence of women on literary style and genre could be bridged or closed though attention to the orality-literacy-print shift . . . early women novelists and other women writers generally worked from outside the oral tradition because of the simple fact that girls were not commonly subjected to the orally based rhetorical training that boys got in school. . . . Certainly, non-rhetorical styles congenial to women writers helped make the novel what it is: more like a conversation than a platform performance.
>
> (159-60)

It seems to me, however, that Ong's guess about the relationship of early women writers to orality is off the mark, at least in France. Or rather, his primary conception of secondary orality (orality that persists after the introduction of writing) is in fact a very narrow, academic, and elite one—and not very "oral" at all. The women who wrote fairy tales were interested in simulating another kind of oral transmission, a practice that Ong never mentions. He suggests, at the end of the passage I've quoted, that women's writing tended to be based on "conversation" rather than on platform rhetoric—but he never acknowledges that conversation, including the ritualized conversation of the salons, is after all an oral practice, too. In his laudable attempt to think about women in relation to orality and writing, he in fact defines the oral tradition in a way that excludes them.

I think we need to develop more nuanced categories of the oral—categories that will permit us to see the ways oral practices that do not derive from the ancient techniques of rhetoric taught in schools continue to leave their traces in written texts. The nostalgia for the oral that permeates most written narratives can take on very different forms. The orality that has left its marks in many fairy tales is rarely the disputational "harangue" of Ong's school-based oratorical rhetoric, and not always the pseudo-folk situation that is sketched in Perrault's frontispiece. Rather the women of the 1690s attempted to reproduce the conversational ambience of the salons that had formed them as writers. As Joan DeJean has shown in *Tender Geographies,* "the conversational style . . . is originally a female concept, invented in the salons and reinscribed in prose fiction when, following Scudéry's example, women found a new power base in the republic of letters" (47). While her claim seems too broad, forgetting the conversational basis of earlier texts like Plato's dialogues or the *Decameron,* DeJean rightly emphasizes the importance of conversation in women's writing of the later seventeenth century in France.

Like the earlier novels by Scudéry or Villedieu, the *conteuses'* tales grew out of the competitive, scintillating dialogues that were an integral part of the salons. First fairy tales were a diversion in the salons, one of the many collaborative "divertissements" that formed part of salon culture, like riddles, metamorphoses, portraits, and "maximes d'amour"; then they were written down. But both practices seem to have continued simultaneously throughout the 1690s; as Roger Chartier has said, "the opposition of oral and written fails to account for the situation that existed from the sixteenth to the eighteenth century when media and multiple practices still overlapped" (170).[13] This was true in popular culture, where evening tale-telling coexisted with the publication of fairy tales in chapbooks and *colporteur* literature. And, I believe, it was equally true in the aristocratic practices of the salons. Tale-telling and tale-writing went on simultaneously, as many of the frontispieces suggest.

Like all oral cultures, the culture of the salons is difficult to recover. We know much more about it than about many other oral cultures, because the participants were literate; they wrote about what went on at the salons in their letters, memoirs, even novels. But it was fluid, ephemeral, constantly changing. The evidence we have of the ways stories were told and received is spotty and unreliable—found mostly in letters like Sévigné's and novels like Segrais's *Les Nouvelles françaises ou les divertissements de la princesse Aurélie* (1656), about the group around the Grande Mademoiselle during her exile at Saint-Fargeau, or La Force's *Jeux d'esprit* (1701), about the "divertissements" that the Princesse de Conti promoted during her exile at Eu in the early seventeenth century. Madame de Sévigné, in her letter of August 6, 1677, suggests all the artificiality and the incongruities of a fairy-tale-telling scene at court—as well as its links with the opera—in order to establish the oral situation in which it took place:

> Mme de Coulanges, qui m'est venue faire ici une fort honnête visite qui durera jusqu'à demain, voulut bien nous faire part des contes avec quoi l'on amuse les dames de Versailles: cela s'appelle les *mitonner.* Elle nous mitonna donc, et nous parla d'une île verte, où l'on élevoit une princesse plus belle que le jour: c'étoient les fées qui souffloient sur elle à tout moment.

> (August 6, 1677: 320)

> [Mme de Coulanges, who has come here to pay me a gracious visit that will last until tomorrow, wanted to acquaint us with the stories that are currently amusing the ladies of Versailles: that is called *cajoling* them. She cajoled us then, and told us about a green island, where a princess more beautiful than the day was being brought up; it was the fairies who breathed on her at every moment.]

Sévigné, with her usual clear-eyed irony, is not much amused by the fantastic fairy-tale, which lasts "une bonne heure" [a good hour]. She makes use of the neologism *mitonner* in order to mock the tone and flavor of the storytelling.[14] In 1677, neither Mme de Coulanges, her court source, or Mme de Sévigné herself thinks of fairy tales as written, but rather as part of a concrete social milieu—far from the homely, domestic milieu sketched in Perrault's frontispiece.

Recently several writers have attempted to look at the conversation of the salons in its relationship to French intellectual and artistic life in the seventeenth and eighteenth centuries.[15] While acknowledging its elusiveness, they have brought out some of its crucial features: the allusive word-play, the emphasis on repartee and collaborative exchange, the emphasis on improvisation, the absence of weighty "sujet." Erica Harth believes that the salons became "a discursive dead end for women" (17)—and, if one is primarily interested in women becoming recognized as philosophers, this is probably true. But I see the discourse or, to use a less weighty term, "talk" of the salons as a literary proving ground—not only for the novel, as DeJean has shown, but also for fairy tales. Just as salon talk influenced the suggestive brush-strokes of Watteau's canvases, it also provided the airy framework for the castles and enchanted islands that were staples of the fairy tales women wrote.

And here I mean "framework" in a rather literal way. Though Perrault often used the dialogue form in his more "serious" works—the ***Parallèle des anciens et des modernes*** (1692), for example—he abandoned it when he wrote his ***Contes,*** preferring to create the naive, solitary voice of "Ma Mère Loye" [Mother Goose]. His women contemporaries, however, saw in the give and take of salon dialogue a useful way to introduce and frame the stories they were writing. Though they may not have collaborated on individual stories (I have found no evidence that they did), they situated themselves and their stories in this sparkling, collaborative interchange. Both Raymonde Robert and Lewis Seifert argue that the framing device was primarily to give a nostalgic illusion of "social cohesion" or class solidarity.[16] I want to argue here, however, that the frames had another, narrative function.

Reading tales like L'Héritier's "The Adroit Princess" (1696) in their original form, in fact, we discover that most later editions and translations have wrenched her tales out of their conversational frame. "The Adroit Princess" is dedicated to Mme de Murat and begins as if L'Héritier were carrying on a dialogue with her:

> Vous faites les plus jolies Nouvelles du monde en Vers; mais en Vers aussi doux que naturels: je voudrois bien, charmante Comtesse, vous en dire une à mon tour; cependant je ne sai si vous pourrez vous en divertir: je suis aujourd'huy de l'humeur du Bourgeois-Gentilhomme; je ne voudrois ni Vers, ni Prose pour vous la conter: point de grands mots, point de brillans, point de rimes; un tour naif m'accomode mieux; en un mot, un récit sans façon et comme on parle. . . .
>
> (229-30)

> [You create the most beautiful "nouvelles" in the world in verse, but in verse as sweet as natural: I would like, charming Countess, to tell you one in my turn; however, I'm not sure it will amuse you: today I feel like [Molière's] Bourgeois Gentilhomme; I don't want to use verse or prose to tell it to you: no grand words, no startling effects, no rhymes; a naive tone suits me better; in a word, a story ["récit," which retains the aura of the oral] told without any ceremony and as one speaks. . . .]

There are lots of interesting things here, particularly L'Héritier's claim that she has used a language that's simple and "naive," a language that is not formal but rather is written "as one speaks." Simplicity, a key word for both Perrault and these women writers when they talk about the language of their tales, is never a pure transcription, but rather a constructed and carefully pruned version of actual speech. Like Perrault, L'Héritier is creating a special, stripped-down language for her tales. Unlike Perrault, however, she does not claim to be reproducing the voice of a peasant story-teller. Rather, she is interested in recapturing the elegant simplicity of the language current in the salons, always characterized as "naive" even at its most artificial and constructed. In his recent chapter, "Origins of the Fairy Tale," Jack Zipes describes the rhetoric of the *conteuses* this way: "they placed great emphasis on certain rules of oration such as naturalness and formlessness. The teller of the tale was to make it 'seem' as though the tale were made up on the spot and did not follow prescribed rules" (21). This assumed "naiveté" and simplicity is a crucial feature of the language promoted in the salons.

And we do not hear this language as a monologue, the uninterrupted voice of a single story-teller. L'Héritier speaks of telling a story *in her turn*; that is, she conceives of story-telling as an exchange. She imagines a situation rather like the situation in the *Decameron* or in Marguerite de Navarre's *Heptaméron,* or in Basile's *Pentamerone,* in which the characters in the frame tell stories. This seems to have been the way fairy-tales played a role in the salons: members of the group took turns, often adding to and elaborating on the tales others had just told. L'Héritier echoes this reciprocal, sometimes competitive, sometimes collaborative story-telling (a version of what Joan DeJean calls "salon writing") in her written tales.[17]

In the earliest novels that included fairy tales—Aulnoy's *Hipolyte, Comte de Duglas* (1690) for example—the tale is always told by a character in the novel, sometimes in very contrived situations. The hero of Aulnoy's novel tells the tale of the "Ile de la Félicité" to an abbess to distract her while her portrait is being painted. He is in disguise as the painter's assistant; his beloved Julie is quasi-imprisoned in the abbey. The tale—a long story that mingles classical references and motifs that the hero remembers from the "contes des fées" he has heard on his travels—seems in part to be a retarding moment, designed to build up the suspense that leads to the lovers' reunion. But it also establishes the convention that many of the later writers of fairy tales follow (though significantly *not* Perrault): the creation of a conversational frame for the tales.

At the height of fairy-tale production, five years later, the tales become a more motivated and "natural" part of the action. In Catherine Bernard's novel *Inés de Cordoüe* (1696), two contrasting fairy tales are told by rival ladies at the Spanish court of the late sixteenth century, each trying to outdo the other. Since the Queen of Spain, Elizabeth, is French—a point that the novel underlines—she has preserved the custom of holding "conversations" for four or five hours a day, and is always thinking up new amusements for the group that gathers in her "cabinet" (6-7). Bernard carefully establishes Elizabeth's salon as the place where the court could escape the legendary severity of Philip II, a retreat to French "galanterie" and arts.[18]

In this milieu, the heroine Inés tells the story of "Le Prince Rosier," a story that features appearances of fairies in miniature chariots of ivory and princes transformed into rosebushes, but that is essentially about the impossibility of unchanging true love. Her rival Leonor responds by telling the story of "Riquet à la Houppe," a story that Perrault also retold; this is also, unlike Perrault's, a tale in which no one lives "happily ever after." Like "Le Prince Rosier," her version of the tale runs counter to the form we expect fairy tales to take. Both women tell stories that are marked by the marvelous: in "Le Prince Rosier" a guardian fairy and miraculous transformations; in **"Riquet à la Houppe"** fairies and a subterranean realm occupied by gnomes. Though the decor is fantastic, the emotional climate is in fact quite grimly realistic: in both "le mariage, selon la coustume, finit tous les agrémens de leur vie" (43) [marriage, as is the custom, ended all the pleasures of their lives].

These stories suggest some of the distinctiveness of the tales the women wrote, their tendency to work against the "happily ever after" we now expect as an ending. But, in the context Bernard provides for them, they also show us the way the tales grew out of salon culture, its diversions and rivalries. Inés's tale, for example, is praised by the Queen and many other members of the court; her rival Leonor, however,

> fit à Inés plusieurs questions sur ce conte avec autant de malice que d'aigreur. Inés y répondit avec une douceur qui acheva de la faire paroistre une personne parfaite.
>
> Le lendemain Leonor se prepara à conter une Fable, & n'oublia rien pour l'emporter s'il se pouvoit sur Inés. . . .
>
> (45)
>
> [asked Ines several questions about the story with as much malice as animosity. Ines answered with

a sweetness that had the effect of making her seem to be a perfect person.

> The next day Leonor got ready to tell a Fable, and did everything she could to make it superior to Ines's. . . .]

To tell a fairy tale well is a way to shine in the salon; Leonor is unable to attract the attention of the Marquis de Lerme, who clearly prefers Inés's story, "Prince Rosier." The entire plot of the novel—incredible though it often seems—is driven by Leonor's jealousy of Inés and her desire for revenge; the tale-telling sessions in the Queen's salon mark the beginning of the conflict between the perfect Inés and her most imperfect competitor.

When they begin writing fairy tales down, then, Aulnoy and Bernard and L'Héritier set them in an oral situation, but an oral situation that is far from the supposed Ur-situation that Perrault evokes in his frontispiece. Aulnoy continues to frame her tales; in the *Nouveaux Contes des fées* (1697), for example, the stories are set in a double frame: first a conversational milieu at Saint Cloud, then a Spanish "nouvelle" *Dom Gabriel Ponce de Leon.*) As the Madame D . . . of the preface (a transparent stand-in for Aulnoy herself) says,

> Voici un cahier tout prêt à vous lire; & pour le rendre plus agreable, j'y ai joint une nouvelle Espagnolle, qui est très-vraye & que je sçai d'original
>
> (7)
>
> [Here is a notebook ready to read to you; and to make it more charming, I have connected to it a Spanish novella, which is very true and also I think original.]

The fictionalized "author" of the tales, after being visited by a nymph, offers to *read* her tales aloud to her listeners; again reading and orality are explicitly invoked together. The conception of the oral that pervades the tales written by women is not the "factitious orality" that Perrault created, the simulation of the supposed stripped-down language of the "folk." And their tales were even less designed for children than Perrault's. Rather their written fairy tales grew primarily out of an aristocratic oral culture, a culture that, though often in opposition to the official culture of the court, always distinguished itself from the culture of the "menu people" as well.[19]

III

This leads to a final series of paradoxes: Perrault in his *Contes* manipulates conventions of the book, both typography and illustration, in order to create the illusion of "folk orality"—in the frontispiece, on the title-page, and in the crude illustrative headpieces of the tales. L'Héritier and the other women writers of the earlier 1690s, on the other hand, rely on the apparent transparency or neutrality of current print practices to carry on what seems to have been a living oral tradition. Instead of surrounding their tales with all the typographical signals of folk origins, they frame them in a conversational setting, a setting that marks their tales as part of an aristocratic and highly literate milieu.

Perrault, like the king in the *Arabian Nights,* pays apparent homage to the skills and cultural power of the female story-teller. He pretends to reproduce her voice, in a peculiar kind of narrative cross-dressing. But he appropriates that voice and that female figure for his own purposes—and, at the same time, represents her as unable to write.[20] The story-teller is female, but the story-writer is male.

Perrault attempts to create the illusion that he is reproducing story-telling as it existed in the oral popular culture of his day; his simulation of its practices became the dominant style and ideology of the fairy tale, as we see in the Grimms' prefaces and most writing on the fairy tale up to our time. But the women who also participated in the invention of the written fairy tale in France created a very different illusion—the illusion that the story is told within the conversational space of the salons. All these writers try to give the impression that the stories are being told aloud. They all simulate oralities, but the oralities they simulate are radically different and their methods of producing the illusion of orality even more so. Perrault simulates the oral by imitating (or inventing) the language and world of the folk and the image and voice of the woman tale-teller. Aulnoy, L'Héritier, and Bernard, however, reject the models of orality and of femininity that Perrault both accepts and promotes. By framing their tales with traces of salon conversation, they represent their tales as part of an aristocratic oral culture. By writing their tales down, they contest the notion that women can only tell the tales that men transcribe and transmit. And, in a final paradox, these women include traces of the oral as part of their attempt to create a new model of femininity: the woman who not only talks—by the fireside to children or in the salon—but also writes.[21]

Notes

1. Marina Warner's book *From the Beast to the Blonde,* which pays considerable attention to these women writers, appeared only after this article was completed. I haven't been able to take full account of her arguments—and my disagreements—here. But I think she is wrong to say that writers like Aulnoy ever assumed the persona of "the lower-class older woman" (166).

2. See Maria Tatar's discussion of various imitations of this scene in Germany and England in the nineteenth century, and the accompanying illustrations (Figures 8-14), in *The Hard Facts,* 106-114. She notes that the middle-class grandmother replaced the lower-class nurse in later illustrations, and that she is sometimes represented then as reading from a book. *Caveat*: the frontispiece in Marina Warner's new book is said to be the Perrault 1697 frontispiece. But it isn't; it must be from a later edition.

3. For a particularly interesting instance of this traditional association, see the discussion of *Les évangiles des quenouilles* [The Gospel of the distaffs], a fifteenth-century MS divided into *viellées,* about the tale-telling and talk of an exclusively lower-class women's group, in Danielle Régnier-Bohler's "Imagining the Self: Exploring Literature." (See also Warner 36-39 and *passim*.)

4. See her essay "Tales as a Mirror," particularly 95-97 and 128-32. Louis Marin's analysis of the frontispiece, in "Les Enjeux," also suggests the ways it plays into Perrault's literary strategies in designing his collection. See also Verdier's article, "Figures de la conteuse."

5. Trinh's chapter "Grandma's Stories" is a remarkable treasure-trove of myth about female story-telling. But see also Karen E. Rowe's "To Spin a Yarn: The Female Voice in Folklore and Fairy Tale," in which she explores—and accepts as a cultural given—the association between women's spinning, weaving, and story-telling. Her argument is more nuanced than many, however, since she recognizes that many stories allegedly told by women are controlled by male "editors" and collectors.

6. See Dégh's *Folktales and Society,* particularly Chapter 6.

7. Occasionally, as in the volume of tales by La Force in the same edition, the publishers use Perrault's frontispiece for tales by the *conteuses.* It seems impossible to determine who chose the frontispieces—publisher or author—and why. But I think that Perrault's frontispiece became a

kind of counter or default position—if you can't find another frontispiece, slap it on any collection of tales—while the other, more unusual frontispieces I have discussed above were consciously selected to show a different kind of tale transmission.

8. On words "in costume" and the effects of the materiality of print in literature for children, see Jeffrey Mehlman, *Walter Benjamin for Children: An Essay on His Radio Years* 6.

9. Gabrielle Verdier, in her "Figures de la conteuse," has studied the frontispieces of later works by Aulnoy in order to show that she rejects the model of the story-telling woman with the spindle in favor of a Sibyl-like figure. But her contention that these frontispieces show women writing seems too simple. (They often seem to be writing and speaking at the same time.) And she does not discuss the traces of salon conversation and practices that are present in the tales written by women.

10. See Perrault, *Contes* 75, and L'Héritier, *Oeuvres meslées* 163-4 (also reprinted in Perrault, vol. 239.

11. See his essay "Who are the Folk?" in *Interpreting Folklore* and Roger Chartier's analogous redefinitions of "popular culture."

12. In his essay "Latin Language Study as a Renaissance Puberty Rite," Ong makes it clear that "oral memory skills" and Latin were taught almost exclusively to boys. But, as far as I can tell, he does not see how narrow—and by the seventeenth century, how un-oral—his definition of "orality" is.

13. See also Ruth Finnegan in *Oral Poetry*: "In practice, interaction between oral and written forms is extremely common, and the idea that the use of writing *automatically* deals a death blow to oral literary forms has nothing to support it" (160). She gives examples from British and American balladry, Irish songs, and American cowboy laments, as well as modern Yugoslavia.

14. The new word "mitonner" derived from cookery, where it means to simmer slowly. (It's related to the word "mie," the soft part of a loaf of bread, the non-crusty part—a word that was also used in seventeenth-century France for a governess, though that is usually thought to be short for "amie.") The word tends to have connotations of flattery, buttering someone up so

that that person will do something for you. (Examples Furetière gives in his *Dictionnaire* of 1693 include "This nephew *mitonne* his uncle, so that he will make his heir," and "this cavalier *mitonne* the old woman, so that she will give him her daughter in marriage.") But the word here seems to have slightly different connotations: the story-tellers at court seem to be treating their audience, the ladies of Versailles, as governesses treat spoiled children, catering to their wishes (perhaps in order to get into their good graces).

15. These include Erica Harth's study of women in the Cartesian tradition and Mary Vidal's work on Watteau. Benedetta Craveri summarizes their efforts and others' in her essay "The Lost Art."

16. See Robert 330-335 and Seifert, "Marvelous Realities" 1. Armine Kotin Mortimer also emphasizes the frame primarily as a representation of a closed and exclusive society.

17. See *Tender Geographies,* 22-24, 71-77. For a brief account of the way these practices affected the transmission of fairy tales, see Jack Zipes's introduction to *Beauties, Beasts, and Enchantment,* particularly 2-4, and his recent "Origins of the Fairy Tale" 20-23. Renate Baader also is helpful in understanding the role fairy tales played in the salons

18. This may be a camouflaged reference to the function of the salons in the late years of Louis XIV's reign, when he was increasingly influenced by the puritanical practices of Mme de Maintenon. See Dorothy R. Thelander's article, "Mother Goose and her Goslings," for a discussion of the "muffled aristocratic disaffection" (493) that the tales reveal.

19. In the dedication to Louis XIV's niece, Perrault argues that he has included tales that show what goes on "dans les moindres familles" [in the least important families] to give her and other potential rulers some idea of what the life of their subjects is like. L'Héritier, on the other hand, explicitly distinguishes her tales from popular ones: she says that tales told and retold by the folk must have picked up impurities, much as pure water picks up garbage as it flows through a dirty canal: "if the people are simple, they are also crude (*grossière*)" (*Oeuvres meslées* 312-3).

20. As Karen Rowe says, often "a male author or collector attributes to a female the original power of articulating silent matter. But having

attributed this transformative artistic intelligence and voice to a woman, the narrator then reclaims for himself . . . the controlling power of retelling, of literary recasting and of dissemination to the folk." (61)

21. My thanks to Margaret Higonnet and Ulrich Knoepflmacher, for their encouragement when I began work on these problems, and to Ruth Solie, for her help in bringing them to a conclusion, however paradoxical. I also learned a great deal from the participants in a Guthrie Workshop at Dartmouth on French and Italian fairy tales (March, 1995).

Works Cited

Aulnoy, Marie-Catherine le Jumel de Barneville, Baronne de. *Histoire d' Hipolyte, comte de Duglas.* 1690. Geneva: Slatkine, 1979.

————. *Nouveaux contes des fees.* 1697. Amsterdam: Estienne Roger, 1725.

Baader, Renate. *Dames de Lettres: Autorinnen des preziösen, hocharistokratischen und 'modernen' Salons (1649-1698).* Stuttgart: Metzler, 1986.

Barchilon, Jacques. *Le conte merveilleux français de 1690 à 1790.* Paris: Champion, 1975.

Bernard, Catherine. *Inés de Cordoüe: Nouvelle Espagnole.* 1696. Geneva: Slatkine, 1979.

Certeau, Michel de. *The Practice of Everyday Life.* Trans. Steven Rendall. Berkeley: U of California P, 1984.

Chartier, Roger. "Texts, Printing, Reading." *The New Cultural History.* Ed. Lynn Hunt. Berkeley: U of California P, 1989. 154-175.

Craveri, Benedetta. "The Lost Art." *New York Review of Books* (December 2, 1993): 40-43.

Dégh, Linda. *Folktales and Society: Story-Telling in a Hungarian Peasant Community.* Trans. Emily M. Schossberger. 1962. Bloomington: Indiana UP, 1969.

DeJean, Joan. *Tender Geographies: Women and the Origins of the Novel in France.* Gender and Culture Series. New York: Columbia UP, 1991.

Dundes, Alan. *Interpreting Folklore.* Bloomington: Indiana UP, 1980.

Finnegan, Ruth. *Oral Poetry: Its Nature, Significance, and Social Context.* Cambridge: Cambridge UP, 1977.

Harth, Erica. *Cartesian Women: Versions and Subversions of Rational Discourse in the Old Regime.* Ithaca: Cornell UP, 1992.

La Force, Charlotte-Rose Caumont. *Les Jeux d'Esprit ou la Promenade de la Princeses de Conti à Eu.* Ed. de la Grange. Paris: Auguste Aubry, 1862.

L'Héritier de Villandon, Marie-Jeanne. *Oeuvres meslées.* Paris: Guignard, 1696.

Marin, Louis. "Les Enjeux d'un frontispice." *L'Esprit Créateur* 27 (1987): 49-57.

Mehlman, Jeffrey. *Walter Benjamin for Children: An Essay on His Radio Years.* Chicago: U of Chicago P, 1993.

Mortimer, Armine Kotin. "La clôture féminine des *Jeux d'Esprit.*" *L'Esprit Créateur* 23 (1983): 107-116.

Ong, Walter J. "Latin Language Study as a Renaissance Puberty Rite." *Rhetoric, Romance, and Technology: Studies in the Interaction of Expression and Culture.* Ithaca: Cornell UP, 1971.

————. *Orality and Literacy: The Technologizing of the Word.* London: Methuen, 1982.

Perrault, Charles. *Contes.* Ed. Gilbert Rouger. Paris: Garnier, 1967.

Régnier-Bohler, Danielle. "Imagining the Self: Exploring Literature." *A History of Private Life.* Ed. Philippe Ariès and Georges Duby. Trans. Arthur Goldhammer. Vol. 2. Cambridge: Harvard UP, 1985.

Robert, Raymonde. *Le Conte de fées littéraire en France de la fin du XVIIIe à la fin du XVIIe siècle.* Nancy: Presses Universitaires de Nancy, 1982.

Rowe, Karen E. "To Spin a Yarn: The Female Voice in Folklore and Fairy Tale." *Fairy Tales and Society: Illusion, Allusion, and Paradigm.* Ed. Ruth B. Bottigheimer. Philadelphia: U of Pennsylvania P, 1986. 53-74.

Seifert, Lewis. "Marvelous Realities: Toward an Understanding of the Merveilleux." Unpublished paper.

————. "The Time That (N)ever Was: Women's Fairy Tales in Seventeenth-Century France." Diss. University of Michigan, 1989.

Sévigné, Marie Rabutin-Chantal, Marquise de. *Correspondance.* Ed. Roger Duchêne. Paris: Gallimard (Pléiade), 1972-78.

Stewart, Susan. *Crimes of Writing: Problems in the Containment of Representation.* New York: Oxford, 1991.

Tatar, Maria. *The Hard Facts of Grimm's Fairy Tales.* Princeton: Princeton UP, 1987.

Thelander, Dorothy R. "Mother Goose and Her Goslings: The France of Louis XIV as Seen through the Fairy Tale." *Journal of Modern History* 54 (September 1982): 467-496.

Trinh T. Minh-ha. *Woman, Native, Other: Writing Postcoloniality and Feminism.* Bloomington: Indiana UP, 1989.

Velay-Vallantin, Catherine. "Tales as a Mirror: Perrault in the *Bibliothèque Bleue.*" *The Culture of Print: Power and the Uses of Print in Early Modern Europe.* Ed. Roger Chartier. Princeton: Princeton UP, 1989. 92-135.

Verdier, Gabrielle. "Figures de la conteuse dans les contes de fées feminins." *XVIIe siècle* 180 (1993): 481-99.

Warner, Marina. *From the Beast to the Blonde: On Fairy Tales and their Tellers.* New York: Farrar, 1995.

Zipes, Jack. Introduction. *Beauties, Beasts, and Enchantment: Classic French Fairy Tales.* New York: Meridian, 1991.

———. "The Origins of the Fairy Tale." *Fairy Tales as Myth/Myth as Fairy Tale.* The Thomas D. Clark Lectures. 1993. Lexington: UP of Kentucky, 1994.

Lisa Brocklebank (essay date fall 2000)

SOURCE: Brocklebank, Lisa. "Rebellious Voices: The Unofficial Discourse of Cross-dressing in d'Aulnoy, de Murat, and Perrault." *Children's Literature Association Quarterly* 25, no. 3 (fall 2000): 127-36.

[*In the following essay, Brocklebank interprets the confusion of gender identity in Perrault's fairy tale "The Counterfeit Marquise" as a critique of social standards.*]

Titles such as "Cinderella," "Sleeping Beauty," "Little Red Riding Hood" and "The Yellow Dwarf" often call to mind contemporary or at least post-eighteenth-century interpretive versions of their original counterparts. Some Disney films, for example, have contributed to the cultural homogenization of the fairy tale genre. In effect, consciously or otherwise, we tend to perceive and evaluate these narratives as *children*'s tales, as stories primarily designed for and consumed by young people. In recent years, for instance, much invaluable criticism has been directed toward the often chauvinistic representation of women within these tales and their possible detrimental effect on today's young readers or viewers.[1] However, in determining the signification and weighing the significance of such literary fairy tales, it is essential that we situate them within their historical and social-cultural milieu—in effect, evaluating the tales in light of the specific discursive formations out of which they arose and with which they were in dialogue. The original reading community of seventeenth-century French fairy tales was not children, but rather adults. More specifically, they were members of court society for, as Henriette-Julie de Murat reveals in her fairy tale "Starlight": "all the intelligentsia of the country spent their time reading nothing else" (159).

These tales, then, deserve examination as prominent and incisive literary and social discourse because they were one of the more popular and prevalent forms of expression during the latter decades of the *ancien régime*. It seems necessary to examine the dynamics behind canon formation: why have these tales come to be regarded as only for the nursery, when their original audience was highly sophisticated members of the French court? It is my contention that the authors of these wonder tales used the "genre" of children's stories not only as a vehicle for the instillment of normative social codes of conduct, but also as a means of voicing an implicit and often explicit social critique. As such, these tales can be regarded, instead, as valuable examples of socio-political commentary.

From the motif of cross-dressing that surfaces in some of the fairy tales produced during this period arises significant statements, challenges, and—most crucially—queries about the nature of the social order. I will examine three non-canonical tales: **"The Counterfeit Marquise,"** attributed to the collaborative efforts of Charles Perrault and Francois-Timoléon de Choisy; "Starlight," by Henriette-Julie de Murat; and "Belle-Belle ou le Chevalier Fortuné," by Marie-Catherine d'Aulnoy. All of these tales employ the cross-dressed figure as a touchstone to contest official order and socially constructed representations of power. In effect, they launch a potent critique of the status quo that begins with an examination of gender norms. I would contend that these tales, by highlighting the performativity of gender and gender relations, also call into question the production of other modes of power that claim a "natural" status to sanctify their existence and dominance. As Judith Butler has revealed in her influential study: "gender is the repeated stylization of the body, a set of repeated acts within a highly rigid regulatory frame that congeal over time to produce the appearance of substance, of a natural sort of being. . . . Gender is a construction that regularly conceals its genesis" (*Gender Trouble* 33, 140).

As the body is synechdotal of the social system, "its boundaries can represent any boundaries which are threatened or precarious" (Douglas 115). The *ancien régime,* in particular, relied heavily upon the symbolic equation between the body politic and the individual body—more specifically, the king's body. Representations of these bodies, moreover, relied upon the audience for whom they were created to imbue them with signification (Outram 4). In this sense, then, it seems plausible to argue that representations of the body within the *ancien régime* were highly performative.[2] To critique the performativity of gender, then, would be tantamount to critiquing all socially constructed identity posited as "natural"—from gender, to the family, to the state. I propose that within the three tales I will examine, the cross-dressed figure functions to indicate a "category crisis"[3]—not only of gender, but of the construction and perpetuation of a social order reliant upon the stylistic construction and representation of the Sun-King.

The reign of Louis XIV set in motion the deliberate and elaborate creation of a kingly image or representation, an official narrative of glory and power that held order in place. However, the permeation of this official narrative gave birth to a secret, shadowy sub-narrative that was in direct opposition to its parent discourse and that was bent on its overthrow. With the apotheosis of the Sun-King and the creation of the theater-state came the clandestine filtering of anti-images—texts, hostile to the monarchical system of representation. Unofficial newspapers, burlesque gazettes, erotic novels, secret histories, satires and songs, epigrams and epitaphs all challenged the monarchically willed and controlled representation of power (Hoffmann 148).

The attacks grew more concentrated as Louis XIV's reign progressed. In the 1660s, four subversive political pamphlets came into print; in the 1670s, six; in the 1680s, sixteen texts circulated; and the 1690s brought forth thirty-five anti-monarchical pamphlets (Burke 146). The creators of these dissenting images remained either anonymous or pseudonymous. Peter Burke identifies two kinds of dissenters: those individuals who presented themselves as loyal subjects making gentle fun of the court and those who openly declared themselves enemies of the king and his regime (146). The literary tactics varied between direct attacks and the implications of "secret histories" revealed to private eyes. The tone of the pieces varied as well, ranging from the moralizing to the cynical. The main subjects included the king's ambition, his lack of moral scruples, his tyranny, vanity, intellec-

tual weakness, and his military and sexual impotence (136-37). Such varied themes combined to form an anti-representation or a dissenting image of the king.

These counter-texts most often concentrated on the military and sexual weakness of the king. The narratives, moreover, closely linked the two themes, so that war became a metaphor for sex, or sex, conversely, became a metaphor for war. In deliberate contrast to the official representation of the royal hero, the unofficial narratives represented Louis XIV as battle shy or as an impotent old man, unsuccessful both in the sexual and military field. The spectacle of impotence hence replaced the potent image of battle (Burke 142). Hoffmann argues that this symbolic emasculation or castration of the Sun-King transformed the monarchy from "omnipotent head to impotent phallus" (7). Thus, the anti-narratives and counter-representations directly disabled and disempowered—at least imaginatively—the representative of social order and, consequently, the order the king represented.

I would argue that the evolution of the French literary fairy tale is intimately connected with these dynamics of representation and counter-representation. Although neither Hoffmann nor Burke even considers the possibility of the fairy tale as one of these anti-images, I would argue that it shares a similar origin, production, and purpose, and therefore expresses equal, if not greater, political dissatisfaction and insidious revolt. The fairy tales first came into print in the mid 1690s at the point Burke defines as the proliferative height of unofficial texts. These fairy tale texts present a fantastic unofficial discourse to counter official discourse. The writers speak from the margins, beyond the reach of official reprimand, eluding censors by encoding their alternative representations in the language of wonder. They build on a heritage of protest, encompassing within their discourse various strains of dissent and subversion to challenge not only the monarchy but also the inequalities of the entire system.

The first writers of fairy tales inherited the reformist vision of the *précieuses* and continued their subversive expression of rebellious instincts.[4] In the mid-seventeenth century, the interest of the *salonières* in manipulating language and meaning through riddles and word games led them to folklore; as a result, they turned to folk-tales as an innovative means of expressing their desires and championing their views (Anderson and Zinsser 22). As they told these stories to one another, the narratives of metamorphosis and wondrous change began to shift and metamorphose themselves, assuming, with each telling, hues of the teller's own life, the shapes of her own monsters and ogres, and visions of her own wishful resolutions. The *salonières* began to tell tales that questioned the standards that governed their lives, continuing the themes of *préciosité* such as freedom of choice in marriage, fidelity, and justice. Through the disparity between the ideal world of the tales and the world from which the tales arose, the *salonières* expressed their discontent with the status quo. In these tales, then, the fantastic and the political often became inextricably linked, and the ideological bent of the tales is either quietly or overtly subversive.

By the 1690s, these salon fairy tales were so prevalent and popular that the tellers began to write them down for public consumption, thus effectively transforming the oral tale into the literary tale and transferring it from the private sphere of the salon to the public sphere of society (Zipes, *Beauties* 3). Zipes links the publicization of the fairy tale to the tenuous political situation of the time. In 1688, France entered a period of severe political crisis. The policies of Louis XIV caused an increase in debt, taxation, and poor living conditions that, in turn, resulted in a more austere manner of life for the aristocracy and bourgeoisie, as well as increasing the abject conditions of the peasants. Concomitantly, Louis XIV became more and more despotic and absolutist. The combination of these two factors produced a situation ripe for backlash and protest, but also effectively silenced any protest before it was even voiced (5-6). Since censorship disabled writers from directly criticizing Louis XIV, the fairy tale became a means of voicing dissatisfaction and projecting hopes while evading punitive repercussions.

The liminal space that the fairy tale occupied resulted not only from its political marginality but also from its generic marginality. It occupied the as yet undefined area between oral popular culture and literary tradition (Canepa 12). This status enabled the tale to become a means of expressing social criticism that the censors would not have tolerated in more canonical genres. The literary aesthetics that the *précieuses* and their inheritors developed in their narratives—be they romance novels or fairy tales—were distinctly anti-classical (Zipes, *Beauties* 4). The *salonières* thus wrote their tales both on the margins of the literary establishment and in direct opposition to the predominant aesthetic and literary canon. Hence, in the contemporary literary and aesthetic debate known as the *Querelle des Anciens et des Modernes,* the women

writers of the wonder tales implicitly situated themselves on the side of the *Modernes* (Seifert 7).

These women writers also continued in the path of the *précieuses* through their reappropriation of language and of a distinctly gendered storytelling tradition. By recalling the oral connection of the tales, they invoked the original dynamics of the genre that pitted common people against established authority. In this vein, by writing under the alibi of "old wives" or "governesses" they spoke in a type of ventriloquy through the mouths of those either at the bottom of or outside the social order. From this position on the outside (which only magnified their own position) they could direct their criticism against society while remaining safely disguised. Significantly, the writers assumed female spokespieces, entitling their collections "*contes de quenouilles*" [tales of the distaff], "*contes de vieilles*" [old wives' tales], and "*contes de ma mère L'oye*" [Mother Goose tales]. This appropriation of female voices served two purposes. First, it set up the image of a mother or nurse telling tales to children, contributing further to the evasion of censors by disguising adult material as children's stories of allegedly peasant origins. Second, it created and provided access to a conventionally "female" realm of language, wisdom, and knowledge.

Significantly, these writers who appropriated a marginalized form and adopted the voice of outsiders were themselves marginalized. Mme Murat, author of "Starlight," was born Henriette Julie de Castelnau in 1670 in Brittany (Barchilon 170). At the age of fifteen, her father gave her in marriage to the comte de Murat, and she moved to Paris. Although she embraced (some thought with reckless abandon) the life of the French court, Murat remained strongly influenced by the traditions and folklore of her native Brittany. On more than one occasion, she caused a sensation by wearing a traditional Breton costume in court (Zipes, *Beauties* 129). Her wit, independence, and nonconformity soon won her enemies. Indeed, her own husband and family denounced her for her unruly behaviour, including the charge that "*elle aime un peu trop sa semblable*" ["she's rather too fond of her own kind"] (Barchilon 71). In 1694, Murat published a political satire targeting Louis XIV's liaison with Mme de Maintenon. Consequently, the King exiled her from Paris, sending her to the Loire Valley, where she remained under house arrest until just before her death (Warner 8). Undaunted by exile, she organized her own salon and began telling her own version of the tales she recalled from her childhood in Brittany. She then proceeded to record these tales in written form, as well as to invent and write original tales. Significantly, then, only after exile did she commence her engagement with tales. Hence, Murat—forced against her will at a young age into an unhappy marriage, demonized by her own husband and family for her "unruly" behavior and threatening sexual proclivities, and exiled by the King for her political criticism—turned to the marginalized fairy tale as a means of expressing her subversive views and opinions. Literally placed outside of the social system, she appropriated a form outside of the literary system to direct criticism against those mechanisms that perpetrated her exclusion.

Mme d'Aulnoy also began writing fairy tales while in exile. Marie-Catherine d'Aulnoy was born in Normandy in 1650. Her mother and her aunt both played influential roles in her formative years by encouraging her to live as independently as possible and by telling her folk-tales (Zipes, *Beauties* 296). At the age of fifteen, she married the Baron d'Aulnoy (De France 13). She lived with the baron at the French court until 1669 when, with the help of her mother and their respective lovers, d'Aulnoy tried to implicate her husband in a crime of high treason against the King, hoping that he would receive the normative punishment of execution. However, their plan backfired; the baron managed both to extricate himself and reveal the perpetrators at the center of the fiasco. As a result, the lovers faced an execution that d'Aulnoy and her mother narrowly escaped by fleeing to Holland, then England, and finally Spain. In 1685, they received the King's permission to return to Paris, where d'Aulnoy proceeded to establish a literary salon that soon became the most popular and highly-frequented salons. In 1690, d'Aulnoy began her literary career, and in 1696 she published *Les Contes de Fées,* which catapulted the fairy tale to an unprecedented height of fashion among its proponents. From this point forward, d'Aulnoy relegated her mischief-making and her issues with patriarchal constraints chiefly to imaginary realms (De France 14 and Zipes, *Beauties* 294-95).

The writing of subversive tales was not, however, limited solely to women. Charles Perrault, whose tales (albeit modified) have achieved a canonical status denied his female counterparts, also wrote *précieux* tales. Author of the highly successful *Contes du temps passé,* published in 1697, Perrault championed the cause of the *contes de fées* (Zarucchi 16). Although readers and scholars alike have traditionally interpreted Perrault's excessive moralizing as "'Victorian prudishness'" (Barchilon and Flinders 81), I would argue that his sardonic jocularity mocks the very conventions it purports to uphold. In this vein, although the epigrammatic morals at the end of his tales seemingly fulfill the conventional pedagogical imperative, they in fact interrogate the very precepts that they ostensibly uphold. Perrault could thus evade the censors by disguising his criticism as fatherly moral and social advice for young ladies of the court. He did, however, publicly enlist himself as a supporter of women through his publication of *Apologie des Femmes* (1694) which, in the form of a father advising his son to marry, gives an impassioned defense of women (Barchilon and Flinders 54-55).

Interestingly, Perrault also borrowed the female figure as a spokespiece. The frontispiece of his *Contes de ma Mère l'Oye* portrays a peasant woman spinning and telling stories to a group of children sitting by the fireplace (Barchilon 90). By thus imaginatively assuming the role and voice of a woman to tell his tales, Perrault positioned himself in line with the female writers, both on the outside, looking in, and at the bottom of the hierarchy, criticizing those at the apex. Although **"The Counterfeit Marquise"** has never been included in a Perrault collection, past scholarship has persuasively argued for the plausibility of his collaboration on the tale with its accepted author, the Abbé de Choisy—a libertine priest, courtier, historian, deputy ambassador to Siam, and an infamous transvestite whose memoirs chronicle his adventures in cross-dressing.[5]

The authors themselves cross-dress by assuming a female narrative persona in **"The Counterfeit Marquise"**: "Nowadays it is the fashion for women to display their wit in print and I have no wish to be behind the times" (123). By establishing such a narrative persona, they draw upon the oral aspects of the literary fairy tale in both its folk background and its salon setting. They evoke the atmosphere of women telling stories to other women in stories that comment upon their society and express a utopian vision. Perrault, in his other fairy tales, also transvestizes himself under the name *Ma Mère l'Oye.* I would argue that it is not unfeasible that he may have intentionally borrowed the name, and hence the persona, of *Mère Folle* from the "Abbeys of Misrule." In French cities, men often played the part of the unruly woman officer of Misrule during these carnivalesque festivals. Men used this disguise to draw upon the symbolic power of the unruly woman, employing her license to inveigh against unjust rule. In addition to providing access to this role, the disguise validated their riotous behavior and freed them from responsibility for their actions (Zeamon Davis 139). Perrault and de Choisy's use of the female narrative persona thus draws upon a long tradition of protest and misrule while at the same time dissociating them from it.

Their narrative persona evokes, as well, the relationship between the storyteller and audience by giving "lessons" and addressing herself to "ladies" (123). Most significantly, however, the creation of a teller-audience relationship enables the narrator of **"The Counterfeit Marquise"** to specify that she has exclusive and eye-witness access to secret knowledge: "do not begin to doubt what I am going to tell you. I saw it all, heard it all, know it all; I witnessed these events myself" (124). Through this claim, the authors seem to indicate that the tale belongs to the unofficial literature of "secret histories" that purported to contain inside information revealed to private eyes. The tale thus aligns itself with the unofficial discourse aimed at creating an anti-image of the king and the monarchy. The drag voice then positions itself on the margins from where it can challenge the status quo. It mocks socio-political conventions, representations, and images, suggesting that they are just as artificial as "she" is. "We women all have our little mannerisms. Femininity betrays itself beneath the stiffest of styles. . . . The attentive reader is sure to detect a certain softness, a characteristic frailty, which we are born with and lapse into repeatedly. Too much is not to be expected of us" (123). This deliberately satirical parody of "femininity"—voiced by a male—undermines the precepts it purportedly conveys and shows how constructed it is. It thus presents a paradox: femininity, rather than being something "which we are born with," is but a "style." Through drag, the narrator highlights the stylization of gender, and underscores the ostensible moral of the tale: "you still know only by appearances, which are often deceptive" (139).

During a great Carnival ball in **"The Counterfeit Marquise,"** the handsome Prince Sionad appears dressed as a woman. The tale extends this temporary instance of officially sanctioned cross-dressing, bringing the carnivalesque disruption of masking, hidden identity, and festive disregard for all propriety into the daily realm. It tells the tale of little Marianne—born a boy but raised a girl. Her mother, the Marquise de Banneville, loses her husband in battle and fears the same fate for her yet unborn child, should it be a boy. Her fears prove correct, for her child is, indeed, a boy. She determines to correct "nature," however, and tells everyone that her baby is a girl. She teaches the child "everything a girl of noble birth

should know: dancing; music; the harpsichord" and, since she possesses "so fine a mind," proceeds to teach her the "male" subjects of "languages, history, even modern philosophy" (125). The marquise teaches her daughter so well that no one, not even Marianne herself, suspects her identity. The tale thus emphasizes the fact that gender behavior, far from being innate, results rather from learning and acculturation.

Marianne happily lives her life as a female, and only when she falls in love with the handsome Marquis de Bercour does her mother reveal the truth: she was born a male although "habit has given [her] a different nature" (141). Marianne decides to marry the Marquis anyway. However, the potentially explosive nature of their marriage is defused when the Marquis reveals that he, in fact, is a female in disguise. Yet although they may resolve their incongruities by both resorting to their "natural" gender, they so enjoy their customary gender that they decide to maintain the facade and so happily sustain a double cross-dressed marriage.

Throughout the tale, Perrault and de Choisy indulge in a fetishistic detailing of clothing, adornments, and toilette. Through their concentration on the semiotics of clothing, they highlight the performativity of social roles by implying that not only gender itself, but also the social order upheld by prestige consumption, is a representation and charade. When Marianne enters young adulthood, her male sex still remains unapparent for "she had been a little constricted from infancy with an iron corset, to widen her hips and lift her bosom" (125). The text proceeds to elaborately enumerate Marianne's toilette. Her suitors voyeuristically watch her literally "making herself up," "putting herself together," and "painting her face" (126). These phrases, in addition to the following, point to the artificiality of the processes by which we distinguish gender or, for that matter, power relations in general:

> Her chambermaids would do her hair, but she would always add some new embellishment herself. Her blonde hair tumbled over her shoulders in great curls. . . . She would herself, with exquisite grace, put pendants in her ears, either of pearls, rubies, or diamonds—all of which suited her to perfection. She wore beauty spots [and] when putting them on she made a great show of consulting now one suitor, now another, as to which would suit her best.
>
> (126)

Her mother, observing the toilette, congratulates herself on her ingenuity: "he is twelve years old" (126).

Significantly, the descriptions of the Marquis de Ber-cour do not differ greatly from those of Marianne. When Marianne first sees him, his "dazzling diamond earrings and three or four beauty spots" immediately attract her (132). Ironically, Marianne's mother expresses objections to his appearance: "he is too conscious of his looks, and that is not becoming in a man. He might as well dress as a girl" (132). Marianne responds that "these days young men are always doing themselves up like girls" (133). This exchange highlights the importance of clothing to the distinction of sex and illuminates how tenuous is our ability to distinguish. The clothing styles of different sexes often converge during times when gender roles are in question. Gender uncertainty thus becomes reflected in the similarity of clothing. As Majorie Garber remarks in her discussion of sumptuary legislation, the monitoring of gender and class through dress codes becomes fraught with anxiety during periods of social unrest (21-40). It therefore seems highly probable that de Choisy and Perrault, despite the glib jocularity of their narrative, may have in fact intended their tale to be interpreted on a deeper level as social commentary. For through their portrayal of cross-dressing, they highlight the dependence of gender construction upon sumptuary laws and the performance of pre-established roles.

Moreover, in the cultural milieu of the *ancien régime,* to play with sexual signifiers threatened to disrupt much more than gender binaries. Seventeenth-century France saw the elaborate cultivation of outward appearances as a tool of social differentiation and as an indispensable instrument in maintaining social position. The display of rank through outward form shaped, regulated, and controlled court life, and became the visual and material site of struggle for status and prestige (Elias 63). The more elaborate and significant the classifications and differentiations of dress, the more vested social identity and signification became in clothing and the easier it became to interrogate these classifications via transgression. Any confusion of this classification system threatened to collapse the very structures that maintained social order. For a woman to appropriate the signifiers of masculinity, or vice versa, would call into question specifically gender categories and more generally the entire social system of categorization that included gender, class, race, and the divinely sanctioned status of the monarchy itself. Therefore, in the tales of the French writers, the cross-dressed figure holds the potential to thwart socio-political authority.

Henriette-Julie de Murat's "Starlight" similarly exploits the topsy-turvy potential of clothing by showing how the wearing of a "uniform"—either by those who are not fulfilling their role or by those who are not acting according to the definitions imposed by this dress—can be a means of questioning the behavioral assumptions associated with it and of protesting its necessity. Through her portrayal of the extraordinary customs of the fairy tale world, Murat mocks the conventions of her own society. Indeed, the tale draws attention to itself as a source of social criticism. When a fairy, disguised as a cat, addresses Starlight—the imprisoned heroine—the narrator intervenes, explaining that the reader should not be surprised that Starlight "didn't faint" when she heard a talking cat (159). She is unfazed, the narrator proceeds to reveal, by the phenomenon of a talking cat because she had "greatly improved her mind by reading fairy-tales" (159). Through this aside, Murat both emphasizes the oral aspect of the tale (in terms of the dynamic relationship between teller and audience), thus aligning herself with the rebellious peasant tellers, and establishes the connection between the other world and the "real world." By reading tales, the heroine of her tale improves her life and transforms her situation.

Through this depiction of the interrelationship between the primary and secondary worlds within the text itself, Murat creates a mirror representation of the effects she sees her text having on the reader and, through the reader, on society. Hence, the narrator posits the fairy tale as a source of valuable wisdom and knowledge and advises the reader to pay attention: this tale extends beyond its surface role of amusement—embedded within lies a significant message. By insidiously voicing her comment through the mouthpiece of a character in the narrative, Murat can champion the subversive nature of the tale while eluding the political censors. The narrator adds that "all the intelligentsia of that country spent their time reading nothing else" (159). This second allusion serves a three-fold purpose: first, it illuminates the status and role of the fairy tale within France at the time; underneath its guise as a harmless tale for children, it addresses an adult readership of a distinctly elite class, namely the members of the court. The seemingly frivolous, escapist fantasies therefore served an ulterior purpose and held as their mandate the creation of a counter-culture, or subculture. Second, the allusion imbues the fairy tale world with the same characteristics as the French court, hence, implying that any satirical/critical portrayal of events in the otherworld reflects and comments directly upon the conditions of the "real" world. Third, the textual comment situates the tale on the side of the *Modernes,* in the *Querelle des Anciens et des Modernes.* This "Modern" partisanship occurs yet again within the tale in the description of the courtiers' reaction to the ambiguous remarks of a centaur:

> it was soon being said that he was amazingly clever. Those who understood him least praised him most; some fools learnt his sayings by heart, and bigger fools wrote them down. That is the origin of all those books that people only pretend to understand, and of the form of speech that was later called persiflage, a word no academy so far has been able to define.
>
> (167-68)

Within this comment lies a fairly explicit jab at the elitism of the *Académie,* at their denial of higher education to women, and at their denigration of vulgar and local writing in favor of Greek and Latin.

The plot of the tale—that of star-crossed lovers fleeing the conditions impeding their union, overcoming various obstacles, and reuniting happily in the end—borrows from the *précieux* romantic plots of improbable adventure in the quest for *tendresse.* As well as the conventional narrative depiction of *tendresse*—or perfect, unconquerable love—the tale espouses the *précieux* social concerns with arranged marriages and male-female relations. It adds to the roster of these concerns a more overriding social criticism of war and the monarchy. Thus, through the fairy tale Murat takes issue with this "time of madness when the fools set the tone" (168).

The dangers of forced and unhappy marriages abound in the tale. The tale opens with the dilemma of unfortunate lovers. Prince Izmir's father prohibits him from marrying the girl he loves because she is but a captured slave. The two lovers flee together; however, when a storm capsizes their ship, the sea separates the lovers, carrying Starlight to the shore of an unknown city. The king of the country comes to her rescue and bring her back to the palace where he and the queen treat her as if she were their own daughter—as, indeed, she is. It comes to light that Starlight is their long-lost daughter, abducted by the enemy army that sacked their city many years ago. Unfortunately, the happiness of their family reunion proves short-lived. When the king discovers Starlight's secret identity, he arranges a politically advantageous marriage between her and a neighboring emperor. Starlight explains that she has promised to be faithful

to Izmir and cannot belong to another. The callous king ignores her tears and protestations. Although the queen sympathizes with Starlight's plight, she "could think of no remedy: Starlight must obey" (184). Only through fairy intervention does Starlight escape this imprisoning marriage. In these two instances, the tale criticizes the inability to choose one's marriage partner freely and the arranging of marriages for political or economic benefit.

"Starlight" offers a fairly unambiguous portrayal of the sexes. Through the fantastic portrayal, the tale seeks to imaginatively rectify the inequalities of male-female relations in the primary world. The power relations between Prince Izmir's parents presents an inversive vision that disrupts not only the prescribed roles within a marriage, but also the prescribed roles within a state. King Peacemaker yields to the greater authority of his wife. The queen, in fact, commands more force and power than the king and controls his decisions and actions; she can "easily persuade her husband to allow her to do as she wished" (152). The male/female relationship within marriage—as an expression of service, rule, and sovereignty—serves as an icon for other similarly hierarchical relationships, such as master/subject, sovereign/subject and public/domestic (Zeamon Davis 129). These dynamics imply that the microcosm of the domestic sphere stands as an icon of the state, so that an "ordered" relationship between the sexes within the home stands for order in the state. The potential disruption of gender roles on this small scale would then threaten to disrupt the stability of the state as a whole. Moreover, Peacemaker's subservience to the Queen suggests a political as well as a sexual impotence. It is the Queen who grips the scepter and wields the phallic tongue. Curiously, the tale seems to undermine its own subversive portrayal by depicting the Queen in demonic terms—relegating her to the role of evil, jealous (prospective) mother-in-law, underscoring her acerbic and conniving traits, and painting her as "naturally arrogant and ill-tempered" (152). Perhaps her demonization serves as a deliberate mask or cover-up, for to portray a man in service of his wife, or a king in service of a powerful and politically ruthless woman, would hold too many overtly incendiary possibilities.

Indeed, all the men in the tale exhibit barbaric natures to varying degrees. Starlight, inadvertently finding herself in the Forest of the Centaurs, at first expresses alarm at finding herself amid "such creatures" (164) but then decides to trust them, rationalizing: "Men have schemed to destroy me . . . and the only man I might turn to is not in a position to help me; so why not put these creatures to the test? They are perhaps less barbarous" (164). Her rationalization proves correct, for the half man-half beast centaurs prove far more gracious, refined, compassionate, competent, and peaceful than any other "fully human" males the story portrays. The human men are beastly in comparison.

Their beastliness manifests itself chiefly in the arena of warfare. The kingdom of King Peacemaker is constantly at war with that of King Warmonger. King Peacemaker's actions fail to live up to the promise of his name. Each year, King Warmonger asks King Peacemaker to honor certain treaties he had agreed to, and each year King Peacemaker refuses. Notably, not only does King Peacemaker fail to fulfill the kingly role denoted by his title, but he also fails to embrace the opposite. In deliberate contrast to the official image of king as warrior-hero, the tale presents Peacemaker as battle-shy. The aging king can no longer fight his own battle; he must have the young, virile Izmir act as his substitute sword/(phallus). He disapproves of Prince Izmir's falling in love because it has caused him to lose all interest in his reputation as a "warrior-prince" (149). The use of this term indicates the inextricable link—a least in this secondary world—between war and monarchy, and the crucial role war plays in both the maintenance of power and the self-imaging and self-representation of both the monarchy and masculinity. War serves as a means of accruing honor and as a means through which masculinity is inscribed and upheld: "'the eyes of the whole world are upon you; posterity will hold you responsible for your actions; what will they say of your honor?'" (150). Through battle, the warriors carve out a public image, a representation of themselves which they then present to the public gaze. These comments reveal the performativity of state identity by highlighting the construction of self-representation and imaging and their role in the establishment of power and of the consolidation and ratification of that power through the creation of an iconic object held up to the admiring gaze of the public or the "eyes of the world." Sexual prowess and violence are inextricably connected to the formation of masculinity and this, in turn, plays itself out in a public spectacle. The public, visual nature of Izmir's performance thus suggests that his own sense of masculinity can only exist as such when confirmed by an audience. When Izmir agrees to fight in return for Starlight, he dons "a magnificent suit of armour . . . all shining with gold, rubies, and diamonds" (155). In battle, the "incomparable Izmir" is a sight "fell

and terrible to behold" (156). Rampaging through the field in battlelust, he "swoops like an eagle . . . cutting the arms off some, running others through, and sending heads flying through the air" (156). The vocabulary of war, in this unofficial fantastic representation, serves to ridicule, as opposed to attesting to its power and glory. Although the spectacle of violent bloodshed proves Izmir's "valour and strength" (156), the tale points to the artifice which underlies and upholds this proof. Despite Izmir's recuperation of his masculine and royal identity, King Peacemaker reneges on his promise. Izmir and Starlight therefore flee the country. The lovers become separated when a sea-storm catches their ship and the two fall overboard.

Izmir washes up on the shores of Quietlife Island, so called because not a sound was to be heard there: "everyone spoke in whispers and walked on tiptoe. There were no quarrels and hardly any wars" (173). The utopian world within the fairy tale realm, Quietlife Island reveals the travesties and inadequacies of the tale's world, and thus of French society. It is the World Turned Upside Down—the topsy-turvy land where "normal" social behavior is inverted, not only in terms of war, but in terms of gender norms as well: "When it became absolutely impossible to avoid engaging in combat, only the ladies fought, throwing crab-apples from a distance. The men kept well away: they slept until midday, plied their spinning wheels, tied pretty bows, took children for walks, and made their faces up with rouge and beauty spots" (173). Quietlife Island, therefore, reverses Izmir's idea of socially proper gender behavior, as male and female roles reverse both within marriage and within the state. The amazonian wives are "hunters" and "masterful women," while the men occupy themselves with spinning wheel and bows (174). Izmir, the manly hero and prototype of his society, gallantly offers the women jewels. They, however, take no interest in them, but pass them on to their husbands. When Izmir shares with the men his tragic love story, they cry "their eyes out"; the women, conversely, show a muted sympathy, marked with "firmness" and "severity" (174).

Much disconcerted, Izmir proceeds to the palace, where he hopes to find his terms of reference restored to their proper order. Instead, though, he encounters the king, who lies at ease on a canopy bed, surrounded by perfumes, "listening to his chancellor read him the story of Bluebeard" (175). Meanwhile, his ministers absorb themselves in the all-important task of "teaching the baby princess to walk" (174).

The monarch explains to Izmir that he is resting while the queen occupies herself at war. This "unforgivable" inversion of norms shocks and revolts the manly Izmir (175). To Izmir, war serves as a means of defining masculinity/monarchy. For a woman to enter the battlefield and usurp this terrain not only robs him of this means, but "feminizes" and disempowers him in relation to her "masculinization" and empowerment. He cannot face the challenge which the inhabitants pose to his conceptual paradigm of reality and to his very identity. Hence, he launches a brutal attack on the king—an attack which possesses all the undertones of a rape scene. Izmir tries to reinscribe his threatened sense of masculinity by assaulting the "effeminate king" with his (phallic) "stout lance" (175). His assault achieves the desired result: "The poor king, crying his eyes out, swore to do anything Izmir wanted: he was afraid he would get a second dose of that terrible lance, which Izmir was brandishing" (176). Izmir forces the king to promise to "abolish" their "absurd customs" and to "go to war like other kings" (176). Izmir thus represents the violent conforming impulse of his patriarchal society. He beats the deviants into submission, forcing them to fit the mold. Paradoxically then, to conform to Izmir's sense of order, the king cross-dresses in the queen's armor and rides out to battle with Izmir.

The foreign prince inflicts himself upon the humane "battle" of the islanders. While they throw harmless crab-apples, he lays waste with the aforementioned phallic lance. Horrified by this spectacle, the islanders beg him to cease his slaughter: "Stop, for goodness sake. You can't kill people like that without mercy! All we wanted to do was to chase them away" (177). This passage explicitly critiques the violence of a military and patriarchal society. Society is more peaceful, harmonious, and humane when men act as "women" and women assume the authority usually wielded by men.

Izmir calls their way of life "absurd customs," but to the islanders, his behavior is just as absurd and incomprehensible. To the king of Quietlife Island, their behavior accords with their "laws and customs" and has been the norm since "time immemorial" (175). The "norm," therefore, results from the process of socialization. Whatever is ratified by law and custom, whatever is habitual and known, becomes the accepted way, or the way "things should be." Anything or anyone who deviates from the long-standing tradition is regarded by those who uphold the tradition as the corruption of an inherent value or condition.

Izmir then asks why the king's palace has no staircase. The king responds that his predecessors never had one, and that it was the way things always were. Izmir reacts with characteristic belligerent indignation: "A fine reason for maintaining such a stupid inconvenient custom!" (177). Through her mockery of the ignorant hero, Murat satirizes and comments upon the blindness of her own society. Though Quietlife Island is subversive in its festive aura of a World Turned Upside Down, Murat points out that although its behavior and customs are diametrically opposed to those of the so-called "Upright" world, it still adheres to the same conditions of fixed socialization and ossified concepts of binarism. Through the juxtaposition of the two worlds and two systems, she emphasizes foremost that the disparate behavioral roles of the sexes are primarily a social construct. The different patterns of different societies suggest that gender roles, behavioral norms, and state/political systems are not inherent and prototypical. By thus contesting the precept of a natural and divinely sanctioned order, Murat opens a crack through which dissension and dissatisfaction may filter.

D'Aulnoy also expresses dissatisfaction with both normative gender and political paradigms. "Belle-Belle ou le Chevalier Fortuné" utilizes a cross-dressed amazonian figure to challenge gender orthodoxy. The title of the tale, by including both the heroine's female and male identities, draws attention to the inseparability of seemingly mutually exclusive characteristics and d'Aulnoy's attempt to deconstruct fixed gender binaries. Even before she assumes the outward signifiers of masculinity, Belle-Belle, the eponymous heroine, exhibits traditionally "masculine" behavior through her "extraordinary courage" and her habit of "hunting every day" (d'Aulnoy 566). Once she becomes, outwardly at least, a male, she still retains those qualities prized as the quintessence of feminine virtue, such as politeness, consideration, and charm. While retaining her "feminine" qualities, she epitomizes knightly virtues, earning herself the title of "flower of all chivalry" (581). As a male, Belle-Belle excels at all the duties of a chivalrous knight: "He won the prize at all the tournaments. He killed the most game when he went hunting. He danced at all the balls with more grace and skill than any other courtier. In short, it was delightful to watch him and hear him speak" (577).

Moreover, Belle-Belle accomplishes a series of tasks supposedly exclusive to the male sphere: she travels freely and unharassed, assumes leadership of a motley crew of social outcasts, serves as the king's ambassador, defeats a dragon and, finally, restores to the king his lost possessions. She restores his goods and, through this action, saves his kingdom, accomplishing what the king failed to achieve himself. The tale thus interrogates the construction of gender—not only in terms of "femininity," but also in terms of "masculinity" as well. Of greater implication, however, is that in its questioning of "masculinity," the tale questions, as well, the role of the king, who is the nominal representative of masculine identity.

Like "Starlight," "Belle-Belle" opens with a depiction of the king's inability to fulfill his role. Just as King Peacemaker fails to keep the peace, or even to participate in the war, the monarch in "Belle-Belle" is "besieged" and "conquered" by the enemy emperor, who "took possession" of his "treasures" and "ravaged" his kingdom (564). His military defeat thus bears the distinct connotations of a sexual defeat depicted, as it is, in terms of rape and emasculation. His military inability comes under scrutiny yet again further on in the narrative. He neglects to even attempt to conquer the dragon that threatens his kingdom or to regain his lost possessions from the enemy emperor. Rather than undertaking these missions himself, he sends his page, the chevalier Fortuné (Belle-Belle), who successfully accomplishes these tasks and who, moreover, is a woman.

In one particularly emblematic scene, the chevalier places the dragon which "he" captured at the feet of the king, so that the monarch can strike the final blow himself. The king then "drew his sword and terminated the existence of one of his most cruel enemies" (585). This public performance of sovereign power draws "shouts of joy" from the crowd of spectators (585). The spectacle of the king plunging his phallic sword into the breast of his enemy highlights the dynamics of the construction of power both within the tale and within the *ancien régime*. This act of valor and strength restores the king's potency and recreates a public image of supreme unvanquishable glory and might. This public image, in turn, maintains the stability of the social order. However, d'Aulnoy has a woman, dressed as a man, orchestrate the whole deliberate performance. In so doing, the author reveals the elaborate construction behind the king's image and the dependence of order upon the upholding of this representation. Additionally, she discloses that the power that places the king at the apex depends directly upon those at the bottom of the social hierarchy. Without this rigid hierarchicalization, the nebulous aura of *gloire* surrounding the king would dissipate. Yet, by having a cross-dresser as the or-

chestrator, d'Aulnoy not only deconstructs the very order that this image supposedly upholds, but also shifts the seat of power from the male to the female and from the king to the peasant, thus emasculating the male king and empowering the female peasant.

Hence, it becomes apparent that d'Aulnoy, like Murat and, less overtly, Perrault and de Choisy, utilizes the cross-dressed figure to combine a critique of gender roles with a critique of normative socio-political paradigms. By thus attacking the monarchical system of representation, these ostensibly children's tales reveal themselves as belonging to the unofficial discourse of anti-monarchical texts. Or do these tales necessarily hold such an unequivocally incendiary potential? Perrault and de Choisy, for example, were undeniably invested in the very culture they rebelled against. De Choisy, for one, served as an integral part of Louis XIV's entourage, accompanying the king to Siam and attending the coronation ball of Pope Innocent XI—albeit dressed as a woman (Ackroyd 9). Perrault, in turn, began his literary career as a public poet, lauding the monarch in official texts that contributed to the construction of the image of the Sun King (Barchilon and Flinders 24). Could **"The Counterfeit Marquise"**—or either of the other tales—in fact function in the service of official culture? Perhaps they could serve as safety-valves by providing a vehicle through which audiences could express their discontent in imaginary realms, diffusing the possibility of taking action in reality. The cross-dressed figure, moreover, shares the same ambiguous discursive space as the tales. Both the text of the body and the text of the tale seek to rewrite reality through alternative representations yet, paradoxically, ones which seem categorically dependent on that which they seek to subvert. While attempting to contest the official, they still derive from and imitate its language in terms of narrative, gender, and politics. Ultimately however, while these tales of cross-dressing may not succeed in overtly subverting the status quo, they do at least open up space for the interrogation of hegemonic laws surrounding both gender and monarchy.

Notes

The author wishes to offer thanks to Kieran Kealy, Matt Farish, and two anonymous reviewers for their useful comments on this essay.

1. Examples of such critiques can be found in the essays in the list of Works Cited by Marcia K. Lieberman, Karen E. Rowe, Kay Stone, and Jack Zipes, "Breaking the Disney Spell."

2. I use "performative" in Butler's sense of the term, whereby performativity acts as "the reit-

erative and citational practice by which discourse produces the effects that it names" (*Bodies* 2).

3. Marjorie Garber argues that the presence of a cross-dressed figure in a text can testify to a "category crisis" or a failure of definitional distinction, i.e., conceiving of gender in binaric modes (16).

4. The *précieuses* were a group of subversive women writers and intellectuals dedicated to a revolt against dominant culture. During the reign of Louis XIII the *précieuses* instituted the salon to provide a milieu in which a woman could develop her intellectual talents and where she would receive acceptance and encouragement. The salon came to provide an intellectual shelter for dissident views and opinions, thus placing itself outside the court and often in opposition to it. For further discussion of the *précieuses* see: Ian Maclean's *Woman Triumphant* and Wendy Gibson's *Women in Seventeenth-Century France.*

5. "The Counterfeit Marquise" was first published in the February 1695 issue of the *Mercure galant* under the title *L'Histoire de la marquise-marquis Banneville*. A year later, the February 1696 issue of the *Mercure* published Perrault's "*La Belle au bois dormant*" with the preface that: "*On doit ce petit ouvrage à la même personne qui a écrit l'histoire de la Petite Marquise*" ["we owe this little piece of work to the same person who wrote the story of the 'Petite Marquise'"] (qtd. in Van der Cruysse 346). Jeanne Roche-Mazon, while acknowledging the possibility of Perrault's involvement in the authorship of the text, speculates that he transmitted the manuscript to the editor of the *Mercure galant* as a favor for his friend, the Abbé de Choisy, neither confirming nor denying that he was the author. (See J. Roche-Mazon 513-42.) In seeking to expand the Perrault canon to include this tale, I cite Foucault's argument regarding the necessity of suspending unities such as the oeuvre, for "the oeuvre can be regarded neither as a certain unity, nor as a homogeneous unity" (*The Archeology of Knowledge,* 24).

Works Cited

Ackroyd, Peter. *Dressing Up: Transvestism and Drag: The History of an Obsession*. Norwich: Jarrold and Sons, 1979.

Anderson, Bonnie S., and Judith P. Zinsser. *A History of their Own: Women in Europe from Prehistory to the Present*. Vol. 1. New York: Harper, 1988.

Barchilon, Jacques. *Le conte merveilleux français de 1690 à 1790: cent ans de féerie et de poésie ignorées de l'histoire littéraire*. Paris: Librarie Honore Champion, 1975.

Barchilon, Jacques, and Peter Flinders. *Charles Perrault*. Boston: Twayne, 1981.

Burke, Peter. *The Fabrication of Louis XIV.* New Haven: Yale UP, 1992.

Butler, Judith. *Gender Trouble: Feminism and the Subversion of Identity*. New York: Routledge, 1990.

———. *Bodies that Matter: On the Discursive Limits of "Sex."* New York: Routledge, 1993.

Canepa, Nancy L. *Out of the Woods: The Origins of the Literary Fairy-Tale in Italy and France*. Detroit: Wayne State UP, 1997.

d'Aulnoy, Marie-Catherine. "Belle-Belle ou le Chevalier Fortuné." *Beauties, Beasts, and Enchantment: Classic French Fairy Tales*. Ed. and trans. Jack Zipes. New York: New American Library, 1989. 564-98.

De France, Anne. *Les contes de fées et les nouvelles de Madame d'Aulnoy (1690-1698): L'imaginaire feminin a rebours de la tradition*. Geneve: Librairie Droz, 1998.

de Murat, Henriette-Julie. "Starlight." Trans. Terence Cave. *Wonder Tales: Six Stories of Enchantment*. Ed. Marina Warner. New York: Farrar, Straus, and Giroux, 1996. 149-87.

Douglas, Mary. *Purity and Danger: An Analysis of the Concepts of Pollution and Taboo*. London: Routledge, 1966.

Elias, Norbert. *The Court Society*. Oxford: Basil Blackwell, 1983.

Foucault, Michel. *The Archaeology of Knowledge*. New York: Pantheon, 1972.

Garber, Marjorie. *Vested Interests: Cross-dressing and Cultural Anxiety*. New York: Routledge, 1997.

Gibson, Wendy. *Women in Seventeenth-Century France*. New York: St. Martin's, 1989.

Hoffmann, Kathryn A. *Society of Pleasures: Interdisciplinary Readings in Pleasure and Power during the Reign of Louis XIV*. New York: St. Martin's, 1997.

Lieberman, Marcia K. "Some Day My Prince Will Come: Female Acculturation through the Fairy Tale." *Don't Bet on the Prince*. Ed. Jack Zipes. New York: Routledge, 1987. 185-200.

Maclean, Ian. *Woman Triumphant: Feminism in French Literature, 1610-1652.* Oxford: Clarendon, 1977.

Outram, Dorinda. *The Body and the French Revolution: Sex, Class, and Political Culture.* New Haven: Yale UP, 1989.

Perrault, Charles, and Francois-Timoléon de Choisy. "The Counterfeit Marquise." Trans. Ranjit Bolt. *Wonder Tales: Six Stories of Enchantment.* Ed. Marina Warner. New York: Farrar, Straus, and Giroux, 1996. 123-47.

Roche-Mazon, J. *"Une collaboration inattendue au XVIIe siecle: l'abbé de Choisy et Charles Perrault."* *Mercure de France* (Feb. 1928): 513-42.

Rowe, Karen E. "Feminism and Fairy Tales." *Folk and Fairy Tales.* 2nd ed. Ed. Martin Hallett and Barbara Karasek. Peterborough, Ont.: Broadview, 1996. 325-45.

Seifert, Lewis C. *Fairy-Tales, Sexuality, and Gender in France, 1690-1715.* Cambridge: Cambridge UP, 1996.

Stone, Kay. "Things Walt Disney Never Told Us." *Women and Folklore.* Ed. Claire R. Farrer. Austin: U of Texas P, 1975. 42-50.

Van der Cruysse, Dirk. *L'Abbé de Choisy: Androgyne et mandarin.* Paris: Librairie Artheme Fayard, 1995.

Warner, Marina, ed. *Wonder Tales: Six Stories of Enchantment.* New York: Farrar, Straus, and Giroux, 1996.

Zarucchi, Jeanne Morgan, ed. *Charles Perrault: Memoirs of My Life.* Columbia: U of Missouri P, 1989.

Zeamon Davis, Natalie. *Society and Culture in Early Modern France.* Stanford: Stanford UP, 1975.

Zipes, Jack. *Beauties, Beasts, and Enchantment: Classic French Fairy-Tales.* New York: New American Library, 1989.

———. "Breaking the Disney Spell." *From Mouse to Mermaid: The Politics of Film, Gender, and Culture.* Ed. Elizabeth Bell, Lynda Haas, and Laura Sells. Bloomington: Indiana UP, 1995. 21-42.

Ruth B. Bottigheimer (essay date 2002)

SOURCE: Bottigheimer, Ruth B. "Misperceived Perceptions: Perrault's Fairy Tales and English Children's Literature." *Children's Literature* 30 (2002): 1-18.

[In the following essay, Bottigheimer traces the publication history of eighteenth-century children's literature, contending that Perrault's fairy tales reached their peak popularity much later than originally supposed.]

The place of Charles Perrault's fairy tales in the development of English children's literature has been both misunderstood and overrated. This view of Perrault's role in children's literature has a history. In the libraries I've scoured for books written for and read by children in eighteenth-century England, Perrault's fairy tales have been more an absence than a presence. This observation, however, is not enough to support so fundamental a redefinition of the early history of English children's literature. What can—and does—support my argument is book history, whose perceptions and methodologies I use here.

Let me offer one example of how book history is able to correct misperceptions that have arisen from the way books are listed in published library catalogs. Catalogs take their data from title pages, but title pages can be misleading. For example, what if one publisher, after a year of dismal sales, sold his books to another publisher, who then inserted a new title page and sent the books newly titled but otherwise unchanged out into bookshops? The catalog would record two dates of publication for one printing. Book history, in contrast, would use its resources to identify the book's text and its title page and to recognize that only one printing had, in fact, taken place. This is not an imagined example; it actually happened with a 1764 printing of Perrault's tales.

Unraveling an eighteenth-century printing practice like the reissue of 1764/65 requires a methodology and a vocabulary uncommon in the study of children's literature. "Printruns," "sheets," and "fingerprints" all play a role in explicating the relative popularity of individual books in the eighteenth century. The argument that follows has a slow pace, and for that I apologize. I am urging a fundamental change in long-held views, and I want to build my case carefully and persuasively.

* * *

With clockwork regularity literary anthologies and course textbooks imply, suggest, or assert that eighteenth-century English children's literature was rooted in fairy tales, specifically those of Charles Perrault. Harvey Darton, whose richly documented history of English children's literature has provided the guiding direction for countless other accounts, wrote that Perrault's tales "have been naturalized citizens of the British nursery" since they were translated by Robert Samber in 1729 (88). In *Classics of Children's Literature,* John Griffith and Charles Frey put five of Perrault's tales—**"Sleeping Beauty,"**

"**Little Red Riding Hood,**" "**Blue Beard,**" "**Puss in Boots,**" and "**Cinderella**"—front and center and claim that they "grew steadily in popularity" once they were translated into English (3). Little wonder that Geoffrey Summerfield could comfortably state without further proof or elaboration that "these tales of Perrault soon passed into England, and in Robert Samber's translation were frequently reprinted throughout the eighteenth century" (44). Summerfield's easy acceptance of the Perrault paradigm characterizes both lay and scholarly perceptions.

The chronology of the publishing history of Perrault's tales in England would appear to substantiate such claims. Translated by Robert Samber and published in London in 1729, those tales preceded the 1740s printings of children's books by London's Thomas Boreman, Mary Cooper, and John Newbery by a good ten to fifteen years. But this simple chronological sequence has made it all too easy for generations of literary historians to leap directly to the conclusion that Perrault's prior appearance represented a point of origin. Exploring late seventeenth- and early- to mid-eighteenth-century English children's literature presents a disturbing disjunction between scholarly claims of Perrault's precedence and the mood evident in the literature itself.

Over the past several years I have undertaken a journey of discovery to research libraries in the United States, Canada, and England. My study of hundreds of books published for children between 1670 and 1770 has led, among other things, to a sense that it is necessary to revise fundamentally the place that Perrault's fairy stories occupy in the early history of English children's literature. The history of fairies and fairy literature in England encourages such revision; scholarship in such newly emerging fields as book and publishing history supports it; and most significantly, the evidence of children's literature itself requires it.[1]

The fairies of Charles Perrault's *Histories* [*Histoires ou Contes du temps passé, avec des moralitez* were preceded by centuries of England's own imps and phantoms as well as by decades of Mme d'Aulnoy's supernaturals (Palmer, Palmer and Palmer, Verdier). By the time Perrault's supernatural protagonists arrived on English soil in such fairy tales as "**The Fairy,**" "**Sleeping Beauty in the Wood,**" and "**Cinderilla**" ["**Cinderella**"] [*sic*], they represented England's third generation of fairies,[2] one which eventually overlaid both England's native fairy population (calendared by Reginald Scot) and Mme

d'Aulnoy's successfully imported and disseminated fairy traditions. Perrault's tales provided the basis for the modern canon of fairy tales. That is not in doubt. But the ultimate success of Perrault's fairy tales has blinded generations of scholars to the fact that they conquered the field with near-glacial slowness. The reasons for Perrault's tardy success implicate genre and gender, while more far-reaching explanations rest on patterns of book consumption and book marketing.

Perrault's fairy tales differed fundamentally from the traditional fairy fictions of Mme d'Aulnoy. Unlike her tales, Perrault's stories generally obfuscated sex. And differing even more fundamentally from a dystopic tale like Mme d'Aulnoy's "History of Adolphus," in which Time brutally strangled the hero in the concluding paragraphs, Perrault's (rare) violence was wrought only upon the wicked. ("**Red Riding Hood**" is, of course, not a fairy tale but a warning tale.) Best of all for late-eighteenth-century propriety, every one of Perrault's fairy tales had a hero or heroine who was virtuous, at least in formal terms, and ended with a clearly set out moral. The morals themselves were sometimes wry, sometimes ironic, and always worldly, yet on the surface they and the fairy tales' endings regularly stressed the importance and utility of goodness. Whatever internal contradictions might on occasion disturb the smooth flow of a moral, the overt message of the majority of Perrault's tales was that happy endings crowned virtuous lives.

Mme d'Aulnoy further explored the narrative consequences of human intrusions into fairyland and of fairy entries into human life in stories like "Graciosa and Percinet," "The Fair One with Golden Locks," and "The Hobgoblin Prince." Perrault, in contrast, examined the social life of human beings, the obstacles to whose easy success were swept away either by earthly kings or by fairy magic. In his stories a fairy made roses, pearls, and diamonds fall from the mouth of a kindly but ill-treated daughter ("**The Fairy**"); a fairy godmother created a coach from a "pompion" ("**Cinderilla**"); and another fairy made the hideous Riquet appear handsome and transformed his beloved but stupid Princess into a sensible woman ("**Riquet a la Houpe**"). Only one of Perrault's fairy tales—"**Sleeping Beauty in the Wood**"—resembled Mme d'Aulnoy's stories in that a good fairy and a malevolent one pitted their magic against one another in a contest of wills that produced repercussions in the lives of the tale's human protagonists.

The date of Perrault's first translation into English, 1729, is generally cited as the moment of its initial success in England. It is easily demonstrated that

Perrault's tales were translated and published in London in 1729, but many important facts in conjunction with its fallaciously claimed success have been eagerly, perhaps willfully, overlooked. To explore the question of the popularity of Perrault's tales, we need to return to the world of print as it existed in publishing centers in Paris, the Lowlands, and London at the end of the seventeenth and beginning of the eighteenth centuries.

Within a few months of the January 1697 appearance of Perrault's fairy tales in Paris, his stories had been pirated by the Amsterdam publisher Jaques [*sic*] Desbordes. Desbordes's book claimed to be a faithful copy of the French edition ("suivante la copie a Paris"), yet its publisher misspelled the author's name ("Perreault") even as he added Perrault's illustrious title ("de l'Academie François"). Desbordes's book sold well enough on the Continent to justify a second printing in 1700 and a third in 1708. In 1711 Estienne Roger, another Amsterdam publisher, produced a six-volume compendium of French fairy fictions and fairy tales. Volume 5, entitled *Les Chevaliers Errans par Madame la Comtesse D***,* included Perrault's tales and five others by Mme D'Auneuil;[3] the sixth volume bore the title of Perrault's oeuvre, *Histoires ou Contes des Temps Passé,* and was attributed to "Perreault," but with an insouciant disregard for authorship, it contained not a single one of Perrault's tales!

Perhaps it was volume 5, *Les Chevaliers Errans [Les Chevaliers Errans par Madame la Comtesse D***]*, in Estienne Roger's set of fairy tales that caught Jaques Desbordes's eye and led him to calculate that Perrault's tales could be made even more attractive by adding a traditional and lengthy fairy fiction. Whatever his reason, in 1716 Desbordes added "L'adroite Princesse ou les aventures de Finette," which had been written by Perrault's niece, Marie-Jeanne L'Héritier de Villandon. Desbordes finally spelled Perrault's name correctly and published *Histoires ou Contes du temps Passé, Avec des Moralitez. Par M. Perrault. Nouvelle Edition augmentée d'une Nouvelle, à la fin. Suivant la Copie de Paris.* His successor firm republished it in 1721 and 1729.

In 1729 Robert Samber's word-for-word translation of Perrault's tales appeared in London. It included, in the printer's fanciful typography, **"The Little Red Riding-Hood," "The Blue-Beard," "The Fairy," "The Sleeping Beauty in the Wood," "The Master Cat: or, Puss in Boots," "Cinderilla: or, The Little Glass Slipper," "Riquet a la Houpe,"** and **"Little Poucet, and His Two Brothers."** Samber worked from Desbordes's Dutch edition, similarly including Mlle L'Héritier's "Discreet Princess; or, the Adventures of Finetta. A Novel."[4] Mlle L'Héritier had originally addressed "L'adroite Princesse" to another French author of fairy fictions, Mme de Murat. Samber's Englishing of the book extended to the novel's dedicatee, and so on the separate title page that preceded the "novel," he addressed "The Discreet Princess" to "The Right Hon. Lady Mary Montagu," daughter of John, Duke of Montagu.

Perrault's own tales are so familiar that I needn't repeat their plots here, but Mlle L'Héritier's "Discreet Princess" has fallen from the canon and requires a brief retelling so that modern readers may understand the full reach of Samber's book as it appeared in London in 1729:

> Once upon a time there were three princesses, idle Drone-illa, prattling Babillarde, and virtuous Finetta. After their mother's death, their father feared both for his daughters' well-being and for their virtue, and so having had a fairy make a glass distaff for each of his daughters that would break if its owner acted dishonorably, he locked them all into a high tower and forbade them to receive guests. Lazy Drone-illa and prattling Babillarde were distraught at their isolation, but Finetta spent her days contentedly, reading and sewing.
>
> One day Drone-illa and Babillarde hauled up a wizened old woman who had begged entry to their tower. The "old woman" was, in fact, the crafty Prince Riche-cautelle, who easily seduced first Drone-illa and then Babillarde. The virtuous Finetta, however, repulsed his advances and defended herself with Boccaccian trickery, dropping him into a stinking sewer. To avenge his honor, Riche-cautelle had Finetta kidnapped and carried to a mountaintop, down which he proposed to roll her in a barrel studded with knives and nails. Instead, Finetta kicked *him* into the barrel and rolled him down the slope. When Finetta returned home, she found that her two sisters had each given birth to a son born of her "marriage" night with Riche-cautelle. To conceal her sisters' shame Finetta, dressed as a man, carried the two children in boxes to the capital, and left them behind as "ointment" for the prince's wounds. Once again bested by Finetta, Riche-cautelle made his noble brother, Prince Bel-a-Voir, Swear to marry Finetta and kill her on their wedding night.
>
> Finetta, whom a fairy had warned to always be on her guard because "distrust is the mother of security" (141), substituted a straw dummy for herself in the marriage bed. From a hiding place

she saw her husband stab it murderously, even though in so doing he lamented his act and declared that he intended to kill himself afterward. Finetta hindered his suicidal resolve, and they lived long and happily together.

Robert Samber claimed that the story, "though entirely fabulous . . . wrap[s] up and infold[s] most excellent morality, which is the very end, and ultimate scope and design of Fable" (140). At its conclusion, he repeated his warm approval of the novel's "great deal of good morality," for which reason, he said, it "ought to be told to little children in their very infancy, to inspire them betimes with Virtue" (201-2). A strange sort of morality, we may well conclude.

Few London parents, however, seem to have told, or read, these stories to their infants, as the following publishing history will demonstrate. Montagu and Pote, the book's publishers, took twelve years to issue a second English-language edition; a third appeared nine years after that, in 1750.

To counterbalance a century's baseless claims, it is worth carrying out a simple mathematical calculation based on reasonable numbers and rational assumptions. In the eighteenth century a print run of 1,000 books was the general maximum for the commercial market. Smaller print runs were common, but larger print runs were generally reserved for subsidized Bible printings and the like. Rational commercial practices dictated that publishers would not and did not reissue a book while stocks remained unsold on their shelves. Conversely, publishers quickly reprinted sheets when they had sold out.

Based on the commercial premises that guided publishing and republishing, we may reasonably conclude that 1,000 copies of the English-language edition of Perrault's *Histories* were sold between 1729 and 1741. That works out to about 83 books of Perrault's fairy tales sold per year over a twelve-year period (1729-41). Between 1741 and 1750 the rate of sale increased slightly to 111 books per year. Before declaring this a bestseller, however, one must remember that England's population numbered approximately seven million with large numbers of English-speakers in Wales, Scotland, and Ireland. Perrault's book in its English translation reached a very small fraction of England's population, approximately 1/3,500. When James Hodges, at the Looking Glass, facing St. Magnus Church, London-Bridge, reissued *Histories or Tales of Passed Times* in 1750, his sales of all-English Perrault tales plummeted. It took aver-

age sales of 52.6 copies a year to clear the shelves to make way for another such edition nineteen years later, in 1769!

Perrault's *Histories* had a second publishing history in England as a dual-language textbook. England had long had a market for dual-language textbooks, of which Johan Amos Comenius's *Orbis Pictus* is perhaps the most famous representative. In England his Latin-English catalog of the (principally) secular world was one of several Latin-English textbooks on the market for Latin-learning English pupils. However, with the increasing popularity of a grand European tour to crown eighteenth-century aristocratic boys' education, French displaced Latin as the language of choice in dual-language schoolbooks in England, and new French-English books like Faerno's *Fables* and Hübner's *Youth's Scripture Kalendar* found a market there.

It was to England's dual-language textbook market that England's first publishers of Perrault's tales turned in 1737 to repair their financial damage when commercial sales of the English-only edition evidently failed to cover their printing costs. They restored Perrault's French to create a dual-language book, "very proper to be read by young Children at Boarding Schools, that are to learn the *French* Tongue, as well as in private Families." Unlike the single-language English translation of Perrault's tales, the textbook flourished. If they printed 1,000 copies per print run, then the dual-language textbook sold three times as well as the English-language children's book, at a gratifying average rate of 250 copies per year, sales that justified reprinting it four years later, in 1741.

The surviving books of Perrault's tales, with their scribblings and signatures, suggest yet another consideration, gender. In the English-language and dual-language editions of Perrault's tales that I have inspected, my tally to date hints that girls more often owned English-language editions, boys French or dual-language ones. The evidence, though sparse, is tantalizing, because it corroborates the publishing history of Mme Leprince de Beaumont's girl-centered *Magasin des Enfans,* whose English translation swiftly supplanted and far outsold the French original in England.

In 1741 and after, however, sales of Perrault's dual-language *Histories* apparently slowed down, because the book was not reprinted again until 1750. In that year Montagu and Pote yielded their rights for Perrault's *Histories* to James Hodges, who supposedly printed an edition "in *French* and *English.* Price Bound 2s. 6d" (according to an advertisement in his 1750 English edition). But Hodges's 1750 dual-language edition of Perrault's *Histories* must have sold even more slowly than had the ones published by Montagu and Pote in 1735 and 1741, if indeed the dual-language edition was ever published at all. If it was not published, then the overall sales for Perrault's tales in dual-language editions fall even lower. A summary of this publishing history is listed below.

ENGLISH-LANGUAGE EDITIONS

PUBLISHER AND YEAR	AVERAGE SALES
MONTAGU AND POTE, 1729	83/YEAR
MONTAGU AND POTE, 1741	111/YEAR
JAMES HODGES, 1750	?
B. COLLINS, 1763	?

DUAL-LANGUAGE EDITIONS

PUBLISHER AND YEAR	AVERAGE SALES
MONTAGU AND POTE, 1737	250/YEAR
MONTAGU AND POTE, 1741	111/YEAR
JAMES HODGES, 1750	71/YEAR
J. MELVIL, 1764 (= VAN OS 1765)	VERY FEW

One may well wonder why Perrault's tales lost market appeal in both their English- and dual-language editions. Because sales dipped when James Hodges took over publication, it is tempting to conclude that his books were in some way inferior. But, in fact, they differed very little from the Montagu and Pote editions in paper quality, and they had exactly the same illustrations. One explanation lies in the differing manner in which textbooks and children's books are used over time. Textbooks have a way of saturating the market because students hand their books on. That observation is consistent with the textbook's diminishing sales between 1737 and 1764. But why are sales of the English-language edition also so low? These books addressed a leisure market, in which a book was a present, something to be treasured and kept, something that one purchased anew to give as a gift. For this market, it is likely that the changing temper of the times had a powerful effect on book choice: after 1750 strong anti-French sentiment animated an English public exasperated by continuing conflicts with France.

After Perrault's fairy tales foundered as a textbook at mid-century, a publisher with access to provincial markets, J. Melvil of London and Exeter, took up Perrault's *Histories* and brought out a dual-language edition in 1764. His sales must have been poor, too, because a publisher with offices in London and The Hague, Van Os, ended up with Melvil's unillustrated, and unsold, sheets, that is, the large pieces of paper with several pages printed on each, which, when folded, produce a fascicle, or section of a book. That Melvil's 1764 sheets were reissued by Van Os in 1765 can be demonstrated by identifying the printing's "fingerprint," the letters that appear directly above a designated marker, usually A2 or A3. Van Os substituted roughly executed and reversed copies of previously published illustrations, inserted them between the pages, and provided Melvil's sheets with a new title page, *Mother Goose's Tales,* a title first given Perrault's tales by another Dutch publisher, Jean Neaulme, twenty years before. Melvil's disposal of his unsold sheets was probably an act of desperation. But what readers should note is that sales for Perrault's *Histories* were low for the English editions and steadily declined for the dual-language textbooks from 1729 to the 1760s, that is, during precisely the period in which English children's literature was beginning to assume its modern form.

James Hodges, as mentioned earlier, also brought out an English-language edition of Perrault's *Histories* in 1750. This edition should be investigated carefully because there is evidence that in 1763 B. Collins published *Mother Goose's Tales* in Salisbury, with provincial sales augmented by a Mrs. Maynard in Devizes, and with London sales managed by W. Bristow in St. Paul's Church-Yard.[5] The question to be raised here is whether Hodges's and Collins's sheets are one and the same, as were Melvil's and Van Os's (a bellwether for sluggish sales) or whether the two books represent separate print runs (and hence higher rates of sale). If Bristow's London sales were successful, then they would have set the commercial possibilities of fairy tales before the very eyes of John Newbery, a point to which I will return later.

Chapbooks are another possible place to search for tales from Perrault's *Histories.* It is far easier, however, to find assertions in histories of children's literature that Perrault's tales were widely disseminated by the chapbook trade to England's children by the mid-eighteenth century than it is to actually locate chapbook copies of those tales. It is true that Perrault's *Histoires* were common in *France*'s chapbooks, the *Bibliothèque bleue,* between 1725 and 1775. But it wasn't until well after 1750 that isolated tales from Perrault's oeuvre begin to turn up in the Dicey Brothers' chapbook printing catalogs from Aldermary Church-Yard in London.[6] Gilles Duval, a

French historian of English chapbooks, carefully assessed eighteenth-century chapbook content and characterized Perrault's tales as Johnny-come-latelys ("adaptées tardivement").[7] In so doing he flatly contradicted generations of assumptions and assertions about the role of Perrault's tales in the originary years of English children's literature in the first half of the eighteenth century.

Diehard defenders of the hypothesis that Perrault's tales were preeminent would probably explain the absence of Perrault's fairy tales from English chapbooks as the result of his tales having been so beloved that they were read to shreds. Book history, however, demolishes that argument: avid eighteenth-century chapbook collectors left no Perrault tales in collections that they assembled before 1750. Nor are Perrault's tales found in the records of eighteenth-century circulating libraries in child-friendly formats. Instead, as Matthew O. Grenby found, they were "designed for an adult market . . . in multi-volume editions costing several shillings."[8]

Miscellanies for children offer a final potential entry point to be investigated in an analysis of the role of Perrault's tales in the emergence of English children's literature. We don't expect to find fairy tales in such books as *Every Youth His Own Moralist* (J. Shatwell, 1771) or *Vice in Its Proper Shape* (Francis Newbery [1767]). But to modern minds there is at least the hint of a promise of fairy tales in books with titles like *A Christmass[sic]-Box for Masters and Misses* (London: Mary Boreman, 1746), *The Amusing Instructor: or, Tales and Fables in Prose and Verse* (W. Harris, 1769), *Mrs. Lovechild's Golden Present, to all the little Masters and Misses, of Europe, Asia, Africa, and America* (Francis Newbery [1770]), or Don Stephano Bunyano's *Prettiest Book for Children; Being the History of the Enchanted Castle* (J. Coote, 1770). The magic and the otherworldly characters that these books introduced, however, drew not at all on Perrault's fairies and fairy tales but on England's old heroes and giants.[9] John Newbery flirted with fairy tales in *Short Histories for the Improvement of the Mind* (1760)—not Perrault's, however, but the highly moralized ones by François Fénelon.

One other miscellany remains to be investigated, Mme Leprince de Beaumont's *Magasin des Enfans* (1756). Soon translated into English as *Magasin des Enfans, or, The Young Misses Magazine,* it retained its half-French, half-English title for decades and was published well into the nineteenth century. Alternating fairy fictions and moral tales with geography, an-

cient history, and Bible histories, the book valorized *history* (histoire) over *tale* (conte) in both structure and commentary. When it came to magic transformations in the service of love, Mme Leprince de Beaumont substantially revised Perrault's **"Riquet a la Houpe"** and then composed her own highly moralized and still popular story of female beauty and male hideosity, "Beauty and the Beast." In other words, she too rejected Perrault's oeuvre.

When John Newbery copublished B. Collins's *Pretty Book for Boys and Girls* in 1743, he associated himself with a book in which both the warning tale **"Red Riding Hood"** and the fairy godmother of **"Cinderilla"** appeared, as Elizabeth Johnson reports in her catalog description of the Ball Collection of Children's Literature at the University of Indiana. Both tales were still in the 1756 *Pretty Book,* touted as "the seventh edition," along with "Fortunatus" and "The Effect of Good Nature. A Family Tale," a retelling of Perrault's **"Diamonds and Toads,"** a quintessentially normative narrative of good behavior rewarded.

Several questions arise in connection with the B. Collins book of 1743 and following editions. Was "the seventh edition" really a seventh edition, or was that an early example of an advertising device meant to suggest market success and therefore desirability, something that one often finds in eighteenth-century publishing? Scholarly inquiries like these make *A Pretty Book for Boys and Girls* an avenue to explore.

It is at this point that John Locke's often-cited disapproval of fairy tales becomes relevant. If we accept the evidence of the Collins provincial imprint, then we are led to the inevitable conclusion that both early and late in his publishing career Newbery's Lockean anti-fairy inclinations were directed more against England's own fairies than against French imports. The second, and equally inevitable, conclusion is that if Newbery, a canny publisher as John Buck has demonstrated, had believed before 1767 that Perrault's fairy tales would have sold well as a whole, then he would have offered them for sale. The possibility that he went in with Collins in 1743 on a book that included **"Cinderilla,"** but that he himself didn't turn towards Perrault again until more than twenty years later suggests that he assessed England's market for such literature and concluded that Perrault was unprofitable.

What *is* verifiable is that Perrault's **"Puss in Boots,"** the quintessential modern rags-to-riches fairy tale, appeared in a commercially successful miscellany (commercially successful by my definition means successive editions within a few years of each other) in 1767, when John Newbery included it in his gaily harum-scarum *The Fairing*.[10] Schooled as we all are to understand John Newbery as the ultimate Lockean producer of rationally based and socially useful books for children and as a publisher who doubted the suitability of fairy tales for children, we scarcely expect to find Perrauldian magic instead of Lockean literacy leading to wealth in one of Mr. Newbery's books. As an aside it is worth noting that Newbery invited one of England's own supernaturals, Queen Mab, to advertise his *Lilliputian Magazine* in 1750 (Pickering, 1981, 223), but during his entire publishing career he otherwise staved off the English imps and gnomes whom Locke had excoriated. Another London publisher, John Marshall, did the same thing. Samuel Pickering Jr. has interesting things to say in this regard. He tells us that Marshall assured buyers that his children's books were entirely divested of the prejudicial nonsense of hobgoblins, witches, and fairies.[11] The fact that Marshall eventually published Perrault's tales demonstrates that he too distinguished between England's fairy population and those in Perrault's fairy tales.

John Newbery's use of Queen Mab as a spokesperson tells us a lot about the market he addressed. Not a profound innovator, Newbery was rather an improver and popularizer of existing genres and characters, as Buck's thorough study of Newbery's literary merchandising makes clear. Consequently, his turning to Queen Mab early in his career tells us that she was a stock figure whose familiarity to his readers made her a useful advertising vehicle.

Newbery's 1767 introduction of Perrault's **"Puss in Boots"** into *The Fairing* was, however, a far more significant inclusion than Queen Mab, and it is legitimate to wonder why Newbery finally took this significant step. Although he had worked together with Collins over the years, he had *not* been part of the 1763 Collins-based consortium that brought Perrault's fairy tales to Mr. Bristow's shop in St. Paul's Church-Yard. But he could hardly have missed either knowing that Mr. Bristow was selling **Mother Goose** or seeing little customers walking out of Mr. Bristow's shop with copies of the book in their hands. And so if **Mother Goose** was a commercial hit at Mr. Bristow's shop just across the way, it would have been a natural move for Mr. Newbery, who habitually added to his list from genres that were in popular demand (Buck, passim), to tap into Perrault's tales for his own books.

The year 1767 thus represents the point at which it may be asserted that Perrault's tales entered the ranks of mainstream (i.e., London produced and distributed) English children's literature. The year 1767 postdates the 1744 publication of *A Little Pretty Pocket-Book*, usually cited as the beginning of modern English children's literature, by more than twenty years. In the context of the history of children's literature as a whole, the late date (at the end of John Newbery's publishing career) at which fairy tales became a mainstream constituent in children's literature means that we need to think of the emergence of the genre as a generation-long process. It was, above all, a process that responded to market opportunities and market tastes. It can be said to have begun with Newbery's little primers and to have achieved much of its potential with Newbery's acknowledgement of Perrault.

Two years later, in 1769, Perrault's *Histories or Tales of Past Times, Told by Mother Goose with Morals* was finally both printed and published as a children's book in London. (Earlier B. Collins editions had been printed in Salisbury in the provinces and distributed, i.e., published, in London.) Gone now was the sexually problematic "Discreet Princess," which leads to the conclusion that London's middle and upper-middle classes really did not want their children to know about Prince Riche-cautelle's "pernicious pleasure" (1729 161), or about Droneilla's immoral welcome of the knavish Riche-cautelle "for her husband . . . [with] no greater formalities than those which are the conclusion of marriage" (163), or about Riche-cautelle's caddish bedding of Drone-illa at night and Babillarde in the morning (168). Perrault's tales must have become far more attractive to middle-class English book buyers when the repellent images, affronting references, and negative examples of Mlle L'Héritier's "novel" disappeared from its pages. It is certainly noteworthy that the disappearance of Mlle L'Héritier's novel coincided exactly with an increased sales rate of Perrault's fairy tales.

By 1769, forty years after its first appearance in England, both Perrault's book and the times had changed. John Newbery had died and his heirs had taken over his publishing firm. Even at this late date, the publishers of Perrault's fairy tales were still giving signs of skittishness about the financial risk of their venture: three firms—John Newbery's successor firm Newbery and Carnan, B. Collins from Salisbury, and S. Crowder of London—carefully spread the risk by joining together in the undertaking.

Successful production of Perrault's fairy tales as a whole (rather than as individual stories) in England can be said to have begun in Salisbury in 1763 with B. Collins's **Mother Goose** and to have continued in London in 1769 with the Newbery-Carnan-Collins-Crowder team. From this point onward, Perrault's tales began their spectacular commercial ascent, blazing glory and trailing success. Whatever concerns Newbery, Carnan, Collins, and Crowder might have had about the market acceptability of Perrault's fairy tales in 1769 must have been dispelled by subsequent developments. Perrault's stories captured imaginations and markets, and chapbook editions of individual Perrault tales abounded in the late eighteenth and early nineteenth centuries.[12]

Why has Perrault's point of impact on English children's literature been misdated? One reason is that research tools available for the study of children's literature, although improving, still remain limited: reference books often repeat predecessors' views; catalog information is incomplete in such long-standard references as the pre-1956 National Union Catalog; and even the British Library's far more inclusive catalog presents another stumbling block by utilizing eighteenth-century title page practices. Meant to enhance the public's perception of a book's success, eighteenth-century publishers often misleadingly and intentionally numbered the printing of different kinds of books sequentially. With reference to the publishing history of Perrault's fairy tales in England, James Hodges called his 1750 reissue of Montagu and Pote's Samber 1729 English translation not the third edition, which would have accurately reflected the real situation, but "the fourth edition," because he counted in two dual-language schoolbook editions as second and third editions.

The nineteenth century mythologized fairy tales and saw in them expressions of nationhood, evidence of unbroken connection with the childhood of mankind, and proof of a sacred social cohesion that transcended class boundaries, with nursemaids telling children stories from time immemorial. Few nineteenth- or twentieth-century scholars have questioned this set of beliefs, and, as a consequence, what has become firmly embedded in histories of children's literature is not evidence itself but *beliefs* about evidence.

This exploration of English, French, and Englished French fairy tales in conjunction with the development of books for English children in the first three quarters of the eighteenth century leads to two fundamental revisions to the history of English children's literature.[13] First, Perrault's tales became "popular" in London's print trade only in the 1760s. Second, our old friend John Newbery did not eschew fairy tales to the end of his life. On the contrary, he introduced Perrault's magic when he saw that it sold. In both cases, market profitability took precedence over Lockean ideology in an increasingly mercantile world of publishing.

Notes

Postscript: Matthew O. Grenby of de Montfort University in England, who has recently investigated children's literature in eighteenth-century English lending libraries, has also noted a general absence of fairy tales in this period. Grenby's work will be published in a forthcoming issue of *Book History*.

1. Space does not permit me to include here my research on Mme d'Aulnoy. In brief, however, the d'Aulnoy material was first marketed to economically and socially privileged buyers, later to merchant readers, and finally to artisanal and child readers. As the collection of tales moved downmarket in social and/or economic terms, its prose was altered to address the consumers its publishers sought.

2. For a learned and lively discussion and a broad sample of seventeenth-, eighteenth-, and nineteenth-century sentiment about fairies, fairy fictions, and fairy tales, see Samuel Pickering Jr., *John Locke and Children's Books*, chap. 2. Broader access to popular publications of this period in the last twenty years has required modifying some of Pickering's conclusions.

3. "Les Chevaliers Errans," "La Princesse Zamée," "Le Prince Elmedor," "Zalmayde," and "Le Prince de Numidie."

4. Justin Schiller says that Samber worked from the 1716 Desbordes edition published in Amsterdam (Schiller, Entry no. 17), but Samber could have used the 1721 or 1729 Desbordes editions.

5. This information comes from Carpenter and Prichard, *Oxford Companion to Children's Literature*, 251, but I myself have not seen such a volume, nor do I know of any documentation of its contents, i.e., whether it included or excluded "The Discreet Princess."

6. Nicholas Tucker alludes to (undated) fairy tales' chapbook associations in "Fairy Tales and Their Early Opponents," 107-8.

7. Duval, *Littérature de colportage*, 68.

8. Matthew O. Grenby, "Children's Books in British Circulating Libraries, 1748-1848," *Book History* (forthcoming).

9. Although it is not his purpose, Andrew O'Malley describes the same result in "The Coach and Six" (2000 passim), which is devoted to book size and contents in what he terms "transitional" books of the eighteenth century. Duval, of course, treats eighteenth-century English chapbook content far more extensively.

10. "Puss in Boots" may have appeared even earlier than 1767 because the 1767 edition, according to its complete title, is a "new edition," i.e., the publisher claims that it had also appeared previously. But the complete title also claims that it has "additions," and so we can't be sure that "Puss in Boots" appeared before 1767 until we can examine an earlier edition.

11. Pickering, *John Locke and Children's Books*, 41.

12. See Schiller, "Charles Perrault and His 'Contes des Fées,'" Entry no. 36.

13. The evidence here also reveals that the popular (as opposed to textbook) emergence of Perrault's tales seems to have originated in the provinces and thus to have reversed the usual direction, from London outwards. This is, in itself, worthy of note in the history of the book.

Works Cited

Note: The fingerprint for some books has been included after basic bibliographic information.

Aulnoy, Marie Catherine Jumelle de Berneville, Comtesse d'. *The History of Adolphus, Prince of Russia; And the Princess of Happiness. By a Person of Quality. With a Collection of Songs and Love-Verses. By Several Hands.* London: R. T. near Stationers-Hall, 1691.

————, [and Chevalier de Mailly]. *The Diverting Works of the Countess D'Anois, Author of the Ladies Travels to Spain. Containing I. The Memoires of Her own Life. II. All Her Spanish Novels and Histories. III. Her Letters. IV. Tales of the Fairies in three Parts Complete. Newly done into English.* London: Printed for John Nicholson at the Kings Arms; And John Sprint at the Bell in Little Brittain, Andrew Bell at the Cross Keys and Bible in Cornhill; and for Samuel Burows [*sic*], 1707.

Buck, John D. C. "John Newbery and Literary Merchandising, 1744-1767." Ph.D. diss., University of California, Los Angeles, 1972.

Comenius, Johann Amos. *Orbis Sensualium Pictus.* Trans. Charles Hoole (1610-67). Reproduction of 1727 (text) and 1728 (title page) London editions. Syracuse: C. W. Bardeen, 1887.

Darton, F. J. Harvey. *Children's Books in England: Five Centuries of Social Life.* 3d ed., rev. by Brian Alderson. Cambridge: Cambridge University Press, 1982.

Duval, Gilles. *Littérature de colportage et imaginire collectif en Angleterre à l'époque des Dicey (1720-v. 1800).* Talence: Presses Universitaires de Bordeaux, 1991.

[Faerno, Gabriello]. *Fables in English and French Verse.* Trans. Charles Perrault. London: Davis, 1741.

Griffin, John, and Charles Frey, eds. *Classics of Children's Literature.* 4th ed. Upper Saddle River, N.J.: Prentice-Hall, 1995.

Hübner, Johann. *Youth's Scripture Kalendar: or, Select sacred stories for every Sunday throughout the Year in French and English: The Former, By the Reverend I. P. Aubaret, Maitre de Langues at the Prussian Court; And the Latter, By a gentleman of Oxford, To Which is annexed a succinct Historical account, in Both Languages, of the Four Most Holy Evangelists, Matthew, Mark, Luke, and John, the Whole Calculated for the use of schools.* London: T. Caslon, 1759.

Johnson, Elizabeth L. *For Your Amusement and Instruction: The Elisabeth Ball Collection of Historical Children's Materials.* Bloomington, Ind.: Lilly Library, 1987.

Leprince de Beaumont, Marie. *Magasin des Enfans, ou dialogues entre une sage gouvernante et plusieurs de ses élèves.* London: J. Haberkorn, 1756. Rare Books Collection, University of California, Los Angeles (hereafter UCLA).

————. *Magasin des Enfans, or, The Young Misses Magazine containing Dialogues between a Governess and Several Young Ladies of Quality.* London: B. Long and T. Pridden, 1759. UCLA.

[Newbery, John?] *The Fairing: or, A Golden Toy for Children of all Sizes and Denominations. In which they may see all the Fun of the Fair, And at home be as happy as if they were there. Adorned with Variety of Cuts, from Original Drawings. A New Edition, with Additions.* London: J. Newbery, 1767. UCLA.

Newbery, John, ed. *Short Stories for the Improvement of the Mind.* London: J. Newbery, 1760. Cotsen Collection of Children's Books, Princeton University (hereafter Cotsen).

O'Malley, Andrew. "The Coach and Six: Chapbook Residue in Late Eighteenth-Century Children's Literature." *Lion and the Unicorn* 24.1 (2000): 18-44.

Opie, Iona, and Peter Opie, eds. *The Classic Fairy Tales.* London: Oxford University Press, 1974.

Palmer, Melvin. "Mme d'Aulnoy in England." *Comparative Literature* 27.3 (summer 1975): 237-53.

Palmer, Melvin, and Nancy Palmer. "English Editions of French *Contes de Fees* Attributed to Mme d'Aulnoy." *Studies in Bibliography* 27 (1974): 227-32.

————. "The French Conte de Fée in England." *Studies in Short Fiction* 11 (winter 1974): 35-44.

Perrault, Charles (by date)

————. *Histoires ou Contes du Temps Passé. Avec des Moralitez. Par le Fils de Monsieur Perreault* [sic] *de l'Academie François. Suivante la Copie a Paris.* Amsterdam: [Jaques Desbordes], 1697. Cotsen.

————. *Histoires, ou Contes du temps passé. Avec des Moralitez. Par le Fils de Monsieur Perreault* [sic] *de l'Academie François. Suivant la Copie a Paris.* Amsterdam: [Jaques Desbordes?] 1700. Cotsen.

————. *Contes de Monsieur Perrault Avec des Moralitez.* Paris: Chez la Veuve Barbin, 1707. Cotsen.

————. *Histoires, ou Contes du tems* [sic] *passé. Avec des Moralitez. Par le Fils de Monsieur Perreault* [sic] *de l'Academie François. Suivant la Copie a Paris.* Amsterdam: Jaques Desbordes, 1708. Cotsen.

————. *Les Chevaliers Errans par Madame la Comtess D***.* Amsterdam: Estienne Roger, 1710. Houghton Library, Harvard University.

————. *Histoires, ou Contes du tems* [sic] *passé. Avec des Moralitez. Par M. Perrault. Nouvelle Edition augmentée d'une Nouvelle, à la fin. Suivant la Copie de Paris.* Amsterdam: Chez Jaques Desbordes, 1716. Cotsen.

————. *Histoires ou Contes du tems* [sic] *Passé, Avec des Moralitez. Par M. Perrault. Nouvelle Edition augmentée d'une Nouvelle, à la fin. Suivant la Copie de Paris.* Amsterdam: Chez la Veuve de Jaq. Desbordes, 1721.

————. *Histoires ou Contes du tems* [sic] *passé, Avec des Moralitez. Par M. Perrault. Nouvelle Edition augmentée d'une Nouvelle à la fin. Suivant la Copie de Paris.* Amsterdam: Jaques Desbordes, 1729. fingerprint A2 = _bob, A3 = _la_. Cotsen.

————. *Histories, or Tales of Past Times. With Morals. By M. Perrault. Translated into English.* London: Printed for L. Pote and R. Montagu, 1729. [Morgan]

————. *Histories, or Tales of Passed Times. With Morals. Written in French by M. Perrault, And Englished by R. S. Gent. The Second Edition, Corrected. Histoires ou Contes du Tems* [sic] *Passe. Avec des Moralitez. Par M. Perrault. Augmentée d'une Nouvelle, viz. L'Adroite Princesse. Troisieme Edition* [sic] London: Printed for R. Montagu at the Book Ware-House, that End of Great Queen-Street, next Drury Lane, and J. Pote, at Eton, 1737. fingerprint B3 = ceefst. Cotsen.

————. *Histories, or Tales of Passed Times. With morals. Written in French by M. Perrault, And Englished by R. S. Gent. The Third Edition. Corrected. With Cuts to every Tale.* London: Printed for R. Montagu, at the Book Ware-House, that End of Great-Queen-Street, next Drury-Lane, and J. Pote, at Eton, 1741. fingerprint B2 = *iffer. Cotsen.

————. *Contes De Ma Mere L'Oye. Mother Goose's Tales.* The Hague: Jean Neaulme, 1745. Cotsen.

————. *Histories, or Tales of Passed Times. With Morals written in French by M. Perrault, And Englished by R. S. Gent. The Fourth Edition, Corrected. With Cuts to every Tale.* London: For James Hodges, at the Looking-Glass, facing St. Magnus Church, London-Bridge, 1750. Morgan Library, New York.

————. *Contes De Ma Mere L'Oye. Ornée de neuf belles Figures de Cuivre. Sixieme Edition.* The Hague: Pierre Van Os, 1759. fingerprint A2 = ron_A3 = *t_de. Cotsen.

————. *Mother Goose's Tales.* Salisbury: B. Collins; Devizes: Mrs. Maynard; London: Mr. Bristow, 1763. See note 6, above.

————. *Tales of Passed Times by Mother Goose. With Morals. In French by M. Perrault, And Englished by R. S. Gent, To which is added a New one, viz. The Discreet Princess. The Sixth Edition, Corrected, and adorned with fine Cuts.* London: Printed for J. Melvil, Bookseller in Exeter change in the Strand, 1764. fingerprint A4 = pero. Cotsen.

————. *Mother Goose's Tales, in French and English, with Morals. Written in French by M. Perrault, and Englished by R. S. Gent. To which is added a*

New One, viz. The Discreet Princess. The Sixth Edition, Corrected, and adorned with fine Cuts. Hague: Printed for Van Os and Sold by J. Pridden at the Feathers in Fleetstreet, London, 1765. fingerprint A4 = pero. Cotsen.

————. *Histories or Tales of Past Times, told by Mother Goose. With Morals. Written in French by M. Perrault, and Englished by G. M. Gent. The Fifth Edition, corrected.* Salisbury: Printed and sold by B. Collins, also by [London:] Newbery and Carnan in St. Paul's Church-Yard; and S. Crowder, in Pater-Noster-Row, [1769]. fingerprint A3 = ich_. Cotsen.

————. *Tales of Past Times, by Old Mother Goose with Morals.* London: W. Osborne & T. Griffin, [ca. 1780].

Pickering, Samuel Jr. *John Locke and Children's Books in Eighteenth-Century England.* Knoxville: University of Tennessee Press, 1981.

A Pretty Book for Children, 7th ed. London: J. Newbery, J. Hodges, and B. Collins, 1756. fingerprint B3 = plig. Cotsen.

Schiller, Justin. "Charles Perrault and His 'Contes des Fées': Rare and Collectible Editions Published between 1691-1826 with Related Publications of This Genre, Being Contributions Toward a Bibliography Assembled 1977-1994 as the Personal Library of Justin G. Schiller." Kingston, N.Y., 1995. Xeroxed typescript. Cotsen.

Scot, Reginald. *The discouerie of witchcraft, Wherein the lewde dealing of witches, and witch mongers is notablie detected, the knauerie of coniurors, the impietie of inchantors, the follies of soothsaiers, the impudent falshood of cousenors, the infidelitie of atheists, the petilent practice of Pythonists, the curiosities of figure casters, the vanitie of dreamers, the beggerlie art of Alcumystrie, the abhomination of idolatrie, the horrible art of poisoning, the vertue and power of naturall magike, and all the conueniences of Legerdemaine and iuggling are deciphered, and many other things opened, which have long lien hidden, howbeit verie necessarie to be knowne. Heerevnto is added a treatise vpon the nature and substance of spirits and diuills, Ec.: all latelie written by Reginald Scot Esquire.* London: William Brome, 1584.

Summerfield, Geoffrey. *Fantasy and Reason: Children's Literature in the Eighteenth Century.* Athens: University of Georgia Press, 1985.

Tucker, Nicholas. "Fairy Tales and Their Early Opponents." In Mary Hilton, Morag Styles, and Victor Watson, eds., *Opening the Nursery Door: Reading, Writing, and Childhood 1600-1900.* London: Routledge, 1997. 104-16.

Verdier, Gabrielle. "Comment l'auteur des 'Fées à la mode' devint 'Mother Bunch': Métamorphoses de la Comtesse d'Aulnoy en Angleterre." *Marvels and Tales* 10.2 (1996): 285-309.

TITLE COMMENTARY

📖 **"CENDRILLON OU LA PETITE PANTOUFFLE DE VERRE" (1697; "CINDERELLA, OR THE LITTLE GLASS SLIPPER")**

Timothy C. Murray (essay date December 1976)

SOURCE: Murray, Timothy C. "A Marvelous Guide to Anamorphosis: *Cendrillon ou La Petite Pantoufle de Verre.*" *MLN* 91, no. 6 (December 1976): 1276-295.

[*In the following essay, Murray investigates the significance of voyeurism, sexual desire, and memory in "Cendrillon ou la petite pantoufle de verre."*]

The voyeur. A spectator of desires. One who is lured to a certain class of literature for contemplation, comprehension, and satisfaction. The body of literature particularly suited to his wants: the *merveilleux*. The fairy tale, for instance, opens to its viewer a supernatural world of dreams and visions, some desirable and enticing, others grotesque and repulsive, but all compelling and enchanting. The *merveilleux* seduces the voyeur with striking and seemingly illogical visions which nevertheless, as Marie Françoise Christout lucidly perceives, "possède en fait sa propre logique intérieure qui n'est pas celle de la vie courante, et conserve le souci d'une vraisemblance personnelle, base de son pouvoir suggestif, volontaire ou non."[1] The fairy tale is a manifestation of the voyeur's projections of unrealized possibilities of existence—unknown to the voyeur in their extraordinary form, but akin to his desires in their verisimilitude. The voyeuristic reading of a fairy tale, a veritable consumption of an unreal but satisfying universe, is indeed a manifestation of "la tension extrême de l'être . . . conjonction de la réalité et du désir." The voyeur of the *merveilleux* amuses himself by means of "l'imagination subjective delivrée par des états exceptionnels et l'imagination objective créant spontanément le mythe, le conte."[2] A private vision of the extraordinary narrative of a fairy tale, Christout implies, allows for the fulfillment of unknown desires;

the unconscious is revealed; the desired perception is realized. The *merveilleux* itself is an object of desire. It is an indirect vision of elementary patterns of the unconscious through which desire is structured and verified by the voyeur.

Anamorphosis, the particular vision suitable for voyeurism, distorts the fairy tale's narrative structure so that particular objects of perception may be isolated for the close observation of the voyeur. The objects of isolation range from proper names to moments of narrative action. As a group these objects create a distorted textual image unrecognizable unless viewed by the proper restoring device. Yet, the voyeuristic reader is enticed by the isolated objects whose naked forms remain suspended from the narrative's supportive context. As Jurgis Baltrusaitis explains in his illuminating discussion of anamorphosis in art, the voyeur is fascinated by the anamorphic "incertitude des choses visibles."[3] The attraction of such uncertain images is a dominant topic in Jacques Lacan's *Le Séminaire XI*. In his brief discussion of Baltrusaitis and anamorphosis, Lacan explains that these anamorphic forms are uncertain because they stand out as signifiers of the voyeur's dreams and wants, as "quelque chose de symbolique de la fonction du manque."[4] Through close evaluation of the seductive objects that assume the form of his dreams, the voyeur is able to make sense of his unconscious projections. The voyeur's successful decoding of his projections restores the distorted image of the text and satisfies the desires that enchanted him to experience the *merveilleux*.

The central role of anamorphosis in the reading of a fairy tale is best discussed in terms of a specific tale. A text ideally suited for this purpose is Perrault's **"Cendrillon ou La Petite Pantoufle de Verre"** in the 1697 edition of *Histoires ou Contes du Temps Passé*.[5] My critical reading of **"Cendrillon"** will first delineate the two narratives of transformation and kinship that convey the logic of the *merveilleux*. Only after presenting these structures as crucial in establishing for the reader the tale's "souci d'une vraisemblance personnelle," will I emphasize their acute inadequacy as objects of the viewer's desire. Cendrillon will then be shown to invite a voyeuristic mode of reading. For the tale is structured to isolate ambiguous objects of vision for the seduction of the voyeur. The repeated surfacing of these objects forces the viewer to acknowledge his attraction to their seductive images. The form of **"Cendrillon"** is anamorphic, one that elicits and structures projections of desire. Furthermore, **"Cendrillon"** will be shown to

verify Todorov's contention that "ce qui distingue le conte de fées est une certaine écriture, non le statut de surnaturel."[6] The writing of **"Cendrillon,"** like that of this essay, not only depends on the inadequacy of its own logical structures, but also instructs the voyeur how to become aroused and satisfied through its reading.

Seduction of the reader is the task of all bodies of writing. The narrative of any fairy tale has a particular logic contributing to the allure of the *merveilleux*. Marc Soriano and Michel Serres have presented insightful explications of the logic found in the narrative of **"Cendrillon."**[7] Soriano emphasizes **"Cendrillon"**'s rational tone, which is exemplified by the scene in which the Marraine readies Cendrillon for her first ball. The preparatory spells highlighting this scene follow a strict and logical correspondence: the six mice are transformed into "six chevaux, d'un beau gris de souris pommelé," and the rat, chosen for his "maîtresse barbe," becomes a large coachman "qui avait une des plus belles moustaches qu'on ait jamais vues." The visual correspondance between the objects, before and after metamorphosis, contributes to a metonymical fluidity in the narrative. However unreal the spells may seem, the contiguous relation between, say, the rat and the coachman establishes a clear visual image of the logic underlying the marvelous process of metamorphosis. This metonymical fluidity is enhanced on a philological level. Serres emphasizes the correspondance between certain original objects—*citrouille*—their latin synonyms—*cucurbita*—and the synonym's reference to the transformed objects: "*currus-véhicule à courir-cucurri, de curro.*" The contiguity of the language of metamorphosis adds to the clarity of the visual image of metamorphosis. Visual and verbal structures of metonymy facilitate a smooth narrative movement from element A to element Ā, from mangy mouse to dapple-grey horse. The interior logic of **"Cendrillon,"** then, provides the framework through which a clear perception of the *merveilleux* can be enjoyed by the viewer.

Vladimir Propp asserts that the primary function of "folk-logic" is to order the narrative in such a way that the individual characters and episodes are "defined from the point of view of [their] significance for the course of action."[8] The subordination of **"Cendrillon"**'s various episodes to their role in effecting the end point of the narrative is aided by an element common to the logic of the *merveilleux*: the "effet du miroir." The process of mirroring duplicates a certain character or episode for the sake of narrative economy. Mirroring clarifies the object of duplication and catalyzes the narrative away from concentration on the object. For instance, Soriano describes the narration of **"Cendrillon"**'s balls in terms of the "effet du miroir." While there are two balls, only the first receives a unique narration. However, this one episode is retold twice—once from Cendrillon's perspective, and again from the viewpoint of the resentful stepsisters. The narration of the second ball is but an expanded repetition of the account of the first ball. In this case, mirroring both contributes to character development for the sake of *pathos* ("le fils du Roi en était fort en peine") and moves the focus of attention away from striking moments of narrative *caesurae* ("Il se fit alors un grand silence"). Mirroring is a constant element of narrative logic in **"Cendrillon."** Whether the object of reflection comprises a small section of metonymic structure—the Marraine's first "coup de sa baguette"—or a large segment of narrative—the first ball—the logical effect is the virtual negation of any textual element as valuable in itself.

The "effet du miroir" and the metonymic structures of logic contribute to a clear outline of **"Cendrillon"**'s form, but neutralize any particular moments within the text. A closed form results. Although the viewer is attracted by the exposed form of an elongated textual body, the synchronic narrative works to shield particular areas of fascination from the desirous eyes of the voyeur.

The voyeur, however, is charmed by the moral appendage attached to the body of **"Cendrillon"**'s narrative. While the morality is an integral part of any tale in Perrault's collection, it is remarkably different from the structure of the narrative proper. Unlike the prose of the narrative, the morality's verse does not encourage a causal progression of images, an elongation of text. Instead, it trains the eye on a vertical moment of poetry. Nor is the verse a mere addition to the form of **"Cendrillon"**'s narrative. The morality is a projection onto form—the manifestation of a "translator's" desire for interpretation. Perrault's morality works to insert private meaning into the synchronic narrative. In Louis Marin's words,

> La moralité nous donne à lire le récit comme un text chiffré dans lequel l'événement est plus et autre chose que lui-même . . . surtout *après* le récit, elle appartient à un autre ordre de lecture . . . qui, en donnant son sens, induit à une relecture: celle-ci doit permettre de vérifier la moralité, de décoder le récit selon le code que la moralité nous donne. Nous ne lisons plus le récit, nous le traduisons.[9]

Perrault's code for translation suggests an alternative to the priorities established by Cendrillon's synchronic narrative. Although the first morality appears to confirm a central concern with Cendrillon's transformation—"La bonne grâce est le vrai don des Fées," the other morality suggests that *all* persons are the natural recipients of *bonne grâce* which "on reçoit du Ciel en partage." Here, the matter of kinship, "Ou des parrains ou des marraines" takes precedence over Cendrillon's individual transformation. A rereading of the narrative, directed by the morality's code for translation, results in a contraction of the elongated narrative. The voyeur is treated to the accentuation of previously disguised structures. The text reveals an alluring diachronic narrative: Cendrillon's realization of the elementary structures of kinship.

The opening narrative of **"Cendrillon"** outlines a specific structure of kinship. "Un Gentilhomme" marries "une femme, la plus hautaine et la plus fière qu'on eût jamais vue." The man's entrance into a matrilineal household strips him of all rights to authority "parce que sa femme le gouvernait entièrement." The wife's dominant character of "mauvaise humeur" is imitated by her two daughters who "lui ressemblaient en toutes choses." Virtual castration of the husband/father by the wife underlines the axis of matrilineal filiation that the text introduces. Such a matrilineal structure, writes Lévi-Strauss, "ne reconnaît aucun lien social de parenté entre un enfant et son père; et dans le clan de sa femme—dont ses enfants font partie—il est lui-même un 'visiteur', un 'homme-du-dehors' ou un 'étranger'."[10] The father is alienated from his stepdaughters and from Cendrillon, his daughter from a previous marriage. Although Cendrillon appears to descend from a family of matrilineal filiation ("elle tenait cela de sa Mère") her new maternal family cannot accommodate a young girl "d'une douceur et d'une bonté sans exemple." Cendrillon's tenderness represents a maternal image which challenges the arrogant demeanor of her stepmother ("sa mère . . . la meilleure personne du monde" as opposed to "une femme, la plus hautaine . . .."). Adoption of Cendrillon into the family would render the two sisters, the stepmother's doubles, "encore plus haïssables." Exogamic alliance is forsaken for Cendrillon's humiliating bondage. The initial kinship structure of **"Cendrillon"** excludes alliance for consanguinity, exogamy for endogamy, masculinity for femininity, compassion for "mauvaise humeur."

The diachronic opening up of a closed synchronic narrative first reveals a closed system of endogamic kinship. Yet, Perrault's insistence on the role of "ou des parrains ou des marraines" points to the exist-ence of two more patterns of kinship which displace the first. From the moment of the Marraine's appear-ance in the text, the stepmother disappears from the narrative. The Marraine enters the narrative as the substitute for Cendrillon's "positive" mother. The seventeenth-century *marraine,* according to Furetière, was responsible for the maintenance of "une alliance spirituelle entre la marraine et son filleul."[11] In addi-tion, Furetière defines the responsibilities of the *mar-raine* to be synonymous with those of the *parrain.* In the context of Cendrillon's original matrilineal envi-ronment, the Marraine serves both the function of substitute mother and that of maternal uncle.[12] While the Marraine's maternal function is to insure the spiri-tual protection of Cendrillon, her avuncular role is to make available those primary elements missing in the narrative's initial kinship structure: exogamic alli-ance and masculinity. The Marraine as mother and uncle joins the King in consenting to the exogamic marriage of Cendrillon and the Prince. Cendrillon's bondage to a nefarious matrilineal household is eradi-cated by her acceptance into a society of balanced kinship in which masculinity and tenderness are endorsed.

Although the stepmother of "mauvaise humeur" dis-appears from the text with the introduction of the Marraine, the two stepsisters, the doubles of the step-mother, continue to stand outside of the new exo-gamic structure illustrated by Figure 2. However, the marriage of Cendrillon catalyzes a third pattern of kinship incorporating the stepdaughters into the exogamic/patrilineal society. Just as the stepmother is replaced by the Marraine, the Marraine's role is adopted by Cendrillon at the time of her marriage. It is now Cendrillon who plays the double role of mother and uncle to the stepsisters. Cendrillon, the maternal figure "les priait de l'aimer bien toujours." Cendrillon, the maternal uncle "les maria dès le jour même à deux grands Seigneurs de la Cour." Figure 3, then, illustrates the end point of the diachronic narrative. Cendrillon fulfills her role as mother/maternal uncle by joining the fils du Roi as go-between in the marriage of her two stepsisters. Exo-gamic alliance and patrilineal filiation "de bon coeur" reign às the ultimate diachronic structures in **"Cendrillon."**

The diachronic narrative provides the voyeur with particular areas of visual concentration. The three main narrative segments present differing attitudes of parental affirmation or negation and varying struc-tures of sexual alliance. Yet, we might still question

the effectiveness of the diachronic narrative in cata-lyzing the voyeur into a realization of his subjective visions. Although the diachronic structures are present in the text for visual consumption, the logic of their presentation works to deny the voyeur's per-sonal realization of the various kinship forms in the narrative. The diachronic narrative is, like the syn-chronic narrative, dependent on the logic of the "effet du miroir." Figures 1-3 provide an illustration of the repetitive and contiguous relationship between the three kinship structures in the text. As it works in the synchronic narrative, the "effet du miroir" establishes the diachronic narrative as the unfolding of the ac-tion up to the end point of Figure 3. Particular mo-ments of the diachronic narrative self-consume upon completion of their metonymical function. The move-ment of both narratives, then, shows the voyeur struc-tures of closed form—those elongated in the syn-chronic narrative, and those contracted in the diachronic narrative. In both cases, only the final nar-rative segments signifying the end point of the tale receive narrative emphasis. Consequently, **"Cendril-lon"** presents the voyeur with parallel narratives whose particular interior meanings are subordinated to the structural emphasis on narrative progression. The logic of the narratives works to frustrate voy-euristic concentration on the separate moments that attract the viewer.

But what are these "particular interior meanings" and why are they so essential to the observance of **"Cen-drillon"**? Would it not suffice to conclude this article with the following statement: Perrault's code for translation enables the voyeur to penetrate the el-ementary structures of kinship signified by **"Cendril-lon"**'s synchronic narrative; the diachronic narrative, furthermore, implies a "positive" sexual fulfillment that, according to Christout, "conserve le souci d'une vraisemblance personelle, base de son pouvoir sug-gestif, volontaire ou non"? In my opening remarks, I suggested that the *merveilleux* is most appealing to the voyeur because it presents and isolates particular signifiers that assume the form of his desires. The voyeur, however, is not seduced by the end vision, the image of superimposed layers of narrative struc-ture—a synchronic signifier and a diachronic signified. What fascinates the voyeur is the marvel-ous surfacing of specific moments of signification in the text. New signs of desire constantly surface be-tween **"Cendrillon"**'s two narratives of transforma-tion and kinship. These are projections that remain isolated outside of the metonymical movement of the narratives. As projections, they are clear to the voy-eur in form, but unclear in meaning. While the textual isolation of such a sign as, say, the proper name Cendrillon attracts the eyes of the voyeur, its ambiguous connotations challenge the certainty of the voyeur's vision. By grafting from Lacan, we can say, for instance, that the proper name Cendrillon functions as a *"colophon du doute."* "Le colophon, dans un vieux texte," Lacan reminds us, "c'est cette petite main indicative qu'on imprimait dans la marge, du temps où l'on avait encore une typographie. Le colophon de doute fait partie du texte."[13] The colophon is doubtful because its significations are constantly multiplied and challenged. As will be demonstrated, the voyeur's attention remains focused on such ambiguous signs of desire. A narrative of signification results that oscillates between a clear presentation of the signs of desire and an emphasis on the uncertainty of their inconstant meanings. The two superimposed narratives relying on the "effet du miroir" reflect a third narrative of anamorphosis.

To the voyeur, the text is reducible to the simultaneous vision of various forms of signification. The difficulty lies in his structuralization and verification of these forms as lasting manifestations of the unconscious. Interestingly enough, **"Cendrillon"** is structured to aid the voyeur in this process. While presenting its viewer with vascillating objects of fascination, the text instructs its reader in modes of vision for the comprehension of the *merveilleux.*

The text assists the voyeur by stressing introductory signs that function as indicators of the narrative of anamorphosis—*le colophon des colophons de doute.* This colophon is isolated in the title: **"Cendrillon ou La Petite Pantoufle de Verre."** As colophon, the title signals a motivated anamorphic viewing of the text. It is the keyhole through which we see the various *colophons de doute.* While this was shaped by the translator, Perrault, for the voyeur's entrance into the text, it is a very sophisticated device. Easy entry is deterred. Because experience is most often the best aid in the manipulation of a tricky lock, we might discuss the function of the title in terms of a previously established theory of signification. Roland Barthes, for example, might refer to this keyhole as "the outline of an economy of signification." The initial shape of the keyhole, comprised of language material, "introduces a certain order at the level of the first (significant) articulation."[14] The order of the first signification, or the shape of the keyhole is relatively clear. Upon viewing the title, our immediate response might be to search for the key marked "Cendrillon" that is shaped to open the traditional text concerning "la jeune fille sacrifiée par ses parents au profit de

soeurs injustement choyées."[15] Yet, closer observation of the keyhole will disclose a more elaborate lock. It requires a key shaped both for the tumbler "Cendrillon" and for the tumbler "La Petite Pantoufle de Verre." This double title must be clarified in order to attain clear vision through the keyhole. Leading questions must be answered: Why does the "Pantoufle de Verre" receive textual prominence? What is the significance of the juxtaposition of "Cendrillon" and "Pantoufle"? Why are the signs "Cendrillon" and "Pantoufle" equated by the conjunction *ou*? As these questions indicate, the first articulation of the text introduces an order of ambiguity—the outline of anamorphic signification.

While this outline is ambiguous, its purpose is to aid the voyeur in seeing through the keyhole. The motivation provided by the title **"Cendrillon ou La Petite Pantoufle de Verre"** can be appreciated by considering a certain function of the sign of signification. In *Elements of Semiology,* Barthes moves beyond Saussure to posit the signification's power of motivation:

> from signified to signifier, there is a certain motivation in the (restricted) case of onomatopoeia . . . and also every time a series of signs is created by the tongue through the imitation of a certain prototype of composition or derivation.[16]

In choosing his title, Perrault outlined a series of onomatopoeic significations. In addition, these significations point to the composition of the text—its oscillation from one narrative to another—and to its derivation—the main characters' projections of desire that are the foundation of the narrative. We will now profit from a detailed analysis of the outline **"Cendrillon ou La Petite Pantoufle de Verre."**

Let us begin with **"Cendrillon,"** the sign and the *jeune fille.* Who is the *jeune fille* in Perrault's text? We receive little information about her background. We know her only as a girl *without* a name, *without* a mother, *without* a father, *without* a family. But more importantly, she is a girl *without* a Self. Her exceptional gentleness and kindness are virtues inherited from her mother, the best person in the world. The *jeune fille* is an image, a form of beauty, but one lacking a reflective interior. The proper name Cendrillon, assigned by a stepsister, signifies the *jeune fille* who lacks sense, who has never known herself, or who has forgotten herself: *cendres-y-ont. Cendres,* as Furetière indicates, "se prend . . . pour la *mort* . . . ou la *memoire* de la personne."[17] Cendrillon is a living ghost. She must remember her repressed identity for revivification.

The process of remembrance is discussed by Lacan in "Du reseau des signifiants." He informs us that remembrance depends on "le système perception-conscience." By confronting memory with "les traces de perception," the subject revitalizes structures of desire that lay forgotten. Recollection, however, can only occur by means of the subsequent erasure of perception which deprives memory from the "other" that has rekindled it.[18] A "certitude" of vision is replaced by a doubt of perception. However, it is not the perception itself that is doubted, but the *conscience,* the recollection of "tout ce qu'il en est du contenu de l'inconscient." Yet, doubt isolates and verifies the signs of the unconscious:

> c'est là que Freud met l'accent de toute sa force—le doute, c'est l'appui de sa certitude. Il le motive—c'est justement là, dit-il, signe qu'il y a quelque chose à préserver.[19]

Repetition of the process *perception-conscience-doute* clarifies a "forme qui n'est pas claire." Remembrance, says Lacan, is contingent on repetition.[20] It is through the repetition of *perception-conscience-doute* that Cendrillon becomes certain of her name—the signification of both her *mort* and her *memoire.*

Cendrillon sits in the ashes because she "n'osait s'en plaindre à son père." Her condition of loss—both of her family and of her Self—is emphasized by this motif of isolation. In contrast, Cendrillon's interaction with her stepsisters facilitates the process of remembrance. The first instance of Cendrillon's verbal contact with the stepsisters occurs when "elles [les deux soeurs] appelèrent Cendrillon pour lui demander son avis, car elle avait le goût bon. Cendrillon les conseilla le mieux du monde." Cendrillon's helpful advice provides "les traces de perception" that stimulate the remembrance of her Self. The activation of her memory is underlined by her offer to "les coiffer." Furetière indicates that *coeffer* meant "s'entêter, se preoccuper en faveur de quelque chose, se coeffer de nouvelles opinions."[21] Cendrillon's aggressiveness in offering advice, suggested by this play on *coeffer,* points to an initial surfacing of her advisory capacity as mother/avunculate. However, her identity as a counselor is denied by the stepsisters: "vous vous moquez de moi"—"Tu as raison." This negation of Cendrillon's worth stimulates the interior process of remembrance. The *traces de perception* in the form of a spoken dialogue disappear. But the "*raison*" for doubt remains. Cendrillon's spoken dialogue is continued by an interior dialogue that ponders her reality as *marraine.*

I would like to suggest that such a pondering is implied in Perrault's narrative insertion: "Une autre que Cendrillon les aurait coiffées de travers; mais elle était bonne, et elle les coiffa parfaitement bien." This reassertion of Cendrillon's worth as *coiffeuse* signifies the process of remembrance. It not only suggests the act of advising which provides the *traces de perception,* but it also implies the subsequent doubt and *conscience* resulting from the sisters' negation of Cendrillon. The *Petit Robert* lists the following definition "par analogie" of *coiffer*: *recouvrir, surmonter.* In Cendrillon's case, *recouvrir* is to conceal again, to doubt her identity as *marraine. Surmonter* is the potential overcoming, surmounting of doubt. The act of *coiffant* stands out in the text as a striking *colophon de doute.* It is a sign of Cendrillon's sense which she and the voyeur must verify.

A second instance of Cendrillon's remembrance is provided by her first interaction with her Marraine. Cendrillon renews her efforts to *coiffer* by offering advice to her Marraine. It is Cendrillon who suggests that a rat would make a suitable coachman. She literally assumes the role of *marraine* by excelling in the logic peculiar to "ou des parrains ou des marraines." The importance of this moment is stressed by Perrault's subtle shift in the use of possessive pronouns. Up to the time of Cendrillon's suggestion, her Marraine is consistently referred to as "*Sa* Marraine." After the Marraine's affirmation of Cendrillon's identity as *marraine,* the Marraine loses her possessive pronoun. She becomes "*la* Marraine," or "*la* Fée." This grammatical shift suggests that Cendrillon has, for the moment, come into her own as *marraine.* Furthermore, the Marraine's affirmation of Cendrillon's identity—"Tu as raison"—is particularly poignant because it is the same phrase with which the stepsisters negated Cendrillon's identity as *coiffeuse.* The anaphoric use of this phrase isolates it as a *colophon de doute.* It is used to signify both *recouvrir* and *surmonter.* In fact, Cendrillon's *raison* is again the catalyst of doubt.

Her vocal discomfort concerning "mes vilains habits" thrusts Cendrillon back into the dependence on her Marraine. At this moment in the text, the passive pronoun returns. "*Sa* Marraine" outfits Cendrillon in "des habits de drap d'or" that allow her entrance into the exogamic court. The Marraine also issues the proscription "de ne pas passer minuit." This proscription can easily be described as the act of signification symbolized by the ambiguous *ou* in the title. On the one hand, Cendrillon is provided with "une paire de pantoufles de verre." These slippers of *vair* (a Renaissance term for coat of arms) suggest Cendrillon's preordained place in court. The proscription, however, requires Cendrillon to return to her home of *cendres*. She must continue the process of remembrance. Although Cendrillon's remembrance of her Self depends on her liberation from endogamic bonds, she must return to her family to enact her obligations as *marraine*. The proscription, then, is the colophon signifying the ambiguity inherent in the juxtaposition and equation of **"Cendrillon ou La Petite Pantoufle de Verre."**

Because remembrance is contingent on repetition, neither Cendrillon nor the voyeur can fully realize the sense of the proscription without repeated visions of its ambiguous signification. At the first ball, Cendrillon successfully maintains her position of mediation. She arouses the desire of the Prince and she watches over the sisters by offering "mille honnêtetés. . . ." However, her behavior at the second ball provides the viewer with a prime example of poor voyeuristic perception. Cendrillon centers all of her attention on her new object of desire: "Le fils du Roi fut toujours auprès d'elle . . . la jeune Demoiselle ne s'ennuyait point." She is obsessed with a physical body that lacks full sense outside of the context of her kinship responsibilities. Consequently, Cendrillon forgets both the proscription and her identity as *marraine*. She regains the air of a lost *Paysanne*: "rien ne lui étant resté de toute sa magnificence qu'une de ses petites pantoufles."

As a result of this latest loss of memory, the "jeune fille fort mal vêtue" truly personifies **"Cendrillon ou La Petite Pantoufle de Verre."** While she resumes the role of Cendrillon at home, her lost slipper is the object of attention at court. The oscillation between Cendrillon's appearance at home and at court is temporarily suspended. She now remains visible to the voyeur in both societies. The quality of vision depends on the flexibility of the voyeur's gaze.

The Prince, for instance, is deprived of Cendrillon, the visual object of his desire. The intensity of his desire is not fully apparent until the disappearance of those *traces de perception* signifying Cendrillon. Only after the Prince loses Cendrillon ("Le Prince la suivit, mais il ne put l'attraper") does the realization of his desire occur: "qu'assurément il était fort amoureux de la belle personne à qui appartenait la petite pantoufle." This desire is realized through a displacement of vision. The Prince ignores all the mundane objects of perception around him in order to gaze in wonder at the *pantoufle de verre*. This slipper is the anamorphic *glass* through which the Prince can now see all that he misses: "il n'avait fait que *la* regarder pendant tout le reste du Bal." "La" is the heart of the slipper, Cendrillon. Cendrillon is the sign of the Prince's *cendre*. According to Furetière, "on dit figurément, qu'une coeur est réduit en cendre; pour dire, qu'il est consumé d'amour."[22] The Prince's anamorphic vision signifies the recognition of his love for Cendrillon. Furthermore, this gazing at the shoe is a phantasm of the marital consummation of this love. As a phantasmic image, the *pantoufle de verre/vair* (*fourrure*) assumes the fetishistic quality of the foot which is described by Freud:

> the foot or shoe owes its preference as a fetish to the circumstances that the inquisitive boy peered at the woman's genitals from below, from her legs up; fur and velvet . . . are a fixation of the sight of the public hair, which should have been followed by the longed-for sight of the female member.[23]

The sexual act is represented by the Prince's anamorphic gaze at this shoe. Prolonged anamorphic vision "dans sa fonction pulsatile et étalée," Lacan suggests, is the projection of "le symbole phallique, le fantôme anamorphique."[24] This voyeuristic penetration of Cendrillon's vaginal shoe is a concrete sign of the Prince's suppressed desire. His realization of this desire results in his exogamic marriage to Cendrillon.

"La petite pantoufle de verre" is also the sign of Cendrillon's dual role as mother and maternal uncle. The fact that Cendrillon's reunion with "la petite pantoufle" represents her motherhood requires no reiteration. Yet, Cendrillon cannot experience exogamic motherhood unless her avuncular responsibilities are simultaneously fulfilled. This remembrance is contingent on Cendrillon's anamorphic understanding of her own *pantoufle*. While watching her sisters fail to fit the shoe, Cendrillon "*reconnut*" the significance of her slipper. Her penetration of the slipper fulfills the liberating task for which the sisters are impotent: "elle y entrait sans peine, et qu'elle y était juste comme de cire." This penetration of her own vagina signifies Cendrillon's remembrance of her Self as both mother and uncle. Through the sharp vision and penetration of her shoe, Cendrillon attains her longed for moment of anamorphic insight which, according to Baltrusaitis, "est muable et flexible comme la cire."[25] Signifying both mother and uncle, **"Cendrillon ou La Petite Pantoufle de Verre"** opens the household to flexible exogamic relations.[26]

Cendrillon's exogamic wholeness facilitates the stepsisters' appropriation of anamorphic insight. By viewing Cendrillon's symbolic act of hermaphroditic copulation, the stepsisters are struck by a tableau that expresses their repressed kinship to Cendrillon. Cendrillon fulfills their wishes for a compassionate mother and a responsible father. These desires make their first textual appearance in the form of the proper names which the sisters assign to the "pauvre fille": "Cucendron," "Cendrillon." These names are unrealized articulations of the sisters' unconscious longing for a balanced and liberating exogamic kinship. The psychological significance of name-giving is discussed by Lévi-Strauss in *The Savage Mind*:

> At one extreme the name is an identifying mark which, by the application of a rule, establishes that the individual who *is named* is a member of a preordained class (a social group in a system of groups, a status by birth in a system of statuses). At the other extreme, the name is a free creation on the part of the individual who *gives the name* and expresses a transitory and subjective state of his own by means of the person he names . . . The choice seems only to be between identifying someone else by assigning him to a class or, under cover of giving him a name, identifying oneself through him.[27]

The name Cucendron designates the *jeune fille* to be a member of a family not accepted by those who assign her this name. *Cucendron* is the mark of the *jeune fille*'s death or separation from her proper family. Furthermore, this name which is "si malhonnête" reflects the antagonism of the name-giver towards the class represented by the named. The name Cucendron expresses the stepsisters' hostility towards outside lineages. It also expresses a defensive attitude towards "les bonnes qualités de cette jeune enfant" and towards Cendrillon's potential authority as avunculate. The more affectionate name Cendrillon, however, refers to the entirely different "transitory and subjective state" of the cadette who assigns the name. The cadette suffers from the joint loss of Self and compassionate parentage implied by the name *Cendres-y-ont*. Like the *jeune fille,* the cadette must realize her suppressed desire before she can be freed from the state of her endogamic death. The cadette's enunciation of this desire is also the articulation of the Ainée's desire. Being doubles, the sisters' thoughts and actions are inter-referential. The stepsisters oscillate between their antagonism signified by the name Cucendron and their desired kinship expressed in the name Cendrillon. At one moment in the text, their unconscious dependence on Cendrillon is expressed when "elles appèlerent Cendrillon pour lui demander son avis." Yet, they maintain their barrier of antagonism towards Cendrillon's potential avuncular authority as *coiffeuse*: "on rirait bien si on

voyait un Cucendron aller au Bal." At a later point in the text, the stepsisters narrate their unrealized vision of Cendrillon's maternal/avuncular position: "il y est venu la plus belle Princesse . . . elle nous a donné des oranges et des citrons." However, their defensive antagonism hinders their interpretation of this vision. They react negatively to Cendrillon's suggestion that she borrow her sister's house robe. Were Cendrillon to wear or appropriate this garment, a sign of the sister's shallow identity, she would literally transform the signification carried by the robe. For the transference of this garment from a stepsister to Cendrillon would be a sign of reciprocal exchange in return for the gift of prized fruits. The act of a willing exchange would signify a mutual feeling of compassion, kinship, and obligation between the three women. The possibility of the stepsisters' realization and purging of their *cendre* is denied by their reversion to the use of Cucendron: "Pretez votre habit à un vilain Cucendron comme cela: il faudrait que je fusse bien folle." The stepsisters' repetitive failure to appropriate the significance of their name-giving provides another textual example of the aberration of sense. On the other hand, their increasing familiarity with the forms of behavior associated with "Cucendron" and "Cendrillon" serves as a referent through which they can clarify these names as signs of desire.

The stepsisters' remembrance is finally achieved as a result of their vision of Cendrillon's recognition and penetration of her slipper. The stepsisters are unable to fit the liberating shoe. Although their thwarted attempts represent an actualization of their desires for exogamic kinship, the fact that "elles ne purent en venir à bout" certifies their lack of avuncular power. They themselves can neither realize nor effect their kinship desires without the aid of an avuncular mediator. They are bound to their endogamic heritage of *mauvaise humeur.* The responsibility of mediation belongs to Cendrillon the *coiffeuse*. Her successful penetration of the shoe posits Cendrillon's authority over the inept sisters. This striking vision of her power as mother and uncle thrusts the sisters into a realization of their own positions. They are dependent both on Cendrillon's power as advisor and protector and on her maternal compassion represented by "la belle personne qu'elles avaient vue au Bal."

The stepsisters realize the subjective significance of the proper name Cendrillon. In recognizing "Cendrillon" as a symbol of desired kinship, they express their willing submission to her avuncular authority. "Elles se jetèrent à ses pieds pour lui demander pardon de tous les mauvais traitements qu'elles avaient fait souffrir." This act of penitence represents the complete actualization of the desires expressed in either the name Cu*cendron* or *Cendr*illon. As well as referring to death, forgetfulness, and burning love, *cendre* means to "faire penitence; se mortifier."[28] Through the assignation of proper names, *par don,* the two sisters express their desire for *pardon.* To go one step further, I might suggest that in name-giving, the two sisters unconsciously assume the role of *marraine.* "C'est d'ordinaire," writes Furetière, "la marraine qui nomme les filles."[29] By the illegitimate undertaking of the *marraine*'s duties, the two sisters express their desire to be the recipients of a *marraine*'s "bonne grace." Remembrance allows the two sisters to satisfy these repressed wants. Anamorphic vision makes clear their desires for protective parentage, exogamic marriage, and balanced sexuality.

For the Prince, Cendrillon, and the two sisters, the realization and the satisfaction of sexual and kinship desires depends on their anamorphic vision of the signs of desire: **"Cendrillon ou La Petite Pantoufle de Verre."** These signs appear in many different forms throughout the text. The success of anamorphic vision depends on the voyeur's ability to attribute sense to a collection of oscillating and seemingly contradictory signs of signification. The fairy tale **"Cendrillon ou La Petite Pantoufle de Verre"** presents a striking illustration of the process of anamorphic remembrance described by Baltrusaitis:

> toute une série de phénomènes curieux où les objets se doublent, se déforment et se déplacent, comme dans les mains d'un prestidigateur, sont réunis autour d'une grande idée . . . Ils rendent certaine l'incertitude et, par cela, ils appartiennent à un réseau de témoignages sur la nécessité de réviser les conceptions et les valeurs.[30]

An anamorphic approach to the reading of **"Cendrillon ou La Petite Pantoufle de Verre"** requires the voyeur to challenge the form of the text. The meaning of this fairy tale does not consist of two superimposed layers of logical narration. The value of the narrative is thrown into question by a plethora of ambiguous signs and moments that stand outside of the causal/metonymic movement of both the synchronic and diachronic narratives. These moments are all projections of unrealized possibilities of existence—for the characters of the tale as well as for the voyeur looking into the tale. The allure of the *merveilleux* lies in the voyeur's potential remembrance of these uncertain visions. Attempts to clarify the many textual significations found in **"Cendrillon ou La Petite Pantoufle de Verre"** may confuse and frustrate the

voyeur. However, such doubt, as we have seen in our analysis of the tale, works to isolate and structure significations of suppressed desire. Through such structuralization, the voyeur verifies and satisfies his desires. *Ils rendent certain l'incertitude.*

The intriguing sense of **"Cendrillon"**—*sens-drille-ont* (meanings have a text)—consists in the tale's mode of instructing the voyeur how to see anamorphically. The text is constructed to remind the voyeur what it is that he wants to see. He is not so much fascinated by bodies of narrative as he is seduced by isolated and enticing structures of desire: *la petite pan-touffe de vers* (the small excerpt [print-bunch] of verse). He is teased by visions that he longs to experience: scenes of manipulation, sexual fantasies, kinship roles, moments of remembrance. The best method of appropriating these visions is illustrated by textual examples of poor and insightful anamorphic observation. Most importantly, the text's presentation of the process of remembrance constantly instructs the voyeur that his visions are projections of his own desires.

Perrault's edition of **"Cendrillon ou La Petite Pantoufle de Verre"** stands out as an example of "le vrai don des Fées." "Pour engager un coeur, pour en venir à bout," the text is both an illustrated guide to anamorphic vision and an exercise book that encourages the student to practice his lessons in voyeuristic reading. Moreover, Perrault reminds his students of their dependence on his instruction. In the *autre moralité,* he insists that the possession of intelligence, courage, and good sense are worthless traits "si vous n'avez, pour les faire valoir, Ou des parrains ou des marrains." Perrault is the *parrain* who instructs the reader in methods of projecting their own sense onto the foreign and meaningless form of **"Cendrillon ou La Petite Pantoufle de Verre."** He provides the voyeur with moralities pointing to the different shapes of the textual body. The anamorphic order of these shapes is outlined in Perrault's title that serves as the index for his tale of instruction. Attentiveness to Perrault's lesson is the prerequisite to an exogamic relationship with the text. The subsequent anamorphic reading is "muable et flexible comme la cire." The voyeur satisfies his desire for the *merveilleux.*

Notes

1. Marie-Françoise Christout, *Le merveilleux et le "théâtre de silence"* (La Haye: Mouton, 1965), p. 11.

2. Christout, p. 7.

3. Jurgis Baltrusaitis, *ANAMORPHOSE ou magie artificielle des effets merveilleux* (Paris: Olivier Perrin, 1969), p. 70.

4. Jacques Lacan, *Le Séminaire, livre XI: Les quatre concepts fondamentaux de la psychanalyse* (Paris: Seuil, 1973), p. 82.

5. Perrault, *Histoires ou Contes du Temps Passé avec des moralités* in *Contes* (Paris: Garnier, 1967). Any emphasis of excerpts is mine.

6. Tzvetan Todorov, *Introduction à la littérature fantastique* (Paris: Seuil, 1970), p. 59.

7. Marc Soriano, "Cendrillon" in *Les Contes de Perrault: culture savante et traditions populaires* (Paris: Gallimard, 1968), pp. 141-147.

   Michel Serres, "Traduction mot à mot: Cendrillon" in *Hermes I: La Communication* (Paris: Minuit, 1968), pp. 214-218.

8. Vladimir Propp, *Morphology of the Folktale,* trans. Laurence Scott (Austin: Univ. of Texas Press, 1968), p. 21.

9. Louis Marin, *Études Sémiologiques* (Paris: Klincksieck, 1971), p. 300.

10. Claude Lévi-Strauss, *Les Structures Élémentaires de la Parenté* (La Haye: Mouton, 1967), p. 120.

11. Antoine Furetière, *Dictionnaire Universel,* Tome III (La Haye: 1727).

12. Lévi-Strauss analyzes "the problem of the avunculate" in "Structural Analysis in Linguistics and Anthropology," *Structural Anthropology,* trans. Claire Jacobsen and Brooke Grundfest Schoepf (New York: Basic Books, 1963), pp. 39 ff.

13. In referring to Freud, Lacan writes that "il nous invite à intégrer au texte du rêve ce que j'appellerai *le colophon de doute* . . . Cela nous indique que Freud place sa certitude, *Gewissheit,* dans la seule constellation des signifiants tels qu'ils résultent du récit, du commentaire, de l'association, peu importe la rétractation." *Séminaire XI,* p. 45.

   In *Écrits I* (Paris: Seuil, 1966), p. 274, Lacan appears to describe the *colophon de doute* when writing that ". . . la structure métaphorique, indiquant que c'est dans la substitution du signifiant au signifiant que se produit un effet de signification qui est de poésie ou de création, autrement dit d'avènement de la signification en question."

14. Roland Barthes, *Elements of Semiology,* trans. Annette Lavers and Colin Smith (Boston: Beacon Press, 1970), p. 53.

15. Such is the description of "le personnage de Cendrillon" offered by G. Rouger in his foreword to our edition of "Cendrillon ou La Petite Pantoufle de Verre," p. 154.

16. Barthes, *Elements of Semiology,* pp. 50-51.

17. Furetière, Tome I. My emphasis.

18. In "Du reseau des signifiants," *Séminaire XI,* p. 46, Lacan writes:

    Freud déduit de son expérience la nécessité de séparer absolument perception et conscience—pour que ça [les traces de perception] passe dans la mémoire, il faut d'abord que ça soit effacé dans la perception, et réciproquement.

19. Lacan, "Du sujet de la certitude," *Séminaire XI,* p. 36.

20. Lacan, "Du reseau des signifiants," p. 50.

21. Furetière, Tome I.

22. Ibid.

23. Sigmund Freud, "Fetishism," in *The Standard Edition,* Vol. XXI, trans. James Strachey (London: Hogarth Press, 1961), p. 155.

24. Lacan, "L'anamorphose," *Séminaire XI,* p. 83.

25. Baltrusaitis, p. 69.

26. Perrault emphasizes this realization by means of the final deletion of the Marraine's possessive pronoun. Cendrillon is equal with "La Marraine" as one of the number of "des parrains ou des marraines."

27. Lévi-Strauss, *The Savage Mind* (Chicago: Univ. of Chicago Press, 1966), p. 181.

28. Furetière, Tome I.

29. Furetière, Tome III.

30. Baltrusaitis, p. 69.

Bonnie Cullen (essay date 2003)

SOURCE: Cullen, Bonnie. "For Whom the Shoe Fits: Cinderella in the Hands of Victorian Illustrators and Writers." *Lion and the Unicorn* 27 (2003): 57-82.

[*In the following essay, Cullen maintains that Perrault's version of "Cinderella" became more popular than other renditions because it was easier to adapt to the pantomime performances of nineteenth-century England.*]

"Cinderella" is a story we all know. Despite a range of oral tales from many cultures, and some distinctly different literary incarnations, one "Cinderella" eclipsed the others in English. In 1950, Disney Studios produced this version in cinematic form. In this way it is now perpetuated globally.

Fixed in print, a folktale becomes a different creation, losing the nuances of performance and gaining the literary conventions of its day. When illustration is added, another level of interpretation is formed and perpetuated.

The narrative now popularly known as "Cinderella" was published originally with only one picture—Cinderella fleeing from the ball, leaving her slipper behind. As it was propagated in English books during the nineteenth century, this tale began to acquire what we might call signature images.[1]

Studying surviving editions of "Cinderella" dating from the eighteenth through the early twentieth century in the British Library and the Victoria and Albert Museum's National Art Library, I discovered a great variety of treatments. Nevertheless, in many English versions, both writers and illustrators seem to be constructing an ideology that was also being developed in visual art and in the popular press.[2]

By the early twentieth century, a fairly standard form of "Cinderella" had emerged in most English editions—an adaptation of the French tale written by Charles Perrault and published in 1698: **"Cendrillon ou la Petite Pentoufle de Verre."** Perrault's tale had been addressed largely to an adult and highly sophisticated audience. By the late eighteenth century, however, it had been watered down in English cheap editions, or chapbooks, read by adults and children alike. At the beginning of the nineteenth century, it entered the realm of popular entertainment in pantomime theater.

Why Perrault's story, above all others? Considering its origins, there were many contestants for the dominant tale. **"Cinderella"** is really a large family of tales first analyzed by folklorists in the nineteenth century. Studying more than 300 related narratives from Europe and Asia, Marian Roalfe Cox identified Cinderella stories according to the presence of certain themes: an abused child, rescue through some reincarnation of the dead mother, recognition, and marriage.

The earliest known Cinderella story is actually a literary version from ninth-century China. Already it has the familiar elements. Yeh-hsien (Cinderella) has lost both her father and mother and seeks consolation from a pet fish. Her cruel stepmother eats the fish and buries the bones. A man comes from the sky advising her to find and save the bones—she will get whatever she wishes for.

When her stepmother and stepsister leave for a festival, Yeh-hsien follows them in a cloak of kingfisher feathers and gold shoes. She loses a shoe, the shoe is found, and given to a king. A search for the foot small enough to fit the shoe ensues. Yeh-hsien is finally shown to be the rightful owner and marries the king (Ting 4-5).

In most early Cinderella tales, the dead mother hovers protectively, reincarnated as a cow, a fish, or a tree. Her relationship with the grieving daughter is as significant as the girl's triumph. Occasionally the protagonist is male. The shoe is not always the means of identification, although it is extremely common, as is the use of some magic garment (Philip).

By the sixteenth century, Cinderella appears in print in the West.[3] One major debut is in Basile's seventeenth-century collection, *Il Pentamerone (Lo cunto de li cunti),* as the feisty "Gatta Cenerentola" or "Cat Cinderella." Zezolla (Cinderella) kills her wicked stepmother with the help of a governess, but when the governess marries Zezolla's father, the girl is mistreated again. A fairy in a tree supplies magic clothes and a coach for a feast where Zezolla captures a king's heart.

In Basile's tale, the dead mother is no longer a significant presence, although she might be vaguely identified with the fairy. While close to some oral versions, his bawdy narrative is full of intricate metaphors and clearly written for an adult audience (Canepa 14-15). The book was published in Neapolitan dialect, which probably limited its dissemination in print (Canepa 12; Opie and Opie 20-21), although Basile's stories may have passed into the oral repertoire and traveled in other languages.

During the ancien régime of Louis the XIV, folktales were transformed into a new literary genre, the fairy tale. Narrated as a kind of conversational game in the salons of the *précieuses,* by the end of the century they were being written down (Zipes, *Beauties* 1-9; Warner 167-70). Two distinct versions of **"Cinderella"** issued from the pens of Charles Perrault and the Countess d'Aulnoy.

Marie-Catherine Le Jumel de Barneville, Baronne d'Aulnoy,[4] was a feminist and writer, the first to publish her stories as "fairy tales," or literary versions of popular folktales. Her Cinderella, "Finette Cendron," is both altruistic and spirited. When their parents abandon Finette and her sisters, she engineers daring escapes for all three. They plot against her, but Finette remains loyal. With a godmother's help she finds some magnificent clothing and triumphs at the ball. She loses a shoe and gallops back to claim it, but refuses to marry the prince until her parents' kingdom, which they lost, is restored (d'Aulnoy, *Fairy Tales* 227-45).

Perrault's **"Cendrillon"** [**"Cendrillon ou la petite pantoufle de verre"**] is quite a different lady. He dubs her chief virtue "la bonne grace," i.e., in the face of adversity she is generous, long-suffering, charming and good-humored; the ideal bride, from the gentleman's perspective.

A bland protagonist perhaps, but Perrault exhibits his wit. Cendrillon plays her own tricks on the sisters, asking one if she can borrow a dress to see the mysterious princess at the next ball. He also writes tongue-in-cheek. The slipper, evoking female virginity, is made of glass in his tale. Not only is it fragile and extremely pure, but Perrault hints that visual proof will be necessary.

Perrault's position as a member of the French Academy may have led him to adopt this tone for tales of the peasant class (Warner 168-70). He also shifts the spotlight to the fairy godmother, giving her a dominant role. In the ancien régime, fairies were equated with powerful women at court (232-34). D'Aulnoy's fairy is sympathetic and dignified, asking Finette to be her lady's maid and comb her hair. Her magic is in providing the necessary items, whether or not she is present. Perrault's elaborate description of rat-and-pumpkin tricks is a spoof: his fairy godmother is a witch.

D'Aulnoy called her stories *Les Contes des Fées* or "tales about the fairies," evoking those powerful women with whom they were so popular. Perrault published his as **Contes de Ma Mère l'Oye,** or **Mother Goose Tales.** Warner, who argues that fairy tales were originally a women's genre, says in doing so he distanced himself from the tales, and related the *salonières* to the "old wives" who originally told them (18, 234).

Was this more than an amusing literary duel? Both Zipes and Warner describe these devotees of the fairy tale as disaffected aristocrats and haute bourgeoisie couching their malaise in children's stories as Louis XIV grew oppressive and distant. Tales of the folk, their misfortunes reversed by magical transformation, were inherently subversive and utopian. Retold by the literati, they also served to undermine the bias toward classical literature maintained by the French Academy (Zipes, *Beauties* 1-8; Warner 168-69).

As a cover, both writers appended concluding morals in verse form. On the surface, this invoked tradition: folktales for children also served a didactic function. D'Aulnoy exhorts her readers to "overpower" the selfish with kindness (*Fairy Tales,* 245). Perrault's verses, by contrast, are the final coup in his ironic development. First he advises: much better than beauty (of which, nonetheless, "we can never tire"), is "la bonne grace" in order to "win a heart, and conquer a Ball," concluding that "Without it you've nothing; with it, all." Then he parries with: it's all very well to have shrewdness, wit, good breeding, talents, and so forth, but unless you have a "willing godmother, or godfather" who can "spread your talents further," you'll never get ahead (Philip 15-16). Or in other words, it's not *what* you know, it's *who* you know. Hiding as "Mother Goose," then, Perrault effects a subtle male coup within the circle of fairy tale devotees, most of whom were women.[5]

When literary Cinderellas began to appear in English in the eighteenth century, it was Madame d'Aulnoy's story that took the lead. Several translations of her works preceded the first appearance of "Finette Cendron" in *A Collection of Novels and Tales, Written by that Celebrated Wit of France, the Countess d'Anois* (1721-22). Perrault's **Contes** did not appear in English until 1729.

By the nineteenth century, the tables had turned, apparently. Only seven English editions of d'Aulnoy's tales survive in the British Library; not all contain "Finette." There are over thirty editions of Perrault's **"Cinderella"** as a separate volume, besides its inclusion with the tales. Perrault's story was also adapted for pantomime and plays.

Perrault's version faced new competition, however. Searching for an antidote to bourgeois life—the stale "getting and spending," as Wordsworth put it—Romantics turned to nature. Might not the oral tales of country folk contain some primal wisdom? How closely they transcribed their originals is debated, but the Grimm brothers believed they were collecting rather than writing stories as they prepared their editions of *Die Kinder- und Hausmärchen* in 1812 (Warner 188-93). Their "Cinderella," "Aschenputtel," is indeed close to folk versions such as the Scottish tale, "Rashin Coatie" (Opie and Opie 117-18).

Mourning and revenge underlie "Aschenputtel": the heroine plants a tree on her mother's grave and tends it lovingly. A bird in the tree answers her calls for help. She begs for a dress, attends the feast and attracts the prince. The sisters cheat at the slipper test, cutting off parts of their feet, but birds reveal their deceit and at the wedding, peck out the sisters' eyes.

"Primal" tales had their opponents. With the first English translation, in volume two of *German Popular Stories* (1826), the brutal eye-pecking disappeared. During the previous century, the market for printed tales had expanded through chapbooks, devoured by a new audience of young readers as well as adults. By the end of the eighteenth century there was a movement in England to sanitize children's literature. Mrs. Trimmer, reviewing children's books for middle-class families, argued that the often brutal tales "excite . . . groundless fears" and "serve no moral purpose" (2: 185-86). This explains the intrusion of religious motifs, such as praying and church architecture, in chapbook illustration from the early nineteenth century, and the relative scarcity of expensive editions at the time.[6]

Fairy tales would not go away, however. Those who wanted to imbue them with bourgeois morality faced equally vociferous champions of "pure" tales. "A child," Ruskin wrote, "should not need to chose between right and wrong. It should not be capable of wrong . . ." Innocent, children could be "fortif[ied] . . . against the glacial cold of selfish science" with the "inextinguishable life" of the folk tradition (83). As Zipes points out, arguments about fairy tales became part of the greater "Condition of England" debate on the effects of the Industrial Revolution (*Victorian Fairy Tales* xvi-xxix).

In the case of **"Cinderella,"** it was a somewhat revised Perrault that prevailed in Victorian England. Illustrated editions abound, and while improvising textually and creating a cycle of pictures, they retain his major motifs. Nor did two new editions of Basile, by Taylor in 1847, and Sir Richard Burton, in 1893, affect the dominance of Perrault's story.

By studying how English writers and illustrators contributed to the discourse that produced this "Victorian Cinderella," I hoped to discover why Perrault's tale is the one that has prevailed, and what lay behind the "messages" woven into it during the nineteenth century.[7]

When Perrault's **"Cendrillon"** first appears in English in 1729, it is in a complete volume of his stories giving both French text and the translation. The engravings—one per tale—are copied from the original *Contes,* and repeated for the English text. They stage the ball scene, with Cinderella running away, looking over her shoulder at the prince, who kneels to pick up the slipper.

This edition is reissued with slight changes, but Perrault's tale is not particularly prominent during the eighteenth century. Enterprising chapbook publishers see a market for more extensive illustration, however. *The Choice Gift: Containing the Story of Princess Fair-Start, and Prince Cherry and Cinderella* (c. 1775-99) from Dublin has several pictures for Cinderella, although they are generic woodblocks not designed specifically for the story.

By the early nineteenth century Perrault's **"Cinderella"** appears to be a big hit. Publishers invest in lavish illustration. The earliest example, an engraved booklet with captions and foldout flaps, is curious. Dated February 24, 1804, *Cinderilla: or, the Little Glass Slipper* adds a dose of classical mythology. It opens at the court of Venus where the Prince, struck by Cupid's arrow, sees "chaste Diana." The familiar Cinderella tale follows, enhanced with more classical motifs, including a Roman matron (the fairy godmother) in a Pompeian landscape.

The book's specific date is as unusual as its classical elements—many nineteenth-century books have no date at all. The explanation must be Cinderella's new popularity in pantomime theater. **"Cinderella"** was first performed at Drury Lane, 10 January, 1804.[8] *A Program of the Overture & Songs to the Allegorical Pantomimic SPECTACLE* from Drury Lane (1804) combines the same elements: Venus, Diana, the Prince, and the Cinderella story.

This is not so odd a melange as it first appears. Early pantomime was a hodgepodge of mythology, harlequinade and chapbook tales (Hartnoll, *Oxford Companion to the Theatre* 625). Occasionally, "panto" scenes drift into other editions of Perrault's text, as in an 1816 Cinderella from the New Juvenile Library with engravings showing a Roman-looking fairy godmother and theatrical settings.

Chapbooks convey quite a different tone, introducing religious elements. One from Banbury, *The Interesting Story of Cinderella and Her Glass Slipper* (c. 1814), follows Perrault's text fairly closely but opens with a woodcut of Cinderella praying.[9] Another from York, *Adventures of the Beautiful Little Maid Cinderilla; or, The History of a Glass Slipper* . . . (c. 1820), adds a frontispiece depicting feminine primping and a verse about sin, pride and dress.

Despite this new emphasis on moralizing, Perrault's concluding verses disappear from English versions at the beginning of the nineteenth century, although they persist in some French and Spanish editions.[10] Clearly, his tongue-in-cheek remarks to the French court did not suit the wider audience of English readers.

One very significant change to Perrault's original is the treatment of the stepsisters. Perrault never describes them as ugly (Whalley 54). Although he confides Cinderella is "a hundred times" prettier than her sisters, he focuses on nobility of being as her superior quality.

It was the English, apparently, who first portrayed the sisters as old hags. An Evans chapbook (c. 1810) calls them "deform'd and ordinary," adding that they can scarcely read or pray. The crude woodcuts drive the point home. Some expensive editions also try this formula. One from John Harris (c. 1828)[11] with hand-colored prints and a verse text opens, "What females are these . . . ?" beneath a cut of ugly stepsisters gesturing to Cinderella. The fairy godmother appears as a tiny witch floating on a cloud.

The "ugly stepsisters" theme does not take hold until about 1870, however. Most illustrators show three ladies (also the norm in French and Spanish editions); Cinderella is often distinguished by gesture and dress.

During the '30s and '40s, chapbooks continue to follow Perrault's story fairly closely, but sometimes a preachy conclusion is appended. The wording in this edition "Corrected, and Adapted for Juvenile readers By a Lady" and published by Dean and Munday is typical:

> The amiable qualities of Cinderella were as conspicuous after as they had been before marriage, by means of which she retained the love of her husband, and gained the esteem of the court, and the good-will of all who knew her.[12]

Woodcuts now show the godmother as a witch, but the stepsisters are not usually distinguished as ugly. A fairly standard cycle of scenes is established by this time: Cinderella by the hearth; Cinderella doing the sisters' hair; the godmother's appearance; the ball and/or Cinderella running from the prince; the slipper trial, and marriage.

At mid-century, writers and illustrators take fresh approaches in expensive editions. Cruikshank revamps the entire story for his 1854 Fairy Library edition, adding temperance sermons and describing the wedding in detail, as if for a society newspaper. He opens with the family suffering hard times. The stepmother is a gambler and Cinderella's father is in debtor's prison.

An adaptation for young thespians by Julia Corner with engravings by E. H. Forrester entitled *Cinderella and the Glass Slipper, or, Pride Punished . . .* (1854) shows the heroine as a Victorian lady seated before a rather grand fireplace with caryatids. Fairies become a preoccupation of the Victorian age around this time, and one might expect a reinterpretation of the godmother. With a few exceptions, her portrayal as a witch persists.[13]

The most significant changes around mid-century involve Cinderella herself. Perrault's is the least active of the early Cinderellas—Finette is a virago, feisty Zezolla kills her stepmother, and Aschenputtel tends her mother's grave and asks for help. Yet Cendrillon has a sense of fun, as well as some ideas—she suggests using a rat when the fairy godmother cannot think how to produce a coachman.

Whatever vivacity she may have had, at mid-century it has been purged by most English illustrators and writers. Early nineteenth-century pictures show her and the prince gaily dancing; she now averts her eyes as she takes his hand and physical contrasts between them are accentuated, as in the 1852 edition illustrated by "M. J. R."[14] Cruikshank's lively lass is one exception—but such a consummate caricaturist could hardly produce a bland protagonist.

Writers leave out both her joke and her suggestions to the godmother. Chapbooks insert new phrases emphasizing her marital state. Wording in *The History of Cinderella and the Little Glass Slipper* (c. 1850) is typical: "Cinderella made a most excellent wife, . . . universally loved and respected for her sweet temper and charming disposition."

Most extreme is the Cinderella in the 1854 *Home Treasury* series, a veritable Madonna praying by the fire. Sir Henry Cole, who wrote the text and commissioned the illustrators, was the first Director of the Victoria & Albert Museum, an institution dedicated to improving public taste. His text includes an injunction from the dying mother: bear everything, and you will be happy. His fairy godmother is an old beggar woman whom Cinderella feeds—noblesse oblige. Discreetly, Cole used a pseudonym.

That Cole got into the act with his own editions suggests the popularity of the fairy tale genre as a means of instilling middle-class values, including aesthetic ones. In a handwritten notice inserted into one of the *Home Treasury* volumes, Cole states that "one object" of the series "was to place good pictures before my own and other children," explaining that he got Royal Academicians to produce lithographs for the first editions.[15]

In the 1840s, pictorial reportage took off with the debut of *Punch* and the *Illustrated London News*. Caricature and social satire were enormously popular, and illustrators forged considerable reputations. Painters like the Pre-Raphaelites also worked on books, and as the century progressed, some improvised so much that their imagery seems to be either independent of, or leading the text (Vaughan).

Banking on the popularity of illustrators, publishers began producing "toybooks" for children. These were paperbacks with elaborate imagery accompanied by narrative captions. Developments in woodblock printing made colored illustration on a large scale feasible and relatively cheap. Toybooks were marketed in collectible series often featuring the artist.

Walter Crane's 1873 toybook *Cinderella* is a Pre-Raphaelite beauty. The sisters have graying hair and irregular features, although they are not called ugly in the captions. The text concludes with the sisters vowing to work harder:

> We'll work ourselves, and never have another kitchen maid.
> We have been idle all our lives,—we'll try another way,
> And be industrious instead—it really seems to pay.

This is also a line from a Victorian pantomime, suggesting again a crossfertilization between panto and books.

In later nineteenth-century versions, some illustrators exploit the "ugly stepsister" theme. An elaborate 1892 satire by Lieutenant-Colonel Seccombe (who also worked for *Punch*) caricatures the sisters as bald hags who draw and sing horribly. Cinderella, by contrast, is demure and pretty, blushing when she enters the ball where "she hoped to have joined the gay party unseen." Their milieu looks distinctly middle-class, and the sisters, returning from the ball, dispute the cab fare.[16]

Two notable exceptions to this trend involved women in production: an expensive Warne picture book from 1878, written by Laura Valentine and illustrated by Weir and Gunston; and an Arts & Crafts-style book from 1894 edited by Grace Rhys.

By the early twentieth century, Cinderella's youthful beauty, rather than her behavior, is her chief asset in most editions. Books open with such phrases as "Cinderella was a pretty girl . . . and she had a slim figure and very, very nice feet and ankles. . . ." Millicent Sowerby, who wrote this lavishly illustrated edition around 1910-15, adds that the sad heroine dries her eyes because sobbing spoils her looks.[17] Rackham presents a energetic young girl ironing vigorously, her short hair tied up in a scarf; the stepmother is an overbearing matron with lorgnette. The sisters adopt ungainly postures, their noses, hands and feet exaggerated through his use of silhouette technique.[18]

For this deluxe 1919 edition (aimed at both the English and American markets), the publisher, C. S. Evans, rewrites the story. He follows the basic plot, fleshing out details and developing its emotional possibilities. Cinderella remembers her mother, for example, and there is a scene in which she and the prince spy each other years before the ball. Rackham's frontispiece (in rags, she gazes wistfully through a window) recalls the melodramatic style of contemporary silent films.

A far cry from Perrault's witticisms! Why the shift from "la bonne grace" and moral rectitude to beauty, and what was so compelling about the ugly stepsisters?

During the nineteenth century, two theories about human appearance were circulating. Physiognomy, developed by Johann Lavater (1741-1801), held that character is revealed in facial features. Similarly, phrenology argued that "faculties" such as benevolence reside in recognizable portions of the skull. Developed by Frans Joseph Gall (1758-1828), this pseudoscientific system was popularized in art circles by George Combe's *Phrenology applied to Painting and Sculpture* (1855) (Cowling 44-45).

Although somewhat discredited among educated thinkers later in the nineteenth century, phrenology and physiognomy were common beliefs in Victorian society, underlying the popularity of caricature in illustrated magazines like *Punch* (Cowling 25-39, chapter 4). Even Dickens fell prey to these theories for a time, according to Michael Hollington.

The Evans chapbook published around 1810-20 was apparently taking this line, linking the sister's deformity (in both text and pictures) with their inability to read or pray. Lectures on phrenology were popular early in the century among the self-educated working classes in such venues as the Mechanics' Institutes (McLaren 86-97). The same audience would have formed a significant part of the chapbook market. The similar treatment in the more expensive Harris edition suggests the concept was circulating among the middle classes at an early date as well.

By the 1850s, art critics were reading "beauty of face and form . . . as a badge of respectability," according to Cowling (350), who examines the application of these theories in Victorian painting. Considering such ideas prevailed in "high art" during the 1850s, as Cowling demonstrates (232-44) with Frith's *Derby Day* (1858) (London, Tate Gallery), it is hardly surprising that illustrators followed suit, particularly those aiming to corner the "polite" market.

Cole's 1859 "Cinderella" spelled it out for the middle classes: Cinderella grew more beautiful, while the sisters' "temper and cruelty . . . marked their features with ugliness" (102); his illustrator used the more subtle approach of academy-style drawing rather than the caricature favored in the popular press.

With color printing and the expansion of the market through toybook editions in following decades, imagery had an even greater impact. What had been subtle at mid-century was often exaggerated. Pantomime fed the appetite for comic spinsters. The ugly stepsisters made their theatrical debut in the 1860s.[19] They became as popular as "Cinders" in the show, now called *Cinderella; or, the Lover, the Lackey, and the Little Glass Slipper.*

That Perrault's tale entered pantomime at the beginning of the century indicates its appeal to English nineteenth-century audiences. Its popularity as public entertainment helps explain its continued prominence in books. In fact, the genres were feeding each other: in this case the ugly stepsisters, debuting in print and illustrations in the first half of the century, were put on stage in the second half.

As for Cinderella, her idealized features and passive poses of the 1850s were the visual equivalent of a contemporary poem about the perfect fiancée:

> She came, and seem'd a morning rose . . .
> And, with a faint, indignant flush,
> And fainter smile, she gave her hand,
> But not her eyes, then state apart,
> As if to make me understand
> The honour of her vanquish'd heart . . .
>
> (Patmore 145)

In a study of Victorian imagery, Lynda Nead argues that definitions of domesticity and gender, propagated

in art, fueled the middleclass drive for hegemony in Britain during the 1850s. Establishing class identity through a code of respectability was part of the process.

According to this code, men act; women respond, or as Ruskin put it, order and praise. Further, a man's realm is the public sphere, whereas women are naturally suited to the home. Laws regulating marriage, the national census, imagery and literature all served to define a woman's ultimate role as wife and mother, her pleasure, self-sacrifice and devotion (Nead 12-47).

Whether or not Henry Cole imagined he was reviving traditional lore in designing the *Home Treasury* series,[20] his conception was purely Victorian: "[Cinderella] was most happy in the love of her husband, the esteem of the court, and the good will of all who knew her." His illustrators expunged all active portrayals, excepting the moment when she hears the clock. The image is strikingly reminiscent of Holman Hunt's *Awakening Conscience* (1853) (London, Tate Gallery), an exposition of temptation and denial.[21]

Another change during the century, interesting in this context, is that the slipper test is offered not just to the gentry, as in Perrault's text, but to all ladies of the realm. This implied that all marriageable women were potential Cinderellas.

That Cinderella came to signify a Victorian ideal of "femininity" is revealed in an argument Dickens had with Cruikshank in 1853. Cruikshank, ever the teetotaler, decided to plead the cause by writing and etching his own editions of fairy tales, beginning with "Hop 'o my Thumb." Dickens, a "purist," was livid.[22] Dickens retorted with a parody of **"Cinderella"** in his magazine, *Household Words*. Lampooning both teetotalers and feminists in the story, he concluded with a morose vision:

> She [Cinderella] also threw open the right of voting, and
> of being elected to public offices, and of making the laws,
> to the whole of her sex; who thus came to be always gloriously occupied with public life
> and whom nobody dared to love . . .

adding a Wordsworthian plea for the "pure" fairy tale:

> The world is too much with us, early and late.
> Leave this precious old escape from it alone.
>
> (97-100)[23]

Dickens's parody of Cinderella as a suffragist is revealing, particularly when he becomes sarcastic and emotional: women active in public life are unlovable.

At that moment, their ranks were growing and a feminist movement was underway (Thompson). In 1865, women were granted the legal right to own property, and by the 1870s, some were getting involved in local politics (Levine 19, 57).

The suffragist wave was also cresting. By 1919 (the date of Rackham's edition), women in England got the vote. It is possible that the popularity of Cinderella's ugly stepsisters in both books and pantomime during the second half of the nineteenth century related to a growing displeasure with women not disposed (or able) to emulate the ideal associated with Cinderella. That displeasure might also turn to threat. Increasingly, the sisters age. Perrault's conclusion, in which the sisters are married off, disappears from several editions of the story.[24] Whether the ugly stepsisters invoked feminists, suffragists or merely "old maids" would have depended on individual readers. The equation of female beauty with success, and ugliness with defeat, was a subliminal message difficult to avoid.

As for the fairy godmother, Perrault gives no physical description, although he associates her with witchcraft through her magic spells. A great majority of English illustrators pick up on Perrault's implications, portraying her as a witch, or at least an old woman with a stick. Her appearance is never threatening. Some artists use her for a dash of comedy—Cruikshank's tiny witch, orchestrating a parade of mice and lizards, is a brilliant example.[25]

For readers at the dawn of the Industrial Revolution, Perrault's step-by-step delineation of fairy technology must have been compelling. With a stroke, he demystifies magical powers for the modern world, and gets a good laugh, too. In fact, one reason Perrault's tale prevailed was its suitability for a modern audience. During the nineteenth century, the market for literary fairy tales in England was increasingly urban and middleclass. Perrault focuses on the social sphere, rather than the forest.[26] He delineates hairdos, costume, behavior at the ball and reactions to Cendrillon's appearance with the ironic tone of a society reporter.

D'Aulnoy's Finette is busy slaying ogres and galloping through the mud, while in "Aschenputtel" there is blood from the sisters' mutilated feet. Romantics like Ruskin favored the rugged terrain of folktales, but as Mrs. Trimmer's remarks indicate, "polite" readers were concerned about "improving" young minds to function effectively in society.

More important, perhaps, Perrault's tale prevailed in English because it was the best vehicle for Victorian notions of femininity. D'Aulnoy's heroine liberates herself though female power, both magical and human. Folk Cinderellas like Aschenputtel also take action, advised by incarnations of their lost mothers. Perrault's Cendrillon is the least active, and he shifts the spotlight to her fairy godmother, whose magic is as amusing as it is powerful.

Whether or not the oral fairy tale had been a female genre, as Warner argues, by the nineteenth century the fairy tale in print was increasingly dominated by male writers and illustrators in an industry controlled by male publishers. That even some women writers followed the "party line" with canonical Cinderellas shows how powerful a formula it was for the middleclass market of nineteenth-century England.

It is interesting to note that Disney's revival of **"Cinderella,"** which repeats the Victorian interpretation of Perrault's story, came out in 1950: a time when women, indispensable in the workforce during the war years, were being urged back home with imagery of ideal wives and mothers. There have been attempts to reclaim the tale in recent years in both print and film. Yet the canonical tale, with its Victorian ideology, persists.

Whether Perrault would have liked the self-abnegating heroine in the Disney film, he might have enjoyed this update of his vision: Cendrillon triumphs through a rather complicated process of fairy technology. Pumpkin, lizard and mice are transformed, while her identity is enhanced, like a digital capture adjusted with imaging software. Only her body and the glass slippers are material.

At the stroke of midnight, her virtual reality dress, coach, and attendants all vanish, while the slippers remain. The question arises: who is the real Cinderella—the domestic drudge, or the simulated princess? Is the servant, an identity forced upon her, more real than the woman so perfect her foot fits the slipper?

In the end, it is the simulated princess, not the drudge, who captures the prince's heart. Of the author, Angela Carter, Marina Warner writes, "Her crucial insight is that women . . . produce themselves as 'women,' and that this is often the result of *force majeure*, of using what you have to get by. The fairy tale transformations of Cinders into princess represent what a girl has to do to stay alive" (195).

In the twenty-first century, producing and projecting oneself with technology is becoming the modus operandi for both genders. Simulation through computer technology is the latest form: the coach and finery that can mutate or dissolve instantaneously on the screen.

With no material substance behind an image or configuration, simulation produces a new "crisis of substance," or lack of faith in any identity beyond appearances. Or as Baudrillard put it, we are living an "'aesthetic' hallucination of reality" (Woolley 209). Perrault's little joke—"Prospects grim? Get a fairy!"—is even funnier today.

Notes

1. Illustrators may invent tabulae rasae, of course; they may also, as some cheap editions with woodblocks indicate, recycle generic pictures. But popular narratives that are frequently illustrated tend to generate a cycle of pictorial motifs. Kurt Weitzmann examined this phenomenon in *Illustrations in Roll and Codex*. He was concerned with classical and early Christian illustration, but the process can be observed into the twentieth century for certain well-known narratives. Modern editions of "Cinderella" often depict the same scenes—Cinderella losing her slipper, the fairy godmother transforming the pumpkin, and so forth.

2. I am taking the position that art and literature actively construct rather than merely reflect meaning in cultures. See Nead's discussion regarding the visual arts (4-5) and Zipes's analysis of current literary theory and the fairy tale genre (*Fairy Tales and the Art of Subversion* ch.1).

3. Zipes (*Oxford Companion* 95) names Bonaventure des Périer's *Les Nouvelles Recréations et joyeux devis* (1558) as the first. Warner shows a German illustration from the early sixteenth century but doesn't discuss it (204).

4. Also known as La Mothe in some English editions. See the discussion of her work and life in Warner (284-86), Zipes, *Beauties* (introduction), and Opie and Opie (14-15).

5. Perrault employs an ironic tone when depicting older women in some of his other *contes* as well. Knoepflmacher analyzes his barbs at female sexuality and matriarchal figures (14-19).

6. Whalley and Chester suggest chapbooks were instrumental in preserving fairy tales during this period of middleclass disapproval (94). Andrew

O'Malley analyzes this trend toward "sanitization" in depth, identifying "hybrid" works that contain elements of "plebeian culture" alongside middle-class pedagogy.

7. Meaning in folk and fairy tales is problematic, however. Similar stories appear in many different cultures, and folktales also appear to have common structures, as Propp pointed out. There may well be universal messages encoded in them. Bruno Bettelheim argued that fairy tales guide children through difficult stages in personality development, for instance. In his view, "Cinderella" is about losing one's nurturing mother and Oedipal issues.

   Bettelheim did note that emphasis varies with different narrators. One "Cinderella" theme he identified is "striving for higher goals." The version that prevails in English editions ridicules this notion by showing that influence makes the difference; hence its popularity in what he called our "cynical age" (262).

   Whatever archetypal messages "Cinderella" may hold, I shall be concerned with the meanings constructed by specific narrators and illustrators during a specific period in time. Warner critiques Propp's approach with regard to "Cinderella" (238), and Zipes summarizes the issues surrounding an historical versus a "universal" approach to fairy tales, in *The Oxford Companion to Fairy Tales* (xvii-xix).

   Current theory would also argue that despite the narrative, audiences are not monolithic. One story may console an ill-treated stepdaughter while entertaining misogynists: reception generates ever more "Cinderellas of the mind." I do not address the problem of audience reception in this paper.

8. Information kindly supplied by Keith Ludwick, the Theatre Museum, London.

9. Pearson (42) dated this chapbook 1814, attributing the design to George Cruikshank.

10. They survive in the 1836 edition of the *Contes* illustrated by N. Thomas and the 1867 edition illustrated by Gustave Doré, as well as the 1883 edition from Barcelona.

11. Date from notes by J. I. W., in the facsimile of an identical edition by the Scolar Press, *Cinderella; or The Little Glass Slipper,* London, 1977.

12. Similar wording appears in the Edinburgh *Cinderella* (c. 1840) and the 1889 edition illustrated by W. Gibbons.

13. One notable example with a fairy for the god-mother is the 1852 edition illustrated by "M. J. R." On the popularity of fairy painting, see the excellent catalogue to the 1997 Royal Academy exhibit, *Victorian Fairy Painting*.

14. The demure heroines in the 1854 edition illustrated by Forrester and the Routledge edition written by "Aunt Mavor" should be compared with the dancing cinderellas in the Banbury chapbook and the John Harris edition. Chapbooks at mid-century sometimes repeat the earlier formula, however. Later French illustrators such as Doré (1867) and Gerbault (1898) also portray a more subdued heroine than Thomas's pumpkin-toting girl in the 1836 *Contes*.

15. The process proved expensive and in later volumes he had to resort to colored woodblocks "with inferior results," according to a note dated 16 January, 1880, and signed "Henry Cole" in an 1846 edition of *Traditional Nursery Songs of England* now in the British National Art Library collection.

16. Other depictions, varying in subtlety, appear in Cole's edition, on the cover of the Cassell Story Book edition (c. 1869), and in *The Cinderella Nursery Story Book* (1878) and *The Surprising Adventures of Cinderella* (1889). Gerbault's illustrations for the 1898 French edition also contrast an attractive Cinderella with disagreeable stepsisters and a domineering stepmother.

17. Similar treatments are used for the versions published by W. Collins, 1903, Blackie & Son, c. 1904, and the French edition from Librairie Renouard, 1898.

18. Rackham may have got the idea for the step-mother from Gerbault's illustrations in the Librairie Renouard *Contes*.

19. The ugly sisters were introduced at the Royal Strand Theater, December 26, 1860 according to *Pickering's Encyclopaedia of Pantomime*.

20. A view taken by Alison Lurie and Justin Schiller in *Classics of Children's Literature, 1621-1932*.

21. Cole's *Home Treasury* series began in 1843 but the volume with "Cinderella" is dated 1859.

22. While Dickens helped develop a new type of literary fairy tale as an indictment of industrial society, he was also a protector of traditional tales. Zipes suggests he had personal as well as political reasons—fairy tales were a consolation in his sad childhood (*Victorian Fairy Tales* xx-xxi). Harry Stone studies Dickens's relationship to fairy tales in *Dickens and the Invisible World*.

Dickens's objections may have been as much artistic as anything. Cruikshank was a consummate illustrator, but his sermonizing in the text was extremely crude.

23. Cruikshank forged ahead with *Cinderella*. He neither idealized the heroine nor parodied the sisters in his etchings, but continued teetotaling in the text, defending himself with "Notice to the Public" at the end of the book. Their friendship never recovered.

24. Among them, Cole's and Crane's versions, and the Cassell and Ward editions. Rackham includes it, however.

25. The priestess-like figure from early pantomime style versions disappears quickly, and at mid-century some editions leave the godmother out of the imagery altogether, putting the focus on Cinderella and the social realm. Those illustrators who interpret her afresh show an angel, a fairy, or an ancient dame with a wimple.

Powerful women as positive agents are not common in nineteenth-century imagery, except where their power involves sacrifice—Joan of Arc, for instance. Dangerous women like Morgan le Fay, and the femme fatale type grow popular toward the end of the century, but the original model for the godmother—the *précieuse*—is absent from the scene.

For fairy interpretations see the edition illustrated by "M. J. R." and published by Addey & Co. around mid-century, as well as Crane's toy-book edition; the Routledge toybook shows an ancient dame in medieval settings.

26. I am grateful to Will Vaughan for his suggestions regarding the social appeal of Perrault's story for a Victorian audience.

Bibliography of Folk and Fairy Tales

[Arranged chronologically; editions designated V&A are in the National Art Library, BL in the British Library.]

Perrault, Charles. *Contes de Ma Mère l'Oye, Histoires ou Contes du Temps Passé (Par le Fils de Monsieur Perreault)*. Paris: 1698. (BL C.57.a.20).

d'Aulnoy, Marie-Catherine, Countess. *A Collection of novels and tales, written by that celebrated wit of France, the Countess d'Anois*. London: W. Taylor and W. Chetwood, 1721.

Perrault, Charles. *Histories, or Tales of Passed Times . . . With Morals.* By M. Perrault. Translated into English. London: J. Pote + R. Montagu, 1729.

Perrault, Charles. *Stories or Tales of passed times, with morals. Written in French by M. Perrault, and Englished by R. S. Gent.* [Trans. Robert Samber] The Second Edition, Corrected. Trans. Robert Samber. London: R. Montague & J. Pote, 1737.

Perrault, Charles. *Tales of passed times by Mother Goose. With Morals. Written in French by M. Perrault, and Englished by R. S. Gent. To which is added a new one, viz. The Discreet Princess.* Trans. G. Miege. London: printed for T. Boosay, 1796.

The Choice Gift: Containing the Story of Princess Fair-Start, and Prince Cherry and Cinderella . . . Dublin: Wm Jones, 1775-99. (V&A Renier MB.CHOG.JO0).

Cinderilla: or, The Little Glass Slipper. London: G. Thompson, November 22, 1804. (V&A 60.Z.497 (g)).

Cinderella; or, The Little Glass Slipper. London: John Evans, [c. 1810, n.d.]. (BL CH. 800/276 (6)).

The Interesting Story of Cinderella and Her Glass Slipper. Ill. George Cruikshank [?]. Banbury: J. G. Rusher, [c. 1814, n.d.]. (V&A M.B.CIND RU0).

Cinderella; or, the Little Glass Slipper. London: New Juvenile Library, 1816. (BL 12202.aa.26).

Adventures of the Beautiful Little Maid Cinderilla; or, the History of a Glass Slipper: To Which is Added an Historical Description of the Cat. York: J. Kendrew, c. 1820. (V&A Renier MB.CIND.KE.10).

Cinderella, or, the Little Glass Slipper. Glasgow: William Gage [c. 1825-40, n.d.]. (V&A MB.CIND.GA0).

Grimm, Jacob and Wilhelm. *German Popular Stories.* Trans. Edgar Taylor. vol. 2. London: J. Robins, 1826.

Cinderella; or, the Little Glass Slipper. London: John Harris, [c. 1828, n.d.]. (BL 012806 ee. 31. (1). Fac. ed. London: Scolar P, 1977.

Cinderella; or, the Little Glass Slipper . . . a New Edition, Corrected, and Adapted for Juvenile Readers By a Lady. London: Dean and Munday, [c. 1820-40, n.d.]. (V&A Renier ren.coll.O).

Contes de Perrault. Ed. Paul L. Jacob. Ill. N. Thomas. Paris: L. Mame, 1836. (BL 12430.g.13).

Cinderella; Or, The Little Glass Slipper. Edinburgh: William Gage, [c. 1840, n.d.]. (V&A MB.CIND. TU0).

The History of Cinderella. England: Otley, 1840 [?]. (V&A Renier MB.CIND.YO0).

Basile, Giambattista. *The Pentamerone, or the Story of Stories, Fun for the Little Ones.* Tran. J. E. Taylor. London, 1847.

The History of Cinderella and the Little Glass Slipper. London: W. S. Johnson, [c 1850, n.d.]. (V&A Renier EC.CIND.18505.JO0).

Contes des Fées. Paris: Chez Aubert, 1850. (V&A 60.A.63).

History of Cinderella, or the Little Glass Slipper. New And Improved Series No. 45. Glasgow: n.p., 1852. (V&A 60.R.Box 11 vii).

Cinderella or the Little Glass Slipper. Ill. "M. J. R." London: Addey and Co., 1852. (BL 12806. g. 12).

Cruikshank, George. *Cinderella and the Glass Slipper. Edited and Illustrated with Ten Subjects, Designed and Etched on Steel by G. Cruikshank.* G. Cruikshank's Fairy Library. London: D. Bogue, 1854. (V&A 60.X.163).

Corner, Julia. *Cinderella and the Glass Slipper, or, Pride Punished. An Entertainment for Young People. By Miss Corner, and Embellished by Alfred Crowquill, Esq.* [Ill. E. H. Forrester]. London: Dean & Son, 1854. (V&A 60 F. 122).

D'Aulnoy, Marie Catherine, Countess (also La Mothe). *Fairy Tales by the Countess D'Aulnoy.* Trans. J. R. Planché. London: 1855.

Mavor, Aunt. *Cin-der-ella and the Lit-tle Glass Slipper.* London: G. Routledge & Co., [c 1855- 60, n.d.]. (V&A 60.R. Box 5).

Summerly, Felix [Sir Henry Cole]. "Cinderella, or the Little Glass Slipper." *The Home Treasury of Old Story Books.* Ill. J. Absolon. London: Sampson Low, Son, and Co., 1859. (V&A 60.X.122).

Les Contes de Perrault. Illus. Gustave Doré. Paris: J. Hetzel, 1867.

Cinderella; or the Little Glass Slipper. Cassell's Fairy Story Books. London: Cassell, Petter & Galpin, [c. 1869, n.d.]. (V&A 60.y.154).

Cinderella; or the Little Glass Slipper. Routledge's Shilling Toy Books. London: G. Routledge, [c. 1870, n.d.]. (V&A 60.W.274).

Crane, Walter. *Cinderella.* Walter Crane's Toybooks. London: G. Routledge & Sons, 1873. (V&A 60.R.Box XIV (viii)).

The Cinderella Nursery Story Book. London: Ward, Lock & Co., 1878. (BL 128 œ08.d.9).

Valentine, Laura. *Aunt Louisa's Favourite Toy Book.* Ill. Harrison Weir and W. Gunston. London: Warne, 1878. (V&A Renier B.LB.WARN.1878).

Seccombe, Thomas Strong. *The Good Old Story of Cinderella Re-told in Rhyme . . .* Ill. Thomas Seccombe. London: F. Warne, 1882. (BL 12810.d.14).

Cuentos de Hadas por Carlos Perrault. Barcelona: Libreria de Juan y Antoni Bastinos, 1883. (BL 1609/1961).

The Surprising Adventures of Cinderella. Ill. W. Gibbons. London and Sydney: Griffith, Farrar, Okden & Welsh, 1889. (BL 12800. f. 45/7).

Basile, Giambattista. *The Pentameron.* Trans. Richard Burton. 2 vols. London, 1893.

Cinderella, or the Little Glass Slipper. Banbury Cross Series. Ed. Grace Rhys. Ill. Robert Anning Bell. London: J. M. Dent, 1894. (BL 012808.ee.51).

Les Contes de Perrault. Ed. Henri Laurens. Ill. H. Gerbault. Paris: Librairie Renouard, 1898. (BL 12430.l.28).

Cinderella. Ill. W. G. Miller. London and Glasgow: W. Collins Sons & Co., 1903. (BL 12812.c.12).

The Old Nursery Stories and Rhymes. Ill. John Hassall. N.p.: Blackie & Son Ltd., c. 1904. (BL 12812.c.41).

Sowerby, Millicent. *Cinderella.* London: Humphry Milford, [c. 1910-15]. (V&A 60.cc.39).

Evans, C. S. *Cinderella.* Ill. Arthur Rackham. London: W. Heinemann, 1919. (BL 12410.r.5).

Basile, Giambattista. *The Pentamerone of Giambattista Basile.* Trans. Benedetto Croce. Ed. and Trans. N. M. Penzer. Vol. 1. London: John Lane, 1932.

Works Cited

Bettelheim, Bruno. *The Uses of Enchantment.* New York: Knopf, 1976.

Canepa, Nancy L. *From Court to Forest. Giambattista Basile's Lo Cunto de li Cunti and the Birth of the Literary Fairy Tale.* Detroit: Wayne State UP, 1999.

Cowling, Mary. *The Artist as Anthropologist.* Cambridge: Cambridge UP, 1989.

Cox, Marian Roalfe. *Cinderella: Three Hundred and Forty-five Variants.* Publications of the Folk-lore Society (no. 31). London, 1893.

Dickens, Charles. *Household Words* 184. 1 Oct. 1853: 97-100.

Hartnoll, Phyllis, ed. *The Oxford Companion to the Theatre.* 4th ed. Oxford: Oxford UP, 1983.

Hollington, Michael. "Dickens, 'Phiz' and Physiognomy." *Imagination on a Long Rein, English Literature Illustrated.* Ed. Joachim Möller. Marburg: Jonas, 1988. 125-35.

Knoepflmacher, U. C. "Repudiating 'Sleeping Beauty'." *Girls, Boys, Books, Toys: Gender in Children's Literature.* Ed. Beverly Lyon Clark and Margaret R. Higonnet. Baltimore: Johns Hopkins UP, 1999. 11-24.

Levine, Philippa. *Victorian Feminism 1850-1900.* London: Hutchinson Education, 1987.

Lurie, Alison, and Justin Schiller. *Classics of Children's Literature, 1621-1932.* New York: n.p., 1977.

Maas, Jeremy, Charlotte Gere, et al. *Victorian Fairy Painting.* London: Royal Academy of Arts, in association with Merrell Holbertson Publishers, 1997.

McLaren, Angus. "Phrenology: Medium and Message." *Journal of Modern History* 46.1 (Mar. 1974): 86-97.

Nead, Lynda. *Myths of Sexuality: Representations of Women in Victorian Britain.* London: B. Blackwell, 1988.

O'Malley, Andrew. "The Coach and Six: Chapbook Residue in Late Eighteenth-Century Children's Literature." *The Lion and the Unicorn* 24.1 (Jan. 2000): 18-44.

Opie, Iona, and Peter Opie. *The Classic Fairy Tales.* Oxford: Book Club Associates by arrangement with Oxford UP, 1992.

Patmore, Coventry. *The Poems of Coventry Patmore.* Ed. Frederick Page. London: Oxford UP, 1949.

Pearson, Edwin. *Banbury Chap Books.* London, 1890.

Philip, Neil. *The Cinderella Story.* Harmondsworth: Penguin, 1989.

Pickering, David, ed. *Encyclopaedia of Pantomime.* Andover: Gale Research, 1993.

Program of the Overture & Songs to the Allegorical Pantomimic SPECTACLE. London: Theatre Royal, Drury Lane, 1804.

Propp, Vladimir Y. *Morphology of the Folktale.* Trans. L. Scott. 2nd ed. Austin: U of Texas P, 1968.

Ruskin, John. "Fairy Stories." Ed. Lance Salway. *Signal* (May 1972): 81-86.

Stone, Harry. *Dickens and the Invisible World.* Bloomington: Indiana UP, 1978.

Thompson, Dorothy. "Women, Work, and Politics in Nineteenth-Century England: The Problem of Authority." *Equal or Different: Women's Politics 1800-1914.* Ed. Jane Rendall. Oxford: Basil Blackwell, 1987.

Ting, Nai-Tung. *The Cinderella Cycle in China and Indo-China.* F. F. Communications no. 213. Helsinki: Suomalainen, 1974.

Trimmer, Sarah. *The Guardian of Education.* 5 vols. London: J. Johnson, 1801-05.

Vaughan, William. "Incongruous Disciples: The Pre-Raphaelites and the Moxon Tennyson." *Imagination on a Long Rein, English Literature Illustrated.* Ed. Joachim Möller. Marburg: Jonas, 1988. 148-60.

Warner, Marina. *From the Beast to the Blond.* London: Vintage, 1995.

Weitzmann, Kurt. *Illustrations in Roll and Codex.* Princeton: Princeton UP, 1947.

Whalley, Irene. "The Cinderella Story." *Signal: Approaches to Children's Books* (May 1972): 49-62.

Whalley, Joyce, and Tessa Chester. *A History of Children's Book Illustration.* London: Murray, 1988.

Woolley, Benjamin. *Virtual Worlds: A Journey in Hype and Hyperreality.* Oxford: Blackwell, 1992.

Zipes, Jack David. *Beauties, Beasts, and Enchantment: Classic French Fairy Tales.* New York: New American Library, 1989.

———. *Fairy Tales and the Art of Subversion: The Classical Genre for Children and the Process of Civilization.* New York: Wildman Press, 1983.

———. *The Oxford Companion to Fairy Tales.* Oxford: Oxford UP, 2000.

———. *Victorian Fairy Tales: The Revolt of the Fairies and Elves.* New York: Methuen, 1987.

📖 "LE PETIT CHAPERON ROUGE" (1697; "LITTLE RED RIDING HOOD")

Bill Delaney (essay date winter 2006)

SOURCE: Delaney, Bill. "Perrault's *Little Red Riding Hood*." *Explicator* 64, no. 2 (winter 2006): 69-71.

[*In the following essay, Delaney traces the literary origins of Perrault's version of "Little Red Riding Hood."*]

"Little Red Riding Hood" began as an oral folk tale and continued to be told to children for centuries before being published in a French version by Charles Perrault in 1697, and then in 1812 in the German version by Jacob and Wilhelm Grimm.

Over the years, scholars have piled an entire cosmos of meanings on this small girl's shoulders. Some call her tale a seasonal myth, an allegory of the sun swallowed by night, or the personification of Good triumphing over Evil. Her basket of wine and cakes, it's said, represents Christian Communion; her red cape stands for menstrual blood. Some see the tale in Freudian terms as the Ego overcome by the Id; others see it as symbolic of the relationship between Man and Woman. And inevitably the tale has been a vehicle for imparting sexual ethics in keeping with the social fabric of the times. Tellers have consciously and subconsciously manipulated the plot to portray a seduction by a temptress, the rape of a virgin or the passage of a young girl into womanhood.[1]

It is hard to believe that the anonymous creator of the tale would have had the slightest notion of what Freudians, Jungians, anthropologists, deconstructionists, and others have read into it. The story is worth examining because it reveals the genius of the original storyteller. It is noteworthy that Catherine Orenstein assumes that Perrault's version "must be a truncated, fragmentary version of the original oral tale."[2] The same applies to the version by the brothers Grimm because it was derived from Perrault.[3]

Much has been made of the fact that the little girl wears a red riding hood. This is undoubtedly because it seems odd that a peasant child whose wardrobe is probably limited to one faded dress should own such a luxury garment as a cloak intended to be worn for riding. Her mother would be lucky to own a cow, much less a horse. No father is mentioned. We suspect that this is an exceptionally poor family. It is highly unlikely that, as Perrault suggests, her mother would have made her daughter such a garment. The mother would have made something more practical if she had had the material to make anything at all. More probably in the original oral version, the little girl was given the red riding hood by some local Lady Bountiful whose daughter had outgrown it, and the little girl wears it all the time because she has never owned anything so beautiful before. When she wears the garment she probably fantasizes that she is rich and is riding her very own pony.

In analyzing a story, as in analyzing a dream, it is often the most incongruous element that can be the most revealing. The most incongruous element here is the fact that a little peasant girl who might not even own a pair of shoes, nevertheless, owns a scarlet hooded cloak, possibly lined with silk. If the red riding hood symbolizes anything, it suggests that the girl lives in a fantasy world, which explains why she does not hear her mother when she is told to go straight to her grandmother's house and not to talk to strangers.

The story is called **"Little Red Riding Hood,"** and the little girl is called Little Red Riding Hood because she wears that famous garment all the time. It is extremely important to note that her name is certainly not Little Red Riding Hood. She is *called* Little Red Riding Hood by those who know her, and this name keeps appearing in the story from the title to the last scene in the story. We can assume that no one outside her immediate circle knows her unusual nickname. When she meets the wolf in the forest, it is natural for him to ask her name. In trying to start a conversation with a small child we still ask, "What's your name?" and "How old are you?" The wolf obviously could not know her or her nickname, although both Perrault and the brothers Grimm take it for granted that he does. The fact that she does not recognize the wolf as a wolf proves they have never met before. Furthermore, if they had met before, he probably would have eaten her on the spot, and there would have been no story, or at least a different story.

The little girl has been cautioned not to talk to strangers, but she has not really listened because she lives in a fantasy world in which she is a rich girl riding her own pony. She naïvely tells the wolf that she is *called* Little Red Riding Hood. With this information, the wolf hurries off to the grandmother's house while the little girl, who did not hear her mother's other piece of advice, "amused herself by gathering nuts, running after the butterflies, and making nosegays of the wild flowers which she found."[4] This, of course, gives the wolf plenty of time to get to the grandmother's cottage where what transpired is well known.

An old woman who lives all alone in a forest inhabited by wolves is likely to be frightened and suspicious. When the wolf knocks at her door, her dialogue writes itself—which is another aspect of the genius of the original storyteller, quite probably a grandmother herself. The timid old lady asks, "Who's there?" Because the little girl has given the stranger a vital piece of information, the wolf easily gains entrance. He disguises his voice and says, "It is your granddaughter, Little Red Riding Hood." The nickname acts like a secret password, as the grandmother naturally assumes that no stranger would know it. The words "Little Red Riding Hood" take on an ominous tone which should send chills down the spines of children listening to the tale.

Thus, the little red riding hood and the nickname Little Red Riding Hood are a brilliant device to impress the hearer with the principal moral of the tale: *Do not talk to strangers because you never know what you might say that can be used against you.* Many grownups have learned to their regret that it is not only children who need to be reminded of this moral.

> Now, as then, 'tis simple truth—
> Sweetest tongue has sharpest tooth![5]

Notes

1. Catherine Orenstein, *Little Red Riding Hood Uncloaked: Sex, Morality, and the Evolution of a Fairy Tale* (New York: Basic, 2002) 4.

2. Orenstein 3.

3. Orenstein 3.

4. Charles Perrault, "Little Red Riding Hood," *Little Red Riding Hood: A Casebook,* ed. Alan Dundes (Madison: U of Wisconsin P, 1989) 5.

5. Perrault, "Little Red Riding Hood," Orenstein 19.

Works Cited

Dundes, Alan, ed. *Little Red Riding Hood: A Casebook.* Madison: U of Wisconsin P, 1989.

Grimm, Jacob, and Wilhelm. *The Complete Fairy Tales of the Brothers Grimm.* Trans. Jack Zipes. New York: Bantam, 1987.

Orenstein, Catherine. *Little Red Riding Hood Uncloaked: Sex, Morality, and the Evolution of a Fairy Tale.* New York: Basic, 2002.

Perrault, Charles. *Perrault's Complete Fairy Tales.* Trans. A. E. Johnson. Harmondsworth, Eng.: Kestrel, 1962.

CINDERELLA: AND OTHER TALES FROM PERRAULT (1989)

Karen Little (review date February 1990)

SOURCE: Little, Karen. Review of *Cinderella: And Other Tales from Perrault,* by Charles Perrault, illustrated by Michael Hague. *School Library Journal* 36, no. 2 (February 1990): 84.

Gr. 1-4—In these eight familiar tales, [*Cinderella: And Other Tales from Perrault,*] the uncredited translations follow the French closely, except for a few deleted passages, retaining much of the formal, literary style of the originals. Each tale bears an emblematic title page and one or two full-page paintings illustrating standard moments: the Prince discovers the Sleeping Beauty, a simpering Red Riding Hood meets the wolf in the wood, Master Cat confronts the Ogre, Cinderella flees down the palace steps. The ink and watercolor paintings bear Hague's trademarks: the rich dusky palette filling the page, the misshapen figures and their placement in the foreground, and a tendency to overembellish, in this case with a repeated stylized floral border whose bright color and crisp style clash with the romanticized pictures.

CINDERELLA, PUSS IN BOOTS, AND OTHER FAVORITE TALES (2000)

Nina Lindsay (review date August 2000)

SOURCE: Lindsay, Nina. Review of *Cinderella, Puss in Boots, and Other Favorite Tales,* by Charles Perrault, translated by A. E. Johnson. *School Library Journal* 46, no. 8 (August 2000): 174-75.

K-Gr. 4—New translations of often-adapted Perrault tales, first published in 1697 as *Histoires ou contes du temps passé avec des moralités.* [In *Cinderella, Puss in Boots, and Other Favorite Tales,*] Johnson provides a fresh look at **"Little Red Riding Hood," "The Fairies"** (also known as **"Diamonds and Toads"**), **"Puss in Boots," "Blue Beard," "Cinderella," "Ricky of the Tuft," "The Sleeping Beauty,"** and **"Little Tom Thumb."** Children may have forgotten, or may never have known, that Little Red Riding Hood gets eaten by the wolf and that Sleeping Beauty's awakening is only the beginning of her story. Perrault's morals in verse also allow readers to rethink the tales. Each story is illustrated by a different French artist on partial spreads and in spot art on every page. The large text and use of white space add to the sense of elegance in the design. A short introduction lends some context to the translation, although John Bierhorst's *The Glass Slipper: Charles Perrault's Tales from Times Past* (Four Winds, 1981; o.p.) provides a much more intriguing and informative afterword and bibliography. As it contains the same eight tales, libraries that already own that book may not need this new one even though it is colorful and enticing. Libraries without such a collection should easily find use for this bright new translation of long-ago stories.

CINDERELLA (2005)

April Spisak (review date December 2005)

SOURCE: Spisak, April. Review of *Cinderella,* by Charles Perrault, retold and illustrated by Barbara McClintock. *Bulletin of the Center for Children's Books* 59, no. 4 (December 2005): 197.

McClintock's adaptation of **Cinderella** is faithful to the Charles Perrault version of the tale: Cinderella is dutifully principled: she obeys her elders, resists the temptation to respond unkindly to the cruelties of her stepfamily, and forgives all (even playing matchmaker for her stepsisters) after her virtue is rewarded with the requisite happy ending. However, this is not an exact replication, and distinctive touches abound in the text and illustrations: the fairy godmother's outburst of "Foomus Baloomus" is an unexpected magic phrase, and McClintock's own cat Pip puts in an appearance on almost every page. The art is reminiscent of the era of Kate Greenaway, Walter Crane, and Randolph Caldecott, brimming with old-fashioned charm. Exquisite details in the illustrations draw from historical Paris with extravagantly opulent costumes, stunning castles, and the quiet tree-lined streets of the middle class. The divergent lives of Cinderella and her stepfamily are established through the judicious use of white space that literally shrinks the world of the beleaguered heroine and contrasts with double-page spreads that draw from an elegantly colorful palette to portray the world of the privileged nobility. Cinderella has been adapted and retold around the world for hundreds of years, but the sumptuous artwork, elegant retelling, and reliable source references make this notable version a necessary purchase.

FURTHER READING

Criticism

Beckett, Sandra L. "Recycling Red Riding Hood in the Americas." In *Interdisciplinary and Cross-Cultural Narratives in North America,* edited by Mark Cronlund Anderson and Irene Maria F. Blayer, pp. 7-28. New York: Peter Lang, 2005.

 Assesses Perrault's influence on the history of the "Little Red Riding Hood" fairy tale.

Johnson, Sharon P. "The Toleration and Erotization of Rape: Interpreting Charles Perrault's 'Le Petit chaperon rouge' within Seventeenth- and Eighteenth-Century French Jurisprudence." *Women's Studies* 32, no. 3 (April-May 2003): 325-52.

 Analyzes "Le Petit chaperon rouge" from a philosophical perspective.

Koch, E. R. Review of *Seeing through the Mother Goose Tales: Visual Turns in the Writings of Charles Perrault,* by Philip Lewis. *Choice* 34, no. 8 (April 1997): 1344.

Lauds Philip Lewis's book as "a landmark work that presents both a new vision of 17th-century intellectual history and also important new readings of Perrault's tales."

Menninghaus, Winfried. *In Praise of Nonsense: Kant and Bluebeard,* translated by Henry Pickford. Stanford, Calif.: Stanford University Press, 1999, 257 p.

Explores arabesque and nonsensical imagery in Perrault's "Bluebeard."

Roth, Elizabeth Elam. "From the Beautiful to the Sublime: Postmodern Transformation in *The Sleeping Beauty.*" *Children's Literature Association Quarterly* 23, no. 4 (winter 1998-99): 210-13.

Examines a Royal Ballet Company production of *The Sleeping Beauty* designed by Maria Bjørnson.

Ruddick, Nicholas. "'Not So Very Blue, After All': Resisting the Temptation to Correct Charles Perrault's 'Bluebeard.'" *Journal of the Fantastic in the Arts* 15, no. 4 (2004): 346-57.

Discusses Perrault's "Bluebeard" in the context of seventeenth-century French literature.

Additional coverage of Perrault's life and career is contained in the following sources published by Gale: *Beacham's Guide to Literature for Young Adults,* **Vol. 4;** *Children's Literature Review,* **Vol. 79;** *Dictionary of Literary Biography,* **Vol. 268;** *Guide to French Literature, Beginnings to 1789;* *Literature Criticism from 1400 to 1800,* **Vols. 2, 56;** *Literature Resource Center;* *Major Authors and Illustrators for Children and Young Adults,* **Eds. 1, 2;** *Reference Guide to World Literature,* **Eds. 2, 3;** *Something about the Author,* **Vol. 25; and** *Writers for Children.***

Jonathan Stroud
1970-

English author of puzzle books, juvenile nonfiction, and juvenile and young adult novels.

The following entry presents an overview of Stroud's career through 2006.

INTRODUCTION

Stroud's popular "Bartimaeus Trilogy" of young adult novels has attracted frequent comparisons to the J. K. Rowling's Harry Potter series and has garnered critical acclaim for its complex characterization, dark, edgy narration, and success in subverting fantasy genre expectations. Set in a modern world where politically motivated "magicians" hold elite positions due to their ability to control demons and imps, the three novels in the series—*The Amulet of Samarkand* (2003), *The Golem's Eye* (2004), and *Ptolemy's Gate* (2005)—relate the adventures of a young magician's apprentice and the "djinni" (or genie) Bartimaeus who begrudgingly aids him. The novels in the "Bartimaeus Trilogy" eschew the normative fantasy genre stereotype of the altruistic wizard by casting its magicians as part of a vain, powerless elite who exploit the abilities of a demonic slave caste to wield power over average citizens, adding levels of ambiguity and complexity to the texts that many fantasy works for young readers generally avoid. The first book in the trilogy, *The Amulet of Samarkand,* has received a notable book citation from the American Library Association, a top ten fantasy books for youth citation from *Booklist,* and a *Horn Book/Boston Globe* Award honor citation.

BIOGRAPHICAL INFORMATION

Stroud was born on October 27, 1970, in Bedford, England, the son of a civil engineer and a history teacher. From a young age, he began writing his own fantasy game-books, comics, poetry, and plays. Stroud attended the University of York, where he studied English literature, graduating with a B.A. in 1992. From 1994 to 1998, he worked as an editor for children's book publisher Walker Books Ltd. in London, where he was encouraged to write as well as edit. His first published work, *Justin Credible's Word Play World,* a children's picture puzzle book illustrated by Caroline Holden, was published by Walker Books in 1994. Stroud's next two books, *The Lost Treasure of Captain Blood: How the Infamous Spammes Escaped the Jaws of Death and Won a Vast and Glorious Fortune* (1996) and *The Viking Saga of Harri Bristlebeard: A Heroic Puzzle Adventure* (1997), are also picture puzzle books. In 1998 Stroud began working as an editor for Kingfisher Books, which subsequently served as the publisher of several of his later works. In the fall of 2001, Stroud quit his job as editor in order to work full time on the writing of *The Amulet of Samarkand,* his first juvenile novel, while his wife Gina, a book designer, supported him. Stroud lives in Hertfordshire, a suburb of London, with his wife and two children.

MAJOR WORKS

One of Stroud's first publications, *The Lost Treasure of Captain Blood,* illustrated by Cathy Gale, is a picture puzzle book in which a crew of pirates gets the better of a group of villains. The puzzle element of the story is that each page presents a question or puzzle that the child is encouraged to answer or solve, although this is not necessary to following the story. The plot of the similarly formatted *The Viking Saga of Harri Bristlebeard,* also illustrated by Cathy Gale, concerns a quest to retrieve a magic banner stolen by a dragon, while each page presents questions based on simple riddles or visual observations. Stroud's first novel for young readers, *Buried Fire* (1999), follows two brothers, Michael and Stephen MacIntyre, their sister Sarah, and a local priest who discover a dark secret entombed beneath their quiet English village. His next work, *The Leap* (2001), tells the story of a girl named Charlie whose best-friend Max drowns in a mill-pool, though, after a series of bizarre dreams, Charlie comes to believe that something more supernatural is to blame for Max's disappearance. In 2003 Stroud published *The Siege,* a minimalist fantasy about three friends who allow their imaginations to run wild in the ruins of an abandoned caste.

Released that same year, *The Amulet of Samarkand,* the first book in the "Bartimaeus Trilogy," is narrated from the dual perspectives of a young magical novice and Bartimaeus, a five-thousand-year-old djinni who is given to speaking in sarcastic wisecracks and haughty, humorous footnotes. In Stroud's fantastic alternate reality, the modern-day British Empire is run not by politicians but by magicians. Humiliatingly for Bartimaeus, the djinni has been summoned to this enchanted London to serve a twelve-year-old apprentice to one such magician. This apprentice, named Nathaniel, needs Bartimaeus's help to get revenge on one of London's most powerful magicians, Simon Lovelace, who has humiliated Nathaniel in public. The proper form of revenge, Nathaniel decides, involves stealing one of Lovelace's magical trinkets, the Amulet of Samarkand, which protects its bearer from others' spells. Stealing the amulet proves trivially easy for Bartimaeus, but this act sets in motion a series of other potentially dangerous events. Not everyone is happy with the magicians' oligarchical, nondemocratic government, Bartimaeus and Nathaniel discover, and now some of them are plotting to overthrow it, much to Nathaniel's dismay.

The Amulet of Samarkand was followed by *The Golem's Eye,* which picks up the action two years later. Nathaniel has graduated from his apprenticeship and is now a full-fledged member of the magical government, with a post in the Department of Internal Affairs. In this position, Nathaniel is responsible for quashing resistance to the government, which is quite a challenge at this time. Besides the Resistance movement Nathaniel and Bartimaeus stumbled into in *The Amulet of Samarkand,* a mysterious magician within the government has turned traitor and summoned a golem bent on destroying the city of London. Plus, a psychopathic afrit—an evil demon—has taken up residence in the skeleton of a famous wizard. A third major character is added in *The Golem's Eye*: Kitty Jones, a teenage member of the Resistance who was introduced in *The Amulet of Samarkand.* She is impervious to magic, a gift with which she was born, and events in her past have made her a motivated and effective leader of the Resistance. In alternating chapters, Kitty and Nathaniel provide readers with two radically different perspectives on the government and the morality of resistance to it. Although

Bartimaeus is still magically enslaved to Nathaniel, by the end of *The Golem's Eye,* it is clear that his sympathies lie with Kitty and the Resistance, not with his master. The djinni has no fewer reasons than the oppressed commoners to hope for the end of the magicians' government and his freedom.

CRITICAL RECEPTION

Critics have seemed compelled to make comparisons between Stroud's "Bartimaeus Trilogy" and Rowling's Harry Potter series, both of which center around a young, orphaned magician-in-training. Michelle Pauli has noted, "Jonathan Stroud is the latest in a long line of children's authors to be blessed—or burdened—with that hopeful publisher's tag, 'the next J. K. Rowling.'" However, Pauli has also remarked that *The Amulet of Samarkand* is "a darker and more rumbustious read than Rowling's Potter stories, with a wickedly satirical edge." Stroud has won particular praise from readers and reviewers for his ability to subvert the many expectations and stereotypes of the popular "magician's apprentice" fantasy genre. Noted fantasy author Diana Wynne Jones, in her review of *The Amulet of Samarkand,* has stated that, "[w]hat makes this book so unusual is the way Jonathan Stroud has upended the various traditions he draws on. . . . Stroud has turned the well-known tradition of the magician's apprentice, the boy who attempts to perform his master's magic on his own, upside down." Many critics have also commented on the complex characterizations in the "Bartimaeus Trilogy," noting how Stroud paints his ostensible protagonist Nathaniel as a morally ambivalent figure who, often times, fails to attract the reader's sympathy. Suzi Feay has remarked that Nathaniel is "an intriguingly flawed boy, but Stroud has no interest in creating a two-dimensional hero, or in flattering his juvenile readers, which gives his novel quite a sharp tang." The subsequent books in the trilogy have attracted similar praise. Reviewers have particularly praised the further development of Kitty in *The Golem's Eye,* with Timnah Card commenting that, "Resistance fighter Kitty, introduced in the first volume and now forced into action as a major player in the struggle for power, infuses the tale with moral complexity as she consistently chooses idealistic heroism over practical self-preservation, winning Bartimaeus's admiration and providing the more easily corruptible Nathaniel with both a foil and a reason to doubt the wisdom of his own choices." Reviewing

Ptolemy's Gate, Martha V. Parravano has lauded Stroud's conclusion to the "Bartimaeus Trilogy," asserting that, "Stroud builds to a thrilling, inventive climax. The final scene manages to take the reader completely by surprise and yet seem, in retrospect, inevitable: a stunning end to a justly acclaimed trilogy.

PRINCIPAL WORKS

Justin Credible's Word Play World [illustrations by Caroline Holden] (puzzle book) 1994

The Lost Treasure of Captain Blood: How the Infamous Spammes Escaped the Jaws of Death and Won a Vast and Glorious Fortune [illustrations by Cathy Gale] (puzzle book) 1996

The Viking Saga of Harri Bristlebeard: A Heroic Puzzle Adventure [illustrations by Cathy Gale] (puzzle book) 1997

Buried Fire (juvenile novel) 1999

Sightseers: Ancient Rome—A Guide to the Glory of Imperial Rome (juvenile nonfiction) 2000

The Leap (juvenile novel) 2001

*The Amulet of Samarkand (young adult novel) 2003

The Last Siege (juvenile novel) 2003

*The Golem's Eye (young adult novel) 2004

*Ptolemy's Gate (young adult novel) 2005

*These titles make up the Bartimaeus Trilogy.

AUTHOR COMMENTARY

Jonathan Stroud and Martha Irvine (interview date 24 November 2003)

SOURCE: Stroud, Jonathan, and Martha Irvine. "Is Bartimaeus the Next Harry Potter?" *Seattle Times* (24 November 2003): E5.

[*In the following interview, Stroud discusses* The Amulet of Samarkand *with a group of children at a book-signing event in Illinois.*]

Naperville, Ill.—Jonathan Stroud stands before his young bookstore audience with colored markers and big pad of paper. He wants to know what they think a traditional magician looks like.

"Tall, pointy hat," one girl says.

"Long beard," says another.

"Magic wand."

"Curly shoes."

"Right!" Stroud says, quickly adding each component to his drawing.

And that, he tells them, is exactly the sort of magician he didn't want in his new book, *The Amulet of Samarkand,* the first installment in what he's calling the *Bartimaeus Trilogy.*

Some in the book world see so much promise in the series that they've deemed it "the next 'Harry Potter.'" The first book recently released both in Stroud's native England and the United States is already being turned into a movie by Miramax Films, sister company to the Disney affiliates that are publishing the book in this country.

Stroud, a 33-year-old author who lives just outside London, is well aware of the inevitable comparisons to J. K. Rowling's wildly popular "Harry Potter" series. As a former children's book editor, he knew magic was a hot topic when he began writing this book.

"The problem was wanting to do something different," he says of the idea, which came to him as he walked home from work in the rain one evening more than two years ago.

OUT OF THE BLUE

"I was trudging along, feeling very depressed about life, carrying heavy shopping bags," he tells his young audience. And then the idea and book's main characters came to him.

After arriving home, he sat down and almost immediately wrote the first three chapters "It all just came out of nowhere."

The magicians in his story are, in fact, the bad guys.

"And they look something like this," Stroud tells the audience, flipping his paper pad to a new page and drawing another figure. The crowd of young people and parents who've gathered at Anderson's Bookshop in Naperville, Ill., smile and laugh.

This time, the magician is a youngish man in a business suit, carrying a briefcase. His name is Simon Lovelace, and he's the book's main villain. "I suspect he has all kinds of evil traits," Stroud says with a smirk.

The protagonists are Nathaniel, a young apprentice magician who wavers between doing good and evil, and Bartimaeus, a "djinni" or, in the Western world, a "genie." But Bartimaeus is no eager-to-please do-gooder flowing out of a bottle.

DISTINGUISHING FEATURES

Stroud, a tall, dark-haired chap with a friendly face, had a cheeky glint in his eye when he sat down to discuss his book in an interview with The Associated Press.

"I wanted my 'djinni' to be tougher," he says of the shape-shifting Bartimaeus, who can appear as anything, from a bird or human being to a slithering puff of smoke. "He's not a virtuous goody-goody. He's a slightly more edgy portrayal of a hero."

And an unlikely hero at that. Narrating some of the story himself, Bartimaeus is a cocky, larger-than-life personality whom Nathaniel conjures up in the book's first chapter. Nathaniel orders Bartimaeus to steal an amulet necklace from Lovelace, a powerful and pompous figure who humiliated him when he was a young boy. And the adventure moves on from there.

"At the point I started writing, I didn't even know what the amulet did," Stroud says, and he's not about to tell. You'll have to read the book.

Writing children's books full time was something he'd thought about doing since graduating from the University of York with a degree in English literature in 1992. He wrote in his spare time, publishing three children's books in England. But *The Amulet of Samarkand* was his first try at writing fantasy, and was the book he thought might give him his big break.

Shortly after dashing out the first chapters in fall 2001, Stroud decided to leave his editing job. He gave himself a year to "make good" while wife Gina, a book designer, supported the couple.

QUICK IMPRESSION

Stroud's agent began circulating those first few chapters. And when Jonathan Burnham, Miramax Books' editor-in-chief, read them, he immediately hopped on a plane from New York to London to take part in a bidding war for the American rights to the book and movie.

"There was something about the writing that woke me up. He's funny and quirky," Burnham says of Stroud. "The quality of the prose is really the very, very best. It's like the very best adult fiction."

Burnham believes the book will appeal both to adults and children. And that's why he was willing to offer a "substantial six figure deal" for both the book and the movie.

The first print run for the book was 100,000, 25,000 more than *The Thief Lord,* the debut novel by German author Cornelia Funke. Her book, billed by some as last year's "next 'Harry Potter,'" has sold a half-million copies and had a consistently strong presence on *The New York Times* list of children's best sellers. This year, Funke released the first of her own trilogy, titled *Inkheart.*

So though his book is already being readied for its third print run Stroud has some hefty competition.

Meanwhile, the screenplay for his book is already in the process of being written, with hopes of having a movie out by early 2005. Hossein Amini, who wrote the Academy Award-nominated screenplay for *The Wings of a Dove,* is writing the script.

So far, ***The Amulet of Samarkand*** has been a hit with many reviewers.

STARK CONTRASTS

One compared it to *Gulliver's Travels* because of its political undertones. (Some see the book as a critique of British Prime Minister Tony Blair, though Stroud said he never intended that.) Others critics say too much is being made of the Harry Potter comparisons.

"Despite a few basic similarities, ***The Amulet of Samarkand*** is more than just a Harry Potter wannabe," said one reviewer from Australia's *Sydney Morning Herald.* "Nathaniel fills the basic Harry Potter, new-to-magic, young-orphan requirements, but . . . it's the deviations that make things interesting. Hell-bent on revenge, Nathaniel is not a noble kid and, like his power-hungry adversaries, he is willing to use and abuse to get what he wants."

Megan Coley, an 11-year-old who came to Stroud's reading in Naperville, says she thinks the book might be too complicated for readers younger than her. But she says older kids will like the book "because of the characters and the setting."

"I think that Bartimaeus will be close to or as big as Harry Potter, but not bigger," says Megan who "can't wait for the second book to come out."

Stroud says the trilogy's second installment will focus more on Bartimaeus and Kitty, a girl who is neither magician nor djinni.

With his deadline fast approaching, he's been lugging his second manuscript cross country during his book tour, trying to find a few spare moments to read and edit it.

Jonathan Stroud and Michelle Pauli (interview date 12 January 2004)

SOURCE: Stroud, Jonathan, and Michelle Pauli. "Airy Escapes." *Guardian Unlimited* (online edition) http://books.guardian.co.uk/departments/sciencefiction/story/0,,1121611,00.html (12 January 2004).

[*In the following interview, Stroud discusses his conception of the central characters in* The Amulet of Samarkand.]

Jonathan Stroud is the latest in a long line of children's authors to be blessed—or burdened—with that hopeful publisher's tag, "the next J K Rowling".

His children's book, *The Amulet of Samarkand,* is a page-turning tale about a young boy apprentice in a magical world which has garnered a US film and rights deal of £1.3m, but there the comparison ends.

For a start, Stroud is no newcomer to the scene. He has worked in children's publishing for a number of years, and Amulet is his fourth children's book. It is also a darker and more rumbustious read than Rowling's Potter stories, with a wickedly satirical edge.

The first volume in a trilogy, *Amulet* is set in an alternate England ruled by corrupt magicians who summon demons—djinn—to do their bidding. Nathaniel, from whose perspective half the story is told, is an 11-year-old apprentice to a cruel magician politician. Behind his master's back, he succeeds in summoning a djinni, Bartimaeus, and concocts a plan to seek revenge. The wise-cracking Bartimaeus narrates the other half of the tale.

This reversal of the traditional magical narrative was the starting point for Stroud's conception of the series. He explains that the idea for the book came to him very clearly.

"I was strolling along one wet October Saturday, thinking about fantasy fiction and how to get a new angle on it. My first thought was that instead of having a story in which all magicians were good—there are already lots of Dumbledores and Gandalfs out there—it would be unusual to have a story in which most magicians were fairly corrupt and in a position of power, ruling over society."

"I decided that to further make it different, the narrator would be a djinni who is enslaved to one of these magicians. So you reverse the normal case whereby the human magicians are the heroes; here they are the evildoers and the poor old demon is in fact the guy we identify with."

Bartimaeus is indeed the most appealing character in the book. By turns pompous, caring, irascible and wise, his cynical and witty asides give the story an edge which broadens its appeal beyond average children's fantasy.

Stroud's identification with Bartimaeus is evident from the affection with which he describes his creation.

"He is all about lightness—literally. He has no real form, he can be smoke or he can be a bird flying, he's constantly moving and his language too is constantly shifting from being serious to being sarcastic to being informative to being derisory."

Stroud has taken the unusual step of making the young apprentice, Nathaniel, a much more ambivalent character than his co-protagonist. Single-minded in his ambition to become part of the magical political elite, there is something of the young William Hague about the boy. The reader is caught between sympathy for his harsh upbringing and dismay at his treatment of Bartimaeus.

For Stroud it was essential for Nathaniel to be a complex enough character to act as a foil to Bartimaeus.

"The whole dynamic revolves around Bart and Nathaniel's relationship. Sometimes we may well sympathise with Nathaniel for what he's been through, and at other times we'll think he's a complete sod and want Bart to come out on top because he's been enslaved and is a cheeky character. Each is seeking to gain advantage over the other."

Amulet has another unusual feature for a children's book—footnotes. Some provide background information on the alternate reality the characters inhabit, others supply cheap gags and derisive asides. There is a danger that they might interrupt the flow of the story, but they work best when used to undercut the narrative.

"Using footnotes means you can constantly subvert whatever's going on in the main text and keep everything a bit light. The danger with a lot of fantasy fiction is that it's all about good and evil, with a good guy and a bad guy, and some kind of cosmic significance. That's quite weighty. I think you need the text to have some kind of inherent lightness, like the bubbles in an Aero, which keep the narrative motoring and the reader happy."

While the dynamic between the apprentice and his djinni will hold the interest of older readers, it is the high action quotient which is likely to appeal to Stroud's core audience—boys of 10 upwards—as well as the executives at Miramax.

The book is powered by explosions, chase sequences and a torture scene set in the Tower of London as it races towards a climax.

Stroud hopes that the book "pushes the right buttons for boy readers—some boys might not like reading books with lots of character development but they certainly don't mind reading books with lots of sequences of things being blown up."

There is something of Bartimaeus in his creator. Despite Stroud's sudden success and the potential crossover appeal of *Amulet*, he is wary of the "highfalutin, slightly pretentious aspect of the literary world". As he puts it, "children's books are my natural home."

Jonathan Stroud and Rick Margolis (interview date January 2006)

SOURCE: Stroud, Jonathan, and Rick Margolis. "I Dream of Djinni: British Author Jonathan Stroud Talks about the Best-Selling Bartimaeus Trilogy." *School Library Journal* 52, no. 1 (January 2006): 45.

[*In the following interview, Stroud discusses the origins of the Bartimaeus Trilogy and his writing career.*]

[*Margolis*]: *How did you come up with the idea for a trilogy about a smart-alecky djinni and a young magician?*

[Stroud]: I was walking home from a particularly boring and tedious shopping trip in my hometown, and I was turning things over in my mind. I suddenly decided I would create a hero who was a djinni and have as his enemy a young magician who was a politician. A contemporary England that was run by magicians really appealed to me.

I raced home and began writing down some notes. And within a few days I wrote the first four chapters of *The Amulet of Samarkand,* pretty much exactly

as they are right now. The whole voice of Bartimaeus just came out. I had no idea what the story was going to be, but his voice was living in a way I've never experienced before. It was with his voice that the whole trilogy began.

If I were to interview Bartimaeus, what would he say about you?

He'd probably patronize me, and say I was a hard worker, who devoted many hours of my time to doing the very best that I could. He would certainly imply that my effort was fairly middling to poor compared to something he could have done in five minutes. He would certainly emphasize the fact that after a couple days of inspiration, when I wrote the first four chapters, everything slowed up immensely and it took me a month to work out the actual plot of the three books and then three years of solid work. He would find that all a little bit amusing.

I heard that you were a children's book editor before you became a full-time writer.

Pretty much within the month I had the idea for Bartimaeus, I handed in my notice as an editor. That was actually a coincidence. I had another book that I was writing, a book called *The Last Siege.* I couldn't finish it because I was working four days a week as an editor. I finally got so fed up, I said I would give up my job and give myself a year to write and see if I could make it work financially.

Coincidentally, within that very same time span, I had the beginning of this idea for the series about Bartimaeus. All I had was those first four chapters actually of *The Amulet of Samarkand.* I was excited by it, but my agent kept it quiet. I gave up my job and finished the other book and then I began working on Bartimaeus. Halfway through the following year, I had written about 100 pages and that was when I showed it to publishers for the first time in the U.K. and U.S.

Variety reported that Miramax paid close to $3 million for the book and film rights. Were you shocked?

Totally. It was the most remarkable and bizarre month of my life. I spent the first half of that year essentially in seclusion, just finishing one book and writing the beginning of *The Amulet.* When I finally sent it out to various publishers, there was suddenly a massive amount of interest—more interest than I ever had had for any of my other books by a factor of 10. Jonathan Burnham of Miramax Books in the States heard about it and he came motoring over to try and get the publishing rights for the States. Meanwhile, [Miramax chief] Harvey Weinstein read it and was interested in buying the film rights. So over a period of a month, I went from this little, private project to suddenly selling the movie and book rights. It was just the strangest sensation. I remember wandering around for days with a silly grin on my face. Nothing was real; it was kind of like a dream world I suddenly entered. Then again, what actually kept me going was the realization I now had to write the book. I couldn't go out and party.

TITLE COMMENTARY

THE LOST TREASURE OF CAPTAIN BLOOD: HOW THE INFAMOUS SPAMMES ESCAPED THE JAWS OF DEATH AND WON A VAST AND GLORIOUS FORTUNE (1996)

Lynne Babbage (review date March 1997)

SOURCE: Babbage, Lynne. Review of *The Lost Treasure of Captain Blood: How the Infamous Spammes Escaped the Jaws of Death and Won a Vast and Glorious Fortune,* by Jonathan Stroud, illustrated by Cathy Gale. *Magpies* 12, no. 1 (March 1997): 30.

Subtitled *How the infamous Spammes escaped the jaws of death and won a vast and glorious fortune,* this exuberant picture puzzle book [*The Lost Treasure of Captain Blood*] has a crew of villainous pirates who outwit the even more villainous baddies. The reader is asked on each double page to solve the numerous puzzles before progressing. They range from simple observation tasks such as counting the dwindling number of ship's rats and finding the spy to eliminating the eight false hiding spots marked on the map to reveal the true treasure one. Each spread is covered in a large painting with much activity going on and speech bubbles of text. There are also comic-style strips of two or three frames which advance the plot. Puzzle instructions are given in boxed captions with black backgrounds which stand out from the surrounding busyness.

The overall effect is much more complicated than books such as the *Where's Wally?* series and is obviously intended for an older readership. Because the text is broken up into such small and scattered snip-

pets, reluctant readers may well find this an attractive book. Its subject matter, fast-paced action and overall appearance make it appealing, and an inability to solve some of the puzzles is not a deterrent. Some of the answers (but not all) are given on the next page. The only minor quibble is the wording of some of the text. Some of the instructions and answers are addressed directly to the reader and sound a little patronising to an adult but this is not a major issue. Young readers may well spend several hours poring over this book. Not only will their reading skills be put to the test but also their problem solving, lateral thinking and powers of observation.

THE VIKING SAGA OF HARRI BRISTLEBEARD: A HEROIC PUZZLE ADVENTURE (1997)

John Sigwald (review date October 1997)

SOURCE: Sigwald, John. Review of *The Viking Saga of Harri Bristlebeard: A Heroic Puzzle Adventure,* by Jonathan Stroud, illustrated by Cathy Gale. *School Library Journal* 43, no. 10 (October 1997): 112.

Gr. 1-3—Requiring a hefty mix of patience and persistence, this *Where's Waldo?*-like offering [*The Viking Saga of Harri Bristlebeard: A Heroic Puzzle Adventure*] adds occasional simple riddles and memory tests to the compulsory multiple (and often tiny) character searches on every page. Loosely a story about a quest to retrieve a magic banner stolen by a dragon years ago, *Viking Saga* is a slight improvement on Stroud and Gale's *The Lost Treasure of Captain Blood* (Candlewick, 1996). Like its predecessor, it is presented in an oversized, picture-book format and features a comic-strip story line (dialogue balloons and all). An omniscient raven narrator tucked away in the corner; a longhouse lemming and his growing band of buddies; Hilda, the blond supergirl who disguises herself to join Harri's crew; Fenrir, the loyal and fearless wolf; and a large and busy main scene all revolve around the good-hearted but rather bumbling Harri and his faithful companions. A rainy-day diversion for kids who can color inside the lines.

BURIED FIRE (1999)

Heather Lisowski (review date May 2005)

SOURCE: Lisowski, Heather. Review of *Buried Fire,* by Jonathan Stroud. *KLIATT* 39, no. 3 (May 2005): 36.

Deep beneath a hilltop in the English countryside, a dragon sleeps. It is neither a peaceful nor a willing slumber. Michael McIntyre sleeps on the hill above, blissfully unaware of the change that is about to take place in his life. For as Michael sleeps, the dragon dreams, and a single reptilian thought rises from the earth to envelop the boy. When Michael awakens, he finds that he has the ability to see people's true identities. As the days pass, he realizes that he also has three other gifts: the gift of fire, the gift of flying, and the gift of mind control. Michael takes his brother Stephen to the hilltop to initiate him into the small group of villagers who have been changed by the dragon. However, Stephen resists the use of his gifts. Meanwhile, the Reverend Tom Aubrey of St. Wyndham church has made an interesting discovery in his churchyard; the arm of a large Celtic cross has been lifted from the ground. What he does not realize is that this cross bound the dragon into the earth, and with its removal the dragon's power has increased.

Although **Buried Fire** has exciting fantasy elements, it is not a book that will appeal to all. The point of view within the text shifts from character to character, creating a fractured narrative that would be hard for a lower-level reader to follow comfortably. Also, the victory at the end of the story becomes dependent upon some minor secondary characters that are not terribly well developed, and as a result the conclusion feels convenient. However, the tale itself *is* intriguing. Although the dragon is the core menace of the story, the humans who are acting on his behalf reflect the real conflict. Their interpersonal relationships remain human while their actions become reptilian. This thriller will appeal to those fantasy fans who are strong readers. It will especially appeal to those who eagerly await the final volume in Jonathan Stroud's Bartimaeus trilogy.

SIGHTSEERS: ANCIENT ROME—A GUIDE TO THE GLORY OF IMPERIAL ROME (2000)

Cynthia M. Sturgis (review date September 2000)

SOURCE: Sturgis, Cynthia M. Review of *Sightseers: Ancient Rome—A Guide to the Glory of Imperial Rome,* by Jonathan Stroud. *School Library Journal* 46, no. 9 (September 2000): 257.

Gr. 4-7—Like any handbook for tourists, [*Sightseers: Ancient Rome—A Guide to the Glory of Imperial Rome,*] this travel guide to an ancient world includes essential information on accommodations, shopping, key sites, etc. Sidebars describe local customs and offer safety guidelines for sightseers. Even a foldout tour map of the city is included. A concluding "Survival guide" warns readers/tourists about Roman views on law enforcement and how to stay out of trouble. Lots of full-color illustrations and photographs of artifacts combined with a breezy, amusing text result in a delightful, tongue-in-cheek, but informative overview of Roman culture and life. Look to Mike Corbishley's *Ancient Rome* (Facts on File, 1989) for a more straightforward source.

THE AMULET OF SAMARKAND (2003)

Publishers Weekly (review date 21 July 2003)

SOURCE: Review of *The Amulet of Samarkand,* by Jonathan Stroud. *Publishers Weekly* 250, no. 29 (21 July 2003): 196.

A seemingly omniscient narrator begins [**The Amulet of Samarkand,**] this darkly tantalizing tale set in modern-day London, ushering readers into a room where the temperature plunges, ice forms on the curtains and ceiling, and the scent of brimstone fills the air. Suddenly, the voice reveals itself as the djinn Bartimaeus, appearing in front of Nathaniel, the 10-year-old magician who has summoned him ("Hey, it was his first time. I wanted to scare him," Bartimaeus explains). The djinn thinks of himself as rather omniscient, having been present for some major historical moments (as he explains in various footnotes, he gave an anklet to Nefertiti and offered tips to legendary architects—"Not that my advice was always taken: check out the Leaning Tower of Pisa"). Debut novelist Stroud plunges readers into a quickly thickening plot: Nathaniel commands Bartimaeus to steal the Amulet of Samarkand from Simon Lovelace, a task that the djinn completes with some ease. Other factors quickly become more interesting: the motive for the boy's charge, how Simon came by the Amulet and the fallout from the theft. What these reveal about the characters of Simon and Nathaniel makes for engrossing reading. Stroud also introduces the fascinating workings of the "seven planes" (magicians can see three of them only with special spectacles), the pecking order of magical beings, and the requirements of various spells and enchantments—plus the intrigue behind a group of commoners mounting a Resistance (this loose end, presumably, will be explored in the remainder of the planned Bartimaeus trilogy). The author plants enough seeds that readers will eagerly anticipate the next two volumes. Ages 10-up.

Kirkus Reviews (review date 1 October 2003)

SOURCE: Review of *The Amulet of Samarkand*, by Jonathan Stroud. *Kirkus Reviews* 71, no. 19 (1 October 2003): 1231.

In a contemporary London full of magic, a thrilling adventure unfolds [in ***The Amulet of Samarkand***]. Twelve-year-old Nathaniel is apprenticed to a politician (which means magician), but early emotional pain leads him toward hardness and anger. Arrogantly summoning a djinni to help him steal an amulet from slickly evil Simon Lovelace, he's swept into a swirl of events involving conspiracy at the highest government level. Nathaniel's perspective alternates with that of Bartimaeus, the cocky, sardonic djinni. No character is wholly likable or trustworthy, which contributes to the intrigue. Many chapters end in suspense, suddenly switching narrators at key moments to create a real page-turner. Readers will hope that Stroud follows up on certain questions—is it slavery to use a djinni? will shaky looming international politics affect the empire? who deserves our alliance? and *who* are the mysterious children ostensibly running an underground resistance?—in the next installment, sure to be eagerly awaited.

Anita L. Burkam (review date November-December 2003)

SOURCE: Burkam, Anita L. Review of *The Amulet of Samarkand*, by Jonathan Stroud. *Horn Book Magazine* 79, no. 6 (November-December 2003): 757.

The magicians ruling the British empire in [***The Amulet of Samarkand,***] this anachronistic modern fantasy derive their powers from demons—marids, afrits, djinn, imps—who, though summoned to work the magicians' wills, are always looking for a loophole through which to destroy them. Bartimaeus, a smart-mouthed bruiser of a djinni, called by a stripling magician to steal the Amulet of Samarkand, finds just such a loophole when he learns his master's secret birthname. Nathaniel, however, manages to regain the upper hand with a time-delayed spell: Bartimaeus must protect the apprentice magician long enough to get the spell removed or spend eternity in a tobacco tin. Through guile, teamwork, and dumb luck the ambitious but green kid and the "Spenser for Hire"-type djinni uncover and foil a coup attempt masterminded by Simon Lovelace, the powerful and ruthless magician who is after them for stealing the Amulet. The pace never slows in this wisecracking adventure; chapters in Bartimaeus's lively first person (with indulgent explanatory footnotes) alternate with third-person chapters on Nathaniel's adolescent insecurities and desires. Stroud has created a compelling fantasy story in a well-realized world, but it is the complementary characters of Bartimaeus and Nathaniel that will keep readers coming back for the rest of the projected trilogy.

Suzi Feay (review date 7 December 2003)

SOURCE: Feay, Suzi. Review of *The Amulet of Samarkand*, by Jonathan Stroud. *Independent Sunday* (7 December 2003): 18.

Critics of J K Rowling can't fault her amazingly fertile comic imagination or the page-turning power of her stories. But the excitement of the plots isn't matched by the quality of her prose, which is rarely more than efficient.

Step forward Jonathan Stroud—in [***The Amulet of Samarkand,***] the first book of his projected Bartimaeus trilogy, he brings together a fabulist's facility with a rollicking relish in creating good sentences. The demon, or djinni, Bartimaeus, has spent centuries honing his world-weary sarcasm, often racing down into the footnotes the better to express his lofty wit. Stroud's England is not unlike Rowling's, in that magicians and non-magical folk exist side by side, but Stroud has reversed the balance: the arrogant magicians hold the power and they are far from benevolent. Young readers will enjoy the exciting magical set-pieces and phantasmagorical battles, while their elders will be amused by the antics of a ruling class who come on like New Labour with wands.

The trouble begins when young magician's apprentice Nathaniel summons the age-old demon Bartimaeus with an outrageous request: to retrieve the titular Amulet from the smarmy yet fearsome wizard Simon Lovelace, who has offended him. Nathaniel is awfully young to be setting magical feuds in motion—he's an intriguingly flawed boy, but Stroud has no interest in creating a two-dimensional hero, or in flattering his juvenile readers, which gives his novel quite a sharp tang.

Bartimaeus is bound by ancient laws so, much as he'd love to ignore the puny little scamp, he can't: Nathaniel is word-perfect in his spells. Unlike the notoriously hard-of-understanding Harry Potter, Nathaniel is a brain-box, a swot, and it's as much as Bartimaeus can do to outwit him. The boy and the shapeshifting demon (one minute he takes the form of an Egyptian slave, the next he's a gargoyle on the roof of Westminster Abbey) form the ultimate mismatched-buddy team as they battle the forces of evil. Not that Bartimaeus gives a damn about that, of course.

Diana Wynne Jones (review date 13 December 2003)

SOURCE: Jones, Diana Wynne. "The Djinni's Tale." *Guardian* (13 December 2003): 32.

[*In the following review, noted fantasy author Wynne Jones lauds* The Amulet of Samarkand *and compliments Stroud for turning "the well-known tradition of the magician's apprentice, the boy who attempts to perform his master's magic on his own, upside down."*]

[*The Amulet of Samarkand,* t]his first volume in a promised trilogy is set in an alternate England—at least, I hope it's not ours—where the ruling classes are cold-hearted, self-centred magicians who derive their power from their ability to summon demons (djinn, afrits, imps) and coerce them into following their orders.

Half the story is told by a djinni, Bartimaeus, who is summoned by an 11-year-old apprentice and commanded to steal the Amulet of Samarkand from an unscrupulous government minister. Bartimaeus's efforts to follow his orders and, later, to deal with the consequences, while resenting every moment of his adventures, have you on the edge of your seat. His narrative is splendidly amplified by footnotes that add historical depth, wry humour and smug pride to his already packed story.

The other half of the story shows how the apprentice, Nathaniel, was torn from his parents as a five-year-old and dumped in the household of an uncaring master to be force-fed with magical learning. You are just beginning to think you understand how the magician politicians of this world grow up so nasty, when Nathaniel suddenly—albeit arrogantly—begins to display some decent qualities.

Bartimaeus is exasperated, but—and it is a measure of how subtly excellent this book is that you don't spot this immediately—he is forced into a concealed and grudging respect. Together boy and djinni try to retrieve the mess they have made in a thunderously exciting climax.

What makes this book so unusual is the way Jonathan Stroud has upended the various traditions he draws on. He pays homage to *The Arabian Nights* and to any "ripping yarn" you care to name, but the Charles Dickens of *Oliver Twist* and *David Copperfield* is also in there; and this strange mix is made new by being transposed into a country slightly—but only slightly—reminiscent of Kingsley Amis's *The Alteration.*

This is a world in which there are cars, trains, London buses, repressive government ministries, corrupt politicians and covert revolutionaries, all existing inside a social order very different from our own.

Stroud has turned the well-known tradition of the magician's apprentice, the boy who attempts to perform his master's magic on his own, upside down. Nathaniel succeeds in summoning his djinni and in controlling him. Things get out of hand mostly because Nathaniel is only a boy trying to fight adult magicians. But the truly original touch is the way Stroud alternates Nathaniel's story with the djinni's own knowing and irascible first-person narrative. And Bartimaeus is not perfect, though he considers that he is. He makes mistakes, just as Nathaniel does.

If you know a boy between 10 and 13 (or younger, if you like reading aloud), give him this book for Christmas. This is not to say that girls will not find it enthralling too; just that the sort of cynical derision Bartimaeus displays towards his youthful master, and magicians in general, chimes so well with the mind-set of so many boys of around that age that they'll be demanding the next books in the trilogy for their birthdays. Having said that, I can't wait for volume two either.

Ginny Collier (review date January 2004)

SOURCE: Collier, Ginny. Review of *The Amulet of Samarkand,* by Jonathan Stroud. *School Library Journal* 50, no. 1 (January 2004): 136.

Gr. 5-9—[In *The Amulet of Samarkand,*] Nathaniel has been apprenticed to Mr. Underwood for several years. At the age of 12, he has finally been Named and is on his way to becoming a real magician. Suddenly, London is in an uproar. The Amulet of Samarkand has been stolen from the powerful magician Simon Lovelace. Only Nathaniel knows what really happened because it was he who commanded the 5000-year-old djinni Bartimaeus to steal it for him. Now, with a rebellious demon under his control and all of London searching for the thief, he must figure out a way to keep the amulet hidden. Stroud has woven an intricate fantasy set in an alternative London where the most influential members of society, and even the Prime Minister himself, are magicians. The richly rewarding story unfolds in chapters that alternate between Bartimaeus's first-person narration, which includes arcane and very funny footnotes, and Nathaniel's account, told in third person. There is plenty of action, mystery, and humor to keep readers turning the pages. This title, the first in a trilogy, is a must for fantasy fans, and in particular for those anxious for the next Harry Potter.

Janice M. Del Negro (review date March 2004)

SOURCE: Del Negro, Janice M. Review of *The Amulet of Samarkand,* by Jonathan Stroud. *Bulletin of the Center for Children's Books* 57, no. 7 (March 2004): 298.

[In *The Amulet of Samarkand,* t]he demon Bartimaeus is summoned by precocious magician's apprentice Nathaniel and ordered to retrieve the Amulet of Samarkand from the house of master magician Simon Lovelace. Thus begins the partnership between boy and demon, one that can only be dissolved when Nathaniel releases Bartimaeus from a bond of Perpetual Confinement. Nathaniel is unaware of the real power of the Amulet—he only wants it to avenge himself on Simon Lovelace for embarrassing him at a gathering of magicians—but Lovelace was planning to use the Amulet to assassinate the Prime Minister and take over the Government, and he is not happy at its loss. Lovelace tracks the Amulet, kills Nathaniel's master, and sets a host of magical beings in search of boy and demon. Bartimaeus, sworn to protect Nathaniel, sneaks them both into the conference where Lovelace is planning his coup; in a shattering confrontation the boy retrieves the Amulet and saves the day—and the appropriately grateful Prime Minister. Stroud alternates between Bartimaeus' first-person narration and an omniscient narrator's view of Nathaniel. The demon has a sarcastic tone and highly developed sense of irony, evident not only in his direct narrative but in the footnotes he includes to explain himself to the reader. Fast action and Machiavellian politics shape the plot: the structure of the society and the hierarchy of the magicians within it are clearly delineated. The constant threat of discovery means the tension is high, although Nathaniel's eventual survival and his release of Bartimaeus is never really in doubt. The relationship between Stroud's conflicted apprentice and the mouthy demon, as well as his unusual handling of the formal intricacies of magic, make this novel a standard in the genre of magician-oriented fantasy. Here's hoping Bartimaeus gets another chance to help Nathaniel grow up.

Michael M. Jones (review date March 2004)

SOURCE: Jones, Michael M. Review of *The Amulet of Samarkand,* by Jonathan Stroud. *Chronicle of Higher Education* 26, no. 3 (March 2004): 36.

In an alternate London where magicians rule through the power of the spirits they summon from beyond, one young man's desire for revenge entangles him in the heart of a conspiracy aimed at the highest levels of power [in *The Amulet of Samarkand*]. Still a year away from gaining his official magician's name and being granted a measure of respect, the eleven year old apprentice known as Nathaniel secretly summons an ancient, powerful djinn, Bartimaeus, and commands his newfound servant to steal the fabled Amulet of Samarkand from the magician who wronged him, Simon Lovelace.

What Nathaniel doesn't realize is just how ruthless Lovelace is, or how importantly the Amulet factors into a diabolical scheme. Even with the unwilling aid of Bartimaeus, Nathaniel will be tested to the very limits of his loyalty, resourcefulness, and magical abilities. If the odd pair fail, they, and the rest of London's power structure, will be in for a horrible end indeed.

If I had to label one book as "If you like Harry Potter, you'll like this," it would definitely be *The Amulet of Samarkand.* The first book in the Bartimaeus Trilogy, it's nevertheless structured so that it tells a full story in its own right, leaving just enough loose ends to set up the remainder of the series. Nathaniel and Bartimaeus are the unlikeliest of allies, with only threats and mutual bonds of need keeping them together during the darkest times. One of the most entertaining aspects of this book is that half of it is told from Bartimaeus' viewpoint. Not only is he snarky, over-confident, self-involved and egotistical, he speaks in footnotes, which serve to explain many of the unusual aspects of his world and personal history. The other half of the book focuses on Nathaniel, but even during those times, we never lose track of the fact that this is Bartimaeus' story. I'm eagerly awaiting the next installment of the trilogy.

THE GOLEM'S EYE (2004)

Kirkus Reviews (review date 1 August 2004)

SOURCE: Review of *The Golem's Eye,* by Jonathan Stroud. *Kirkus Reviews* 72, no. 19 (1 August 2004): 749.

Picking up two years after *The Amulet of Samarkand* ended, this sequel [*The Golem's Eye*] continues the original's fast-paced excitement and is enriched by a broader moral view and a third main character. Nathaniel, ambitious teenage magician (politician), works furiously to gain power and credence in London's magician-run government. Slave-djinni Bartimaeus, bound to follow Nathaniel's orders, retains his ultra-sardonic voice (including trademark commentary footnotes). The third viewpoint is that of Kitty, a teenaged member of the Resistance tormenting London's seat of government. Unlike headstrong Nathaniel (never questioning the British Empire's repressive power) and sarcastic Bartimaeus, the fierce, fiery Kitty is easy to root for. Grave-robbing, international spying, a city-smashing golem, exploding demons, and fearsome Night Police all figure in before the end—which of course isn't the end at all. Is there hope for resisting the Empire? Might enslaved djinn be involved? Stay tuned for more thrills.

Jeff Zaleski (review date 16 August 2004)

SOURCE: Zaleski, Jeff. Review of *The Golem's Eye*, by Jonathan Stroud. *Publishers Weekly* 251, no. 33 (16 August 2004): 64.

The sharp-witted shape-shifting djinni returns in Stroud's second volume of the Bartimaeus Trilogy, [*The Golem's Eye*,] this time dealing with a mysterious attacker that is terrorizing London. Nathaniel (aka John Mandrake), now 14, is apprenticed to Jessica Whitwell (as established at the close of the first book), "one of the four most potent magicians in the government." When several terrorist attacks take place, the ruling party blames the Resistance, the young commoner idealists introduced in the previous title. Nathaniel, rapidly rising through the ranks and serving as assistant to the Internal Affairs minister, Julius Tallow, suspects something larger at work. He once again summons Bartimaeus; the djinni's charge: "Pursuit and identification of an unknown enemy of considerable power." When it appears that a golem is behind the attacks, the duo's mission takes them to Prague to uncover the magic behind the creature's appearance. Readers learn more about Kitty, previously met as a member of the Resistance, as the narrative shifts among her, Bartimaeus and Nathaniel. Kitty aids Mr. Pennyfeather, leader of the Resistance, in the group's effort to rob the grave of the legendary magician Gladstone to gain power. Bartimaeus once again steals the spotlight; his pages are the most entertaining (one of his signature footnotes points out

that his guise as a feathered, winged serpent "used to bring the house down in Yucatan"). Although the thrill of discovery of Stroud's magical realm may have worn off slightly, fans of book one will enjoy revisiting this delectably uneasy bond between boy and djinni. Bartimaeus's pointed humor makes for a story worth savoring. Ages 10-up.

Tasha Saecker (review date October 2004)

SOURCE: Saecker, Tasha. Review of *The Golem's Eye*, by Jonathan Stroud. *School Library Journal* 50, no. 10 (October 2004): 178, 180.

Gr. 6 Up—[*The Golem's Eye*, t]his sequel to *The Amulet of Samarkand* (Hyperion, 2003) takes place two years later. Now 14, Nathaniel works in the Department of Internal Affairs trying to stop a group of commoners who are responsible for small rebellions against the magician-run government. As he pursues the elusive Resistance, he discovers that an unknown individual is using ancient magic to control a golem and wreak havoc on the city of London. Meanwhile, readers get a look into the heart of the Resistance through the eyes of Kitty, a resourceful young commoner. She was born with a "resilience" to magic, an ability that drew her to the attention of the rebels, and her motivations for joining them are clearly presented. As events unfold, Nathaniel and Kitty are faced with choices that will test their courage and honor. The third-person narrative switches focus between the two characters. As in the first book, occasional chapters narrated by the demon Bartimaeus add sarcasm and irreverent humor to the text and offer a break from the ever-growing tension. The story, which stands alone nicely, retains all of the strengths of Stroud's first installment and adds many more details to his already vivid fantasy world. The characters are well developed and the action never lets up. A must-purchase for all fantasy collections.

Timnah Card (review date November 2004)

SOURCE: Card, Timnah. Review of *The Golem's Eye*, by Jonathan Stroud. *Bulletin of the Center for Children's Books* 58, no. 3 (November 2004): 148.

[In *The Golem's Eye*, t]he sarcastic djinni Bartimaeus and his ambitious master Nathaniel (from *The Amulet of Samarkand*, BCCB 3/04), in spite of mutual vows to leave each other in peace, are reunited "two years, eight months" later in another race to save London from the terrorist acts of political conspirators and Resistance fighters. Only Nathaniel realizes that certain of the attacks on the city (mysterious, large-scale destructions of valuable property) come from a source other than the grassroots Resistance, a deduction which leads him on an undercover mission to the formerly great magical city of Prague, which was, not coincidentally, the site of the creation of the first golem, centuries before. Mortal danger, international intrigue, and treacherous allies keep the temperature high throughout this supersized sequel, while Bartimaeus' acid commentary and wry footnotes add pepper to the pot. Resistance fighter Kitty, introduced in the first volume and now forced into action as a major player in the struggle for power, infuses the tale with moral complexity as she consistently chooses idealistic heroism over practical self-preservation, winning Bartimaeus' admiration and providing the more easily corruptible Nathaniel with both a foil and a reason to doubt the wisdom of his own choices. With a fast-paced, open-ended dénouement assuring readers further high adventure in the next installment, this second book of the trilogy fulfills the potential of the first and promises a satisfying conclusion to come. A list of main characters is provided.

Elizabeth Devereaux (review date 14 November 2004)

SOURCE: Devereaux, Elizabeth. "Of Trolls and Men." *New York Times Book Review* (14 November 2004): 20.

[*In the following review, Devereaux evaluates several works of juvenile fantasy, noting that Stroud's* The Golem's Eye *"heads straight to the top of the class."*]

All good children's fantasy epics are alike; every unsuccessful fantasy epic fails in its own way. Despite settings that range from a land inhabited by water waifs and goblins to a futuristic Europe, the middle installments of five continuing fantasy series look more the same than different. Somehow the authors orchestrate a conflict between good and evil. The good can't be too good, lest the story become too preachy and dull, and the evil can't be too evil, lest the story become too violent or frightening. And, for all the magic, the talking animals, the imaginary creatures and imaginary worlds, a good fantasy must also be original and startle the reader into a new thought or two.

The Bartimaeus Trilogy, Book Two: The Golem's Eye, by Jonathan Stroud, heads straight to the top of the class. To clue in the uninitiated: Bartimaeus is a genie summoned by an apprentice magician named Nathaniel, a precocious boy in the brave-orphan mold. Bartimaeus longs to return to his home in the Other Place but must do Nathaniel's bidding in London (Stroud is British). In this London, however, magicians govern—that is, when they are not scheming against one another or spying on the Czechs, Britain's historic enemies. The author's voice eclipses even this lustrous plot, particularly when Bartimaeus narrates (dedicating a characteristically sardonic footnote to the British Museum, Bartimaeus says it "was home to a million antiquities, several dozen of which were legitimately come by").

In the caesura between the first two books, two years have elapsed, and the characters have evolved. Some fans may be disappointed to see that Bartimaeus's role has been scaled back, but he's too large and too formed a character, perhaps, to occupy center stage without overshadowing the action. Nathaniel, now 14, can seem cold and smug as he leads a government mission to hunt down the Resistance, a band of revolutionaries seeking to return power to the ordinary people. He's still brave, but is he likable? Meanwhile, a seemingly suspicious character from the first book, Kitty, ascends to stake her claim on our sympathies. Kitty belongs to the Resistance, for quite compelling reasons, and it's only a matter of time before Kitty and Nathaniel (and Bartimaeus) divide our loyalties. Amid political intrigues and magic, Kitty and Nathaniel both find their lives threatened.

For all its supernatural complexities, Stroud's book might be strongest for what it reflects of our world. It's not easy to tell who is on the side of good, although many characters have good intentions. As the author confidently tilts the narrative point of view, he magnifies the ambiguity and multiplies the thrills.

By contrast, Clive Barker's *Abarat: Days of Magic, Nights of War* (Joanna Cotler/Harper-Collins, $24.99, ages 12 and up), like its predecessor, *The Thief of Always,* trades heavily on novelty. The author, best known for his adult horror fiction, has spent six years creating the paintings of the rococo creatures used in the color illustrations, among them a villain with three jaws, stacked on top of one another, and a musician with "tendrils of spiraling matter" growing out of his head and back. It's tempting to assume that the paintings preceded the often picaresque plot, which follows young Candy Quackenbush from Chickentown, Minn., through the extravagant oddities of the Abarat islands.

By this second book Candy knows all too well that she will be essential to Abarat's future, and that the supremely evil Christopher Carrion, Lord of Midnight, is out to get her. Barker gets big points for Candy, an unusually natural and winning heroine. Just think "candid" and "candor." But she doesn't have worthy foes. Christopher Carrion and his henchmen come across as cruel yet disappointingly gullible; they're always being betrayed by those to whom they pledge their loyalty, but no one ever wises up. So far "Abarat" reads less like a series than one gigantic novel.

Zizou Corder, the pen name of a British mother and her school-age daughter, keeps sight of the political uses of fantasy in the Lionboy trilogy, the second installment of which is *Lionboy: The Chase* (Dial, $15.99, ages 10 and up). Charlie Ashanti, the boy hero, is biracial and deals (well) with prejudice and hostility, while the plot looks to a future in which a "corporacy" manipulates the public and even perpetuates some illnesses to guarantee demand for various medicines. These elements lurk in the book's foundations; more immediately, Charlie can speak to cats of all kinds, including lions.

As the second adventure begins, Charlie and a troupe of circus lions have hopped the Orient Express in Paris, with a little help from the king of Bulgaria; the idea is for the big cats to return to their own home in Africa and for Charlie to reunite with his parents, who have been kidnapped from their house in London and who, he believes, are being held in Venice. But all sorts of people are after him, still others are after the lions, and can Charlie protect the lions from a mysterious plan to consolidate the doge's power over Venice?

In terms of its questing structure and whole-cloth fantasy setting, the most traditional of these series would be "The Edge Chronicles," written by Paul Stewart and illustrated by Chris Riddell. The third book, *The Edge Chronicles: Midnight over Sanctaphrax* (David Fickling/Random House, $12.95, ages 10 to 12), could stand on its own; it might be argued that with each book this series has grown swifter, tenser and more tightly written, and that readers would do well to start in the middle. The hero, Twig, has progressed from Ugly Duckling beginnings as the foundling of wood trolls to discover his true destiny as a sky-pirate captain. Serving Sanctaphrax, the floating city of the academics, Twig leads his crew on a dangerous mission into a weather "vortex" and learns what he must do to save his world—only to suffer a catastrophe that scatters his crew and erases his last memory. Stewart doles out lots of deaths and scary sequences, but he modulates the terror by changing the scenery rapidly and keeping Twig and child readers too busy to stay frightened or upset.

G. P. Taylor's *Wormwood* (Putnam, $17.99, ages 12 and up) may be more fairly termed a companion book than a sequel to his earlier "Shadowmancer," hailed as the Christian Harry Potter. The protagonists and locales of the two novels differ, but the larger setting and message are identical, as is the pivotal character, an angel named Abram Rickards (eventually revealed as Raphael). Taylor stretches the allegorical trappings mighty thin—who needs clashes between mere good and evil when you can have biblical devils and angels duking it out over eternal stakes? As in "Shadowmancer," the plot of "Wormwood" hinges on a supernatural device (in this case, a book that tempts an 18th-century scientist in London) that could bring all of creation under the sway of the forces of evil.

A lurid, even somewhat sadistic flavor taints this enterprise. In the opening scenes, maddened hounds rip the flesh of panicked Londoners; not long after, the young heroine receives an eye-shaped wound on her palm, "the deep black line around the blood-red center oozing thick green mucus." These flourishes signal greater gore to come. Most unsettling of all, the sole representative of heaven, Abram/Raphael, traffics in death with a vengeance equal in intensity, if not purpose, to that of the bad guys: "I am nothing but an assassin for righteousness," he explains. Don't look for faith, hope or charity. Abram/Raphael doesn't attract, he strikes the deepest fear in the other characters.

The theology aside, dread is a poor substitute for inspiration when it comes to fantasy, especially fantasy for children. When a children's fantasy succeeds, as most of these books do, the reader gets a great story—and an opportunity to grow a little braver, a little stronger, a little more attuned to the possibilities of moral choice.

Kristi Elle Jemtegaard (review date January-February 2005)

SOURCE: Jemtegaard, Kristi Elle. Review of *The Golem's Eye,* by Jonathan Stroud. *Horn Book Magazine* 81, no. 1 (January-February 2005): 122.

In Book Two of the Bartimaeus Trilogy, [*The Golem's Eye,*] the action ricochets between the ancient streets of Prague and the rooftops of London. Fourteen-year-old Nathaniel may be two years older, but his pursuit of power within the ruling community of magicians is no less reckless or impetuous. As unexplained dangers bubble beneath the surface and ever-stronger pockets of resistance crop up, Nathaniel once again calls on forces stronger than his own. Jones's virtuoso portrayal of Bartimaeus (the first-person narrator of this complex web of political intrigue and internecine warfare) allows the five-thousand-year-old djinni's languid sarcasm to shape both the tale and the actors in it. Jones's confident pacing keeps the drama moving forward through the novel's many descriptive passages and overlapping scenes.

Don D'Ammassa (review date February 2005)

SOURCE: D'Ammassa, Don. Review of *The Golem's Eye,* by Jonathan Stroud. *Chronicle* 27, no. 2 (February 2005): 32.

The sequel to *The Amulet of Samarkand* [*The Golem's Eye*] is even more complex and exciting. Bartimaeus is a genie summoned by young Nathaniel, who has magical powers, who accompanies him on a series of adventures in a magical alternate version of our world, this time taking him out of London and across into continental Europe, where he must discover the secrets of his homeland's enemies from the inside. There are times when I thought the author was talking down to his audience a bit, a common problem in children's literature, but not so noticeably that it seriously interfered with my ability to enjoy the story, which is inventive, adventurous, and quite often suspenseful. A considerable step up from the first volume and a good omen for the next and final book in the trilogy.

Michael M. Jones (review date March 2005)

SOURCE: Jones, Michael M. Review of *The Golem's Eye,* by Jonathan Stroud. *Chronicle* 27, no. 3 (March 2005): 45.

[In *The Golem's Eye,*] two years after the events chronicled in *The Amulet of Samarkand,* young magician Nathaniel has, in his adult guise of John Mandrake, risen quickly in the ranks of London's magician-ruled government, becoming the assistant to Julius Tallow, Head of Internal Affairs. In this role, Nathaniel has been appointed to track down the Resistance, a group of ordinary humans dedicated to stealing magical artifacts and disrupting the strict rule of the magicians. So far, he's not doing so well, feeling the pressure from all sides from those envious of his success or fearful of his talents. Things get worse when a magical creature of unknown origins begins to cut a swathe of destruction through magician-held interests, just as the Resistance steps up their own efforts. Nathaniel is forced to go back on an earlier promise, and once again summon the Djinn, Bartimaeus, who helped him two years ago. It's not a partnership either are eager to resume, made all the more tense by Nathaniel's new attitude and drive to succeed.

Told in alternating chapters from the viewpoints of Nathaniel, Bartimaeus, and Kitty, one of the Resistance, *The Golem's Eye* is another captivating adventure set in a world where magic has dictated the course of events across the world for centuries. As events unfold, and Nathaniel's journey takes him from London, to darkly atmospheric Prague and back, we learn more of Bartimaeus' storied history, and discover just what brought Kitty to this point in her life. Conspiracies and mysteries abound, and magic fills the air as Stroud weaves a thoroughly entertaining tale. This is the series I recommend, without hesitation, to those who like Harry Potter. The characters are memorable and complex. Stroud unafraid to exploit their flaws. While some readers might be disappointed by Nathaniel's emotional growth (and resultant change in attitude and morals), it's only logical under the circumstances, and there's plenty of time for him to come around in the third book in the trilogy, which can't come too soon for me.

PTOLEMY'S GATE (2005)

Kirkus Reviews (review date 15 December 2005)

SOURCE: Review of *Ptolemy's Gate,* by Jonathan Stroud. *Kirkus Reviews* 73, no. 24 (15 December 2005): 1328.

The trilogy wraps up with excitement, adventure, and an unexpected wallop of heart and soul [in *Ptolemy's Gate*]. Three years have passed since Bartimaeus told Nathaniel that Kitty was killed by a golem. Nathaniel lives as John Mandrake now, coldly producing government propaganda. Mandrake continues to summon Bartimaeus as a slave-djinni despite the suffering it causes. Commoners (including Kitty, secretly alive) stumblingly rebel against the magicians (politicians). But when a real uprising bursts forth, it takes a shocking form and requires stunning sacrifices and terrifying levels of trust from all three protagonists. Bartimaeus's trademark footnotes are less snarky this time, including those in the chapters about his relationship with Ptolemy in Egypt from 126 to 124 B.C. The djinni, and the rare humans who care, don't solve one profound problem: Magicians get their power from summoning unwilling djinni into slavery. However, Stroud masterfully weaves together four characters and an unearthly realm of existence in an explosive culmination that reaches back to the first two volumes and infuses them with layers of psychological and moral complexity. The volumes in this trilogy should be read in order.

Publishers Weekly (review date 23 January 2006)

SOURCE: Review of *Ptolemy's Gate,* by Jonathan Stroud. *Publishers Weekly* 253, no. 4 (23 January 2006): 208.

Three years have passed since the events of **The Golem's Eye,** but there's more trouble than ever in the young magician Nathaniel's London [in *Ptolemy's Gate*]. At 17, he's climbed to the highest ranks of the British government but his now-"crippling" workload includes trying to sell an unpopular war in the American wilderness to the commoners who must fight it, and battling terrorist attacks and political corruption on the homefront. There's enough of an explosive plot in this final installment of Stroud's trilogy to fuel several novels. After two years of nonstop service to Nathaniel (known as John Mandrake), Bartimaeus has had it: "Irritable and jaded, with a perpetual itch in my essence that I cannot scratch," is how the djinni puts it. Kitty, the commoner and former Resistance leader, plays the Hermione Granger role of social conscience here: her new mission is to break the bonds that enslave the djinn to the ruling magician elite. The narrative shifts among these three, although as usual, Bartimaeus—even in his melancholy mood—steals the show. (It is an unusual novel whose best lines appear in the footnotes, but the djinni's wisecracking asides continue to be well worth the disruption in narrative flow.) This final volume fills in Bartimaeus's backstory, exposing a vulnerability not seen before, and preparing readers—after a galloping run against imps, Pestilence, Detonations, shields, charms and countercharms—for a potent ending that is at once unexpected and wholly earned.

April Spisak (review date February 2006)

SOURCE: Spisak, April. Review of *Ptolemy's Gate,* by Jonathan Stroud. *Bulletin of the Center of Children's Books* 59, no. 6 (February 2006): 287.

[In *Ptolemy's Gate,*] Kitty, Bartimaeus, and Nathaniel return as the central triad in this final volume of the Bartimaeus Trilogy (**Amulet of Samarkand,** BCCB 3/04, **Golem's Eye,** BCCB 11/04). Things have

changed a great deal, though, as Kitty (member of the rebel forces against the manipulative government) is now in hiding and assumed dead, Nathaniel seeks escape from his past and suffocates under increasing power and responsibility, and djinn Bartimaeus' strength is nearly sapped after almost two years of magical servitude. Though none of them wishes to see the others, they are drawn together again because of an imminent risk to themselves and to all humans as djinn and demons have learned how to overtake living bodies and break free of their masters' limitation on their earthly access. The first half of the novel builds toward a dramatic showdown between the human magicians and their summoned slaves (the djinn, demons, imps, and other powerful but restricted creatures from the Other Place) who chafe under being ruled. Readers hoping for a thrilling conclusion from such a dynamic trilogy will not be disappointed, and they'll likely be genuinely shocked by the tragedy that befalls one of the three main characters. The sense of loyalty between these fractious three remains strong until the end, and it is this consistent virtue across the series that leads to the only ending possible when all other attempts have failed and humanity is on the line. Stroud's fast-paced narration and suspenseful story arc are as solid and effective as in the previous volumes, and long-suffering djinn Bartimaeus shines as one of the most satisfyingly irascible, self-involved, and witty (and not quite villainous) heroes since Dahl's Willy Wonka.

Martha V. Parravano (review date March-April 2006)

SOURCE: Parravano, Martha V. Review of *Ptolemy's Gate,* by Jonathan Stroud. *Horn Book Magazine* 82, no. 2 (March-April 2006): 195.

[*Ptolemy's Gate,* t]his closing installment is the best yet, as the fates of the djinni Bartimaeus, the magician John Mandrake (true name: Nathaniel), and the commoner Kitty Jones grow ever more tightly entwined. The situation in Stroud's alternate-universe London has gone from bad to worse, with an unpopular overseas war draining men and resources; the ruling magicians corrupt; and the populace increasingly desperate. Now in hiding, Kitty is secretly learning all she can about Ptolemy, an ancient-Egyptian scholar whom Bartimaeus served—and loved—who aspired to break the cycle of enslavement between spirits and humans. Meanwhile, Bartimaeus, his essence sadly diminished by two years' continual service in the material world, seeks his release; Nathaniel, now a cynical top minister, needs him to investigate a plot to overthrow the government. When the attempted coup goes horribly wrong and powerful demons ravage the city, Nathaniel, Bartimaeus, and Kitty find themselves fighting on the same side— and, in the case of Bartimaeus and Nathaniel, even in the same body. Stroud is a masterful storyteller, balancing touching sentiment with humor, explosive action scenes with philosophical musings on human nature. He ties up the loose ends from previous installments (the identity of the government traitor, etc.) early on, freeing the book from the usual duties of a wrap-up volume and allowing it considerable momentum and power. Skillfully intertwining the various plot strands, Stroud builds to a thrilling, inventive climax. The final scene manages to take the reader completely by surprise and yet seem, in retrospect, inevitable: a stunning end to a justly acclaimed trilogy.

FURTHER READING

Criticism

Stroud, Jonathan, and Carl Wilkinson. "On the Verge." *Observer* (28 September 2003): 12

> Stroud discusses his publishing career and the success of *The Amulet of Samarkand.*

Veale, Scott. Review of *The Amulet of Samarkand,* by Jonathan Stroud. *New York Times Book Review* (8 February 2004): 23.

> Evaluates the strengths and weaknesses of *The Amulet of Samarkand.*

Additional coverage of Stroud's life and career is contained in the following sources published by Gale: *Contemporary Authors,* **Vol. 169;** *Contemporary Authors New Revision Series,* **Vol. 144;** *Literature Resource Center;* **and** *Something about the Author,* **Vols. 102, 159.**

How to Use This Index

The main reference

Baum, L(yman) Frank
    1856-1919 .... **15**
---

lists all author entries in this and previous volumes of *Children's Literature Review*.

The cross-references

See also CA 108, 133; DLB 22; JRDA;
MAICYA; MTCW 1; SATA 18, 100; TCLC 7
---

list all author entries in the following Gale biographical and literary sources:

AAL = *Asian American Literature*

AAYA = *Authors & Artists for Young Adults*

AFAW = *African American Writers* (Charles Scribner's Sons, an imprint of The Gale Group)

AFW = *African Writers* (Charles Scribner's Sons, an imprint of The Gale Group)

AITN = *Authors in the News*

AMW = *American Writers* (Charles Scribner's Sons, an imprint of The Gale Group)

AMWR = *American Writers Retrospective Supplement* (Charles Scribner's Sons, an imprint of The Gale Group)

AMWS = *American Writers Supplement* (Charles Scribner's Sons, an imprint of The Gale Group)

ANW = *American Nature Writers* (Charles Scribner's Sons, an imprint of The Gale Group)

AW = *Ancient Writers* (Charles Scribner's Sons, an imprint of The Gale Group)

BEST = *Bestsellers* (quarterly, citations appear as Year: Issue number)

BLC = *Black Literature Criticism*

BLCS = *Black Literature Criticism Supplement*

BPFB = *Beacham's Encyclopedia of Popular Fiction: Biography and Resources*

BRW = *British Writers* (Charles Scribner's Sons, an imprint of The Gale Group)

BRWS = *British Writers Supplement,* (Charles Scribner's Sons, an imprint of The Gale Group)

BW = *Black Writers*

BYA = *Beacham's Guide to Literature for Young Adults*

CA = *Contemporary Authors*

CAAS = *Contemporary Authors Autobiography Series*

CABS = *Contemporary Authors Bibliographical Series*

CAD = *Contemporary American Dramatists* (St. James Press, an imprint of The Gale Group)

CANR = *Contemporary Authors New Revision Series*

CAP = *Contemporary Authors Permanent Series*

CBD = *Contemporary British Dramatists* (St. James Press, an imprint of The Gale Group)

CCA = *Contemporary Canadian Authors*

CD = *Contemporary Dramatists* (St. James Press, an imprint of The Gale Group)

CDALB = *Concise Dictionary of American Literary Biography*

CDALBS = *Concise Dictionary of American Literary Biography Supplement*

CDBLB = *Concise Dictionary of British Literary Biography*

CLC = *Contemporary Literary Criticism*

CMLC = *Classical and Medieval Literature Criticism*

CMW = *St. James Guide to Crime & Mystery Writers* (St. James Press, an imprint of The Gale Group)

CN = *Contemporary Novelists* (St. James Press, an imprint of The Gale Group)

CP = *Contemporary Poets* (St. James Press, an imprint of The Gale Group)

CPW = *Contemporary Popular Writers* (St. James Press, an imprint of The Gale Group)

CSW = *Contemporary Southern Writers* (St. James Press, an imprint of The Gale Group)

CWD = *Contemporary Women Dramatists* (St. James Press, an imprint of The Gale Group)

CWP = *Contemporary Women Poets* (St. James Press, an imprint of The Gale Group)

CWRI = *St. James Guide to Children's Writers* (St. James Press, an imprint of The Gale Group)

CWW = *Contemporary World Writers* (St. James Press, an imprint of The Gale Group)

DA = *DISCovering Authors*

DAB = *DISCovering Authors: British*

DAC = *DISCovering Authors: Canadian*

DAM = *DISCovering Authors: Modules*
    DRAM: *Dramatists Module;* **MST:** *Most-Studied Authors Module;*
    MULT: *Multicultural Authors Module;* **NOV:** *Novelists Module;*
    POET: *Poets Module;* **POP:** *Popular Fiction and Genre Authors Module*
DA3 = *DISCovering Authors 3.0*
DC = *Drama Criticism*
DFS = *Drama for Students*
DLB = *Dictionary of Literary Biography*
DLBD = *Dictionary of Literary Biography Documentary Series*
DLBY = *Dictionary of Literary Biography Yearbook*
DNFS = *Literature of Developing Nations for Students*
EFS = *Epics for Students*
EXPN = *Exploring Novels*
EXPP = *Exploring Poetry*
EXPS = *Exploring Short Stories*
EW = *European Writers* (Charles Scribner's Sons, an imprint of The Gale Group)
FANT = *St. James Guide to Fantasy Writers* (St. James Press, an imprint of The Gale Group)
FW = *Feminist Writers* (St. James Press, an imprint of The Gale Group)
GFL = *Guide to French Literature,* Beginnings to 1789, 1798 to the Present (St. James Press, an imprint of The Gale Group)
GLL = *Gay and Lesbian Literature* (St. James Press, an imprint of The Gale Group)
HGG = *St. James Guide to Horror, Ghost & Gothic Writers* (St. James Press, an imprint of The Gale Group)
HLC = *Hispanic Literature Criticism*
HLCS = *Hispanic Literature Criticism Supplement*
HW = *Hispanic Writers*
IDFW = *International Dictionary of Films and Filmmakers: Writers and Production Artists* (St. James Press, an imprint of The Gale Group)
IDTP = *International Dictionary of Theatre: Playwrights* (St. James Press, an imprint of The Gale Group)
LAIT = *Literature and Its Times*
LAW = *Latin American Writers* (Charles Scribner's Sons, an imprint of The Gale Group)
JRDA = *Junior DISCovering Authors*
LC = *Literature Criticism from 1400 to 1800*
MAICYA = *Major Authors and Illustrators for Children and Young Adults*
MAICYA = *Major Authors and Illustrators for Children and Young Adults Supplement*
MAWW = *Modern American Women Writers* (Charles Scribner's Sons, an imprint of The Gale Group)
MJW = *Modern Japanese Writers* (Charles Scribner's Sons, an imprint of The Gale Group)
MTCW = *Major 20th-Century Writers*
NCFS = *Nonfiction Classics for Students*
NCLC = *Nineteenth-Century Literature Criticism*
NFS = *Novels for Students*
NNAL = *Native North American Literature*
PAB = *Poets: American and British* (Charles Scribner's Sons, an imprint of The Gale Group)
PC = *Poetry Criticism*
PFS = *Poetry for Students*
RGAL = *Reference Guide to American Literature* (St. James Press, an imprint of The Gale Group)
RGEL = *Reference Guide to English Literature* (St. James Press, an imprint of The Gale Group)
RGSF = *Reference Guide to Short Fiction* (St. James Press, an imprint of The Gale Group)
RGWL = *Reference Guide to World Literature* (St. James Press, an imprint of The Gale Group)
RHW = *Twentieth-Century Romance and Historical Writers* (St. James Press, an imprint of The Gale Group)
SAAS = *Something about the Author Autobiography Series*
SATA = *Something about the Author*
SFW = *St. James Guide to Science Fiction Writers* (St. James Press, an imprint of The Gale Group)
SSC = *Short Story Criticism*
SSFS = *Short Stories for Students*
TCLC = *Twentieth-Century Literary Criticism*
TCWW = *Twentieth-Century Western Writers* (St. James Press, an imprint of The Gale Group)
WLC = *World Literature Criticism, 1500 to the Present*
WLCS = *World Literature Criticism Supplement*
WLIT = *World Literature and Its Times*
WP = *World Poets* (Charles Scribner's Sons, an imprint of The Gale Group)
YABC = *Yesterday's Authors of Books for Children*
YAW = *St. James Guide to Young Adult Writers* (St. James Press, an imprint of The Gale Group)

CLR Cumulative Author Index

Literary Criticism Series
Cumulative Topic Index

This index lists all topic entries in Gale's *Children's Literature Review* (CLR), *Classical and Medieval Literature Criticism* (CMLC), *Contemporary Literary Criticism* (CLC), *Drama Criticism* (DC), *Literature Criticism from 1400 to 1800* (LC), *Nineteenth-Century Literature Criticism* (NCLC), *Short Story Criticism* (SSC), and *Twentieth-Century Literary Criticism* (TCLC). The index also lists topic entries in the Gale Critical Companion Collection, which includes the following publications: *The Beat Generation* (BG), *Feminism in Literature* (FL), *Gothic Literature* (GL), and *Harlem Renaissance* (HR).

Abbey Theatre in the Irish Literary Renaissance TCLC 154: 1-114
origins and development, 2-14
major figures, 14-30
plays and controversies, 30-59
artistic vision and significance, 59-114

Abolitionist Literature of Cuba and Brazil, Nineteenth-Century NCLC 132: 1-94
overviews, 2-11
origins and development, 11-23
sociopolitical concerns, 23-39
poetry, 39-47
prose, 47-93

The Aborigine in Nineteenth-Century Australian Literature NCLC 120: 1-88
overviews, 2-27
representations of the Aborigine in Australian literature, 27-58
Aboriginal myth, literature, and oral tradition, 58-88

The Aesopic Fable LC 51: 1-100
the British Aesopic Fable, 1-54
the Aesopic tradition in non-English-speaking cultures, 55-66
political uses of the Aesopic fable, 67-88
the evolution of the Aesopic fable, 89-99

Aesop's Fables CLR 115: 1-55
overviews and general studies, 4-29
morality in Aesop's fables, 29-39
historical editions of Aesop's fables, 39-53
reviews of contemporary editions of Aesop's fables, 53-55

African-American Folklore and Literature TCLC 126: 1-67
African-American folk tradition, 1-16
representative writers, 16-34
hallmark works, 35-48
the study of African-American literature and folklore, 48-64

Age of al-Andalus CMLC 81: 1-174
overviews, 1-48
history, society, and culture, 48-127
Andalusī poetry, 127-73

Age of Johnson LC 15: 1-87
Johnson's London, 3-15
aesthetics of neoclassicism, 15-36
"age of prose and reason," 36-45
clubmen and bluestockings, 45-56

printing technology, 56-62
periodicals: "a map of busy life," 62-74
transition, 74-86

The Age of King Alfred the Great CMLC 79: 1-141
overviews and historical background, 4-17
the Alfredian translations, 17-43
King Alfred's prefaces, 43-84
Alfred and Boethius, 84-140

Age of Spenser LC 39: 1-70
overviews and general studies, 2-21
literary style, 22-34
poets and the crown, 34-70

AIDS in Literature CLC 81: 365-416

Alcohol and Literature TCLC 70: 1-58
overview, 2-8
fiction, 8-48
poetry and drama, 48-58

American Abolitionism NCLC 44: 1-73
overviews and general studies, 2-26
abolitionist ideals, 26-46
the literature of abolitionism, 46-72

American Autobiography TCLC 86: 1-115
overviews and general studies, 3-36
American authors and autobiography, 36-82
African-American autobiography, 82-114

American Black Humor Fiction TCLC 54: 1-85
characteristics of black humor, 2-13
origins and development, 13-38
black humor distinguished from related literary trends, 38-60
black humor and society, 60-75
black humor reconsidered, 75-83

American Civil War in Literature NCLC 32: 1-109
overviews and general studies, 2-20
regional perspectives, 20-54
fiction popular during the war, 54-79
the historical novel, 79-108

American Frontier in Literature NCLC 28: 1-103
definitions, 2-12
development, 12-17
nonfiction writing about the frontier, 17-30
frontier fiction, 30-45
frontier protagonists, 45-66

portrayals of Native Americans, 66-86
feminist readings, 86-98
twentieth-century reaction against frontier literature, 98-100

American Humor Writing NCLC 52: 1-59
overviews and general studies, 2-12
the Old Southwest, 12-42
broader impacts, 42-5
women humorists, 45-58

American Naturalism in Short Fiction SSC 77: 1-103
overviews and general studies, 2-30
major authors of American literary Naturalism, 30-102
Ambrose Bierce, 30
Stephen Crane, 30-53
Theodore Dreiser, 53-65
Jack London, 65-80
Frank Norris, 80-9
Edith Wharton, 89-102

American Novel of Manners TCLC 130: 1-42
history of the Novel of Manners in America, 4-10
representative writers, 10-18
relevancy of the Novel of Manners, 18-24
hallmark works in the Novel of Manners, 24-36
Novel of Manners and other media, 36-40

American Mercury, **The** TCLC 74: 1-80

American Popular Song, Golden Age of TCLC 42: 1-49
background and major figures, 2-34
the lyrics of popular songs, 34-47

American Proletarian Literature TCLC 54: 86-175
overviews and general studies, 87-95
American proletarian literature and the American Communist Party, 95-111
ideology and literary merit, 111-17
novels, 117-36
Gastonia, 136-48
drama, 148-54
journalism, 154-9
proletarian literature in the United States, 159-74

American Realism NCLC 120: 89-246
overviews, 91-112
background and sources, 112-72

Topic Index

Topic Index

Topic Index

Topic Index

CLR Cumulative Nationality Index

AMERICAN

Aardema, Verna **17**
Aaseng, Nathan **54**
Adams, Adrienne **73**
Adkins, Jan **7, 77**
Adler, C(arole) S(chwerdtfeger) **78**
Adler, David A. **108**
Adler, Irving **27**
Adoff, Arnold **7**
Alcott, Louisa May **1, 38, 109**
Alda, Arlene **93**
Aldrich, Bess Streeter **70**
Alexander, Lloyd (Chudley) **1, 5, 48**
Alger, Horatio **87**
Aliki **9, 71**
Allard, Harry **85**
Anaya, Rudolfo **129**
Anderson, Poul (William) **58**
Angelou, Maya **53**
Anglund, Joan Walsh **1**
Anthony, Piers **118**
Applegate, K. A. **90**
Armstrong, Jennifer **66**
Armstrong, William H(oward) **1, 117**
Arnold, Caroline **61**
Arnosky, James Edward **15, 93**
Aruego, José (Espiritu) **5**
Ashabranner, Brent (Kenneth) **28**
Asimov, Isaac **12, 79**
Atwater, Florence (Hasseltine Carroll) **19**
Atwater, Richard (Tupper) **19**
Avi **24, 68**
Aylesworth, Jim **89**
Aylesworth, Thomas G(ibbons) **6**
Babbitt, Natalie (Zane Moore) **2, 53**
Bacon, Martha Sherman **3**
Ballard, Robert D(uane) **60**
Bang, Molly Garrett **8**
Barrett, Judi **98**
Barron, T(homas) A(rchibald) **86**
Baum, L(yman) Frank **15, 107**
Baylor, Byrd **3**
Bellairs, John (Anthony) **37**
Beller, Susan Provost **106**
Bemelmans, Ludwig **6, 93**
Benary-Isbert, Margot **12**
Bendick, Jeanne **5**
Berenstain, Jan(ice) **19**
Berenstain, Stan(ley) **19**
Berger, Melvin H. **32**
Bess, Clayton **39**
Bethancourt, T. Ernesto **3**
Bishop, Claire Huchet **80**
Block, Francesca Lia **33, 116**
Blos, Joan W(insor) **18**
Blumberg, Rhoda **21**
Blume, Judy (Sussman) **2, 15, 69**
Bogart, Jo Ellen **59**
Bond, Nancy (Barbara) **11**
Bontemps, Arna(ud Wendell) **6**
Bova, Ben(jamin William) **3, 96**
Boyd, Candy Dawson **50**

Boynton, Sandra **105**
Brancato, Robin F(idler) **32**
Branley, Franklyn M(ansfield) **13**
Brashares, Ann **113**
Brett, Jan (Churchill) **27**
Bridgers, Sue Ellen **18**
Bridwell, Norman **96**
Brink, Carol Ryrie **30**
Brooks, Bruce **25**
Brooks, Gwendolyn (Elizabeth) **27**
Brown, Marcia (Joan) **12**
Brown, Marc (Tolon) **29**
Brown, Margaret Wise **10, 107**
Bruchac, Joseph III **46**
Bryan, Ashley F. **18, 66**
Bunting, Eve **28, 56, 82**
Burch, Robert J(oseph) **63**
Burnett, Frances (Eliza) Hodgson **24, 122**
Burton, Virginia Lee **11**
Butler, Octavia E(stelle) **65**
Byars, Betsy (Cromer) **1, 16, 72**
Cather, Willa **98**
Cabot, Meg **85**
Cadnum, Michael **78**
Caines, Jeannette (Franklin) **24**
Calhoun, Mary **42**
Cameron, Eleanor (Frances) **1, 72**
Cannon, Janell **120**
Card, Orson Scott **116**
Carle, Eric **10, 72**
Carter, Alden R(ichardson) **22**
Cassedy, Sylvia **26**
Catalanotto, Peter **68**
Charlip, Remy **8**
Childress, Alice **14**
Choi, Sook Nyul **53**
Christopher, Matt(hew Frederick) **33, 119**
Ciardi, John (Anthony) **19**
Cisneros, Sandra **123**
Clark, Ann Nolan **16**
Cleary, Beverly (Atlee Bunn) **2, 8, 72**
Cleaver, Bill **6**
Cleaver, Vera (Allen) **6**
Clifton, (Thelma) Lucille **5**
Climo, Shirley **69**
Coatsworth, Elizabeth (Jane) **2**
Cobb, Vicki **2**
Cohen, Daniel (E.) **3, 43**
Cole, Brock **18**
Cole, Joanna **5, 40**
Collier, Christopher **126**
Collier, James Lincoln **3, 126**
Colum, Padraic **36**
Conford, Ellen **10, 71**
Conrad, Pam **18**
Cooney, Barbara **23**
Cooper, Floyd **60**
Cooper, James Fenimore **105**
Corbett, Scott **1**
Corcoran, Barbara (Asenath) **50**
Cormier, Robert (Edmund) **12, 55**
Cox, Palmer **24**
Crane, Stephen **132**

Creech, Sharon **42, 89**
Crews, Donald **7**
Cronin, Doreen **105**
Crutcher, Chris(topher C.) **28**
Cummings, Pat (Marie) **48**
Curry, Jane L(ouise) **31**
Curtis, Christopher Paul **68**
Curtis, Jamie Lee **88**
Cushman, Karen **55**
Dalgliesh, Alice **62**
Daly, Maureen **96**
Danziger, Paula **20**
Daugherty, James (Henry) **78**
d'Aulaire, Edgar Parin **21**
d'Aulaire, Ingri (Mortenson Parin) **21**
Davis, Ossie **56**
Day, Alexandra **22**
de Angeli, Marguerite (Lofft) **1**
DeClements, Barthe (Faith) **23**
DeJong, Meindert **1, 73**
Denslow, W(illiam) W(allace) **15**
dePaola, Tomie **4, 24, 81**
Diaz, David **65**
DiCamillo, Kate **117**
Dillon, Diane (Claire) **44**
Dillon, Leo **44**
Disch, Thomas M(ichael) **18**
Dixon, Franklin W. **61**
Dodge, Mary (Elizabeth) Mapes **62**
Domanska, Janina **40**
Donovan, John **3**
Dorris, Michael (Anthony) **58**
Dorros, Arthur (M.) **42**
Draper, Sharon M(ills) **57**
Dr. Seuss **1, 9, 53, 100**
Duke, Kate **51**
Duncan, Lois **29, 129**
Duvoisin, Roger (Antoine) **23**
Eager, Edward (McMaken) **43**
Ehlert, Lois (Jane) **28**
Emberley, Barbara A(nne) **5**
Emberley, Ed(ward Randolph) **5, 81**
Engdahl, Sylvia Louise **2**
L'Engle, Madeleine (Camp Franklin) **1, 14, 57**
Enright, Elizabeth (Wright) **4**
Epstein, Beryl (M. Williams) **26**
Epstein, Samuel **26**
Estes, Eleanor (Ruth) **2, 70**
Ets, Marie Hall **33**
Falconer, Ian **90**
Feelings, Muriel (Lavita Grey) **5**
Feelings, Tom **5, 58**
Ferry, Charles **34**
Field, Rachel (Lyman) **21**
Fisher, Aileen (Lucia) **49**
Fisher, Dorothy (Frances) Canfield **71,**
Fisher, Leonard Everett **18**
Fitzgerald, John D(ennis) **1**
Fitzhugh, Louise (Perkins) **1, 72**
Flack, Marjorie **28**
Fleischman, (Albert) Sid(ney) **1, 15**
Fleischman, Paul **20, 66**

CLR-134 Title Index

ISBN-13: 978-0-7876-9609-2
ISBN-10: 0-7876-9609-9